THE JEWISH–CHINESE NEXUS

The Jewish–Chinese Nexus explores, through a collection of chapters, the nexus between two of the oldest, intact, starkly contrasting and most interesting civilizations on earth; Jews and Chinese. This volume studies how they are interacting in modernity; how they view each other; what areas of cooperation are evolving between their scholars, activists and politicians; and what talents, qualities and social assets are being recognized on each side for the purpose of cooperation and exchange.

Featuring contributions from some of the most important scholars and activists from China and from around the Jewish Diaspora, the essays purview China-related themes including the fascination of Chinese with Jews, and Judaism and its potential value in Chinese national and religious reconstruction; religious and ethnic identity; and East–West interactions. It deals with the growing Jewish community in China and its impact, as well as the development of Jewish studies in China and the translation of Jewish texts into Chinese and their impact.

The work is a first of its kind, identifying an emerging meeting point between these two peoples, and arguing that, despite the giant contrasts in their national constructs, they have nonetheless other important patterns and themes in common that pave the way for fruitful cooperation and mutual respect. As such, it is indispensable for students of China as well as the Jewish Diaspora and provides useful reading for Western tourists to China.

M. Avrum Ehrlich is a full professor of Jewish Thought at the Center of Judaic and Inter-Religious Studies at the Department of Religion at Shandong University, a government-funded national center for inter-religious research in Jinan, China. Ehrlich is a theologian, social philosopher and scholar of classic Jewish texts as well as being involved in training Chinese scholars to understand and translate Jewish concepts and classics into Chinese.

ROUTLEDGE JEWISH STUDIES SERIES
Series Editor: Oliver Leaman
University of Kentucky

Studies which are interpreted to cover the disciplines of history, sociology, anthropology, culture, politics, philosophy, theology, and religion, as they relate to Jewish affairs. The remit includes texts that have as their primary focus issues, ideas, personalities, and events of relevance to Jews, Jewish life, and the concepts that have characterized Jewish culture both in the past and today. The series is interested in receiving appropriate scripts or proposals.

MEDIEVAL JEWISH PHILOSOPHY
An introduction
Dan Cohn-Sherbok

FACING THE OTHER
The ethics of Emmanuel Levinas
Edited by Seán Hand

MOSES MAIMONIDES
Oliver Leaman

A USER'S GUIDE TO FRANZ ROSENZWEIG'S STAR OF REDEMPTION
Norbert M. Samuelson

ON LIBERTY
Jewish philosophical perspectives
Edited by Daniel H. Frank

REFERRING TO GOD
Jewish and Christian philosophical and theological perspectives
Edited by Paul Helm

JUDAISM, PHILOSOPHY, CULTURE
Selected studies by E. I. J. Rosenthal
Erwin Rosenthal

PHILOSOPHY OF THE TALMUD
Hyam Maccoby

FROM SYNAGOGUE TO CHURCH
The traditional design: its beginning, its definition, its end
John Wilkinson

HIDDEN PHILOSOPHY OF HANNAH ARENDT
Margaret Betz Hull

DECONSTRUCTING THE BIBLE
Abraham ibn Ezra's introduction to the Torah
Irene Lancaster

IMAGE OF THE BLACK IN JEWISH CULTURE
A history of the other
Abraham Melamed

FROM FALASHAS TO ETHIOPIAN JEWS
Daniel Summerfield

PHILOSOPHY IN A TIME OF CRISIS
Don Isaac Abravanel: defender of the faith
Seymour Feldman

JEWS, MUSLIMS AND MASS MEDIA
Mediating the 'other'
Edited by Tudor Parfitt with Yulia Egorova

JEWS OF ETHIOPIA
The birth of an elite
Edited by Emanuela Trevisan Semi and Tudor Parfitt

ART IN ZION
The genesis of national art in Jewish Palestine
Dalia Manor

HEBREW LANGUAGE AND JEWISH THOUGHT
David Patterson

CONTEMPORARY JEWISH PHILOSOPHY
An introduction
Irene Kajon

ANTISEMITISM AND MODERNITY
Innovation and continuity
Hyam Maccoby

JEWS AND INDIA
History, image, perceptions
Yulia Egorova

JEWISH MYSTICISM AND MAGIC
An anthropological perspective
Maureen Bloom

MAIMONIDES' *GUIDE TO THE PERPLEXED*
Silence and salvation
Donald McCallum

MUSCULAR JUDAISM
The Jewish body and the politics of regeneration
Todd Samuel Presner

JEWISH CULTURAL NATIONALISM
David Aberbach

THE JEWISH–CHINESE NEXUS
A meeting of civilizations
Edited by M. Avrum Ehrlich

GERMAN–JEWISH POPULAR CULTURE
BEFORE THE HOLOCAUST
Kafka's kitsch
David Brenner

THE
JEWISH–CHINESE
NEXUS

A meeting of civilizations

Edited by M. Avrum Ehrlich

Routledge
Taylor & Francis Group

LONDON AND NEW YORK

First published 2008
by Routledge
2 Park Square, Milton Park, Abingdon, Oxon, OX14 4RN

Simultaneously published in the USA and Canada
by Routledge
270 Madison Ave, New York NY 10016

*Routledge is an imprint of the Taylor & Francis Group, an informa
business*

Transferred to Digital Printing 2010

© 2008 Editorial selection and matter, Avrum Ehrlich;
individual chapters, the contributors

Typeset in Times New Roman by
Taylor & Francis Books Ltd

British Library Cataloguing in Publication Data
A catalogue record for this book is available from the
British Library

Library of Congress Cataloging in Publication Data
The Jewish-Chinese nexus : a meeting of civilizations / edited by M.
Avrum Ehrlich.
p. cm. – (Routledge Jewish studies series ; 26)
Includes bibliographical references and index.
1. Jews–China–History. 2. China–Ethnic relations. I. Ehrlich, Avrum M.
DS135.C5J46 2008
305.892'4051–dc22
2007048949

ISBN10: 0-415-45715-7 (hbk)
ISBN10: 0-415-59341-7 (pbk)
ISBN10: 0-203-89558-4 (ebk)

ISBN13: 978-0-415-45715-6 (hbk)
ISBN13: 978-0-415-59341-0 (pbk)
ISBN13: 978-0-203-89558-0 (ebk)

CONTENTS

Contributors   x
Chronology of the Jewish–Chinese Nexus   xvi
Foreword and Acknowledgements   xxiii
Introduction to the Jewish–Chinese Nexus   xxvii
Map of China 1   xxxii
Map of China 2   xxxiii

Part I
Contemporary Jews in China   1

1 Overview of the Jewish Presence in Contemporary China   3
   M. AVRUM EHRLICH

2 China's Realities from the Viewpoints of "Foreign Experts"   16
   MATTHIAS MESSMER

3 Contemporary Development of Jewish Life in Asia: A Personal
   Memoir   41
   DAVID C. BUXBAUM

Part II
Comparative Culture and Thought   47

4 Crossing Boundaries Between Confucianism and Judaism   49
   GALIA PATT-SHAMIR AND YAOV RAPOPORT

5 Confucianism and Judaism: a Dialogue in Spite of Differences   61
   GALIA PATT-SHAMIR

6 Judaism and its Referential Value to the Cultural Reconstruction
   of Modern China   72
   FU YOUDE

CONTENTS

7 Rethinking the Nanjing Massacre and its Connection with the
   Holocaust   82
   ZHANG QIANHONG AND JERRY GOTEL

Part III
Chinese Perceptions of Jews   95

8 A Chinese Perspective of Judaism and the Jewish People   97
   FU YOUDE

9 Israel and the Jewish People in Chinese Cyberspace
   Since 2002   103
   ZHANG PING

10 The Influence of Jewish Literature in China   118
   FU XIAOWEI AND WANG YI

Part IV
Jewish Studies and Literature   133

11 Australian Jewry, its Relations with China and the First Steps in
   Jewish Studies   135
   SOL ENCEL AND SUZANNE D. RUTLAND

12 The Developing Role of the Hebrew Bible in Modern China   152
   YIYI CHEN

13 Modern Hebrew Literature in China   164
   ZHONG ZHIQING

Part V
Kaifeng Jewish Descendents   173

14 The Contemporary Condition of the Jewish Descendants of
   Kaifeng   175
   M. AVRUM EHRLICH AND LIANG PINGAN

15 Chinese Government Policy Towards the Descendants of the
   Jews of Kaifeng   197
   XU XIN

16 The Judaism of the Kaifeng Jews and Liberal Judaism
   in America   207
   ANSON LAYTNER

CONTENTS

Part VI
Phenomena of the Jewish–Chinese Nexus   225

17 The Adoption of Chinese Children by Jewish Families and the
    Effect on North American Jewish Identity   227
    DAVID STRAUB

Part VII
China–Israel Relations   237

18 Sino–Israel Relations at the Start of the Second Decade: A View
    from Shanghai and Jerusalem   239
    ILAN MAOR

19 Economic and Cultural Relations Between China and Israel Since
    the Establishment of Diplomatic Relations in 1992   253
    JONATHAN GOLDSTEIN

20 China's Potential Contribution to Middle East Cooperation   268
    LIANG PINGAN

    Bibliography   279
    Index   284

CONTRIBUTORS

M. Avrum Ehrlich is a full professor at the Center of Judaic and Inter-Religious Studies at the Department of Religion at Shandong University, a government-funded national center for inter-religious research in Jinan, China. Ehrlich is a theologian, social philosopher and scholar of Judaism and is involved in training Chinese scholars to understand Jewish texts and concepts. He teaches text-based courses in The Philosophy of the Hebrew Scriptures, Introductory Studies in *Halakha* and *Talmud*, and Readings in Jewish Mysticism in addition to Biblical Hebrew.
His general research subjects include Jewish leadership and transgeneration transfer of authority and ideas, the governing mechanics of religions and messianism in Judaism and Christianity, and he is extending his interest to Chinese thought and religion. Ehrlich studied talmudics and theological studies in Israel where he was ordained a rabbi and read Jewish Philosophy and Political Science at Bar Ilan University. He completed his doctorate on leadership strategies of Hasidic masters at the University of Sydney and was awarded the British Commonwealth Scholarship and the Chevening Scholarship to pursue post-doctoral studies at the department of Social and Political Sciences at Cambridge University and the Krytman scholarship to research at the Cambridge-based Center of Jewish–Christian Relations. He remains a life member of Clare Hall Cambridge. He is author of a number of books on Hasidism, articles on Jewish mysticism, religious sects, biblical commentaries, ethics and politics. He is editor-in-chief of the three volume *Encyclopedia of the Jewish Diaspora* (2008).

David C. Buxbaum has lived, researched and worked in Singapore, Taiwan, Hong Kong and Mainland China for over 40 years. His academic career includes a position at the University of Singapore Law Faculty in 1963, a Fulbright fellow in Taiwan, and research at Academica Sinica. He completed his Ph.D. in law and practices as a lawyer and legal consultant and was an associate professor at the law school of the University of Seattle. He was posted to China and formally invited to work and represent business interests there in 1972, becoming one of the first foreigners to enter China during its opening up period towards the end of the Cultural Revolution. Amongst other things, he consulted the Chinese government in constructing a stable business and legal environment for itself and for foreign investment. Throughout this period, as an observant Jew, he maintained strong ties with the various Jewish communities in the region.

Yiyi Chen is a faculty member at Peking University. His research includes the Hebrew Bible in its Ancient near East context, Ancient Judaism and early interactions between the near East and China, as well as the role of the Bible in Chinese society. His book *The Hebrew Bible, from Textual and Archaeological Perspectives* is the only systematic overview on the subject written in Chinese. He is now working on an introductory textbook for Chinese university students studying the Hebrew Bible. Before joining Peking University, he worked as an IT manager in the Silicon Valley. Chen holds a B.A. from Peking University and an M.A. and Ph.D. from Cornell University.

Sol Encel was professor of sociology at the University of New South Wales from 1966 to 1990. Since 1991, he has been Honorary Research Associate at the Social Policy Research Center, University of NSW and since 2004 at the University of Sydney. He has written or edited more than 20 books on a wide range of social and political issues. His most recent publications include *Continuity, Commitment and Survival*, with Leslie Stein (2003); and *Longevity and Social Change in Australia*, with Allan Borowski and Elizabeth Ozanne (2007).

Fu Xiaowei, is a professor of Comparative Literature and Culture, and director of the Center of Judaic and Chinese Studies at Sichuan International Studies University in Chongqing, China. She is the author of four books, including *What is God: Isaac Bashevis Singer's Creation and his Reception and Influence in China* (2006). Her recent essays include: "Confusing Judaism and Christianity in Contemporary Chinese Letters" (2006); "Misreading, Intentional Fallacy and the Blind Worship of Western Literary Theories" (2004); and "The Principle of Harmony without Uniformity and Religious Compromises in European Integration" (forthcoming).

Fu Youde, is director of the Center for Judaic and Inter-Religious Studies and former dean of the School of Philosophy and Social Development at Shandong University in Jinan, China. He earned his M.A. at Shandong University and Ph.D. at Beijing University and continued his research and writing at Trinity College, Dublin; at Oxford Center for Hebrew and Jewish Studies; and at Leo Baeck College, London. He was a visiting professor at Case Western Reserve University, at Boston University and other American academic institutions. Fu has held numerous notable positions including chairman of the Academic Committee of the Humanities at Shandong University, the Philosophy Society of Shandong and Vice Chair of the Society of Religion of Shandong. He is the author of many books, over 50 articles, and is the coordinator and primary author of a project to translate the great works of Jewish civilization and philosophy into Chinese.

Jonathan Goldstein is a Research Associate of Harvard University's Fairbank Center for East Asian Research and a Professor of East Asian history at the University of West Georgia. His books include *Philadelphia and the China Trade, 1682–1846* (1978), *Georgia's East Asian Connection: into the Twenty-First Century* (1990), *America Views China* (1991), *China and Israel* (1999), and *The Jews of China* (2000).

Jerry Gotel is a Senior History Lecturer at London Jewish Cultural Center and Director of Overseas Projects, mainly focusing on teacher training in Eastern Europe. He received traditional Yeshiva education in 1953–1964, studied at Yeshiva University for one year, graduated in 1968 from Brooklyn College of the City University of N.Y. and has studied at Sorbonne, Pembroke College, and Oxford. He represents Great Britain on the Education Committee of The International Task Force for Holocaust Education, Remembrance, and Research and has received support from the task force to hold three conferences in China on the Holocaust.

Rabbi Anson Laytner is currently the executive director of the Seattle Chapter of the American Jewish Committee. As a volunteer, Laytner serves as President of the Sino–Judaic Institute and edits its journal *Points East*. He also is an adjunct professor with Seattle University's Department of Theology and Religious Studies. Previously, Laytner served as the executive director of Multifaith Works and also headed the Seattle Jewish Federation's Community Relations Council. Laytner is the author of *Arguing with God*, co-author of *The Animals' Lawsuit Against Humanity*, and has written over 70 articles on subjects ranging from Jewish theology to the Arab–Israel conflict to the Chinese Jews. Laytner has a B.A. from York University in Toronto, an M.A. in Hebrew Letters and rabbinic ordination from Hebrew Union College, an M.A. in Not-for-Profit Leadership from Seattle University, and an honorary D.D. from Hebrew Union College.

Liang Pingan completed his M.A. on Jewish and Israeli Studies and is writing his Ph.D. on *Modern Foreign Relations Between Israel and the Global Powers* at Shanghai International Studies University. He is a visiting researcher at the Shanghai Academy of Social Sciences. He first came into contact with Jews when he served as a tour guide and then as Deputy General of Kaifeng International Travel Services over 15 years ago. He later became the Deputy Chief Secretary of the Institute of Kaifeng Jewish History and Culture. He served as a diplomatic attaché to the Chinese embassy in Slovenia and Kuwait. He spent a year learning Hebrew and Jewish culture at Hebrew University's Rothberg International School and was an exchange scholar at Tel Aviv University's Far-Eastern Department. He remains actively engaged in Jewish–Chinese relations and in the welfare of the descendants of the Jews of Kaifeng.

Ilan Maor has held the position of the Director of Economic Department III at the Israeli Foreign Ministry since August 2005, which is responsible for the promotion of economic cooperation between Israel and Asia, Pacific, Russia and the CIS countries, as well as the political aspects of Israel's participation in International Organizations, including the WTO, OECD, and FAO. Maor currently also is heading the Israeli negotiation team with the OECD. From 2001–2005 Ilan Maor served as the Consul General of Israel in Shanghai and in 2004 was the first Israeli diplomat to be listed among the "100 Most Influential People in Israel Economy" by the magazine *The Marker*. Prior to his posting in Shanghai, Maor served in various positions in Jerusalem, Nepal, and Taipei. Maor holds a B.A. in Political Science from Tel Aviv University.

Matthias Messmer studied Political Science, Law and Economics at the University of St. Gallen and received his Ph.D. in Social Sciences at the University of Konstanz in Germany. Later, he spent several years doing research in both China and the U.S. His extensive publications cover China, inter-culture and travel. He is a Senior Research Fellow affiliated with the Institute of Federalism at the University of Fribourg in Switzerland. He currently lives and works as a writer, independent researcher and consultant in Shanghai. Among his publications are, "Sowjetischer und postkommunistischer Antisemitismus" (1997) and "China: Schauplätze west-östlicher Begegnungen" (2007).

Galia Patt-Shamir is a senior lecturer of Chinese philosophy and Comparative Philosophy and Religion in the departments of East-Asian Studies and of Philosophy at Tel Aviv University in Israel. She earned her Ph.D. degree in the Study of Religion in 1997 from Harvard. Her main focus is in the dialogue and understanding among civilizations and individuals and she is involved in practical and theoretical projects to enhance this field of study. She wrote a book on human nature in Chinese philosophies and religions (Hebrew, 2004). Her book *To Broaden the Way – A Confucian–Jewish Dialogue* (2006) focuses on the themes of ultimate, social life, and individual pursuit, as dealt with in both traditions, through religious texts, philosophical methodologies, and literary sources. She also published articles on issues in inter-religious dialogue, Confucian and Neo-Confucian texts, practice and theory, in leading journals such as *Journal of Chinese Philosophy, Philosophy and Literature, Journal of Ecumenical Studies, Dao: A Journal of Comparative Philosophy*.

Yoav Rapoport received an undergraduate degree in Chinese Studies from the Department of East Asian Studies at The Hebrew University in Jerusalem and studied history at Tel Aviv University. He went on to receive a M.A. in Chinese Studies from The Hebrew University and also served as Assistant to the Head of the Department of East Asian Studies. In 1990, Rapoport participated in the first Exchange Student Program between China and Israel, spending a year at Southwest China Normal University in Beibei in Chongqing prefecture and continued his studies at Oxford University in England. He has taught courses in Chinese Literature, History and Philosophy at Tel Aviv University, Department of East Asian Studies and currently works as a freelance translator from Chinese to Hebrew, editor of books about China in Hebrew, and commentator and adviser on Chinese affairs for various Israeli media.

Suzanne D. Rutland is Associate Professor and Chair of the Department of Hebrew, Biblical and Jewish Studies at the University of Sydney. She has published widely on Australian Jewish history, as well as issues relating to the Shoah, Israel and Jews in China. She has also assisted in special exhibitions on the Jews of Shanghai at the Sydney Jewish Museum and the National Maritime Museum and was interviewed for the television program *Compass* on the Jews of Shanghai. Her latest book is *The Jews in Australia* (2005). She has received a major government grant with Prof. Sol Encel to study 'The Political Sociology of Australian Jewry'. She has held numerous leadership positions, including being immediate past president of the Australian Jewish Historical Society, and edits the Sydney edition of the *AJHS Journal*.

David Straub is a visiting researcher at the Center for Judaic and Inter-Religious Studies at Shandong University, received his B.A. at the University of Minnesota, Twin Cities and is a graduate student in the Central Eurasian Studies department at the University of Indiana, Bloomington. He has lived and taught in China since 2001, previously contributed to and was assistant editor of the upcoming *Encyclopaedia of the Jewish Diaspora*, is a specialist on Central Asian and China and has travelled broadly across Asia.

Wang Yi is a professor of Aesthetics and Aesthetic Education, and director of the Institute of Tourism and Aesthetics at Sichuan International Studies University in Chongqing, China. He is the author of seven books and his recent publications include "From Franz Kafka to Isaac Bashevis Singer: Chinese Avant-garde Writers' Turnaround – Focusing on Ma Yuan, Su Tong and Yu Hua" (2005); "From Misreading to the Bottleneck of the Aesthetic Education Theory" (2006); and "An Exegetic Study of the So-called Proposition of Confucian Aesthetics" (2008).

Xu Xin, professor of History of Jewish Culture and director of the Center for Jewish Studies at Nanjing University, is also president of the China Judaic Studies Association and editor-in-chief and a major contributor of the Chinese edition of the *Encyclopedia Judaica*. He teaches courses such as Jewish history, Jewish culture and the world civilization, Holocaust studies, and history of the Jewish Diaspora. He has created graduate-level programs on Jewish history and culture at Nanjing University. He is the author of many books and articles about Judaism in China, and has been a visiting professor at numerous universities in the U.S. Xu is a member of the Center for Judaic and Inter-Religious Studies at Shandong University and in 2003 he was awarded an honorary doctorate by Bar Ilan University in recognition of the work he has done on the research of the Jewish people in China.

Zhang Ping is a member of the academic staff of the Chinese program at Tel Aviv University. He holds a B.A. in Chinese literature from Beijing University and an M.A. in Oriental literature from the Department of Oriental Languages at Beijing University. He completed his Ph.D. in Comparative philosophy at Tel Aviv University and taught at Beijing University, Hebrew University in Jerusalem and Tel Aviv University. His publications include the Chinese translation of *Pirki Avoth*, S. Y. Agnon's stories, academic works on Chinese literature, and comparative studies between Confucianism, Judaism and Hebrew literature.

Zhong Zhiqing is an Associate Professor at the Institute of Foreign Literature at the Chinese Academy of Social Sciences in Beijing, China. She holds a Ph.D. from the Department of Hebrew Literature at Ben-Gurion University and is the author of *A Comparative Study of Hebrew and Chinese Literature in Response to the Catastrophe of World War Two, A Study of Contemporary Israeli Authors*, and a number of essays in Hebrew and Jewish literature. In addition, she has translated Amos Oz's *My Michael, Black Box, A Tale of Love and Darkness*; Yehoshua Kanaz's *After the Holidays*; and Gershon Shaked's *Modern Hebrew Function*. Currently Zhong is working on a national project entitled *20th Century Hebrew Literature in Transition*.

CHRONOLOGY OF THE JEWISH–CHINESE NEXUS

M. Avrum Ehrlich

Since the second century BCE there have been unverified myths and assumptions regarding Jewish merchants entering China at different times and various routes.

781 CE, the earliest known Chinese translation of the Hebrew Bible is carved into a stone stele by a Nestorian sect in what is modern-day Xi'an.

960–1127, during the Northern Song Dynasty Jewish merchants, presumably of Persian origin, passed over the Silk Road into China and began a settlement in Kaifeng, which was, at the time, the Chinese capital. This was the earliest clear documentation of Jews in China. Some came by sea, and gradually penetrated from Zhejiang and Jiangsu provinces to the mainland; some came by land via Persia and India on the Silk Road. The emperor himself gave the earliest Jewish immigrants Chinese names such as Gao, Li, An, Mu, Zhao, Jin, Zhou, and Bai. The ancient Chinese history books called them "shushu," "deya," and "youtai," and their religion was called "you tai jiao." They and the Han people lived together and used their Chinese family names. Some Jews seem to have converted or lived as Muslims, becoming part of the *Hui* nationality of minority Chinese Muslims. Jews were also known by the Han majority as "blue capped Muslims" indicating the Han was not able to easily tell the two groups apart. It is possible that an unknown number of Chinese Jews continued to exist in the shadow of a larger Muslim minority, eating ritually slaughtered meat, avoiding pork, celebrating festivals and the Sabbath, as Muslims.

1163, the first synagogue is established in Kaifeng.

1489, a stone tablet is erected at the Kaifeng synagogue, the earliest existing self-document of the Chinese Jews.

1605, Ai Tian, Kaifeng Jew and holder of the Chinese official title of *juren*, meets Jesuit missionary Matteo Ricci in Beijing. This encounter brings news of the existence of Chinese Jews to both European Jews and Christians.

1642, flooding of the Yellow River devastates the Kaifeng Jewish community, which at this time numbers around 5,000.

1843–44, shortly after the conclusion of the First Opium War the first-known Jews, Samuel Cohen and Jacob Phillips, arrive in Hong Kong. The Hong Kong Jews were engaged in finance and banking.

1850s, after years of decline and repeated floods, disasters and reconstructions, the Kaifeng synagogue falls to its final destruction. This also marks the disintegration of the community as such, yet Jewish identity persists in various forms.

1860s, foreign enclaves in Shanghai and across China are established after the Second Opium War. Thousands of Jews arrive in Shanghai and eventually a number of notable Jewish families, such as the Sassoons, Kadoories, and Hardoons became very wealthy and successful, buying huge tracts of land in what is now the center of Shanghai; Shanghai Jews were mainly engaged in trade.

1899, first Russian Jews settle in Harbin, North-Eastern China, creating a fast-growing community reaching its peak with 13,000 people in 1931.

1900, Shanghai Jews found The Shanghai Society for the Rescue of Chinese Jews, with little results; the Ohel Leah synagogue is consecrated in Hong Kong.

1910, Canadian Anglican Bishop William Charles White establishes the Henan Diocese in Kaifeng. During his 25-year mission, he acquired the land of the former synagogue and the stone steles. He was also involved in a Christian attempt "to re-organize the Chinese Jews of Kaifeng," which was a euphemism for converting them to Christianity.

1920s, a surge in the number of Russian Jews relocated to the northern Chinese city of Harbin, which was at the time occupied by Russia, burgeons its population to 13,000 Jews. Gradually, some moved on to places like Dalian, Tianjin, Qufu, and Qingdao and many moved to Shanghai. Ohel Rachel synagogue was established in Shanghai marking the peak of the Baghdadi community in Shanghai. Russian Jewish immigrants establish the Shanghai Ashkenazi community. The Zionist program was publicly supported by Sun Yatsen, whose eagerness to support what he termed "the civilization of the world" helped to lay the foundations for a fruitful relationship with China, through which numerous political milestones would later be achieved.

1920s, the work of a number of Jewish writers becomes popularized in Chinese literary circles.

1920, revolutionary Chinese leader Sun Yat-Sen writes to the Jewish community in Shanghai that "all lovers of democracy cannot help but support the movement to restore your wonderful and historic nation, which has contributed so much to the civilization of the world, and which rightfully deserves an honorable place in the family of nations."

1922, China votes at the League of Nations, which votes in favor of a Jewish homeland.

1927, the Ohel Moishe Synagogue opens in Shanghai.

1929, Harbin reaches the peak of Jewish immigration and Jews begin to seek other places to which to immigrate, including the U.S., Canada, Australia, and Eretz-Israel.

1938–40, some 20,000 Jewish refugees from Nazi Europe find safe haven in Shanghai, including the entire Mir Yeshiva. This miraculous story evolved to serve as a symbol of friendship between Jews and China, much quoted by diplomats and politicians, especially regarding Sino–Israeli relations. There were ultimately around 40–50,000 Jews living in China. The number of Jews living in Shanghai was about 30,000 souls. The war produced a number of notable examples of Chinese–Jewish cooperation. In 1938, China's consul general in Vienna, General Feng Shan Ho, issued visas to Shanghai for Jews seeking to escape Nazi repression, despite threats from German officials; in total, 4,000 Jewish refugees were granted visas to China; In 1939, Dr. Jacob Rosenfeld, a refugee from Nazi Germany, arrived in Shanghai. In 1941, he joined Mao's Red Army and set up clinics and public health works.

1941–45, thousands of Jewish refugees living in China, mostly in Shanghai, suffer harsh mistreatment during the Japanese occupation of China, in particular after Japan captures Shanghai and Hong Kong.

1945–early 50s, foreign Jews begin to leave China and their numbers dwindle to a few that remain who are married to Chinese, work with the Chinese Communist party and others who do business or continue their often interesting lives. This accelerated after the People's Republic of China was established in 1949. Within the next several years, almost all of the Jews of Shanghai, Harbin and the smaller contemporary communities left for Israel, Australia, the U.S., and Canada.

1950, Israel becomes the first middle-eastern country to recognize the formal establishment of the People's Republic of China in 1949. While Stalin's anti-Semitic terror campaign is in full swing throughout the Soviet Union, lack of opposition towards Jews and Zionists and welcoming words from Mao Zedong leads to increasing numbers of Jews entering China, a trend which would continue.

1955, while many might be tempted to suggest that very little occurred during the so-called cold period (1950–92), it seems this time instead marked the beginning of what is now becoming a relationship of mutual cooperation and development between Israel and China.

1952, two delegates from Kaifeng represent the Jewish community in the National Day celebrations in Beijing. They meet Prime Minister Zhou Enlai and request that Kaifeng Jews be recognized as a national minority. The request was politely denied, yet on a local level, some descendants continued to be recognized as *Youtai ren* (Jews) in their residential documents.

1953, in an official document published on 8 June the central government officially denies Kaifeng Jews ethnic minority statues. This document has continued until this day to be the basis for denying Kaifeng Jews official recognition as "Jews."

1955–56, the P.R.C. seems more interested in pursuing diplomatic relations with other Arab and Third World nations at the price of relations with Israel. It is argued that China chose to focus on its struggles with the Soviet Union, whose attempts to infiltrate the Middle East it strategically opposed. Chinese anti-Israel propaganda, which lasted until 1976, causes many outside of China to paint the P.R.C. as anti-Israel.

1960s, more than a dozen Jewish "Foreign Experts" from American and Europe live in China. All are ardent supporters of the Communist Party and participate in the political campaigns of the decade; these individuals pay dearly for their commitment to Mao's revolution and spend many years in prison. Some remain in China after the opening of China in the 1970s, while others relocate abroad.

1961, first Rabbi of Hong Kong is appointed.

1970s, Wang Yisha, a historian and former curator of Kaifeng Municipal Museum, begins to investigate Chinese Judaism, becoming the first local scholar on Kaifeng Judaism.

1978, China begins to purchase military equipment and technology from Israel, through the efforts of Menachem Begin, Israel's Prime Minister and Shaul Eisenberg, a process marking genuine political commitment to establishing a clear agenda of mutual defense strategy.

1980, the shipment of more significant amounts of Israeli military technology and equipment to China takes place, allowing trade to flourish; it would be the first of many such exchanges to take place throughout the 1980s.

1982, the Harbin Jewish community consists of one elderly resident, Anna Agre.

1985, a Hebrew language program opens at Peking University in Beijing.

1985 Wendy Abraham, one of the first foreign researchers of Chinese Jews visits China and begins research on the Jews of Kaifeng.

1987, the first clandestine meeting between the Chinese and Israeli foreign ministers takes place at the 1987 U.N. Assembly.

Late 1980s, the works of numerous Jewish authors appear in translation in China. The interest in Jewish authors and books about Jews will continue through the 1990s and into the first decade of the twenty-first century.

1990s, hundreds, possibly thousands, of Chinese orphans are adopted by Jewish families across the world, most notably in the United States and Canada, from the early 1990s through to the present day.

1992, China and Israel establish full diplomatic relations after years of secret negotiations and trade. For China, established diplomatic relations with Israel possibly meant greater ability to penetrate into American political economy through Jewish connections. China–Israel relations develop on the basis of four important criteria: Sino–Israeli defense relations, civilian trade relations, agriculture and agricultural technology and science, and technology and education exchanges.

1992, the Kaifeng municipal government allows the founding of The Society for the Research of Jewish History and Culture of Kaifeng, headed by Jewish descendant and scholar Zhao Xiangru; Wang Yisha publishes his detailed study of the Jewish descendants, *Spring and Autumn of the Chinese Jews.*

1992, the first Jewish studies conference is held in China. Many more would continue to be held in Shanghai, Harbin, and Shandong.

1992, a statue of Dr. Rosenfeld is erected in Shandong Province on the ninetieth anniversary of his birth.

1993, Kaifeng municipal government officially authorizes the construction of the synagogue according to its old structure. Officially, it is designated to serve only as a museum rather than as an active synagogue.

1993, the ministries of agriculture in Israel and China sign the "Memorandum of Understanding," and throughout the 1990s the two nations launch several highly successful agriculture experiments, greatly benefiting trade and improving the standards of their cooperation. This year also saw deeper levels of cooperation take place in the fields of water resource management and in purification technologies.

1995, a document is signed between China and Israel endorsing deeper cooperation in education, and students are more openly permitted to travel abroad to participate in scholarly exchanges.

1996, the Construction Office for the Kaifeng Jewish center and museum is closed down by the local government and the reconstruction plan abolished. The local Kaifeng government decides to erase the designation of "Jews" from all the residential documents. Jewish descendants are given the option to choose Hui Moslem Chinese or ethnic Han Chinese as their nationality. This represents the government's vigilance toward any sort of revival of Jewish identity in Kaifeng.

1998, President Bill Clinton sends a delegation of three religious leaders to China. One of them was Rabbi Arthur Schneier, president of the Appeal of Conscience Foundation in New York. When Schneier met with President Jiang Zemin, he made an appeal that China would consider recognizing Judaism – being one of the world's major religions – as an official religion in China, together with the five already recognized religions (Taoism, Buddhism, Protestantism, Catholicism, and Islam). Though this request was not met, it appears some accommodations were made for the growing Jewish community.

1998, Rabbi Shalom Greenberg settles in Shanghai and re-establishes orthodox Jewish communal activities, including synagogue prayers and kosher dining.

1999, the Shanghai Jewish community is allowed to convene for New Year's prayer in the Ohel Rachel synagogue, recently renovated by the local government

1999, trade between Israel and China reaches $550 million.

2000, the "Phalcon" incident, which involves the sale of high-tech Israeli military equipment to China, angers the U.S. government. Despite a personal visit to Israel by Chinese president Jiang Zemin, Israel caves into U.S. demands and agrees to cancel the sale of reconnaissance aircraft to China, causing a substantial rift in Sino–Israeli relations.

2000, the Israeli government posthumously awards Consul General Ho the title of "Righteous Among the Nations."

2001, Rabbi Shimon and Dini Freundlich move to Beijing from Hong Kong and set up a Chabad center and educational facilities.

2002, as violence in the Palestinian–Israeli conflict settles down, commentary on Israel in Chinese cyberspace becomes more diverse; the proliferation of pro-Israeli and Jewish-friendly websites alters the image of Israel in a positive direction for Chinese internet users.

2004, China–Israel trade reaches $2.2 billion, but considering trade with Hong Kong, actual numbers are as high as $5.7 billion.

2004, Israel Vice-Premier Ehud Olmert visits China with a delegation of Israeli businessmen. Included in his itinerary is a visit to his grandfather's grave in Harbin. He and his brother Amram, an agricultural attaché at the Israeli Embassy in Beijing inspect their grandfather's grave in the Harbin Jewish Cemetery and witness the beginning of the restoration of the 700-grave Jewish cemetery.

2005, one-hundred Israelis of Harbin origin return to the city to hold a gala reunion and historical conference at their ancestral city and pay their respects at Rabbi Kisilev's grave.

2006, Heilongjiang Province government and its Academy of Social Sciences hold a conference on Jewish studies and collaborated on a volume appropriately entitled "The Homesick Feeling of the Harbin Jews." The synagogue re-opened as a museum with special exhibits on Albert Einstein, Jacob Rosenfeld, and Israel Epstein.

2004, the Chinese central government's department of higher education sponsors a Center for Judaic studies at Shandong University under the leadership of Professor Fu Youde and begins translating Jewish classics into Chinese and training a generation of scholars in Judaism.

2004, Professor Avrum Ehrlich is appointed a professor of Jewish studies at the department of philosophy at Shandong University teaching Jewish philosophy, Tanach, Talmud, and Kabballah, and supervising masters and doctoral students.

2005, after living six years in Jerusalem without official status, Kaifeng Jewish descendant Jin Guangyuan (Shlomo) and his family complete conversion to Judaism, thereby obtaining Israeli citizenship. This raises hope in Kaifeng that more descendants will be able to make *Aliyah*, the facilitation of which Jerusalem-based institute, *Shavei Yisrael*, has taken up as one of its primary goals.

2005, Shandong University holds its first annual summer school in Jewish studies with over 80 Chinese students attending from all around China studying Jewish history, Hebrew, and Kabballah.

2006, Chinese exports to Israel rose to $2.43 billion and Israeli exports to China totaled more than $958.4 million.

2006, Israel's Chief Sephardi Rabbi, Shlomo Amar visits Shanghai and hopes to convince the Chinese government to recognize Judaism as an official religion.

2006, a new Jewish center, containing a synagogue, a school, a kosher restaurant and women's ritual baths opens in Shanghai.

2007, a new branch of Chabad opens in Pudong District of Shanghai.

2007, a new Jewish center, ritual baths and school open in Beijing under the leadership of Rabbi Freundlich.

2007, in January, Prime Minister Ehud Olmert makes an official visit to Beijing.

2007, the Chinese government institutes new regulations for adoptions, including banning single individuals, gays and lesbians, and those over the age of 50, which will affect many Jewish families seeking to adopt Chinese children.

FOREWORD AND
ACKNOWLEDGEMENTS

I came to China in 2004 to visit the family business my older brother set up in the late 1980s, before the excitement around China's economic prospects had reached the fever point it has today. I gave a talk at the Shanghai Academy of Social Sciences and was subsequently invited to present a paper entitled "Four Models of Jewish Messianism" at a conference held at Shandong University in the city Jinan, capital of Shandong Province.

At that time I knew very little about the extent of Jewish studies in China, although I sensed that there was a remarkable niche to explore and many implications associated with Jewish–Chinese interaction. After delivering my paper, I was approached by the conference organizer, Prof. Fu Youde, Dean of the Department of Philosophy, Director of the Center for Judaic and Inter-Religious Studies and Chairman of the Academic Board of Shandong University, as well as being a well-known philosopher in China.

He described how the Center for Judaic and Inter-Religious Studies had been set up several years earlier and was earmarked by the Central Government's Department of Higher Education in Beijing to become a Key Research Institute in the Social Sciences. There were only 100 such research centers in the whole of China, dedicated to aspects of social studies. The central government deemed the subject to be important and worthy of special attention and it would remain one of its kind in the whole of China.

This initiative was of particular significance because it was in the field of religious studies, which is an especially "delicate" subject for Chinese government sensibilities. He asked me to consider an appointment and, after discussions with the University President, I was offered a full professorship to take up residency in Jinan and teach Jewish classics, Biblical Hebrew, Hebrew Bible, Talmud, Kabballah, and other Jewish texts. I was told this was the first (or perhaps the second) appointment of a foreign academic ever to be made within the ranks of Chinese academe. It did not take me long to realize that this was a unique opportunity to be at the forefront of a new frontier for Jewish studies and Jewish thinking, as well as to open a dialogue with an, until recently, insular civilization.

I understood the implications and the challenges, and the prospects for new areas of discussion, interaction, and inter-civilizational dialogue. Within three months I had organized my affairs in Jerusalem and came to teach and live in Shandong province.

During my three, now approaching four, years in China, many of the perspectives and ideas I had written and thought about matured and contrasted with the different axis of thought in China, taking on new perspectives. Asked to deliver talks in many varied forums, from undergraduates to doctoral seminars, to groups of government officials in various provinces, to the Central Government School in Beijing, where the highest ranking leaders of China's administration are trained, my thoughts on Judaism and Jewish thought moved into new contexts and developed different implications. Another invitation of special interest extended to me was to address a group of high-achieving Chinese expatriates returning to China to find out more about their former homeland and seek their "spiritual" roots. I spoke on the relationship between Jews and the Jewish homeland. At first the audience did not understand the connection between the Jewish Diaspora and themselves. Slowly the prospects of a spiritual relationship between overseas Chinese and the Chinese homeland were understood in a different light, informed by the experiences of Jewish yearnings for Israel.

The Chinese interest in Judaism is surprising and seems to be the beginning of a growing trend. Interest by Chinese officials in these subjects suggests that ideas inherent in Jewish thinking may be borrowed for the reconstruction of Chinese culture, both abroad and within China; as well as spiritual and ethical life, an idea also articulated in Prof. Fu Youde's teaching and writing. Considering the estimated 200 million Chinese living abroad, being potential members of a Chinese Diaspora, the benefits of Chinese–Jewish cultural understanding seem significant indeed.

Apart from my teaching duties, I have also learned. Every day involves a remarkable and steep learning curve. It is no less than fascinating. Not only understanding Chinese culture, customs, philosophy, politics, economics and language, but also discovering that being separated from the world of Jewish and Western life provides a curious and original vantage point to observe and review Jewish thought and theology and customs. From the perspective of a nation that has little to no biblical or Jewish cultural mores or biases, the axis around which Jewish thought revolves becomes more distinct

In my upcoming book entitled *Jews and Judaism in Modern China*, I discuss and analyze in depth the ramifications of Jewish–Chinese interaction and other insights into the Jewish–Chinese nexus. In this volume, the people and scholars contributing to this exchange are brought together to form the core of a burgeoning new discipline.

A foreword would not be complete without a number of thanks. Firstly to Professor Fu Youde, whose leadership and pioneering spirit has paved the possibilities for dialogue between Jews and Chinese and an entry point for

Jewish culture into China. Prof. Fu's consistent support and assistance for my activities and for new initiatives has been much valued, especially in providing me with the working conditions and assistance required to optimize my stay in China. Not as well known outside of China as he should be, I am sure that history will attribute important credit to Fu Youde's work in developing a Jewish–Confucian synthesis. Personally, I am impressed by his demeanor and bravery, and honored by the opportunity to meet and work together with a distinct Confucian gentleman of his rank.

I would like to thank Ms. Shoshannah Zirkin for assisting with the early incarnation of this book and maintaining contact with the contributors and reading over some of their contributions and making suggestions. One of my doctoral students, Ms. Tang Maoqin, has been a helpful assistant for research in the Chinese language and I look forward to seeing her develop as one of a new brand of Chinese–Jewish studies scholars. Mr. David Straub, assistant editor to this volume, was of indispensable help in reading, checking, and commenting on the articles that were submitted, and his six-year stay in Shanghai and other Chinese provinces, as well as his interest in Central Asian countries, puts him in good stead to understand the subject. I would also like to thank Ms. Li Meng of Beijing for permitting me to use the maps of China she designed.

I would like to thank Mr. Harry Triguboff AO, who, born in Darien, China, spent his early childhood in the white Russian Jewish community in Tianjin, south of Beijing, before moving to Australia in 1947 and becoming one of Australia's leading property developers and philanthropists. His support for Jewish–Chinese relations is very much appreciated, and his interest in nurturing students in their studies of Jewish thought and culture in Chinese universities is a testament to his leadership and foresight that an exchange between the Chinese and Jewish civilizations of this sort are assets of profound, even though yet unaccountable, value.

I would like to thank my family's business partner Mr. Cao de Hua (Ward) for his friendship and concern for me during my time in China and his support to the Center for Judaic Studies at Shandong University and to other Jewish institutions in China.

I especially would like to thank my family siblings Paul, Rachel, Simon, Adam, and Miriam for their support for the *Ehrlich Family Fund for the Promotion of Judaic, Inter-Cultural and Academic Exchange in China*. The purpose of the fund was to support the cultural and intellectual exchange between Jews and Chinese at Chinese universities and nurture modern understanding, tolerance and cooperation between the two ancient civilizations. Only time will tell of its success! My brother Adam, who has spent the past 20 years coming to and from China, has been particularly generous in his support for my stay in China and for these initiatives.

These endeavors would not be possible and appreciations sorely incomplete without deep and profound acknowledgement of my father and mother, Professor Frederick and Shirley Rose Ehrlich. Their interest and support for new and pioneering projects, which for some not having visited China and seen its rapid change first-hand may appear bizarre. However, their initiative in developing a fund to support the exchange of students and translation of Jewish literature and their personal support, as well as their efforts in facilitating its success through the building of relations with important Australian and Israeli universities, is testament to their forward thinking attitudes and pioneering spirit, to which I am indebted. I would be grateful if I inherited a fraction of this. It is to them this book is dedicated.

M. Avrum Ehrlich
Jinan, Shandong Province, China

INTRODUCTION TO THE JEWISH–CHINESE NEXUS

M. Avrum Ehrlich

The Jewish immigration to China has fluctuated over the centuries. In the opening pages, I provide a chronology of Jewish–Chinese Relations throughout the ages, which may be used as a reference while reading the other contributions.

Apart from the Persian Jewish traders that settled on the Silk Route from the tenth century (though this date is still debated), most notably in Kaifeng, there were the Baghdadi-Indian Jewish traders who settled in Shanghai, Hong Kong, Singapore and other areas of East Asia, during the 1800s and 1900s; their numbers reached about 10,000 permanent residents, and still more itinerant traders and travelers through. This community left an indelible mark on the cities they sojourned. Their wealth and business empires were legendary and the reputation that Jews still have in Asia is attributed to their acumen and achievements.

Russian Jewish immigration to the northern Chinese city of Harbin in Heilongjiang Province, during the 1900s left an equally striking mark on Chinese consciousness. Reaching 40,000 souls, some of these immigrants later became successful in business, politics, culture and diplomacy in the U.S, Canada, Israel, and Australia. They continue to preserve the Jewish–Chinese legacy in various friendship and support societies around the world. The provincial government and the Harbin local government are very active in attracting Jews back to Harbin for the purpose of investment and tourism. They welcome Jewish pilgrimages to the synagogues and schools and cemetery that they have renovated with great care for this purpose.

The German immigration to Shanghai during the Second World War is also a notable and endearing drama. Jewish German refugees fleeing the imminent slaughter by the Nazis, were rejected from countless safe harbors in enlightened Europe, the U.S, Australia and pre-State Israel, but were ultimately granted permits to enter Shanghai and lived a relatively peaceful decade there. The memory is associated with redemption and opportunity in addition to the allure of the Orient. A highly cultured group of immigrants, the impact they left on the city and on its citizens, its cultural institutions and its economy is only now being represented in Chinese and foreign movies and books dedicated to their memory. This group of refugees proliferated throughout the world, the memory of Shanghai with them.

A disproportionately high number of Jews remained in China and assisted the fledgling Chinese Republic in humanitarian, political, diplomatic, and cultural fields. Matthias Messmer, scholar and researcher residing in Shanghai, in his article on Jewish Foreign Experts in China, relates how some became heroes of the Chinese people, other were venerated and respected till their dying days. A few are still alive, most in their 90s and may serve as a unique bridge between the Jewish and Chinese civilizations. They were some of the only Westerners to remain in China through its period of its isolation from the 1950s–70s. Six of the ten foreign-born members of the Central Government's People's Consultative Conference were at one point Jewish. In an upcoming work entitled *Jews and Judaism in Modern China* (Routledge, 2008), I discuss how this legacy recorded between the two peoples may serve as a remarkable facilitator and psychological marker in the development of a more profound Chinese–Jewish discourse.

The Chinese government is proud of its legacy towards the Jews and, even though Shanghai and Harbin were not under Chinese control during much of the first half of the twentieth century, the association of the Chinese people with the saving of thousands of Jews is an important psychological milestone in the developing relationship between Jews and Chinese. Living together under occupation, suffering as victims of war and humiliation, a mutual feeling of fraternity seems to have developed and is being studied and appreciated on various levels. Prof. Zhang Qianhong, professor of Jewish Studies at Henan University in Kaifeng and Jerry Gotel, Director of overseas projects and senior lecturer at London Jewish Cultural Center, address the sense of fraternity through suffering in their co-authored chapter, Rethinking the Tragedy of the Nanjing Massacre and its Connection with the Jewish Holocaust, Part II, Chapter 4.

While the history of Jews in ancient China is fascinating, it has already been explored. Only when yet unearthed archaeological or documentary material on the Jews of the Silk Route surfaces, or government documents relating to the Baghdadi, Russian and German Jews in China are released, will these historical disciplines re-open with new and exciting vistas. In the meantime, the social and intellectual enmeshing between Jews and Chinese that has emerged in the last decade is expanding into new, and yet unexplored, disciplines in philosophy and sociology, and illuminates a fascinating meeting of civilizations and fusion of ideas and cultures that deserves to be explored.

The most important Jewish presence in China is not so much the physical presence of communities but the role Jewish thought, ideas, literature, and reputation play on the internal cultural dialectics of the Chinese people as they understand, revise, and reconstruct their own culture after the devastation of the Cultural Revolution.

This book brings together chapters on various disparate topics belonging to different academic disciplines from history, sociology, philosophy, theology, and diplomacy, with the thread tying them together in an intriguing and exotic relationship which has been slowly intertwining, between two of the most unlikely and almost antithetical national, cultural, religious, and social collectives. The book focuses on the Jewish–Chinese nexus in modernity and explores some of the areas where the relationship may grow and burgeon. The book illuminates the possible areas of future collaboration and by no means exhausts the subject, rather introduces the possibilities. In Part I, Chapter 1, Overview of the Jewish Presence in Contemporary China, I briefly survey the various Jewish communities and Jewish demography in Chinese cities.

The book includes three chapters on different aspects relating to the descendants of the Jews of Kaifeng. Prof. Xu Xin, a leading Chinese scholar of Judaism at Nanjing University, in Part V, Chapter 2, Chinese Policy Towards the Jews of Kaifeng and their Descendants, explains the evolution of the Chinese government's policy not to officially recognize them as a separate and distinct ethnic minority. This illuminates the trend amongst the descendents to assimilate into the dominant Han ethnic group of Chinese as a way of seeking approval and within traditional Confucian thought and practice as a way of showing its loyalty to the state ideology. Ironically, this was later used against them to exclude them from public recognition as an independent ethnic group.

In Part V, Chapter 1, co-authored with Liang Pingan, a visiting scholar at the Shanghai Academy of Social Sciences and Deputy Chief Secretary of the Institute of Kaifeng Jewish History and Culture, a more detailed description of the status of the contemporary Jewish community in Kaifeng is provided and the developments amongst the Kaifeng Jewish descendants are brought up till the present. Rabbi Anson Laytner, President of the Sino–Judaic Institute of America and editor of Points East in Part V, Chapter 3, presents a theory for the existence of a distinct liberal theology of Kaifeng Judaism. Rabbi Laytner references and compares Kaifeng Judaism with the case of American Jewry and liberal Judaism. In doing so, a bridge of understanding and familiarity forms between two otherwise unreconciled communities of Jews, as well as between American and Chinese culture. By observing common patterns and ideas, the gap and misunderstandings between East and West may be reduced and commonalities identified.

The modern period for Chinese–Jewish relations began somewhere in the 1980s. Some of the first people to enter into business and cultural relations in the late 1970s–80s were individual Jews who arrived to do business, to study Chinese language, culture or politics, or were involved in diplomacy.

In his personal account of this period, Part I, Chapter 3, Dr. David Buxbaum, lawyer and business consultant living in China, describes his role in
developing relations with Chinese officialdom and business communities,
and the burgeoning of Jewish communities and a Jewish presence in which
he has participated over the last 40 years in China.

Prof. Fu Xiaowei, professor of Comparative Literature and Culture, and
director of the Center of Judaic and Chinese Studies at Sichuan International Studies University, and Wang Yi, professor of Aesthetics and Aes-
thetic Education, and director of the Institute of Tourism and Aesthetics at
Sichuan International Studies University, explore the cultural influence of
Jewish authors whose work have been translated into Chinese, as well as
some of the difficulties in transmitting Jewish ideas in the Chinese language.
Prof. Yiyi Chen, associate professor at the Dept of Near Eastern Studies at
Peking University writes a chapter examining the influence of the Hebrew
Bible on Chinese thinking, and surveys where it is studied and the problems
encountered in translating it to express the more Jewish aspects of its content. Prof. Zhong Zhiqing, associate professor of the Institute of Foreign
Literature at the Chinese Academy of Social Sciences explores the growing
interest in modern Israeli literature which is being translated into Chinese
by her and other Chinese scholars and writers. These chapters accentuate
the growing interest in Jewish-related culture and the possibilities that this
will pave the way for a deeper cultural understanding and exchange.

Prof. Fu Youde, dean of China's only state-sponsored center for Judaic
and Inter-Religious Studies at Shandong University and well-known Chinese philosopher, writes a chapter describing a Chinese impression of
Judaism. This is an important contribution as the Chinese perspective of
Jews is different from that in Europe and the U.S and different from how
Jews perceive themselves, but it is equally legitimate and insightful and
interesting.

Prof. Fu Youde also contributes a chapter examining how Judaism can
serve as a model for the reconstruction of Chinese culture especially in the
emergence of a form of Confucianism that can serve China as an ethical
and spiritual framework. This work is deeply meaningful as it opens new
vistas for Jewish–Chinese dialogue and provides an opportunity for Judaism
to view itself, not only as a religion for Jews, but also as a model for cultural
and ethical continuation and renewal. I discuss this subject in more detail in
an upcoming book, mentioned above. Galia Patt-Shamir, senior lecturer of
Chinese philosophy and Comparative Philosophy at Tel Aviv University
together with Mr Yoav Rapoport, Sinologist and Chinese-Hebrew translator, contribute chapters comparing and contrasting Jewish and Confucian
thought.

Profs Suzanne Rutland, Associate Professor and Chair of the Department
of Hebrew, Biblical and Jewish Studies at the University of Sydney and
Emeritus Professor Sol Encel of the University of NSW give an account of

the first steps in developing Jewish studies courses and seminars in China in 1992, which were hosted by Australian Jewish communal figures.

Prof. Zhang Ping of Tel Aviv University, writes on the extent and interest that Judaism and Israel commands on the Chinese internet. The Chinese internet has developed into the most important means for Chinese to express their thoughts and interests and Jewish related issues are emerging out of pure Chinese fascination, not driven by Jewish bodies or groups, and reflects a genuine interest in "the other."

David Straub, a visiting researcher at the center for Judaic and Inter-Religious Studies at Shandong University, contributes a different perspective on the Chinese–Jewish nexus by examining the phenomena of Chinese babies given up for adoption and finding themselves in North American Jewish homes, raised as Jews, and the emergence of a mixed Jewish–Chinese identity. The ramifications of this phenomenon may only be seen in a generation but are no less than fascinating.

Prof. Jonathan Goldstein, professor of East Asian history at the University of West Georgia and research associate at Harvard University's Fairbank Center for East Asian Research, writes about the genesis of Israeli diplomatic relations with China. Ilan Maor, former Israel Consul-General in Shanghai and head of the Asian desk in the Israeli Ministry of Foreign Affairs writes about the development of the State of Israel's economic relationship with China. These chapters open up new areas of Chinese–Israeli–Jewish relations and, though not directly related to culture of philosophic exchange, are tied into the meeting of civilizations and cooperation that invariably paves the way for cultural and ideological exchanges via the exchange of personnel between the countries, and the cultural and political hurdles involved in facilitating successful relations. Liang Pingan contributes another chapter on the role of China in developing Mid-Eastern stability. This too is an interesting area for consideration, as China's emergence as a superpower together with its strong relations with Mid-Eastern oil-rich countries, as well as with Israel, changes the dynamics of Mid-Eastern dialogue with many avenues and ramifications to Israel and the Jewish world. I will discuss this subject more in the above-mentioned book to be published with Routledge towards the end of 2008.

Regarding translations, transliterations, and use of Chinese characters, we have used simplified Chinese characters rather than traditional characters. The system of transliterations used in this book is Pinyin, which is used in Mainland China, rather than the Wade-Giles system used in Taiwan. Hebrew words, if used, are given a brief in-text explanation. We have attached two maps for convenience and other documents that may be of use to readers and scholars.

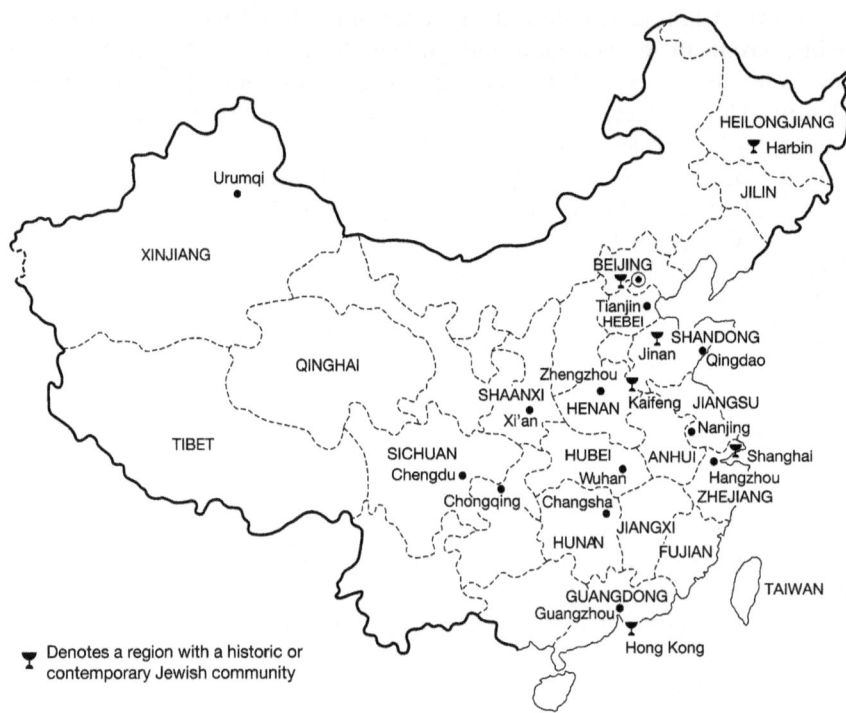

Urumqi

XINJIANG

HEILONGJIANG
♟ Harbin

JILIN

TIBET

QINGHAI

BEIJING
⊙
Tianjin ●
HEBEI
Jinan ♟ SHANDONG
● Qingdao
Zhengzhou
SHAANXI Kaifeng ♟ JIANGSU
Xi'an ● HENAN
Nanjing ♟

SICHUAN HUBEI ♟ Shanghai
Chengdu ● ANHUI
Wuhan ● Hangzhou
Chongqing ● ZHEJIANG
Changsha ●
JIANGXI
HUNAN FUJIAN

TAIWAN

GUANGDONG
Guangzhou ●♟
Hong Kong ●

♟ Denotes a region with a historic or
   contemporary Jewish community

Map 1

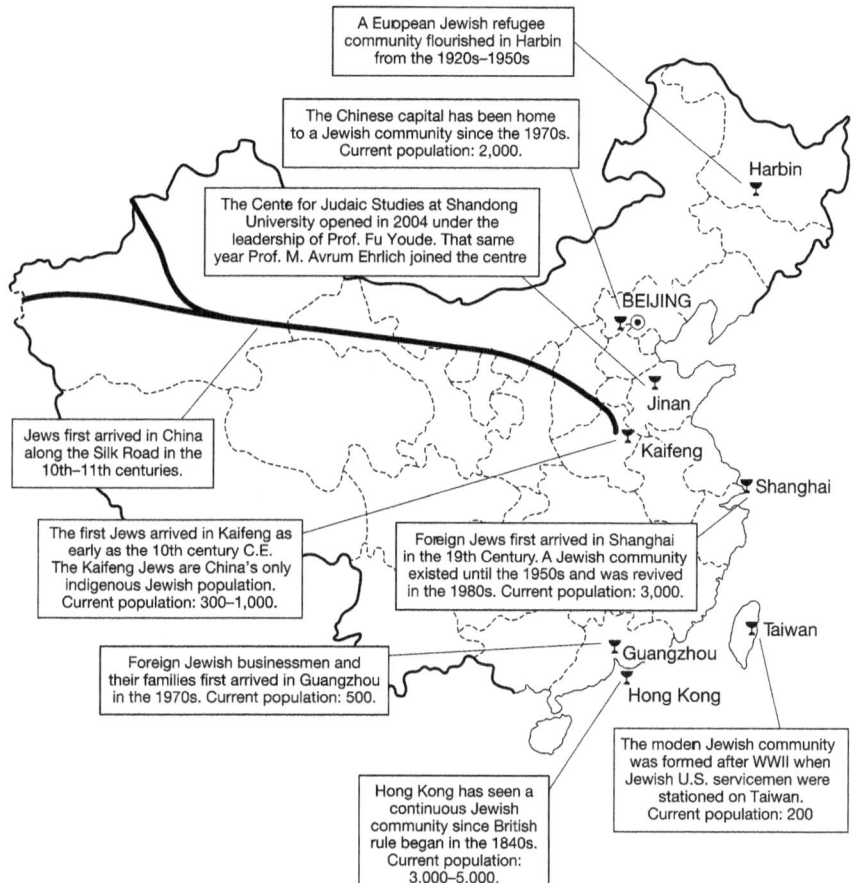

A European Jewish refugee community flourished in Harbin from the 1920s–1950s

The Chinese capital has been home to a Jewish community since the 1970s. Current population: 2,000.

The Cente for Judaic Studies at Shandong University opened in 2004 under the leadership of Prof. Fu Youde. That same year Prof. M. Avrum Ehrlich joined the centre

Jews first arrived in China along the Silk Road in the 10th–11th centuries.

The first Jews arrived in Kaifeng as early as the 10th century C.E. The Kaifeng Jews are China's only indigenous Jewish population. Current population: 300–1,000.

Foreign Jews first arrived in Shanghai in the 19th Century. A Jewish community existed until the 1950s and was revived in the 1980s. Current population: 3,000.

Foreign Jewish businessmen and their families first arrived in Guangzhou in the 1970s. Current population: 500.

The modern Jewish community was formed after WWII when Jewish U.S. servicemen were stationed on Taiwan. Current population: 200

Hong Kong has seen a continuous Jewish community since British rule began in the 1840s. Current population: 3,000–5,000.

Harbin

BEIJING

Jinan

Kaifeng

Shanghai

Taiwan

Guangzhou

Hong Kong

Map 2

Part I

CONTEMPORARY JEWS IN CHINA

1

OVERVIEW OF THE JEWISH PRESENCE IN CONTEMPORARY CHINA

M. Avrum Ehrlich

In his recent book *China – West-östliche Schauplätze, Böhlau* (2007), Matthias Messmer surveys the life and times of Jews who lived in China during the pre-State period. From his depictions, it becomes clear that the Jewish–Chinese nexus was not at all insignificant, in fact, Jews, because of their refugee predicament, were one of the most active foreign elements in China during one of its most turbulent periods of revolution and change. In Part I, Chapter 2 of the present book, Messmer gives detailed descriptions of those Jews who had official status in China as "Foreign Experts". The next paragraphs are an incomplete collation of some of the exceptional people who lived and/or worked in China for varying periods before the establishment of the PRC, and some during the Cultural Revolution. Some of their stories are nothing less than intriguing. Some became national heroes for the Chinese people, others were recognized as heroes of humanity or to the Jewish people. A number of books and movies have already been written about their exploits and adventures, and many more books and movies deserve to be made about those who have till now been forgotten.

It would be appreciated if readers able to furnish more information regarding people left out of this list (or out of Matthias Messmer's chapter) could offer more details about their lives and work, so that future editions of this book can be updated.

Journalists include: Hahn, Emily; Isaacs, Harold R; Peffer, Nathaniel; Sokolsky, George Ephraim; Stein, Gunther; White, Theodore.

Advisors/Couriers/Emissaries include: Borodin, Mikhail; Cohen, Israel; Glassgold, Adolph; Granich, Max; Jordan, Charles; Katz, Rudolf; Margolis, Laura; Rajchman, Ludwik; Shippe, Hans; Siegel, Manuel; Werner, Ruth.

"Adventurers" include: Bennett, Milly; Cohen, Morris Abraham; Lincoln, Ignacz; Trebitsch Prohme, Rayna.

Diplomats include: Einstein, Lewis; Sokobin, Samuel.

Explorers and Travel Writers: Holitscher, Arthur; Katz, Richard; Kisch, Egon Erwin; Schuster, Carl; Stein, Marc Aurel.

Medical Doctors include: Freudmann, Walter; Jensen, Fritz; Robitscher-Hahn, Magdalena; Politzer, Robert; Rosenfeld, Jakob.

Academics/Artists include: Lang, Olga Abramovna; Löwenthal, Rudolf; Reifler, Erwin; Schiff, Friedrich; Tandler, Julius; Weidenreich, Franz.

Jewish Refugees from Nazi-Germany include: Blitz, Karl; Bloch, David Ludwig; Brieger, Lothar; Dawison, Walter; Frank, Ladislaus; Friedländer, Fritz; Friedrichs, Theodor Hinzelmann; Heinz, Hans; Jacoby, Hans Kaim; Rudolf, Julius; Kneucker, Alfred W; Kuttner, Fritz Alex; Lippa, Ernst M; Schwarz, Ernst; Steiner, Karl; Stern, Hellmut; Storfer, Adolf Josef; Tonn, Willy.

Sephardic Jews (long-time residents) in Shanghai include: Ezra, Nissim Elias Benjamin; Hardoon, Silas; Kadoorie, Sir Elly; Sassoon, Sir Victor; Sopher, Arthur and Theodore.

Russian Jews (long-time residents) in Shanghai include: Avshalomov, Aaron; Birman, Meir; Ginsbourg, Anna; Hasser, Judith; Krasno, Rena; Levaco, Michael; Liberman, Jaacov; Schneierson, Vic; Spunt, Georges; Zimmerman, Isabelle.[1]

While the circumstances of history caused eminents to emerge in China, today's circumstances are bringing a different Jewish demography. Presently there are approximately 6,000–7,000 Jews living permanently or temporarily residing in mainland China. These estimates include around 2,000 in Beijing, 3,000 in Shanghai, 500 in Guangdong, 50 in Shandong, 300–1,000 Jewish descendents in Kaifeng, 3,000–5,000 in Hong Kong, and 200 in Taiwan.

Contemporary Jews in China have come from all over the world: Australia, North America, Europe, Israel, and also Russian and Kavkazi Jews. The Jewish presence has diverse expressions and is relatively unorganized. Most are not connected to each other or to the organized Jewish community, though Passover and New Year celebrations draw large crowds to the reform and Chabad events in Beijing, Shanghai, and other places.

There are also large numbers of American, European, and Israeli Jewish tours visiting China for short periods of time. The Jewish tourism industry visiting Shanghai, Beijing, Harbin, and Kaifeng is relatively significant in Jewish numerical terms, with an estimated 5,000 and growing Jewish tourists participating in organized groups per year.

Today, China attracts different types of Jews with different backgrounds, from various countries and cultures, with different languages. The attraction for many people, no less for Jews, are the prospects of meaningful employment opportunities and a cheap alternative to Western cities. Some Jews have come to China in their 'golden age' to work, teach, and live cheaply with their pensions or savings intact. Some have married Chinese women abroad and returned with them to work in China, others married Chinese in China and remained. Most Jews come as skilled professionals for large multinational corporations or for their own private or family businesses.

Many come for trade fairs and live in China for short periods. Some Jewish individuals moved to China to establish businesses and have since settled, and others are here for long periods of time, from five to ten years. A large number of people remain in China for two to three years before moving on or returning to their homes. Many decide to remain longer, developing business or employment relations, mastering Chinese and building lives in China. Gradually, the community of permanent residents is growing, families are being raised in China and children are speaking English, Hebrew, and Chinese from birth.

An unknown number of Jewish business people come to China throughout the year, many have their own businesses and have Chinese partners manufacturing for them, others have joint ventures and investments in China. A growing number of multinational companies are entering China, as well as large Israeli investments seeking opportunity. Over 70 Israeli businesses are registered with the nascent Israel China Chamber of Commerce in Beijing, and there are more who have a presence in China with no coordination or contact with other Israelis.

El Al flies from Tel Aviv to Beijing three times per week, at an average of 300 people per flight; the annual number of entries into China with El Al amounts to about 43,000. Other flights through Russia and Turkey are popular routes for Israelis flying directly to China. There are also other entry points through Shanghai and Hong Kong and the overland routes through West China.

Still more small groups of Israelis come for short study periods of three months to a year, especially those studying Chinese medicine, acupuncture, massage, and pressure point therapy, and often live in Chengdu in Sichuan province and other cities famous for these disciplines. Some come to learn Kung Fu or to work. There is a growing trend for students of East Asia to study in Chinese universities, mainly in Beijing.

In response to the growing expatriate communities living in China's major cities, and the need to accommodate their religious faiths, the Chinese government came to an understanding with Chabad that religious and social meetings may convene without government interference, providing they strictly adhere to the rule that no Chinese nationals may attend these activities. Even though the Chinese government does not formally recognize Judaism as a legal religion in China, it has opened relations with the State of Israel and has come to accommodate the Jewish community. The government has accepted the rights of Jews to congregate, but it is strongly opposed to foreign religions evangelizing within China, which sometimes creates problems when Chinese girlfriends or wives of Jews or guests wish to join community events. Unlike other religious denominations like Catholicism, Protestantism, and Islam, the prohibition against proselytizing is in conformity with Jewish norms. The inevitable process of full recognition as a religious denomination seems to be waiting for the right time and the initiative of the Israeli or foreign diplomacy or the initiative of other international Jewish organizations.

Shanghai and Beijing are the major sites of the contemporary evolvement of new Jewish communities in China. In both cases, liberal congregations were established first with Chabad moving in to Shanghai in 1998 and later to Beijing in 2001. The reform movement has had a presence in Beijing for about 25 years, initiated by Ms Roberta Lipson, a long-time resident of Beijing.

Today, Chabad represents the most dominant organized Jewish presence in China with rabbis in Shanghai, Beijing, and Guangzhou, and new communities and satellite community centers opening up with kindergartens and schools, *mikveh*, kosher food and a hub for community life. A cross-section of Jewish existence is poetically illustrated at Shabbat or festival meal in Beijing, Shanghai, and Guangzhou. An assortment of nationalities may congregate: American, French, Russian, Iranian, Australian, South American, Moroccan, and Israeli Jews doing business in the city; Swiss, French, American, and English students of political science, Chinese culture, and language; and Hasidic Jews from Brooklyn working the garment trade or coming to supervise kosher product manufacturing.

Meanwhile, local governments in Harbin, Tianjin, and Shanghai are commemorating the legacy of their past Jewish populations and funding the renovations of cemeteries, synagogues, and important historical places. Chinese officials are generally proud of their liberal and humane relations towards the Jews during the Nazi persecutions.

The issue of the Jewish descendents of Kaifeng is still a delicate subject for the Chinese government. The sensitivity emerges from fears the Muslim population in the same region may react to this and provoke unrest. Nevertheless, the small Jewish community in Kaifeng draws a large amount of international interest and many journalists, politicians, diplomats, and distinguished Jews from all walks of life have visited the Jewish community of Kaifeng. It must confound the government how such a small group of very poor and nondescript Chinese workers, in an old and underdeveloped Chinese city, can attract the attention and imagination of so many influential foreigners who come to visit.

Guangzhou and Shenzhen in the south draw many Jewish traders and business people to their trade shows, and Chabad has set up a center accommodating them for Shabbat and holidays, as well as catering to Jews that live there permanently. Qingdao and Jinan in Shandong province are developing communities. Qingdao, a coastal city has developed a small, loosely connected community of Israelis involved in trade. Jinan, the capital city of Shandong attracts scholars and tourists coming to Shandong University to teach, research or visit at the Center for Judaic and Inter-Religious Studies and as a place to begin trips to important Confucian and Dao sites in the province.

Many diplomatic, advisory, and government positions in the American, Australian, Argentinean, European Union, and Israeli embassies and consulates are Jews. The Ambassador for the European Union is presently a Jew. Israeli travelers, investors, traders, and foreign experts may constitute up to 40 per cent of the Jewish population of China.

American, Australian, South African, and European business people have come to China to work and stay. Foreign experts, foreign teachers, heads of companies, and senior executives from large multinational corporations now live in major Chinese cities.

With expatriate communities continuously strengthening their presence in many parts of China, and with many people settling down for growing periods of time, it seems that Jewish communities in China are on a road to greater strength and expansion, both in numbers and in terms of influence and stature. These communities are far from being transient.

A large number of Jews re-visit China on "pilgrimages" to the graves of their family members or to revisit places they lived. Jewish heritage tours to Kaifeng, Shanghai, and Harbin attract a few thousand Jews every year. The incoming of so many well-to-do Jewish people to these areas is noted by the local Chinese authorities and they have gone to efforts to ensure the preservation of cemeteries and cultural sites of interest to Jewish tourism. There is still no agreement regarding the property rights over the old Shanghai synagogues and the tracts of land confiscated from Jews and nationalized during modern China's establishment.

The kosher industry in China is a fast-growing business and many of the well-known kosher supervisors work in China, and tens, if not hundreds, of ultra orthodox supervisors come to China every year to ensure the production of kosher products. The sight of ultra orthodox Jews entering into second tier industrialized Chinese cities to check the production of a food line at a factory is an unusual one to behold, and the trend looks as if it will grow.

Jewish studies are being taught and researched in many cities around China. A number of Beijing universities teach Hebrew language; Nanjing University has courses in Jewish History; Henan University in Kaifeng teaches Holocaust Studies; Shanghai Academy of the Social Sciences teaches courses on Israel and Political Studies; Shandong University in Jinan was appointed to set up a key research institute in Jewish studies with its mandate to train a generation of Chinese scholars in Jewish studies and undertake large translation projects making Jewish culture and wisdom available in the Chinese language.[2]

The Chinese attitude towards Jews is very positive. There seems to be a general grassroots sentiment that the Jews are very clever and successful and should be admired. It is very common for a Chinese person to state upon discovering that you are a Jew, "the Jews are the cleverest people in the world." It seems that this is not an affront to the Chinese' own sense that they are the cleverest people in the world. Perhaps the sense that the Jews are too small a group to be perceived as a real threat gives the Chinese the confidence to compliment them so freely. Israel is also seen by many to be brave and innovative. Though its hi-tech industry is active and cooperative with Chinese industries, the cooperation in the area of agriculture has been most successful in winning the estimation of many Chinese, especially in the agriculturally based provinces.

It seems a proportionally large amount of secular Jews return to a more traditional Jewish identity while in China, usually through the aegis of Chabad. The reasons for this may be speculated as due to the sense of isolation of foreigners in China, the pressure to be identified as something else beyond just being a "foreigner" in the eyes of Chinese, and may also be related to the very strong interest and respect that Chinese have for Jews, who may have been embarrassed or hesitant about their identities in their countries of origin, allowing the Jews to become proud of their ethnic association in China.

Beijing

Beijing has a particularly large presence of students scattered in its numerous universities. Many have little to no contact with the Jewish community owing to the city's large size and the universities being far from the foreign business and diplomatic areas where the Jewish community is based. Being the country's capital, the diplomatic corps is very large: the city is home to the largest American Embassy, the second-largest Australian Embassy, and so on for other countries. With these diplomatic missions are proportionately large numbers of Jews; it is estimated that some 30 per cent of the American embassy staff are Jewish, while in the past even the ambassador was Jewish. The current Ambassador to the European Union is Jewish. There are also large numbers of business people, traders, administrators, and consultants working for large companies who are Jewish.

The major industries, trades, and professions of Jewish residents of Beijing include private businesses, executives of global organizations, students, textiles, multinational companies, law firms, engineers, computer consultants, English teachers, and academics. The kosher (and hallal) industry is also growing in China.

There is not yet a chief rabbi of China, but it may be a model for organizing and representing the Jewish communities growing in China to the Beijing authorities. Another suggestion for organizing the Jewish community range is a board of residents and representatives of overseas Jewish interests. There are also suggestions for a Jewish museum and a major center for Jewish studies to be based in Beijing. But various diplomatic hurdles have to be overcome before these milestones can be achieved. It is felt in many quarters that a Jewish–Chinese cultural relationship is important, but the State of Israel is mainly concerned with diplomatic and economic relations.

Roberta Lipson and Alisa Silverstein were some of the first Jews to reside in Beijing over 20 years ago. They built a series of medical services in Beijing and helped found the first Reform Jewish community in 1988. Jewish expatriates began to gather for Shabbat evening services. These services grew so that on the High Holidays a rabbi was brought over from abroad, the Passover *seder* is held at the home of Ms. Lipson with the entire community and other Jews visiting Beijing invited to attend; Shabbat services are attended by a few dozen people.

In 2002, Rabbi Shimon and Dini Freundlich moved to Beijing from Hong Kong and established the second Chabad synagogue in mainland China, after Shanghai. Congregating in the rabbi's family home, tens of people, sometimes a hundred, gather for weekly Shabbat prayers and meals. The people who congregate are mixed, from most parts of the world, students, professionals, diplomats, business people, travelers, tourists, and adventurers. Some are orthodox, others traditional to non-observant. As it is in many international hubs, the mix is eclectic.

In 2003, a Jewish kindergarten or *ganeinu* was set up as part of a different international school. The schools have continually grown and a new education facility was opened up with the support of the Rohr family fund, which included a *mikveh* and a small museum of Chinese Jewry. The rabbi has continually found ways to develop the community and the services for Jews living or visiting Beijing. The kosher industry supports many of these initiatives; kosher food is prepared for Beijing–Tel Aviv flights, for Jewish tourist groups and religious business people, and for the local communities. There is an Israeli and kosher restaurant near the Chabad center.

It should be noted that Chabad discourages the attendance of Chinese nationals at any of its activities. Chinese interested in observing or participating in Jewish meals, even accompanying Jewish friends or intimates, have often been very politely told that this would be in breach of an agreement with the Chinese authorities.

The Russian Azerbaijan Jews in Beijing

In the 1990s, an influx of Jews mainly from the Azerbaijani city of Kuba, along with some from Central Asia and other parts of the Caucasus, with others from Moscow, arrived in Beijing for trade and business purposes. Today, they number about 300, mainly male Jews. Their wives and families are mainly in Azerbaijan, Moscow, and Israel (in Tirat ha Karmel), with other family members in New York. Many arrived in Beijing as young as 17 years old and remained there doing trade, establishing a younger contingent. The average age of people is from about 40 to 50, with people in their 60s living in Beijing. They own their own businesses and gather together in their own restaurants. They have a strong hold on certain industries, including the garment industry and the overland freight cargo trade with Moscow and elsewhere.

Some wives and children have moved to Beijing and their children have begun to attend the Chabad kindergarten and education system. The Russian Azerbaijan Jews identify very proudly, if simply, with their Jewish heritage, often knowing prayers by heart, and are demonstrative about their associations and treat the national Jewish days with earnest. Also, they generally only seek Jewish wives from their home community; marriage to Chinese even if they convert is rare. They like to consider themselves Russian Jews, though they still have proud associations with their region and respect their Rabbi Adam, still in Kuva.

As few from this community speak English, their participation in the Western style Chabad center was not as active, and it was decided to open to a center catering to this community and people living in the more central areas of Beijing. The Chabad rabbi speaks Russian and has come to know the community and its needs well.

Shanghai

Today, most of the Jews in Shanghai come to set up their own trade companies or source goods, to work in international corporations, to teach English, or to study Chinese or Chinese history, culture or business.

As far as Shanghai is an international city and shares in international culture, many Chinese artists and performers, writers, directors, and an array of other professions, collaborate with Jews around the world and there is an active exchange of Jewish–Chinese relations in these disciplines.

There are a large number of Jewish tourists in Shanghai at any given time and a number of interesting sites of Jewish cultural value. A good deal of Shanghai's most expensive properties, its most prestigious downtown shopping streets and the site of the municipal government quarters was once owned by Jews in the first half of the twentieth century. Many books and accounts of life in Shanghai and photo albums and studies of Jewish architecture and music in Shanghai have been produced. Parts of the Jewish ghetto are intact and a museum is housed in one of its synagogues. Discussions with local authorities have taken place as to the extent that this area should be preserved and reconstructed to reflect its Jewish component. The local authorities, while keen to bring Jewish tourism into the city, only allow access to the beautiful Ohel Rachel synagogue in Shanghai and other synagogues. The gravestones from the dismantled Jewish cemetery of Shanghai were found in villages and rivers where the rubble was dumped and many have been restored by the efforts of Dvir Bar Gal, an Israeli artist and journalist residing in Shanghai.

The original Jewish communities and their buildings and properties were nationalized in the early 1950s. The first modern community was a Sephardi *minyan*, this was taken over with the arrival in 1998 of the Chabad Rabbi Shalom Greenberg and his wife. The new Jewish community is a distance from the historic centers of Jewish life, rupturing the sense of continuity between the two. While tourists and travelers may prefer to spend time on the historic Bund waterfront, Hankou ghetto area, or the Nanjing Road shopping area, the long-term residents of Shanghai may prefer to live in the Hongqiao area of villas and more gentile living, next to the domestic airport.

A large number of Jews, mainly Israelis do not identify with the organized Jewish community, but they maintain groupings in different areas of Shanghai.

A new Chabad center has been opened in Pudong, the banking and development area of Shanghai, where many corporations, banks, and multinationals are based and many Jews live.

The Shanghai municipality is proud of Shanghai's role in saving tens of thousands of Jews from the Nazi Holocaust and enjoys a unique sense of friendship and respect for the old Jews of Shanghai. In the major Shanghai municipal museum there is a permanent exhibition on Shanghai's Jews, with a large wall prominently displaying the sentiments "while the enlightened nations of the earth closed their doors to the fate of the Jews running for their life to escape the death camps of Europe, the only city on earth that welcomed them with equality and respect was Shanghai."

The Chinese are generally enthusiastic about meeting Jews and have general and widespread ideas that the Jews are "very clever," "rich," "influential," "upright," "tough negotiators," and so on. There is a renewed interest in Jewish issues and several books, albeit superficial in nature, have come out from Shanghai publishers on Jewish subjects; for example "how to be a Jewish millionaire" and "the secrets to Jewish life". There is a small center for Israel and Jewish studies at the Shanghai Academy of the Social Sciences led by Prof. Pan Guang. He is also the editor of a history and pictorial book commemorating the Jews of Shanghai. This center especially focuses on the study of political issues relating to China and Israel and the Jews; for example, there are papers and studies on Israel–China relations, and on the Jewish Lobby in the U.S.

Many Jews have arrived in Shanghai and have found it convenient to associate with the Jewish community; some have become more identified with religious observance while in Shanghai, with a curiously high number of people becoming orthodox while in Shanghai. This may be attributed to the largesse of the city, to the eclectic mix of people coming to Shabbat dinners at the Chabad center and perceiving the diversity and richness of Jewish life. It also may be attributed to the strong positive affirmation of the Chinese towards Jews, making Jewish identity more attractive.

Many Jewish and Israeli men have met Chinese girlfriends; some have begun to convert to Judaism and some have married and slowly negotiate their mixed Chinese–Jewish identity.

Guangzhou and Shenzhen

Chabad houses have been established in these trade and manufacturing cities in the south of China. Being a mainland extension of Hong Kong and the gateway to Chinese exports, many Jewish-owned businesses and traders come to the trade shows like the famous Canton Fair to see and buy goods. Many have permanent offices and apartments and visit regularly. Since 2006, there has been a permanent Chabad presence and festivals are celebrated together, with kosher food is available for orthodox Jews attending the fairs. These gatherings of Jewish business people have brought together American, Moroccan, Iranian, Syrian, and Russian Jews, not to mention, Israelis, Europeans, South Africans, and Australians.

Macao

As a Portuguese colony, many Portuguese Jews arrived at Macao and, while disguising their faith for the benefit of the Inquisition which functioned there, there are nevertheless still Jewish signs and indications of a Jewish presence.[3]

A handful of American Jewish China traders lived in Macao from approximately 1790 to 1846, when Canton itself was closed off to Western traders. Apart from the fact that these Jews did not attend church or support Christian missionaries, they were indistinguishable from their Christian colleagues in south China. These Jews were, nevertheless, victims of the anti-Semitism of their Christian compatriots. John Heard wrote that Joseph Moses "sports now a ferocious whisker, dirty moustache, and a coat which a Christian would not be seen in." Nathan Kinsman wrote that "it is astonishing to me that Miss King permits that dissipated Jew Moses to gallant her about, [sic] there is no accounting for tastes."

Today, Macao is a gambling haven, an extension of Las Vegas in the orient extending its services to hotels and hospitality, and a growing international conference area. As such, a number of American Jewish property and casino interests have invested in Macao, most notably billionaire businessman and property developer Sheldon Adelson who has also given large amounts of money to Jewish charities in Israel and elsewhere. The city has no organized Jewish community.

Shandong Province

Jinan, the capital of Shandong province is the home to a number of interesting pieces in Jewish–Chinese relations. Dr. Jacob Rosenfeld, who was to become a hero in Chinese history for serving as a doctor in the front lines in the war against the Japanese, and who eventually became the doctor for Mao Zedong, lived and worked in Jinan's well-known Qilu hospital. He was finally buried in Israel and his gravesite has become a quasi-shrine for Chinese government delegations to Israel.

Sam Ginsbourg, who was born in Harbin, later moved to Jinan and served as a professor of Russian literature, at Shandong University, one of China's oldest and most respected academic centers. He penned an autobiography entitled *My First Sixty Years in China*, which tells the fascinating story of Chinese history from the eyes of a Chinese-born person of strong Jewish persuasion, who actively participated in modern Chinese history.

In a somewhat causal relationship, through a related series of events, a center for Jewish studies was set up at Shandong University in the 1990s headed by a well-known Chinese professor of philosophy, Fu Youde. Over a decade, he developed this center to become the foremost institute of Jewish studies and, endorsed and funded by the Chinese Central Government's Higher Education Department, to train a generation of scholars in Jewish thought, language and history, and to undertake large translation programs. In this course of events, the present author was invited to take up a position at Shandong University. A number of Jews live in Jinan, a number of academics, tourists, conference attendees, kosher supervisors, and Jewish traders come through Jinan, which combines a large industrial city, with China's largest agricultural lands and productivity. A number of Israeli businesses have collaborated with Chinese agricultural farms to develop irrigation and greenhouse techniques. Israeli billionaire Yitzhak Tshuva's company Elad recently invested over $220 million in a building project in the city; the deal was signed by his son Elad Tshuva and the company's Far East chairman Pinchas Cohen in 2007.

The Shandong people are generally aware of Jews and grateful for Israeli contributions. Sister-city relationships have been set up between Jinan and Israeli cities and other cooperation is being planned.

A larger number of Israelis and some American Jews have settled in Shandong's coastal city Qingdao, and participate in trade, freight delivery, and manufacturing.

Hong Kong

There are an estimated 3,000–5,000 Jews living on Hong Kong Island, with some in Kowloon.[4] The first Jews arrived in the mid-1800s from Iraq via Bombay. Ashkenazim refugees from Eastern Europe, arrived in the 1880–90s. The numbers dwindled till the 1970s when Hong Kong's strong economic position attracted an influx of Jewish businessmen and professionals, including bankers, lawyers, and academics.

In 1974, Israel appointed its first career Consul-General to Hong Kong and in 1985, the Jewish community was estimated at approximately 230 families, or over 600 people of 25 different nationalities, with High Holy Days with four sets of services for Ashkenazi, Sephardi, Reform, and Chabad. The site of the old historic synagogue, Ohel Leah, was preserved, and a Jewish Club developed in the grounds. The Community founded the Carmel School, an independent non-denominational Jewish day school. In 1997, when the British handed Hong Kong back to the People's Republic of China, the Jewish community lost many families, who felt their futures were at risk. Once the world realized the benign nature of the new Hong Kong government, a wave of migrants arrived, mostly young professionals and their families, and swelled the ranks of the Jewish community.

Free trade, low taxation, and excellent market conditions help make the business environment, where nearly 100 Israeli companies are registered with the Israeli consulate; thirty-seven diamond dealers, thirteen telecom companies, nine high-tech, four information technology and four transportation companies, including El Al and Zim. Twelve companies specialize in banking, security, medical equipment, business development, and import–export.

Hong Kong has five organized congregations. Ohel Leah, housed in a beautiful hundred-year-old synagogue, is modern orthodox. Three other orthodox communities are Chabad, Shuva Israel, and Kehillat Zion; United Jewish Congregation represents Conservative/Reform levels of observance.

The community is well organized. The main funding body is the Ohel Leah Synagogue Charity, which supports the Ohel Leah Synagogue, Jewish Community Center, *mikvah*, *chevra kadisha* (burial society), Jewish Benevolent Society, and cemetery. It gives partial funding to other institutions and congregations.

Major organizations include the JCC (Jewish Community Center). The center houses a library, which includes the Sino–Judaic Collection and archives of material found on the Jews in China and Southeast Asia. The center has two kosher restaurants, a mini-supermarket, function rooms, and a swimming pool. Restaurants are under full-time kosher supervision and the JCC imports a wide range of products from Israel, Australia, South Africa, and the U.S.

Other organizations and services include a *mikvah*, *chevra kadisha*, Jewish Benevolent Society, Jewish Women's Association, United Israel Appeal (UIA), Jewish National Fund (JNF), Israel Chamber of Commerce, Jewish Times Asia, various Ashkenazi and Sephardi Yeshivot, and study halls are active for travelers and traders and local residents.

Taiwan

On the disputed island of Taiwan, there are about 200–300 Jews living mainly in Taipei. The Taiwanese Jewish community includes American,

European, and Israeli businessmen, professionals, students, and teachers. The Taiwanese Jewish community was founded after the Second World War when American Jewish military personnel were stationed in Taiwan and conducted religious services. In the 1960s, Taiwan emerged as a major exporter, and Jewish traders of garments, shoes, and other products began to arrive. At this time, an informal Orthodox congregation began to meet in the *President Hotel* in Taipei and, in the 1970s, a TJC Center was established in the suburbs of Tienmu. The Community obtained official recognition in 1975, when it was allowed to register as a non-profit organization. Among the founders was Yaacov Liberman, a former Russian Jewish refugee in China, who became the community president for the first decade.

At its peak in the late 1970s and early 1980s, the community consisted of more than 50 families. The community is still active today and religious services for Shabbat and holidays are performed at the Ritz Landis Taipei Hotel. Less than ten individuals turn out for weekly services, but on important holidays the congregation numbers 60–100 individuals. The community is served by the only rabbi in Taiwan, Austrian-born Dr. Ephraim. F. Einhorn, who has lived in Taipei for more than 20 years. The Jewish community consists of permanent residents, such as businessmen and high-tech professionals, as well as transient individuals from North America, Israel, Europe, and elsewhere.

Taiwan's booming economy prompted Israel to establish the Israel Economic and Cultural Office (ISECO) in 1993, which is staffed by seven Israelis and nine local employees. Like the trade offices of other countries located in Taiwan, the ISECO functions as a de facto embassy. Despite the growing Israeli presence, the number of Jews in Taiwan has dramatically shrunk as Taiwanese manufacturing industry has gone into decline and been largely exported to mainland China. As industries have relocated abroad, so has the Taiwanese Jewish community.[5]

Notes

1 This list was compiled by Matthias Messmer and is incomplete. Information about any of these individuals or other Jews who have lived in China may be sent to Prof. Avrum Ehrlich or Matthias Mesmer.
2 For a more detailed survey see 'The Growth of Jewish Studies in China,' in M. Avrum Ehrlich, *Jews and Judaism in Modern China*, Routledge, 2008.
3 Jonathan Goldstein, "History of Jews of Macau," in M. Avrum Ehrlich (ed.) *Encyclopaedia of the Jewish Diaspora*, Santa Barbara: ABC CLIO, 2008.
4 Judy Diestal, "History of Jews of Hong Kong," in M. Avrum Ehrlich (ed.) *Encyclopaedia of the Jewish Diaspora*, Santa Barbara: ABC CLIO, 2008.
5 Don Shapiro, "History of Jews of Taiwan," M. Avrum Ehrlich (ed.) *Encyclopaedia of the Jewish Diaspora*, Santa Barbara: ABC CLIO, 2008.

2

CHINA'S REALITIES FROM
THE VIEWPOINTS OF
"FOREIGN EXPERTS"

Matthias Messmer

No one has the norm of norms.

Joseph R. Levenson

The present contribution deals with the biographies and life circumstances of the so-called foreign experts, many of whom were of Jewish origin.[1] Their political attitudes were similar to those of many American and European journalists at that time, as for example Theodore White (Thunder Out of China) or Randall Gould (China in the Sun). Both "groups" – disgusted by the plundering, general corruption and press manipulation of the Guomindang officials in Chongqing, which occurred everywhere, and also thanks to the persuasive power of the communists and a, in many regards, manifestly better economic and political situation in the areas liberated by Mao's troops – moved toward progressive ideas; the longer they were there, the more so.

Dealing with the biographies of these foreign experts brings various aspects to view also for contemporary historical and political science. The life fates of the foreign experts, who until Deng Xiaoping's policy of opening up were long hidden from the view of Western diplomats and journalists, show clearly that the past century was one of ideologies and counter-ideologies, of propaganda and counter-propaganda. Most of these foreign experts passed away in the last few years. Only very few are still alive and have recently been "discovered" by some Western media which have dug out their lives and experiences in Mao's China.[2] One of the most notable and well known of the foreign experts is Israel Epstein, who grew up in Harbin and Tianjin and became a dedicated citizen of the People's Republic of China. Epstein's life has been widely recorded elsewhere, including his autobiography, *My China Eye. Memoirs of a Jew and a Journalist* (2005), and will not be retold here.

After the Chinese Communists took power in 1949, there were no more missionaries, businessmen, adventurers, researchers, and adherents of Chinese exoticism. In the 1950s, Soviet advisors represented the majority of foreign experts stationed in China, but there were also revolutionaries from the Third World, as well as progressively minded Westerners – political refugees, opponents of the expelled Guomindang government, as well as adherents of the ideas of Mao Zedong – in the Middle Kingdom. They were all united by a will and the conviction that they had left their homeland for a good cause, in order to serve China and its people. Called by some the regime's "propagandists" and "useful fools," and by others "idealists" and "brilliant thinkers," they disposed of insight into the politics and society of the newly founded People's Republic such as was otherwise not granted to foreigners since the flight of the Guomindang government from the mainland.[3] That the assessment of the foreign experts, especially in the course of the past few years, has undergone significant changes, is also related to the end of the Cold War: what was once bracketed as political, because it was not regarded as opportune, is today judged more critically and objectively.

Sidney Shapiro: *I Chose China*

Sidney Shapiro, a robust gentleman with a typical New York accent and bright eyes, has lived for several decades in one of the four-cornered Beijing residential courts still spared from the demolition hysteria raging all over in China's cities, the "Siheyuan," at Nanguangfang 24, not far from the banks of Houhai Lake and the former residence of Guo Moruo. The pretty garden is full of roses and cactus plants. The interior of the living room is simply furnished, with many books, ones he wrote and those of his intellectual teachers, Mao Zedong and Deng Xiaoping.[4] Shapiro, born in 1915 in New York's Lower East Side, sought an alternative field of activity during his stay in the Middle Kingdom over the last 50 years: as a translator of Chinese literature, as he has already become known to Western Sinologists, and, less well known, as the editor of a book about the Jews in old China.[5]

In contrast to Epstein, Shapiro does not at first know what he is looking for in China. He, whose parents came from Ukraine and Lithuania, joins the US army in 1941, where he, after law studies, is assigned to a language unit with the main emphasis on Chinese. But only a voyage by ship in April 1947 brings him finally to the Middle Kingdom. Like Epstein, a secularly-oriented Jew ("I left God"), in his childhood he visits the synagogue on holidays. In contrast to the Pole of the same age, he possesses no knowledge of Marxism, but after his arrival in Shanghai he falls head-over-heels in love with an actress who is close to the communists. In his autobiography, *I Chose China* (2000), he, who till then had formed his image of China solely from the American media, recalls his first assessment of the Chinese:

> When I got to China I found that here were people – I'm not
> talking just about the Communists or the political people – who
> were very kindly and considerate, very family-oriented people who,
> if you were their friend, there was absolutely nothing they wouldn't
> do for you, to an embarrassing extent[6]

Shortly before Mao's troops take power, Shapiro and his wife move to Beijing, where he experiences their entry into the city. In a roundabout way, he finds work in the state publishing house Foreign Languages Press, which specializes in the publication of pro-government pamphlets and books. Shapiro is now serving the "new China." He writes about putting an end to prostitution, reducing criminality, land reform, the general cleanup. In the *China Monthly Review*, he defends the entry of Chinese "volunteer" units into the Korean War.[7] Shapiro changes, as he himself said, into a Sinophile, who loves the discussions and study groups of his "danwei" (unit) above everything. Gradually, he knows more and more about Marxism and the ideas of Mao Zedong, but, in contrast to Epstein, he never becomes a member of China's Communist Party. In 1963, he takes Chinese citizenship.

In his autobiography, he attempts to convince Western readers that China must be judged according to its own standards. His explanations are convincing and receive a very personal note; occasionally the presentation seems too self-centered. Many of his ideas appear naive from present-day viewpoints, but one does believe that at the time he really had great hopes for the new socialist morals. As is fitting for a "foreign expert," he unreservedly adopts the official view, for example against religion or the superstitions held by the common people. Shapiro believes in communism, in the "new society" to be created, and criticizes even Mao only when the party line permits this (for example in connection with the policy of the Great Leap Forward).

> Yet swept along by the Chinese revolution, I was coming closer to
> socialism, at least in mental outlook. By the early 1960s I knew that
> in China I had the kind of life I wanted most. I agreed with Chinese aims and policies, I liked the political atmosphere, the cultural
> and social life.[8]

Shapiro adopts without scruples the current propagandistic expressions of that time of the "barking dogs" (referring to Western critics) or the "unleashed" Chiang Kai-shek. Also his opinion on Tibet is consistent, as with Epstein, with the government's position. Finally, he even prostitutes himself as an actor by playing the roles of foreign villains.

Of some interest is Shapiro's report on an inspection trip in December 1980 to the Province of Sichuan, where at the time, the now outlawed, Zhao Ziyang ruled as party boss. His reportage reveals – with quotes from

Chinese academics and factory managers – a rather open critique of state policy that would have been impossible years later.[9] He rather bluntly criticizes the inappropriate reaction of the party leadership to the actions around the protests on Tiananmen Square in 1989. However, like most of the leftover old foreign experts, Shapiro regrets the disintegration of the moral order that existed under Mao. And like some of the foreign experts of Jewish origin, toward the end of his life he reflects on his Jewish roots:

> But here [during his 1989 visit to Israel – author's note] was where it started, the primary essence of me as a Jew began here. I found an origin. This did not make me a Zionist, or a believer in Judaism. I felt it was good for Jews who wanted it to have a country of their own. At the same time I thought it was reasonable for Jews in other lands to continue to be part of other cultures.[10]

Shapiro never regrets his decision to adopt China as his second homeland because, "China offered me the extraordinary chance to experience how with human effort a country can be led from the depths of great humiliation to a decent form of society."[11]

Sidney Rittenberg: *The Man Who Stayed Behind*

For one person a liar, for another a maverick of remarkable charm: Sidney Rittenberg, born in South Carolina in 1921, the son of a prosperous attorney's family, is in any case one of the most mysterious figures within the group of foreign experts.[12] And without doubt the most powerful; according to rumors during the Cultural Revolution he allegedly even pursued the overthrow of Prime Minister Zhou Enlai.[13] Above all, of the group, he sees China's prison walls the longest from inside. Of, in all, 35 years in the Middle Kingdom, he spends almost 16 years in solitary confinement, a truly unusual fate.

Rittenberg's grandfather on his mother's side came from Russia; in his childhood, Rittenberg attends a synagogue and Jewish grade school, but later refers to himself as non-religious. Sid, as he is called by his friends, is a good pupil and effortlessly learns foreign languages, a gift that serves him well in 1942, when he, like Shapiro, is selected by the army for an intensive course in Chinese at Stanford University. Still, during his studies, as a member of the American Communist Party, he gets involved in the causes of cotton factory workers and coal miners, as well as fighting against racial segregation, at that time still widespread. He pays for his engagement with a jail sentence.

In autumn 1945, he is sent by the American army as a translator to Yunnan's capital Kunming. "True, I was a reformer, a revolutionary, almost a zealot for the social causes of the day. But China wasn't one of them. I never dreamed, as so many Americans did, of saving China."[14] Things worked out differently. The reprehensible behavior of an American truck driver to a Chinese girl, as well as the obviously pervasive corruption of the Guomindang drives him, as he himself states later, into the arms of the communists. Whenever he can, he meets their liaison agents: in Shanghai, as an observer of the UNRRA in Hunan, where he observes a terrible famine, and then naturally himself in the area of the new Fourth Army, in the Dabie mountains in the border area of the provinces Hubei and Anhui, where the troops of Li Xiannian, the later state president, sit fast due to a truce negotiated by General George C. Marshall. There Sid, who in the meantime has adopted the Chinese name Li Dunbai (李 敦白) and is serving as a translator, seems to have sensed for the first time an inner drive to intervene in China's domestic politics. He tells Li of his fear that the Americans could deceive the communists by giving them a false sense of security while actually supporting the Guomindang. This was followed by activity as a representative of the United China Relief aid organization in Kalgan, which was then under the control of the later Marshal Nie Rongzhen.

In October 1946, Rittenberg's greatest wish is realized: After a journey of several weeks on foot, horseback and mules, the 25-year-old reaches Yan'an, where for the first time he meets Mao personally: "I could scarcely believe my good fortune. This was the Mao Zedong I had been reading about in the daily press, the Mao whose words I had studied in Stanford. I respected his vision for China and admired his philosophical brilliance."[15] From this moment on, he is the captive of a living icon, of an ideology that fetters him in the truest sense of the world, reduces his own ability to decide to a minimum, and makes him a weak-willed tool, without his being aware of this. Rittenberg, active as an adviser for the English-language radio station, takes the job of liaison man between the communists and the American government. Modesty is not one of his virtues: proud of his role in the revolution, he participates enthusiastically in militant assemblies against large landowners. He finds them necessary in order to bring "the world peace and the oppressed good will." He wants to go farther and farther, put himself fully in the service of this revolution. But where there is a mountain there is also a valley. As a report of the apprehension of Anna Louise Strong by Stalin in early 1949 reaches Yan'an, Rittenberg is arrested on charges of espionage.[16] He personally knows all the higher cadres of the communists and becomes a member of the Chinese Communist Party. He might have even married Wang Guangmei, later married to Liu Shaoqi (who became president of the People's Republic, later labeled a traitor and died in prison during the Cultural Revolution). Rittenberg is nevertheless held for six years in solitary confinement before being released in April 1955, after the Chinese inform him that he had been imprisoned on false charges.

Like other prisoners of the communist system, Rittenberg is subjected to brainwashing. And like other individual Westerners, after his release from prison he expresses a certain understanding for those who let him stew in captivity for so many years.[17] His 1993 autobiography, *The Man Who Stayed Behind*, is a sort of "mea culpa" that the reader will only believe to some extent. He judges too simplistically, at least from today's viewpoint, the situation in Mao's China. And above all he is a person who loves the limelight. After his release, he finds work at Radio Beijing, having access, as he writes, to "top-secret meetings." Rittenberg is a good analyst, but a bad observer. With the exception of a single everyday observation, namely of the various tones of the street sellers known from the pre-war period, the Southerner took note only of the mostly shrill noises of communist politics, and also the volume that seemed to suit him. He is also referred to as a weather vane. Almost guiltily, he admits he believed everything they told him. But again and again his almost morbid urge to stand out emerges, which predestines him to participate in almost all the campaigns of the time. He even participates enthusiastically in the revisionist campaign beginning in the late 1950s following the Hundred Flowers movement. And he and his Chinese wife also emulate those who, in the Great Leap Forward, during which millions of people starved, brought as many cooking pots and as much ironware as they could to local backyard blast furnaces to produce (inferior) steel.

Rittenberg is especially proud, and rightly so, of his participation in the official translation of Mao's works, on which a number of foreign experts worked beside Chinese scholars.[18] "Because of my fame ... I was a speaker in great demand," he comments. He sees himself as a representative of the Chinese position toward the world. It seems strange, given his access to the innermost circles of power, to read that he first heard of the start of the Cultural Revolution on the Voice of America. That again does not prevent him from playing an active role in this vast mass event, which went on for ten years. He, the "international fighter for communism," travels around the whole country, praises the solutions of Chen Boda, one of the leading chief ideologues, gives speeches that are printed in newspapers, and feels like a king-maker. To destroy everything old seems exciting to him, and further stimulates his power instinct. At the start of 1967, he is given the office of Director of Radio Beijing: The foreigner, Rittenberg, has thereby reached the zenith of his power. From there, things can only go downhill. His memories of this period sound like the morbid phrases of someone who no longer knows what he is saying.[19] Christmas 1967 suddenly marks the end of the star allure of the party whip, agitator, string-puller. The Revolution begins to devour its own children, which for Rittenberg, again accused of spying for America, means solitary confinement, this time for all of nine years.

In March 1980, three years after being released, Rittenberg, together with his wife, leaves China for America, without having accepted the Chinese government's offer of a seat on the Chinese People's Political Consultative Conference (although before his departure he served for a short time as an advisor to the Academy of Social Sciences). The non-acceptance of fellow-traveler

Rittenberg sounds like a hollow phrase, in view of the ideals he had held aloft for many decades: "I had come to China to serve humanity, to serve people, to change China, to change the world. I had no intention of spending the rest of my life serving those whom power had corrupted, bought by their perquisites."[20] Rittenberg's chronicle, an undoubtedly valuable historical document, leaves more questions unanswered than it answers. In many ways, it seems like the work of a person who likes to mount the stage and thereby comes under fire. His relationship to Jiang Qing, Mao's widow and member of the Gang of Four, is unclear. Nor can he clear away the accusation that he had denounced foreigners and Chinese. He tries to prove his innocence by pointing to his alleged efforts on behalf of a dissident, Wei Jingsheng, who was convicted in 1979. But he weakens his credibility, because after this he puts the blame on Deng Xiaoping for the increasing corruption of power structures. For him, Mao was a "brilliant, talented tyrant," whom he apparently never liked. The respective motive of his actions, and what was invention, what truth in his comments on his life often remains a mystery. The fact is that in his later years he ran a very successful consulting firm in the US for the purpose of facilitating the access of Western firms to the Chinese market. Perhaps that was the best idea of his life.

Solomon Adler: *The Chinese Economy*

Solomon Adler, who likewise worked on the translation of Volume IV of the Complete Edition of Mao's works, was an economist born in 1909 in Leeds, UK.[21] His parents (his father was an accredited rabbi, but worked as a shop owner) came from Lithuania and had moved to England to give their nine children a better life. Solomon does in fact attend a Jewish school and even has a Bar Mitzvah ceremony, but still rejects Judaism as a religion. With a scholarship, he studies philosophy, politics and economics at Oxford before he earns an M.A. in economics at the London School of Economics. After this, he moves to the US, where he works at the Library of Congress and thereby makes the acquaintance of the later famous Marxist-influenced economist Ji Chaoding, who, on the basis of his theories, advises the Guomindang and later the communists to adopt an active Chinese export policy.[22] For a time in the 1930s, Sol Adler commutes between the US and England, before he finally settles in America and finds work at the Treasury Department. From there he is sent to Chongqing in 1941, where, as a member of the Stabilization Board of China, he attempts to control the worsening inflation. As US Embassy Attaché in Chongqing and later in Nanjing, he becomes familiar through close experience with the Guomindang politicians T.V. Song and H.H. Kung. He also gets along very well with the three Song sisters. In 1947, he returns to the US. Directly after this, he is caught up in the whirlpool of accusations of the China lobby against employees of the American State Department. He is suspended from his job and accused of communist subversion.[23] John K. Fairbank then helps him obtain a research position at Harvard-University.

In 1950, Adler turns his back on the US and returns to the UK, where he does research at the economics faculty of Cambridge University and simultaneously works on his book *The Chinese Economy* (1957).[24] This is the first publication on the economic foundations of China to appear in the West since 1949. At the invitation of Ji Chaoding, he returns to China in 1962. There he works, on the one side, scientifically at the Institute for the World Economy of the Academy of Sciences, and on the other, as an advisor to the Department of Foreign Trade. In contrast to other Western colleagues, he has access to all foreign press publications, from *Le Monde* to the *Herald Tribune*. For the Adlers, according to his wife Pat, life went on even during the Cultural Revolution. Unlike almost all other foreigners, the couple are not bothered, which is also emphasized in an article in *The New York Times*.[25] In May 1981, Adler attends the funeral of Madame Sun – as do among others also Epstein and Max Granich – as a representative of the foreign "Friends of China." In 1994, he passes away in Beijing, hoping "to have contributed some of his knowledge to China."

David Crook: *Revolution in a Chinese Village*

No detailed biographical information was available until recently about another Englishman, David Crook, born in London in 1910.[26] Educated at Cheltenham College in England and also at Columbia University in New York, Crook participated in the Spanish Civil War. He was wounded at the very start and from then on served in the communist underground in Barcelona. As a Soviet KGB agent he is sent to Shanghai in the late 1930s, with the pretence of serving as a journalist and teacher, in order to participate in the hunt for "Trotskyist opponents."[27] After a journey crossing Hong Kong, Vietnam and Yunnan, he finally reaches Chongqing, where he meets his future wife, a missionary's daughter. In 1947, the two enter the "liberated areas," and two years later the couple accepts the invitation of communist functionary Wang Bingnan to teach English to future diplomats in Beijing. In 1959, their book *Revolution in a Chinese Village* appears, in which they report their experience of a mass movement in an ordinary village.[28] During the Cultural Revolution, both David and Isabel Crook are arrested and not released until 1973. Like most other foreign experts, they do not criticize the system for their imprisonment.[29]

Michael Shapiro: *Changing China*

Michael Shapiro, born in 1910 in Ukraine and brought to England at the age of two years, did not possess the title of foreign expert, but was regarded as a friend of China and was given the title of honorary citizen of

Beijing shortly before his death in 1986.[30] On the shelves of his wife's Beijing apartment there are books in Yiddish published in 1906 in Warsaw. Michael's parents were regarded as strictly Orthodox, which was also to find expression in their education of their son. The young man is regarded as a good student and, like Solomon Adler, he also studies at the London School of Economics. Then he becomes active as a party functionary of the English Communist Party, before he travels to China in January 1950 at Mao's request to the sister party, together with three colleagues, on the Trans-Siberian railroad. Shapiro works at the Xinhua press agency as a so-called "polisher," the usual title of a proofreader for translations from Chinese into English. In 1958, his book *Changing China* appears, in which he describes to readers the changes in life in the "new China."[31] Shapiro writes in his foreword that he does not chiefly want to describe China's situation, but rather to explain it. Besides that, under the pseudonym Michael Best, he writes contributions for the communist *British Daily Worker*. Although he had done almost no political work in China, he also disappears behind bars for five years during the Cultural Revolution.

Gerald Tannebaum: Foster Parents' Plan for War Children

Like Sidney Shapiro and Sidney Rittenberg, Gerald Tannebaum, born in 1916 in Baltimore, went to China as part of his service in the US army. Nothing is known of his youth, except that after earning a university degree in 1939 he worked in Chicago in the fields of advertising and broadcasting.[32] After serving as an editor of army newspapers in Hollywood, he is sent to Shanghai late in the summer of 1945 to serve there as acting Director of Armed Forces Radio/China. But only a year later he is discharged from the army and decides to remain in China. He is asked by Madame Sun whether he would like to work for the China Welfare Fund that she had founded, or for its successor organization, the China Welfare Institute. With great engagement, Tannebaum helps to find US sponsors for this project, which originally provides aid to the suffering population in all parts of China, but later concentrates on delivering medicine and other essentials to the "liberated areas."

Tannebaum is simultaneously the Director of the Foster Parents' Plan for War Children in China, an American aid organization whose primary aim is to alleviate the suffering of children most severely victimized by the military conflicts.[33] Tannebaum is one of the foreigners who experienced up close the capture of Shanghai by the communists in spring 1949. His letters impressively describe the takeover of government power by the communists and the attempts of his organization to remain neutral in this internal Chinese conflict. For months he struggles to counter the increasingly gloomy image of China in the American media with his positive experiences:

This is no happenchance. This is the way they [members of the People's Liberation Army – author's note] act all the time. What's more, they are an excellent example for the youngsters. Their discipline is exemplary. It was no propaganda that the PLA soldiers would not touch a needle or a thread which belonged to the people, and which many of the children wrote to their foster parents. It was actual fact.[34]

That is precisely what the American public finds suspect, especially as individual children praise Stalin and the Soviet Union in their letters. Tannebaum, to the contrary, is convinced that all the media reports that reach the US from China are false. Again and again he assures headquarters in New York that it is not a matter of politics, but rather of support for children. In 1950, the program is cancelled due to pressure from the State Department, which provokes Tannebaum to complain:

The American government is making the breach between the Chinese people and the American people wider and wider. All hope is not lost, but as an American sitting in the middle of this, I can tell you plainly that our government has been wrong and if there is anything you can do to correct it, the American people will be ever appreciative to you.[35]

Following this, he continues to work for Madame Sun's projects to further schools, theatres, and hospitals for children. At the same time, he is active as a journalist for the newspaper *China Reconstructs*, co-founded by Israel Epstein. In 1972, he leaves China and settles in the US.

Julian Schuman: *Assignment China*

Julian Schuman, born in Brooklyn in 1920, became known in certain political circles, not for his article "By Rickshaw to Communist China," but rather for his claim that American troops used biological weapons during the Korean War. In 1956, at the peak of McCarthy's anti-communist witch hunt, he is initially accused, along with the journalist and newspaper-owner John W. Powell and his wife Sylvia, of having spread subversive reports. Later this accusation is dropped, and the jury even pleads for treason. In 1961, the American government drops the charges.[36] Schuman, son of an assimilated Ukrainian family, studies French before he, like Sidney Shapiro and Tannebaum, reaches China through military service with intensive language training as a cryptographer. He spends, in all, 35 years in the Middle Kingdom. From 1947 to 1953, he works as a correspondent for various American papers (also for the China Press, which belongs to the Guomindang), above all as an editorial assistant for Powell's *China Weekly*

Review; from 1963–77, he serves as a "polisher," checking Chinese–English translations for Chinese publishing houses, and again 1980–95.[37]

In 1949, Schuman experiences firsthand the fall of Shanghai and other cities to the communists. For the *China Weekly Review*, he reports from locations along the Yangtze, from Kanton (Guangzhou), and even from Taiwan.[38] In the column "Letter from Shanghai," he tries to explain the achievements of the new leadership to domestic and foreign readers, and to respond to what he regards as the one-sided perceptions of American press reports. "Seeing is believing, but hearing must be added in order to understand the new China" is the first sentence of a 1953 contribution he wrote after making a journey of several thousand miles from North to South China.[39]

Praised by both friends and political opponents alike, is the accuracy of the portrayal of a historically important epochal transition in his book *Assignment China* (1956).

> I had seen the death throes of Chiang Kai-shek's China, had witnessed the passing of an old order rooted in four thousand years of tradition. I had lived both in the old and with the new. I had eaten, drunk and passed the time of day with British taipans and American diplomats, with Chiang officials, Mao Tse-tung revolutionaries, impartial political grafters, students on the right and students on the left, impoverished peasants and black-market billionaires.[40]

For Schuman, as one of the very few Western journalists sticking it out in Shanghai, it is clear that speculation about China "as we would like to have it," will get us nowhere: "It would be safer to know her as she really is." Schuman offers the reader this search for truth as the motivation for writing his book. Like other foreign experts praising the start of the "new time," he describes the economic restructuring, for example the land reforms, the attempt to reduce inflation, the struggle of the government against speculators and blackmailers, and other state campaigns.

Schuman dedicates a special chapter – Fruits of Demonology – to Western reportage on China. Similar to publicist Walter Lippmann in the case of the Russian Revolution in 1917, he concludes that Western reports about China do not necessarily show what can be seen, but rather what addressees want to see.[41] He does not want to make any false promises, because he knows about the situation of a country that will require decades to overcome the state of a feudal order of some sort:

From their standpoint China had not become a paradise in the four and a half years since the change. Nor would it in the forty to come. Many still were poor, and would remain so for years. Many millions would continue for years to win their daily subsistence only through arduous labor. Millions would remain inadequately housed and no more than adequately clothed.

Nor can I doubt that there were some victims of injustice while others enjoyed prosperity without having earned it.[42]

Sam Ginsbourg: *My First Sixty Years in China*

Sam Ginsbourg, born in Siberian Tschita in 1914, has something in common with Julian Schuman: He spent several decades in the Middle Kingdom and never regretted this choice. Ginsbourg's father comes from White Russia (now in Belorussia) and flees from the Czar's troops to Tschita, where he amasses a not inconsiderable fortune as a lumber dealer. A few years after Sam's birth, the family moves farther to Harbin, where his father works for the millionaire and coal magnate Skidelsky.[43] Ginsbourg himself refers to his family in his autobiographical notes, *My First Sixty Years in China* (1982), as first of all Russian, although they attended the synagogue on important holidays and during Passover ate matzo instead of bread. In the early 1920s, Father Ginsbourg tries to start doing business in Vladivostok, but is unsuccessful. In 1926, the family journeys by ship to Shanghai, where Sam Ginsbourg will live for over 20 years. He studies at the French Aurora University and later finds a position at a British machine manufacturing company.

In spring 1947 – in the meantime his parents have emigrated to the USA – he decides to move to the "liberated areas" of Shandong.[44] In Wei-fang, the seat of East China University, he initially teaches English, then also Russian. After the university moves to Jinan, he works, besides teaching, as a translator. In 1953, now married to a Chinese woman, Ginsbourg becomes a Chinese citizen:

> From that day on, I was bound not only in thoughts and feelings, but in my status, with the people of China. I was no longer 'a friend'. I was one with the 450 million Chinese. I shared their grief and joys, their defeats and victories, their pride in a great Party, a great Motherland, a great people, a great Republic.[45]

A drop of bitterness: Ginsbourg is never admitted to enter the Chinese Communist Party; he must console himself with membership in the China Democratic League, a sort of faction party.

In Russian Harbin, Sam Ginsbourg is still not acquainted with China, but upon his arrival in Shanghai as a 14-year-old he develops a feeling for Chinese history on patrols through the Chinese city. He learns the names of the various warlords, takes an interest in the Northern campaign and hates Japanese militarism. "But, although not considering myself a Russian any longer, I did not feel any closer to the Chinese people. There was an ever greater admiration, ever deeper sympathy – yes, but it was addressed toward an indeterminate, impersonal mass of people."[46] It is the outbreak of

Japanese–Chinese hostilities in 1937 that sharpens his awareness of the fate of the Chinese: "I sympathized with the Chinese, admired them, pitied them, wanted to know them better and to do something for them." After the proclamation of the People's Republic he takes part in political discussions, in jubilees on the National Holiday ("It was a day when I felt myself freed wholly, completely and thoroughly of the feeling of alienation, rootlessness, not belonging") and in the continual campaigns, for which he does not always show sympathy.[47] In the years of hunger following Mao's Great Leap Forward, Ginsbourg discovers the ability of the Chinese "to take it, to pick themselves up and to go into battle again, always to look ahead and to be optimistic about the future."

During the Cultural Revolution, he is classified as a "monster," then assigned to the category "bourgeois academic authority," and then accused of being a Soviet spy. Despite the hardship that Ginsbourg experiences in those years, he remains optimistic and defends the ruling party and ideology up until the end of his life. For him, the Middle Kingdom has become his homeland:

> But China has accepted me for what I am, in which everything pulls at me and the pull is getting stronger as the years pass. It's not because there's no anti-Semitism in this country … Here I feel myself not a Jew, but a citizen because here it's not things that own me, as they used to in the old society, but I own everything I have.[48]

Hans Müller: *Mi Daifu*

Besides the "Spanish doctors" (doctors from many European countries, mostly Leftist-inclined, who did medical work in Spain during the Civil War in the 1930s and later looked for new challenges in China) and the doctors among the Jewish refugees in Shanghai, there was a further group of "fighters in white coats" who through their work for the good of the Chinese population achieved significance chiefly in the founding years of the People's Republic. Not far from the Beijing Drum Tower, where once the beat of drums announced the change of the night watches, there is an old-fashioned house where Hans Müller, born in 1915 in Düsseldorf, lived for more than 30 years.[49] Today only a spacious, tastefully furnished apartment and a classical study recall the work of "Mi Daifu," or just Doctor Mi, as he was called by the Chinese. After finishing medical studies in Basel in 1939, Hans Müller does not want to return to Germany. A Chinese co-student persuades him to travel to the Far East with him to fight Japanese militarism. His destination is not Shanghai, but Hong Kong. Through Israel Epstein he makes contact with the Chinese Communist Party, which allows him to travel directly to Yan'an. There he works initially in an "International Peace Hospital," before he is transferred to the front at his own request and employed in the headquarters of the CCP-led Eighth Route Army. In the following two years, he personally meets several major Red political figures and military strategists, such as for example Liu Bocheng, called the "one-eyed dragon," and later Marshal of the People's Liberation Army, or China's former Defense Minister Peng Dehuai. For health reasons, Hans Müller has to return to Yan'an in late 1942, as he himself had several times survived severe illnesses.

After the end of the Second World War he wants to return to Europe, but is finally persuaded by friends to remain in China. During the civil war he works as director of the main hospital in the North and North-East China military district (in the city of Chengde). After the founding of the People's Republic, Müller is called to be director of the Third Military Medical University in Changchun, the former Hsinking/Xinjing.[50] Like other foreigners, he experiences, in the meantime in Beijing, as a Chinese citizen and member of the Chinese Communist Party, the Cultural Revolution from the viewpoint of the persecuted and humiliated. In 1972, he becomes Vice-Director of Beijing Medical University. In this function he distinguishes himself as the leader of a research group that, as the first in the history of the People's Republic, produces a vaccine against hepatitis B. For this achievement, but also for his entire life in the service of China, in 1989 he receives the honorary title "Commendable Internationalist Fighter in a White Coat."

Richard Frey alias Stein

Photos on the walls of a beautiful single-family house in a well-guarded, green villa quarter outside the Third Ring Street of Beijing, show Richard Frey, born in 1920 in Vienna (originally named Richard Stein), with the major Chinese political figures Li Peng, Jiang Zemin, and Zhu Rongji: an indisputable sign that this man is respected in China.[51] Like Hans Müller, Richard Frey, whose parents came from Czechoslovakia and Hungary, also spent several decades in China. In contrast to Müller, Frey did not complete his medical studies: As a member of the Austrian Communist Party he has to leave the country in December 1938 within 24 hours, as his name is on a police list. Via Shanghai he reaches Tianjin, where he works in a hospital. Two years later he, likewise, sets out for the "liberated areas." After 1949, Frey is mainly active in the medical-administrative technical area: for example, in the fight against epidemics, for 13 years in Chongqing, and later in Beijing at the Institute for Medical Computer Science, where he works until 1985. Since 1944, Frey has been a member of the Chinese Communist Party, and since the 1950s a Chinese citizen.

Asked about the reasons for his decades-long engagement in China, the Viennese Jew names his political consciousness, which was sharpened especially by the events in Austria in 1933–34. "My parents were anything but communists," he explains. He himself, who had once enjoyed a humanistic education including Greek and Latin, had at the time read many books about the Soviet Union and grew up in the circle around Fritz Jensen. He had never regarded himself as a pacifist. His aim was to fight against National Socialism and Japanese fascism. After the end of the civil war he wanted to help build the "new China." For him, it is clear that socialism gave the Chinese a better life. He justifies the political campaigns in the People's Republic, which claimed countless victims, because they were essential for a higher aim, the Revolution. He argues in a thoroughly Marxist manner: being determines consciousness. If the same conditions prevail in an area, the character of the people will be the same. He experiences Deng Xiaoping's opening-up-policy as a new influence of the West. Evils like corruption, prostitution, and mafia-like robbery appeared again, against which the Chinese had fought in the founding years of the People's Republic. "Socialism," states Frey in conclusion, "is a long epoch whose ultimate destination is still not foreseeable."

Joshua Horn: *Away with all Pests*

In comparison with Müller and Frey, the Englishman Joshua S. Horn spent only a few years, 15 in all, in the Middle Kingdom. Still less is known about him than about his two above-mentioned professional colleagues. The only document is his 1969 published personal recollection, *Away with all Pests*, in which he recounts his experiences in China.[52] In a foreword, Edgar Snow writes that Horn was a humanist with political convictions that he tried to express in his profession. Horn studied in London before working as an anatomy teacher in Cambridge in the early 1930s. Encouraged by W. Somerset Maugham, in 1936–37 he journeys to China to expand his horizons and acquire practical experience. During the Second World War, he serves as a staff doctor for the British Army in France and Holland. In 1954, he decides for political reasons to make his medical knowledge and abilities available to the People's Republic. Until 1969, when he leaves China, he serves the country as a member of a mobile medical team that travels throughout the country to educate the population in the areas of hygiene and disease prevention. In the later years of his stay, he holds a position as Professor for Orthopedics and Traumatology in a Beijing hospital.

His memoirs stem from the worst years of the Cultural Revolution. They are, above all, a report of experiences of meeting people and the story of their diseases. Again and again his political attitudes shine through: "Ever since my student days my political convictions had been getting stronger and more firmly based in Marxist theory." Like other foreigners, Horn also participates in political discussion circles and attempts to comply with the party's ideology and guidelines. For him, however, his patients are his true teachers: "They teach me that human nature is not a fixed, limiting factor to Man's development but that it can change as society changes."[53] As a doctor, he is especially interested in the linkage of Western and traditional Chinese medicine: "The policy of promoting unity between the traditional and modern schools and of combining the best of both, is a correct policy which is benefiting the Chinese people and which, in the fullness of time, will enrich medical science."[54] As well Horn defends the political campaigns from the Great Leap Forward to the Cultural Revolution, which he describes as necessary for the transformation of China from a class society to true socialism and as the "crowning achievement" of Mao Zedong.

Eva Siao: *China – Mein Traum, mein Leben*

"Despite all my critique I love this country as one loves a person even if he or she is not perfect. I ascertain the many terrible events that happen in the world and locate them in World History. But if something bad happens in China, I suffer."[55] With these words in her autobiography *China – Mein Traum, mein Leben* (*China – My Dream, My Life*, 1997) the by-far best-known female foreign expert in the German-speaking world, Eva Siao (Sandberg), born on 8 November 1911 in Breslau, expresses her feelings toward the Middle Kingdom. The foreign country in Asia already surfaces in the childhood dreams of Eva Siao, daughter of a German Jewish physician's family. But the real encounter with China must wait until 1940. Before this lie years of searching and losing her way, which led the "German Jewess" (thus does she refer to herself until the end of her life) across the European continent to the Soviet Union.[56] Eva Siao leaves school a year before graduation because her teacher, a Nazi supporter, one day discovers that this pupil is a Jewess (against her mother's wishes, she attends a synagogue with her uncle and secretly studies Hebrew). Because her brother works as a conductor in Sweden, Eva follows him to Stockholm in 1930, after graduating from the state Institute for Film and Photographic Arts in Munich. In Stockholm, she works in the photographic laboratory of a Russian Jewess and meets Zionists, socialists, and anarchists. At the urging of a friend, she travels to Moscow in 1934, meets among others Isaak Babel and – on an excursion to the Black Sea – also meets the Chinese poet Siao San (Emi Siao), her future husband. After a further six years of inner searching, she travels from Stockholm via Moscow, Urumqi (Wulumuqi) and Lanzhou to Yan'an, where in the meantime Siao San has already resided for a year. Although she can finally be together with her lover after a long separation (and also marries him there), she feels lonely and three years later returns to the Soviet Union.

Between 1944 and 1949, Eva Siao lives in Kazakhstan, Moscow, and Czernowitz, whereby she earns her living chiefly as a photographer. In spring 1949, in Moscow, she is reunited with her husband, whom she directly follows to China, even before the founding of the People's Republic is proclaimed. In Dalian, she initially works for the Chinese–Soviet Friendship Society, before she moves with their children to Beijing. A bit later, she finds work as a photographer for the Soviet Press Agency Tass and for Xinhua, its Chinese counterpart. Her first reportage tour leads her to the cities of the South: Nanjing, Shanghai, Hangzhou, Guangzhou, Changsha, and Wuhan. Her husband Emi is sent in 1951, as Chinese Delegate of the World Peace Council, to Prague, which gives her an opportunity to serve partly as a photographer, partly as an interpreter at various events in Middle and Eastern Europe and to meet major authors from Pablo Neruda to Ilja Ehrenburg, Guo Moruo to Thomas Mann and Arnold Zweig. Eva Siao also makes contacts with publishing houses in the GDR (German Democratic Republic) that will later publish her photo books on Beijing and Tibet.[57] At home again in Beijing, she makes portrait pictures of Mei Lanfang or Li Keran, one of the best-loved contemporary Chinese painters. The constant commuting back and forth between East and West becomes a spiritual battle for her: "I had to harmonize my love of Emi and China, as well as my longing for Europe. On the one hand I had to bring China to Europe, on the other hand let my European friends see China through my eyes, bring China close to them. Only then would my life and my work have a meaning."[58]

Besides being a self-reliant, even headstrong person (she does not participate in the 1957 struggle against the so-called Rightists, and otherwise she can never come to terms with political campaigns) she also reveals her individuality as a photographer: she does not comply with the socialist credo, according to which workers smile cheerfully and are well dressed, but rather with her own subjective understanding in the search for knowledge and truth. In the foreground of her photography is not an educational function, but rather the effort to "find" pictures that express what moves her. Only a subjectively truthful photograph can, in her opinion, make the valuable and essential aspects of a person visible. Between 1958 and 1964, she works as a film correspondent for GDR television in China. Again and again she is disturbed by bureaucratic harassment, which intensifies as the break of China with the Soviet Union (and thereby also with the GDR) becomes increasingly clear. Although in 1964 Eva Siao exchanges her Soviet passport for a Chinese one, this no longer helps her withstand the confusion of the Cultural Revolution. Accused of being a Soviet spy, she spends seven years in solitary confinement. After her rehabilitation she receives another position with Xinhua. With the beginning of the policy of opening up, she travels back and forth through the world to accompany exhibits of her photographs or to give broadcast interviews about her rich, but also difficult, life.

In the epilogue to her autobiography, the independent and sensitive Eva Siao writes: "I see China with critical eyes, but with loving critical eyes. You must have Oriental patience in China. You cannot run your head against the wall."[59] She had to experience this until the end of her life. In China, she says in a personal interview, you always remain a foreigner. "There are a hundred things here that I do not understand."[60] Nevertheless, she tried to make the Middle Kingdom and its people more understandable to the Western public in her quite individual way. Her own legacy to China, the photographic work of three decades, represents a declaration of love to a country that had become her new homeland. Her creativity builds on no system and likewise does not stage pictures, but rather attempts solely to document the lives of people and the cultural objects that surround her throughout her life and to which she feels drawn. Similar to her country-woman Hedda Hammer (later Morrison), who lived in Beijing before 1946, her eyes concentrate on street life in the capital, with its markets, street sellers, artists and handworkers, on the parks or Tiananmen Square.[61] It is astonishing that even after 1949 she prefers to show the viewer a picture of the old China (besides the obligatory pictures of workers who enthusiastically study the texts of Mao or the steel furnaces at the time of the Great Leap Forward): Chinese "Lebenswelten" (life worlds) seem for her to have a timelessness that was not completely destroyed by the Revolution.

Ruth Weiss: *Am Rande der Geschichte*

Ruth Weiss, born in Vienna on 11 December 1908, regards, like Eva Siao, the "new China" with a significantly more critical view than her male for-eign expert colleagues, despite her love for the Middle Kingdom. Never-theless, she was proud at the end of her life to be a Chinese citizen and a member of the Chinese People's Political Consultative Conference.[62] Her father, who took a rigid anti-Soviet attitude, came from Galicia, her mother from Upper Franconia. Not until school is she made aware of her Jewish identity. At the age of ten years, she and her mother travel to her father in Boryslav, in the crude oil region that was given to Poland after the First World War. Three years later, the family returns to Vienna, now burdened by the stigma of "Polish Jews." They decide to take Czech citizenship. Ruth Weiss begins to study German and English literature in Vienna and at the same time works on her numerous other interests, as she relates in her autobiography, *Am Rande der Geschichte* (*On the Edge of History*, 1999): "Probably it was my Jewish origin that gave me a cosmopolitan viewpoint. For a short time I flirted with the idea of emigrating to Palestine in order to possibly join a Kibbutz with other young people."[63]

Ruth Weiss's first contact with China results from the Chinese artworks that are displayed beside others in the Schönbrunn Palace in Vienna. Fur-ther, the performance of Tretjakov's *Roar, China!* and Puccini's *Madame Butterfly* and, finally, similar to Eva Siao, love for a Chinese awakened her interest in the Far East. In 1932, she earns a doctorate in philosophy and acquires the main currents of the various Chinese thought. As quickly as possible she wants to undertake a six-month study trip to China, "alone as a free-lance journalist." With contributions on China in the Austrian media, she tries to increase her market value as a potential Far East correspondent. In a radio report she deals with the question of what China has to say to the twentieth century:

> But what do we know of the people that inhabit that great country, what does Europe know of the Chinese? In countless films which stem from the paper-mâché world of the studios we have got to know them as hypocrites, scoundrels and murderers, in short as the embodiment of the frighteningly uncanny; products of low and even high literature have carried on this characteristic, whereby the public is led astray to these fantastic conceptions and to a rejecting, contemptuous attitude toward the Chinese people, and even the best-educated Europeans often cannot deny their mistrust. This catastrophic error in the judgment of the yellow races stems from the identification of 'foreign' with 'different,' that means 'worse than we.'[64]

In the *Neue Wiener Tageblatt*, she summarizes an interview with a Chinese pedagogue and writes about the traditional Chinese theatre, while she deals with the history of the Jews in the Far East in the Jewish weekly *Die Wahrheit*.[65] In September 1933, she takes a ship to Shanghai. Once there, she soon orients herself to the group around Rewy Alley, Hans Shippe, and other progressive foreigners. With Julius Tandler, the famous Austrian professor and medical expert, she visits factories, "which represent an inferno of exploitation, deplorable conditions and inhumanity." For her, it is clear that she must "place herself on the side of the oppressed." Initially, she continues to write contributions for the *Neue Wiener Tageblatt*, as well as for Powell's *China Weekly Review*.[66] Later she finds a job as a teacher at a Jewish school. The headmaster disapproves that for her Judaism does not mean a religious rite, and so Ruth Weiss must reorient herself. In those years, she meets the American writer Agnes Smedley, the Granichs (two American Leftists), Olga Lang (wife of Karl August Wittfogel), Madame Sun, the Shanghai gangster king Du Yuesheng, and Lu Xun, whom she later memorializes with her book *Lu Xun: A Chinese Writer for All Times* (1985). In 1937, she accepts an invitation from the YWCA to the Province of Sichuan to take over the Secretariat at the local organization of Chengdu and to give instruction in German at a missionary school. This is followed by journalistic activity with the *Chengdu News Bulletin*, English instruction at the Medical University, and, later, a move to Chongqing.

In 1945, Ruth Weiss returns from the interior to Shanghai and a year later travels to the US, where she works for a few months as a secretary in the radio office at the United Nations. But her stay in the West is brief, as she longs so much to return to China. In 1949, she returns via Hong Kong to her elective homeland, first to Tianjin, later to Beijing. There she works initially, like Michael Shapiro, as a "polisher" for the periodical *People's China*, later as a German expert for another governmental magazine, *China im Bild*. Occasionally, she writes contributions for the *Sächsische Zeitung* in Dresden. In contrast to Eva Siao, Ruth Weiss finds the political campaigns "fascinating": "In those years I still believed that the party always spoke the truth, that thus any denunciation was 100% justified! How long one needed to see that that was not at all true will turn out only later – much, much later."[67] As one of only a few foreigners, she is not harassed during the Cultural Revolution. Only much later, when writing her memoirs, does she see her blindness in those times more clearly. She refers to Mao as a "feudal dictator" who tolerated no disagreement, no reasonable debate on opposed opinions. Similar to her fellow countryman Richard Frey, she must realize that after the policy of opening up, many evils of the old society have emerged again, above all corruption and prostitution.

> Nevertheless the situation is not nearly as bad as it was earlier. China is a sovereign country; it makes every effort to stamp out the new plagues. It is to be hoped that the great throw will finally succeed! I will probably not live to see it,

she writes in her autobiography.[68] Ruth Weiss spent almost seventy years in China and there, "despite all the inclemency in the world ... found a new homeland."

Klara Blum: *Der Hirte und die Weberin*

My people live scattered over the whole world,
    Hunted, cursed, driven from country to country.
Your people, if they quietly tend their rice fields,
    Bleed under thieving blows.

In this stanza, Klara Blum, born in Czernowitz on 27 November 1904, portrays her love relationship with the theatre director and journalist Zhu Xiangcheng as a meeting between two ancient peoples who display not only differences, but also commonality.[69] Ruth Weiss once described the four-year-older Klara Blum as a very sensitive person.[70] Precisely this character trait predestines her for a complex perception of China. In comparison with Siao and Weiss, her life fate was the most difficult and saddest. Her childhood in Galicia is not very happy, because her parents often quarrel, and her father puts pressure on her. After the divorce she lives with her mother in Vienna, where the two flee around 1913. After the First World War, she decides for Rumanian citizenship and begins working on a degree in literature and psychology (probably not completed). Simultaneously, she takes part passionately in the

Zionist movement and writes – until 1929 – frequent articles for Jewish papers like the *Ostjüdische Zeitung* in Czernowitz or the *Czernowitzer Allgemeine Zeitung*. In 1929, she resides briefly in Palestine, but can, however, not decide for a long stay there. A bit later she joins the Austrian Social Democratic Party, however, only for three years. From this time on, she sympathizes with the Communist Party, but without ever joining.

In the years after Hitler's seizure of power, Klara Blum receives an award for her poem "Ballad of Duty" (Ballade vom Gehorsam). The prize consists of a two-month study trip to the Soviet Union. This temporary stay will stretch out to eleven years. In 1935, she takes Soviet citizenship, and three years later she becomes a member of the Soviet Writers Union. In 1937, she has – similar to the case of Eva Siao – a fateful meeting with a Chinese, the already mentioned Zhu Xiangcheng, who was born in 1903 in Shanghai, the son of a rich family. The happiness of the lovers from two different cultures and life worlds lasts for only three months, however. In April 1938, Zhu suddenly disappears without taking leave of his lover. Klara Blum tries desperately to obtain permission to leave for China, because she suspects that Zhu had been called home by the Chinese Communist Party – but in vain. She must wait almost ten years before receiving permission, in 1947, to enter China on a roundabout route through Bucharest and Paris with the support of the Jewish Aid Committee, only to learn there that her lover could not be located. Enquiries and questions addressed to government offices by Klara Blum and Zhu's friends are answered with the statement that, out of regard for relationships with the Soviet Union, they should no longer mention the name of the "missing person."[71]

At the start of her "voluntary" emigration to Shanghai, Klara Blum lives in the former "ghetto" of Hongkou, until she finally finds a teaching position at Tongji University (which she must give up after eight months, however). Her love relationship with Zhu Xiangcheng in Moscow has inspired her so much that Chinese motifs occupy the center of her writing from then on. The year the communists take power in China, she writes an autobiographical novel, *Der Hirte und die Weberin* (*The Shepherd and the Weaver Girl*), that she herself calls a memorial to her life. After several political disputes, it appears in 1951 in the GDR.[72] The novel is, according to the publisher Karl Dietz, "written with infinite love for China, building on the mythical background of an old Chinese legend."[73] Lion Feuchtwanger found in it

> the most beautiful descriptions of contemporary China, painted with love and empathy ... , they make the vast country quite transparent with their constantly changing illumination. I knew of no other work that could have given me such a clear picture of the inner landscape of contemporary China.[74]

Chinese places and themes occupy the center, the period spans the years between 1929 (in Shanghai) and 1949 (in Beijing). Klara Blum thereby documents a part of Chinese contemporary history, many descriptions have a direct historical reference, and persons are portrayed realistically. She is enthused not only by the "new China," but also by the beauty and magnificence of its tradition, and does not regard the political break of 1949 as a complete cultural break with the past. Her positive picture of China persists over a longer period of time: in 1939, as well as twenty years later, she writes of a "heroic China."[75]

In this novel, she also reproaches her co-religionists who feel themselves, as Europeans, superior to the Chinese. Her lover's homeland represents for her a paradise, a utopian creation or, as Thomas Lange writes, the "prefiguration of a Jewish-messianic hope of salvation."[76] Chinese communism accordingly represents a substitute for a Zionism that was out of reach for Klara Blum. In *Der Hirte und die Weberin*, she tries to convey the specifically Chinese to her readers, something that for Occidentals will be not just the penetrating smiles of the Chinese or the strict observance of religious practices that often seem superstitious to Westerners. The use of traditional Chinese phrases, as for example "Yuelan" (moon orchid) or "Yueniao" (moon bird), show that she has become better acquainted than others with this country and its culture. The same holds true for the use of specifically Chinese expressions and idioms, for example, "Nin fei xin le" (you are wasting your heart) or "Wan fu" (ten-thousand times luck), which lend the novel an exotic surface. In the novel *Schicksalsüberwinder* (Overcomer of Fate), completed in 1962 but never published, however, she deals with the topic of the "ugly foreigner" in China. Several other former foreign experts also justified staying in the People's Republic after 1949 with reference to the centuries of exploitation of China by Western powers. With their work, they wanted to at least partly make up for what their colonial predecessors had done to the Middle Kingdom.

In 1952, Klara Blum becomes Professor of German Language and Literature at Fudan University in Shanghai and, later in Nanjing, applies for Chinese citizenship, which she receives two years later. From then on, she calls herself Zhu Bailan (white orchid). After an argument with a professor from the GDR, she leaves the former capital and, after 1957, teaches at Zhongshan University in Guangzhou (Canton). At the start of the Cultural Revolution, she is suspected of being a spy. She now feels lonely and helpless:

> Her dream of having a home and the feeling of belonging to a country and a people was totally destroyed. ... She no longer knew where she belonged. She was and remained a stranger, an outsider, despite all efforts. She sank into the deepest sorrow because she had actually not been adopted and accepted by the Chinese and because she was not allowed to belong to them,

the Chinese German philologist Zhidong Yang writes about her situation at that time.[77] In May 1971, Klara Blum passes away, never having denied her belonging to the Jewish people. Still, it was the Middle Kingdom that had given Blum, who came from a multicultural region of Europe, the possibility to experience her Jewish identity without having to play an outsider role. We might get the impression that most persons of Jewish origin who lived in the People's Republic after 1949 had come to China because of their progressive ethos and not because they were Jews. Perhaps, however, they thought progressively because they were of Jewish origin.

Notes

This chapter was translated by James Stuart Brice.

1 The highly political title "Foreign Friend" (外国朋友) was conferred by the Chinese government from the beginning of the 1950s to foreigners who worked in the government.

2 See Sidney Rittenberg, 'An American Who Lived the History of Mao's Rise and Fall,' *Christian Science Monitor*, 29 November 2006, or various internet websites mentioned in this article.

3 On the institution of the "Foreign Experts," not only their meaning in the context of Chinese domestic and foreign policy, see the various contributions of the New Zealander, Anne-Marie Brady: *Red and Expert* (1996); *Insiders and Outsiders* (2000); *Who Friend, Who Enemy?* (1997); *Making the Foreign Serve China* (2002). Cf. also Messmer, *Wirklichkeiten* (2002).

4 Interview with Shapiro on 25 May 2001 in Beijing.

5 Shapiro's translations from Chinese into English "Outlaws of the Marsh" (in Chinese: 水浒传), a classic from the Yuan Dynasty, and Ba Jin's "Family" (in Chinese: 家), etc.

6 Shapiro, *I Chose China* (2000), p. 265.

7 See *China Monthly Review*, August 1951, p. 68f., or November 1951, p. 260.

8 Shapiro, *I Chose China* (2000), p. 159.

9 Shapiro, *Experiment in Sichuan* (1981), e.g. p. 6, 31, 46.

10 Shapiro, *I Chose China* (2000), p. 274.

11 Conversation with Sidney Shapiro on 25 May 2001 in Beijing.

12 He is labeled a "liar" by Sidney Shapiro ("a slippery liar"), see Shapiro, *I Chose China* (2000), p. 298f.

13 Milton/Dall Milton, *Wind Will Not Subside* (1976), p. 304.

14 Rittenberg, *The Man Who Stayed Behind* (1993), p. 17.

15 Ibid., p. 74.

16 Rittenberg helped Anna Louise Strong in 1948 in Yan'an as an interpreter during her conversations with Mao, and believes that his arrest occurred at the behest of the Soviets, whereby he himself was never in the USSR.

17 See Griffin, *Treatment* (1976).

18 See translated Volume IV of the *Collected Works of Mao*. The translation team included Israel Epstein, Frank Coe, Michael Shapiro, and Sol Adler.

19 Rittenberg, *The Man Who Stayed Behind* (1993), p. 371ff.

20 Ibid., p. 446.

21 Solomon Adler, or Sol, as he was called. See also Milton/Dall Milton, *Wind Will Not Subside* (1976), p. 8 und 101.

22 See on Ji Chaoding: Lewis, *Shades* (1999).
23 Adler's name is found, as are, among others, Israel Epstein, Gunther Stein, Max Granich, and Sidney Rittenberg, in the Publication of the Committee on Un-American Activities of the US House of Representatives (*Publications*, 1970, p. 21).
24 Adler, *Chinese Economy* (1957).
25 *New York Times*, 11 July 1970, p. 5.
26 This changed in 2004, when the Crook family suddenly decided to publish the biography of David Crook on the internet < http://www.davidcrook.net >.
27 Hirson, *Cecil Frank Glass* (sine anno), p. 132. The author thanks Professor Tom Grunfeld, State University of New York, for access to this valuable, unpublished document.
28 Crook, *Revolution* (1959).
29 Crook, *30 Years* (1979), p. 59.
30 The information on Michael Shapiro stems from his widow, Liu Jing He, with whom I conversed on 5 September 2001 in Beijing.
31 Shapiro, *Changing China* (1958).
32 Information on Tannebaum was made available to me by his widow Yuanchi Chen. Gerald Tannebaum died in 2001 in Santa Barbara, CA.
33 Foster Parents' Plan (FPP), based in New York, directed projects similar to those in China as well in Europe. See: Shanghai Municipal Archives (SMA), U143 191 (letters of 21 June 1949 to 13 November 1950).
34 Letter from Tannebaum to Edna Blue, the chairman of the FPP in New York, of 15 September 1949, in: SMA, U143 191 (letters from 21 June 1949 to 13 November 1950).
35 Letter from Tannebaum to Edna Blue of 15 February 1950, in: SMA, U143 191 (letters of 21 June 1949 to 13 November 1950).
36 The article "By Rickshaw to Communist China" appeared in: *CWR*, 22. January 1949, p. 188f.
37 Interview with Jonathan Zatkin, 30 May 2001 in Beijing.
38 See *CWR*, 30, April 1949, p. 200ff; *CWR*, 11 February 1950, p. 170ff., as well as 25 February 1950, p. 189f.
39 *China Monthly Review*, February 1953, p. 195.
40 Schuman, *Assignment* (1956), p. 9.
41 Ibid., p. 178.
42 Ibid., p. 217.
43 For Sam Ginsbourg, see his autobiography: *My First Sixty Years in China* (1982).
44 Sam Ginsbourg mentions nothing in his life story about his brother Mark Julius Ginsbourg, except for the fact that the latter was born in 1909 in Barim.
45 Ginsbourg, *Sixty Years* (1962), p. 208.
46 Ibid., p. 81.
47 Ibid., p. 209. At another point he defends the "Three-Anti Campaigns" (1951) and the "Five-Anti-Campaigns" (1953).
48 Ibid., p. 368.
49 On Hans Müller there are a few articles in the Beijing newspaper *Weisheng zhenggong yanjiu* (卫生政工研究); No. 1–4, 1988; Interview with Muller's widow, Koyko Nakamura-Müller, 31 May 2001 in Beijing.
50 This and other biographical details stem from two articles on Hans Müller: Qiu, *Mi-Daifu* (1990), p. 45; and Li, *Dr. Hans Müller* (1992), p. 32.
51 Interview 24 May and 1 June 2001 with Richard Frey, alias Stein, in Beijing.
52 Horn, *Away with all Pests* (1969).
53 Ibid., p. 36.
54 Ibid., p. 80.

55 Siao, *China* (1997), S. 568.
56 Interview with Eva Siao on 2 June 2001 in Beijing. See also < http://www.eva-siao.de/ >.
57 Siao, *Peking* (1956); Siao/Hauser, *Tibet* (1957).
58 Siao, *China* (1997), p. 266.
59 Ibid., p. 570.
60 Conversation with Eva Siao on 2 June 2001 in Beijing.
61 See Siao, *Photographien* (1996), and in comparison Morrison, *Old Peking* (1999).
62 I visited Ruth Weiss on 6 September 2001 at the Friendship Hotel in Beijing.
63 Weiss, *Rande* (1999), p. 36.
64 Radio report of 28 January 1933 by Ruth Weiss on the topic: "What does China have to say to the Twentieth Century?" (unpublished manuscript cordially made available to the author by Dierk Detje, Beijing).
65 *Neues Wiener Tageblatt*, 31 January 1933 (no page reference) and 21 August 1933 (no page reference); Jewish weekly *Die Wahrheit*, 30 June 1933 (no page reference) and 14 July 1933 (no page reference).
66 See "The danger spot in the Far East" (in: *Neues Wiener Tageblatt*, 7 December 1933, no page reference) or, in the same newspaper, "Europeans in Shanghai" (20 January 1934); *China Weekly Review* of 23 December 1933, p. 152 under the title "Do We Want More Political Troubles?"
67 Weiss, *Rande* (1999), p. 314f.
68 Ibid., p. 360.
69 These verses are from the poem "Das nationale Lied" (The national song). See also Yang, *Klara Blum* (1996), p. 25.
70 Cited from: Yang, *Klara Blum* (1996), p. 6.
71 In 1990, it was confirmed that Zhu was arrested in 1938 by Soviet officials and sentenced to eight years in prison. Archival documents reveal he died in a Siberian labor camp in 1943. Klara Blum never gave up hope that she would one day be reunited with her lover.
72 Blum, *Hirte* (1951). See also Yang, *Klara Blum* (1996), p. 162–192.
73 This legend, mentioned for the first time in the classical songbook *Shijing* (诗经).
74 Cited in Yang, *Klara Blum* (1996), p. 20.
75 See Lange, *Wahlverwandtschaften* (1995), p. 194.
76 Ibid., p. 194.
77 Yang, *Klara Blum* (1996), p. 61f.

3

CONTEMPORARY DEVELOPMENT OF JEWISH LIFE IN ASIA

A personal memoir

David C. Buxbaum

In 1963, I was fortunate to have been given a position as an exchange faculty member at the University of Singapore Law Faculty. At the time, I was a fellow at Harvard. Buildings in Singapore of those days were without air conditioning, but had ceiling fans. David Marshall, the previous Prime Minister and a very fine person and Jew, had been sent into exile in Paris by Lee Kuan Yew, Singapore's dictator, in the guise of Prime Minister. Jewish life was still vibrant, indeed the only center of Jewish life in all East, Southeast and South Asia, but was declining. Nevertheless, there were two synagogues, a wonderful Jewish school that my children attended, a *mikvah*, *shochet*, and kosher food. Ms. Nissam, the doyen of the community, was a warm, hospitable and observant Jew. She was most generous with her time, used her ample funds to support the community, and had open house on the Sabbath and Yom Tovim, for all Jewish persons. While it took some time to acclimate to the heat, our family had a wonderful time in Singapore. The needlessly oppressive Singapore government's actions only impinged on our lives a little.

During our stay in Singapore, we made arrangements for our next posting, which was Taiwan. I was to be the senior Fulbright fellow in Taiwan, doing research at Academica Sinica as well as in a village, Ganyuan in Shulin township. However, I first commenced studies to improve my spoken Chinese at the Stanford Center in Taiwan.

There was not much of an organized Jewish Community in Taiwan. We used to pray at the US Army base, which turned a building into a synagogue on Friday and a church on Sunday. There was a get-together each Sunday where the children had Sunday school and the adults ate bagels. There was no Jewish school, so my four children went to Zaixing Elementary School where they became fluent in the Chinese language, two dialects. While there were fine Jewish people on the island in our two postings there in the early 1960s, the community was not organized, and remains so to this day.

In 1966, I was posted to Hong Kong to complete my Ph.D. research. I worked at the University Services Center. The Hong Kong Jewish Community was a great disappointment. The trustees were dominated by one person, and manifested a complete indifference, even a negative attitude, towards Jewish life. The synagogue, beautifully built and as solid as a rock, was not properly maintained. The Jewish Club was not kosher, there was no rabbi, no Jewish school. While there were many wonderful Jewish people in Hong Kong, some having been there for generations, the calculated neglect of the trustees meant that organized Jewish life was at a virtual standstill. In addition, Hong Kong was going through the very destructive beginnings of the so-called Cultural Revolution. There was rioting, murder, and fire bombing in the streets of Hong Kong. Nevertheless, the police did a fine job of restraining the excess of the extreme Leftists; one of whom, most strangely, was honored about 40 years later by the then head of the Hong Kong SAR, Tong Jian Hua. Subsequent to a return to Taiwan, and to Seattle for a brief stint as an Associate Professor in the law school, I was posted to China in April of 1972, particularly to Guangzhou, which was in the throes of the very end of the Cultural Revolution.

I was the first American outside the government to receive an invitation (in those days one only went to China by invitation) to represent business interests. In those days one did not use the word attorney, still a dirty word at the time in China. The Canton Fair brought tens of thousands of foreigners to Guangzhou, the two fairs together occupied almost three months in time, and with visits to other cities, each of which required a separate visa, I was spending much of the year in China. The Dong Fang Hotel eventually permitted us to rent rooms on a long-term basis, which became our business offices and residence, and we were established in some twilight legal status in China.

The Canton fair, where at the time 90 per cent of China's international business with the West and Japan was conducted, brought many persons of Jewish faith to Guangzhou. We would pray together and eat together. There was a peripatetic Jewish life in Guangzhou. At first we were virtually the only foreigners residing in Guangzhou, but gradually others came and, with the advent of the opening of the US Consulate in the Dong Fang Hotel, my children had some foreign friends, namely Dick Williams', the first US Consulate General, children, who resided in the same building.

It was very hard to travel back and forth to Hong Kong during the early seventies. The train was very slow in China, disgusting in Hong Kong, and took a full day from the train station opposite to the Sheraton Hotel in Kowloon to Guangzhou. In addition, visas back and forth were difficult to obtain. Not until the late 1970s did things get easier, and at that time we started spending more time in Hong Kong, especially for the Jewish Sabbath and holidays. David Hirschberg was the Chazan of the community, who had a wonderful voice but was badly mistreated by the trustees of the Ohel Leah Synagogue and trust funds. There was no rabbi in the community. The community itself had felt a need for a stronger Jewish life and were resistant to the trustees' negative acts. Karel Weiss, present in Hong Kong since 1933, Zakki Dweck, Simicha Ben Shay, Arnold, and others started meeting together to study Jewish texts on Saturday. Others, such as Yakov Zion and his wife, joined the group thereafter. Eventually, a rabbi "search committee" was formed, composed of Mark Eijlenberg, Jack Crystal, and myself. We had the impossible task of inviting a rabbi to Hong Kong because of the parsimonious and miserable state in which the trustees kept David Hirshberg. We were turned down by virtually everyone we approached. Finally, one of my daughters, Elisheva Buxbaum, approached Chabad. Rabbi Moshe Kotlarsky advised her how to proceed and, pursuant to his instructions, we wrote to the Lubavitcher Rebbe. He responded with enthusiasm, agreeing to send two young men, unmarried, together, at no cost to the community, except for their room and board. The arrival of these fine men was greeted with enthusiasm by the Jewish community. Mssrs. Gurkov and Avtzon were assisted by the Hong Kong Jewish Community. Persons contributed furniture, phone cards, and other tangible things to make them comfortable. The trustees at first refused to let them stay in the Rabbi's house, which suffered from great neglect (though this was not the trustee's objection). The community put these aspiring rabbis in a hotel, until they were permitted to move to the Rabbi's house. After much time and struggle, the community was finally able to select a rabbi and chose Rabbi. Mordechiai Avtzon as the first real rabbi in Hong Kong for many years. With community participation, the kitchen was koshered, regular religious services were gradually established, meetings with the infirm and ill took place, children's classes were held, and eventually a school was established, and the *mikva* was koshered. The Jewish community came to life and Jewish life started to flourish again in Hong Kong, as it had previously under the distinguished Sassoon family, who were the great builders of Jewish synagogues and schools. There were those who were unhappy, but the bulk of the community was overjoyed. Hong Kong now became the center of Jewish life in East, Southeast and South Asia. From Hong Kong, Jewish life was to revitalize throughout the region.

For the past 50 or so years, the anomaly in Hong Kong has been that the trustees are, without exception, persons who play a very marginal role, if any, in organized Jewish life. Yet their opposition to Jewish activities serves to strengthen the community.

Over the strong resistance of the trustees, there are now four established Jewish *minyans*, two Jewish schools, three kosher restaurants, a regular supply of kosher food, classes for adults, and a very vibrant Jewish life. Several years ago, as a result of a serious mistake by one rabbi, the

Reformed Community was established. It attracts many persons to its activities.

Even today, the trustees are trying to remove a distinguished rabbi by stealth, as head of the Ohel Leah Synagogue. The trustees have tried to tear down the 100-year-old Ohel Leah Synagogue; have secretly amended the trust document twice; have tried to send trust funds out of Hong Kong; have consistently failed to account for trust funds; have, over the objection of the community, sold Jewish land at a substantial value below market price; have themselves entered into contracts to provide fixtures and the like to buildings, built on Jewish land, and in general, have acted badly. Through all this, Jewish life has survived and prospered in Hong Kong. The present head trustee, from an old Hong Kong–Shanghai family, has shown signs of appreciation of Jewish life; this is a new hopeful development in Hong Kong.

In mainland China, organized Jewish life first reappeared in Shanghai, aside from the activities in Guangzhou, above described. Initially, as in Hong Kong, the community itself organized aspects of Jewish life, including Sabbath and festival observance. It established a Jewish organization to manage Jewish life. Chabad started to send young rabbis to assist the community, and a few years ago Rabbi Sholom Greenberg became the permanent rabbi of the community. Before his arrival, meetings commenced with agencies of the Chinese government, including the Public Security Bureau, who were interested in Jewish activities in Shanghai. I was the primary interface with the Chinese government agencies interested in Jewish life; we invited them to our social and religious services, had frank discussions, and developed a position of mutual understanding. The Chinese government permitted the Jewish community to use Ohel Rachel synagogue from time to time, and is contemplating allowing the community to lease the synagogue on a full-time basis. The community has purchased a building for a community center, established a pre-school, is building a *mikva*, and has regular religious services and a vibrant Jewish social and educational life.

Beijing has an excellent Rabbi, Shimon Freudlich, who, together with his wife, have developed organized Jewish life in China's capital city. They are presently building a school and a *mikva*. They have regular religious services, classes for the young and old. They bake fine bread, and Rabbi Freudlich arranges the supervision of *schita* for cows, thereby making kosher meat readily available in China. Beijing also has a long established, but less religious, community, which has conducted services in Beijing for years. The two communities work together in harmony.

The Jewish community in Guangzhou has also purchased a building as a Jewish center. It has organized religious services, and a rabbi and his wife are expected there shortly. The young members of the community are involved in Jewish life, and the Canton Fair and other fairs attract large numbers of Jewish visitors.

Today in Thailand, Singapore, Japan, Philippines, and elsewhere in mainland China, Jewish life is again thriving, as it had in the past. Old synagogues are now in active use, Jewish schools are being established in many locations. New communities are growing up in old locations. In contrast to my arrival in East Asia in 1963, when Singapore was virtually the only center of active Jewish life in East, Southeast and South Asia, today there are dozens of communities establishing centers for Jewish life in Asia. In addition, there has been a developing interest in Jewish life, religion, history, and culture by the peoples of Asia. There are, for example, numerous recently published books in Chinese about all aspects of Jewish life. Centers for studying Jewish history, culture, language, etc., have sprung up in China and elsewhere in Asia.

While Chabad has played the key role in these developments in Asia, many others have contributed to this reformation. For example, the Darwish family and Shuva Yisrael have developed fine centers of Jewish observance and learning in Hong Kong, and have developed successful outreach programs in Thailand and elsewhere. In view of the increasing importance of Asia in the world polity and economy, one can expect continuous development of Jewish life here, with new communities, for example, expected, in Shenzhen and Ningbo in China. The fundamental basis of the development has ever the felt need of the Jewish in a community for a Jewish life and the availability of learned rabbis to come and support this need.

Part II

COMPARATIVE CULTURE AND THOUGHT

4

CROSSING BOUNDARIES BETWEEN CONFUCIANISM AND JUDAISM

Galia Patt-Shamir and Yaov Rapoport

One of the side-currents of increasing globalization in the past hundred years or so is that Chinese and Jews have more and more occasions to meet. Unlike Islam and Christianity, Judaism is an exclusively Middle Eastern and Western phenomenon: very few Jews ever lived in East Asia, and Judaism played no major part in sculpting the history or culture of this part of the world, past or present. When these meetings happen, they turn out quite well. Although both sides expect the others to be very different, after a short intercourse they find the other side to be much more "like us" than they expected. Jews are undoubtedly struck by the Chinese lack of prejudice and preconceptions. The Chinese are completely innocent of anti-Semitism, a concept so deeply ingrained in Christianity and Islam; more the former than the latter, Christianity having stemmed directly from Judaism and bearing a very complex relation to it. Chinese are struck by Jewish perseverance and survival through harsh historical conditions.

Similarities with Judaism appear most frequently in texts identified with one of the philosophical schools of China: Confucianism. This school of thought, although just one of many at the beginning, eventually became the most important and dominant current in Chinese culture as a whole. Without going into great debate about the complex relationships between Confucianism and other schools of thought in China, it will suffice to say that, attractive as other Chinese traditions may seem to individual modern Jews, especially Buddhism and Daoism, Jews rarely draw similarities between these religions and their own. An American Jewish friend once mentioned his desire to lead a Daoist life, floating with the stream. At this point, his wife, returning from the kitchen with the food said, "In this case, I am the stream." The desire to connect Daoism or Buddhism with Judaism is based more on complementary ideas and a wish to add some "missing links" to the chain of tradition, rather than expanding shared ideas.

Regarding Confucianism and Judaism, Katherine K. Young refers to several historical and social features common to Confucianism and Judaism. According to Young, it is important that the kingdoms arose earlier in ancient Israel and in ancient China through warfare and struggles, which enhanced world views in terms of dichotomies of good and evil ways of conduct. In particular, when Jews returned to their homeland the anxiety regarding women increased and, hence, the views regarding family, women's roles, and nature were filled with prejudice. Similarly, China's classical age was characterized by militarism and masculinity.[1] Young also notes that Judaism and Confucianism (together with Hinduism) share certain features because they were "ethnic religions" in their early phase, and generally acknowledged male dominance outside the home. The social structure of ethnic religions was based on kinship relations. During periods of migration, members of the ethnic group attempted to prevent miscegenation in order to preserve their identity as a tribe in line with ideas of cosmic order. This was done by means of stressing the importance of staying within the group by marrying within it.

Indeed, although the scale of the community Confucianism managed to preserve is vast, compared with that of Judaism, Judaism and Confucianism are similar as both are, according to Avrum Ehrlich's suggestion, successful systems for preserving cultural identity over time. (This is also true despite Judaism being an exclusive tradition, which accepts in its fold only those born to it, with a few very specific exceptions, while Confucianism is an inclusive system, accepting into the tradition anybody who is willing to follow, without almost any distinction of race and blood, and always saw itself as meant for all mankind.) The latter is indeed an interesting issue for research. However, the choice in this chapter is to focus on shared ideas as they appear in texts, rather than on historical–anthropological ones, which is to the way Chinese and Jewish communities actually function, today or in different historical periods.

The Language of the *Talmud* and the Language of *Lunyu*

In the first and important Hebrew translation of Confucian *Lunyu* (论语) by Daniel D. Lesley in 1969, the translator makes frequent references to traditional Jewish sources, especially to Talmudic tractate "Avoth," whenever it seems to him helpful for explicating the Confucian text to the Hebrew reader. In some cases, the references to the Jewish text are close or even identical in meaning with specific paragraphs of the Confucian text.[2] An even more sophisticated effort was made more recently by Andrew Plaks, in his masterful Hebrew translation of the Confucian classic *Da Xue* (大学), "Great Learning." Besides being a renowned scholar of Chinese literature, Plaks is also a scholar of Judaism and the parallels he makes between Chinese and Jewish philosophies are even more frequent, and discussed at length. The Hebrew reader may assume that ancient Confucians and ancient Hebrews referred to similar ideas and offered similar moral responses to problems raised in human practice. While this is definitely true to some extent, more importantly the presupposition is that *Talmud* speaks to the Hebrew reader in a language that is similar to that of Confucian classics to their reader. Thus, works of this type try to bring the text to the reader in a *spirit* close to its original context.

Either only an anecdote, or a more significant similarity, the ideas of the ultimate in the two traditions embody an interesting similarity between Confucian humanistic non-theism and Judaism monotheism, in their depiction of the ultimate standard as "way," either *dao* or *halakha*. The follower of *dao* 道 and, likewise, the follower of *halakha* הלכה are both occupied by the search for the way of the past in their walking toward a morally improved future. The Chinese term *dao* is most commonly translated as "way," which depicts the dynamism of a process, of movement, and of change. *Dao* as the way one walks also refers to the doctrine, the method for its realization, and a practice; yet, it is ultimate reality as well, or the law. Similar to *dao*, *halakha* literally refers to walking (*halikah* הליכה) and is manifest as the daily practice of a Jew. It is also the conclusive law of Judaism, and is often used as the ruling at the end of a Talmudic dispute — occasionally it is used in the sense of "a theoretical ruling," but it also has the significance of "a practical ruling" (*halakah le'maaseh* הלכה למעשה) that is implemented in practice and has a practical weight. In the Talmudic language, the word *halakha* refers sometimes to "a law of Moses from Sinai" (*halakah le'Moshe m'Sinai* הלכה למשה מסיני) namely, an oral law, allegedly given directly by God to Moses.)[3]

For the rest of this chapter, we would like to focus on some common grounds that allow the translators to do work of the type mentioned above, and may open ways for a Confucian–Jewish dialogue, which in turn may expand our ideas on human practice, and morality. The similarities should not be addressed before considering the important differences between the traditions.[4] We address hereafter the ideas of tradition, rites, learning, family, and self-cultivation as a communal act.

Tradition Honoring

Jonathan Sacks makes the point that "through tradition and interpretation the past commands the present."[5] While this is said about Judaism, it may be true for Confucianism as well. Talmudic tractate "Avoth" opens with the following statement regarding Jewish teaching, starting with the traditional line of transmission, and immediately moving on to its content.

> Moses received the Torah on Sinai and handed it down to Joshua;
> Joshua to the Elders; the Elders to the prophets; and the prophets

handed it down to the men of the Great Assembly. They said three things: be deliberate in Judgment; raise up many disciples; and make a fence round the Torah. (1.1)[6]

The Torah has passed from God to Moses, then to Joshua and to the whole of the people, by command, so that it will be rooted in the generations by incessant faithful study of the tradition. Other matters are, thus, considered less important, if not an absolute distraction from learning. Secular learning can only be secondary, and is allowed only if it serves Torah study. This strictness of attitude is shown in the story of a person who asked Rabbi Joshua, "Since I have learnt the whole of the Torah, may I study Greek philosophy?" In reply, the Rabbi quoted the verse from Joshua 1.8 saying that the book of the Torah shall not depart out of one's mouth, and one should meditate on it day and night. The Rabbi added the remark: "Go and search at which hour it is neither day nor night and devote it to the study of Greek philosophy" (*Peah* 81.1). The absurd answer is intended to show the absurdity of the question of learning anything that is not part of the tradition.

Rabbi Akivah[7] also believed that tradition (*Massoret* [8]מסורת) is the fence to the Torah ("Avoth" 3:13), namely, it preserves and keeps the doctrine from harm. In *Lunyu* we find reference to two important aspects of learning: learning is learning of the tradition, and the contents of learning. First, regarding tradition, like "Avoth," *Lunyu* stress its centrality:

The Master said: "I transmit but do not innovate; I am truthful in what I say and devoted to antiquity." (7:1)[9]

The Confucian teacher agrees that the doctrine is a transmission of tradition and not an innovation. In 8:8, it is said that learning includes "songs" (or *Odes shi* 诗), "rites" (*li* 礼), and "music" (*yue* 乐), probably with reference to the ancient texts of the *Book of Songs (Shi)*, the traditional collection of rituals that were later gathered into the *Books of Rites (Li)*, and a music canon that has not survived. In this sense, the ideals are set in accordance with past standards; the conduct is ritualistic and in line with the tradition. One's tradition is one's roots; we are connected to it internally, and acting without it is an act of denial of the roots (and consequently the harming of the branches nourished by them.) Contributions and innovations by means of commentary and interpretation are welcome because they serve to improve the understanding of the doctrine. As both Confucian and Jewish sources stress the importance of tradition, the significant status of disciples as spreaders of the tradition necessitates a strong relatedness between old and new. While it is important to be rooted in the tradition, at the same time one has to be able to accept new ideas. Let us take a look at the following Confucian–Jewish pair:

The master said, a man is worthy of being a teacher who gets to know what is new by keeping fresh in his mind what he is already familiar with.

(*Lunyu* 2:11)

The Torah is acquired by forty-eight (things) … hearing and adding thereto.

("Avoth" 6:6)

Preserving the tradition is also an encouragement for reflection and renewal "within the fence." How is the fence kept and strengthened then?

Ritual Practicing

The Greek tradition, a major component of Western tradition, treated religious rituals separately from moral behavior. Rites should be performed because of their divine origin, but the correct moral behavior should be arrived at through philosophy. In Judaism and Confucianism, morality is inseparable from ritual, as the ritual is considered a reflection on morality and a way to internalize it.[10]

Both Confucianism and Judaism have an elaborate system of ceremonies, rituals, and liturgy. It is interesting to compare the Jewish *Shulkhan Arukh* שולחן ערוך with the Confucian *Lijing* 礼经. The *Shulkhan Arukh* (*Set Table*) is the compendium of Jewish customs and laws. It was composed in Israel in the fifteenth century AD, and became a generally accepted authority for Jewish conduct in various situations. The *Shulkhan Arukh* consists of four parts including: laws of prayer and of holidays in *Orach Chayim* אורח חיים ("Way of Life"); diverse laws, including humane-relatedness and dietary laws in *Yoreh De'ah* יורה דעה ("Will Teach Knowledge"); laws of procreation, marriage, and divorce in *Even Ha-Ezer* אבן העזר ("Stone of Help"); and Jewish civil law in *Choshen Mishpat* חושן משפט ("Breastplate of Judgment"). The *Lijing* 礼经 (*Canon of Rites*) is the Confucian collection of rules of conduct, manners, and codes of behavior, dated to around the Han dynasty (specifically the second century BC).[11] It is organized into three parts including: a handbook of the ceremonies, etiquette, and behavior required in worship (in *Yili* 仪礼 "Ceremonials"); a discussion of rites as related to virtues (in *Liji* 礼记 "The Rites Records"); and ideas of government and civil law in light of a utopian system of government attributed to the Zhou dynasty (in *Zhouli* 周礼 "The Rites of Zhou"). A comparison of examples from the two compendiums can be revealed of great use to interested scholars—they are written in a similar voice, one that is simple, authoritative, practicable, and useful. The comparison reveals sometimes surprising similarities, and at other times important differences. The texts deal with the daily practice of the believer, they relate text and practice, and can be helpful for certain comparative studies. The two texts are in an important way *manuals* designed for inner-community use, written in the simplest way to enable the following of instructions. They are not meant to reflect on one's life, only to guide through it. In both collections, ideas are dealt with minimally, while great detail may be given to very specific conducts. How can ideas be internalized in a deeper way in addition to ritual practicing?

Learning[12]

In both systems of thought, studying is a virtue in itself; in both, it is the ultimate way of being an adherent of the tradition. One should aspire to reach a state where she/he can do nothing but study and, if she/he cannot, she/he should spare no effort to give her/his children the chance to do this. For this reason, in both traditions, teachers should take care of their students as best they can, students should respect their teachers, of course, but moreover, to teach or to be taught by someone means a relationship for life.

Learning and teaching have a communal religious aspect in both Confucianism and Judaism, as a direct demand of either the way (*dao* 道) or God (*Elohim* אלוהים). Through learning, one creates oneself as a better community member, a better disciple, and a moral person. Learning is considered a moral practice and one should thus "fix a period for study of the Torah" ("Avoth" 1.15[13]) or "try it out at due intervals" (*Lunyu* 1.1).[14] In both Confucianism and Judaism, learning is a neverending process ("Avoth" 5:25; *Lunyu* 19:6). Both traditions point to the irrelevance of financial or physical worries where learning is concerned (*Lunyu* 15:32; "Avoth" 6.4). Moreover, when one has the right attitude and the desire to learn, learning can occur anywhere, by anyone, according to *Lunyu* (5:28; 7:22) and to the *Talmud* ("Taanit" 7.1; "Avoth" 3.3).

Also, in both traditions, the treatment of those who refuse to commit to learning is quite harsh. In Judaism, those who ask not to learn deserve no less than death ("Avoth" 1.13). Confucius, in a more positive way, demands total devotion to learning, with no deviations from it and a willingness to die for it (*Lunyu* 8:13); those who wish to avoid the difficulty do not deserve his teaching (7:8).

The *Talmud* introduces learning in the opening passage of "Avoth" together with worshipping God and benevolence as three pillars that together support the whole world. The commandment "to love the Lord your God and to serve Him" (Deut. 11.13) receives the comment by Rashi: "to serve means the study of the Torah."

In *Lunyu*, too, we encounter the central place of learning as follows:

> To love benevolence without loving learning is liable to lead to foolishness. To love cleverness without the love of learning is liable to lead to deviation from the right path. (17:8)

The necessity of learning is presented in the Confucian reference in a more "horizontal" description; namely, learning serves as a necessary component in world structure. Even the most central Confucian virtues, if unaccompanied by learning, lead to undesirable results.

Lastly, interestingly, the centrality of learning and the significance of learning relationships is stressed not in its being a duty, but rather in its being pleasure. *Lunyu* opens:

> The Master said, 'Is it not a pleasure, having learned something, to try it out at due intervals? Is it not a joy to have friends come from afar?' (1:1)

Lunyu introduces the main issues of the doctrine as being "gentlemanly," displaying hospitality to friends, and, first and foremost, learning and practicing what is learned. Joy in the act of learning turns out an indication that the learning is not intended for any external goal, except its own sake. Similarly, Torah is studied "for its own name" (*lishmah* לשמה); it cannot have a purpose that is external to it. Learning "for its own name" calls for one to learn out of pure, disinterested motives, and its reward is of a type different from material profit, reputation, or fame. As profit is not offered, one may, and indeed should, simply love it; the benefit will then be one's joy. This attitude is taken directly from the Biblical command to love learning with an attitude of joy (Psalms: 119:72; 119:97).

Filial Piety and the Centrality of Family

Many systems of thought advocate respect for one's parents, yet in Confucianism and Judaism this virtue is made into a basic tenet in the whole structure of human relationships. Family is a source of power in preserving the tradition. By having children, parents may grow and spread tradition; within the family, tradition is transferred and rituals such as holidays or memorial days are practiced and honored. Hence, just like learning, having a family ("building a home") is a *mitzvah* מצווה in Judaism and a compelling commitment and responsibility in Confucianism, where the family unit serves as the root of the way and the primary foundation for the activity of learning. In both traditions, family relations and values are in the core of the general social fabric; the walker of the way either as *dao* or as *halakha* makes the first steps in family relationships.[15] The concern with kinship derives not from a vision of precedence of family members over others; rather, family is a microcosm for moral human relationships. In Confucianism, the virtue of filial piety (*xiao* 孝) is the basis of the family and the primary manifestation of humane relatedness (*ren* 仁). In the second passage of the first chapter of *Lunyu*, it is implied that filial piety is that from which the way grows, namely, filial piety is being human (*ren*) at home. In other words, filial piety can be viewed as the source for the virtue of human-relatedness, the virtue that is considered most vital in Confucianism:[16]

> The gentleman devotes his efforts to the roots, for once the roots are established, the way will grow therefrom. Being good as a son and obedient as a young man is, perhaps, the root of a man's character.
>
> *(Lunyu* 1:2)

In Confucianism, good offspring follow the parents' way when the parents are alive and when they are dead. In 2:5, a student asks about being filial and is answered: "never fail to comply," namely serve one's parents by means of following rites (1:11). Observance in serving father and mother is absolute, such that one ought to argue with them about doing wrong in the gentlest way only. If children's attempts and advice are ignored, they should not become disobedient but always remain reverent, and never complain even if in so doing one becomes exhausted and worn out (4:18).

In Judaism, the value of filial piety (*kibbud horim* כיבוד הורים) appears already in the fifth commandment, next to commandments dealing with worshipping God and preserving the Shabbat. Again, family takes precedence over universal morality:

> [Who has precedence?] Thy poor (thy relatives) or the (general) poor of thy town? Thy poor come first. [Who has precedence?] The poor of thy city or the poor of another town? The poor of thine own town have prior rights.
>
> ("Baba Metziah" 71.1)

The *Talmud* assigns a supremely important religious status to the duty to honor one's parents. It is one of the acts a person performs and enjoys in this world, yet the capital remains in the world to come ("Peah" 1.1). A home in which parents are honored and respected is blessed with divine presence ("Kiddushin" 30.2). Respect for parents must be shown throughout their lives, as well as after their deaths. Reminiscent of the *Lunyu* attitude, we read in the *Talmud*: that "A person must honor his father in life and in death" ("Kiddushin" 31.2).

One should respect parents even when provoked by them, exercise restraint, and do nothing disrespectful. When a rabbi was asked about the limit one must go in honoring parents, he replied that if a father takes his son's purse filled with money and throws it into the sea, the son must show restraint and not put his father to shame (32.1). Because of the priority placed on teaching the tradition, the principal responsibility that rested upon parents was seeing to their children's learning as a biblical command (e.g. Deuteronomy 6.7).

The great importance of family is seen in the Mencian five relationships (*Mengzi* 3A.4), in which three are within family boundaries: affection (*qing* 亲) between father and son, distinction (*bie* 别) between husband and wife, and sequence (*xu* 序) between old and young brothers. There is no similar system of relationships in Judaism; basically the relatedness between man and God (*bein adam la-makom* ביןאדם למקום) is distinguished from inter-personal relationships (*bein adam le-chavero* ביןאדם לחברו). In both traditions, the relationship between husband and wife is constitutive (interestingly, Shulamit Valler in Judaism and Tu Weiming in Confucianism see it as "a division of labor").[17]

In this line, Jewish women's religious duties are centered in the sphere of marriage and family life. In Confucianism, in the human order, women were the foundation for the preservation of the family. Both traditions see pleasure as the very existence of family, especially by being content with what one has and the way it can be preserved. (An interesting religious feature shared by both Confucianism and Judaism, which shows the great value of family is that there is no asceticism in either.[18]) Just like learning, family is to be enjoyed, in a moral way. Let us learn some more about the ideal family member in the broader social context.

Self-Cultivation as a Communal Act

Jews should be satisfied, rewarded, and saved by performing the *Mitzvoth*, the regulations of the religion. These are designed mostly, if not completely, to preserve the Jewish people as such, either positively by helping other members of the Jewish community, or negatively, by differentiating Jews from "Others," with a considerable sacrifice demanded from the individual Jew. Confucians, likewise, should derive satisfaction, reward, and personal salvation by performing rites and making various personal sacrifices for the service and wellbeing of the community in which they live. A Confucian satisfaction from performing a rite or moral act is the most other-worldly aspect of the tradition: one should get a name for himself, so he could be remembered after his death not only by his descendants but also by the community at large.

In this context, one should address individual learning as communal cultivation; in Confucianism as self-cultivation (or self-correction, *xiushen* 修身) and in Judaism as "mending of the world" (*tikkun haolam* תיקון העולם). Both refer to the idea of the human responsibility to make the world a better place through making oneself better, thus preventing strife and conflict. Perhaps the most obvious similarity between Confucianism and Judaism appears in the formulation of the Golden Rule in the negative – "do not do unto others, that which you do not wish for yourself" – as the foundation of a moral community. The identical negative way in which both Golden Rules are formed reveals more than an external similarity.[19]

The accomplished person in both traditions is not only a learner but also a caretaker of others. René Goldman compares the Confucian ideal personality ("noble man" *junzi* 君子[20]) who pursues that which is right (*yi* 义) with the Jewish ideal personality (*zaddik* צדיק) as the follower of right (*zeddek* צדק). Goldman mentions the fact that *zaddik* ("righteous"), derived from *zeddek* צדק, is usually encountered in juxtaposition with *hasid* ("pious" חסיד), a title derived from *hesed* חסד meaning "grace," "benevolence," and "piety," and denoting a devout personality. *Zeddek* (or *zedakah* צדקה) and *hesed* (benevolence) are both divine attributes (e.g. Psalms 92:12). However, through Jewish history the two terms have received various interpretations in the numerous Jewish communities, and the statuses of the personalities represented by them have shifted and changed.[21] Confucianism considers rightness (*yi* 义) and otherness (also translated "benevolence" or "humanity," *ren* 仁) complementary with each other as the two cardinal virtues that characterize the ideal personality either as a *junzi* or a sage (*shengren* 圣人). This ideal personality is an integral part of the community in terms of duties, and has to be first, and foremost, a moral guide. Both Jewish and Confucian exemplary learners are moral exemplars, and yet important differences need to be examined in reference to the source of the human nature as either divine or human. One might also wish to refer to exemplifications by major personalities such as Confucius' disciple Yan Hui (514–483 BC) in Confucianism, or Rabbi Akibah Ben Joseph (AD 50–135) in Judaism, both traditionally praised for not being affected by distress and becoming great scholars.

Needless to say, on the one hand one might find other similarities that seem as important; while, on the other hand, all the above similarities can be disputed on three particular fronts: their exposition here could be alleged not to really be a cardinal feature of the tradition we are talking about, not to be similar enough in both traditions, or to be too universal to the point of being trivial. For instance, filial piety is admittedly much more important in Confucianism than in Judaism. Confucius himself considered it to be superior to any man-made law and, later on, from the incorporation of the Book of Filial Piety into the Confucian Classics, filial piety was accredited with metaphysical qualities. In Judaism, it remained subservient to other, more important laws.

And yet, the similarities previously mentioned show that, across time and region, human beings have shared a very similar sense of morality and self-transcending motives. As we continue to compare cultures, pick up and identify what is common to all mankind, and the realization of sameness amongst human beings is widened, we can hope to prevent those common traits from being used by particular religions, particular nations, to keep their peoples to themselves, and to use them to fight other religions and nations. Herodotus, the father of History, noticed in his travels that fire burns the same way everywhere, but people's ways are very dissimilar.

People all over the world should be aware that their sacred customs are not as unique as they are told, and that their ways are more similar to the rest of mankind, to which their supreme allegiance should lie. And the sooner the better, because our world is a fragile place and all human endeavors and achievements of endless generations could be easily blown to pieces and lost forever as a result of a major clash between opposing religions in the twenty-first century.

Notes

1 Katherine Young, the Introduction in Arvind Sharma, *Women in World Religions,* New York: SUNY, 1987, pp. 9–16.
2 A second translation, which ignores the Jewish context altogether, was published in Hebrew in 2006 by Amira Katz.
3 See Rabbi Adin Steinsaltz, *The Talmud—The Steinsaltz Edition,* New York: Random House, 1989.
4 See Galia Patt-Shamir, "Confucianism and Judaism: A Dialogue in Spite of Differences," in this volume.
5 Jonathan Sacks, *Crisis and Covenant—Jewish Thought after the Holocaust,* New York: Manchester University Press, 1992, p. 268.
6 References to *Talmud* use Abraham Cohen, *Everyone's Talmud—The Major Teaching of the Rabbinic Sages,* New York: Schocken Books, 1949.
7 Rabbi Akivah (died c. 135 CE) was one of the most essential contributors to the early Oral Torah, mainly the *Mishnah* and the *Midrash Halakha.*
8 In Hebrew, *massoret* literally means "that which was transmitted."
9 All references to *Lunyu* use D. C. Lau, *Confucius – The Analects,* London: Penguin Books, 1979.
10 Regarding the important role of rites (or propriety) *li* 礼 in Confucianism see Tu, Weiming, "The Creative Tension Between *Jen* and *Li*," *Philosophy East and West,* 18:1-2, 1968, pp. 29–39.
11 About the authorships of the *Canon of Rites,* as well as for the most extensive discussion on it, see Nylan, Michael, *The Five Confucian Classics,* New Haven: Yale University Press, 2001, pp. 173–178.
12 This section is based on understandings from past work. Patt-Shamir: 2003.
13 "Avoth" as the only non-*halakhic* tractate, prepares one's heart for the full acceptance and observance of the divine commands (*mitzvoth* מצוות), thus chosen here in comparison to *Lunyu* 论语 (*Analects*).
For the sake of brevity, in every reference to Babylonian Talmud (*Talmud Bavli* תלמוד בבלי) hereafter, I will refer only to the specific tractate (*masechet* מסכת) by its Hebrew name. Unless stated otherwise, all citations to *Talmud* use the translation of Cohen, 1949.
14 Unless stated differently, references to *Lunyu* use D. C. Lau, 1979.
15 See René Goldman. 'Moral Leadership in Society: Some Parallels between the Confucian "Nobleman" and the Jewish Zaddik.' *Philosophy East and West,* 1995, 45, 3.
16 See discussion in Galia Patt-Shamir, "Way as Dao; Way as Halakha: Confucianism, Judaism and Way Metaphors," *Dao* 5(2), Summer 2006, pp. 137-158.
17 Tu Weiming. "Probing the 'Three Bonds' and 'Five Relationships'". in S. Walter and G. De Vos (eds.) *Confucianism and the Family,* New York: SUNY, 1998, pp. 121–136; Shulamit Valler, *Women and Womenhood in the Stories of Babylonian Talmud,* (Hebrew), *Hakibbutz Hameuchad.* Tel-Aviv: 1993.

18 Asceticism was known in Biblical time; however, it was forbidden in the period of the *Talmud.*

19 See *Lunyu* 15:24; "Shabbath" 3.1. See discussion in Robert Elliot Allinson, 'Hillel and Confucius: The Proscriptive Formulation of the Golden Rule in the Jewish and Chinese Confucian Ethical Traditions.' *Dao: A Journal of Comparative Philosophy* 3.1, December 2003, pp. 29–41.

20 *Junzi* (君子) is derived from "ruler" (*jun*), meaning, at first, the descendant of a ruling house. Then the term extended to superiority of character, and finally it transformed to be about character alone, meaning "exemplary character."

21 Originally, *zaddik* referred to a just person, and when that term and *hasid* appeared in the Second Temple period *zaddik* was considered superior. Yet in Kabbalah, the whole community is comprised of *Hasidim* whose spiritual leader is a *zaddik*. See Goldman, pp. 333–336. Moreover, *hasid* and *zaddik* need to be juxtaposed with "sagely learner" (*Talmid Chacham* תלמיד חכם).

5

CONFUCIANISM AND JUDAISM

A dialogue in spite of differences

Galia Patt-Shamir

Jewish monotheism is a language about God. For example, when a Jewish person eats a first fruit, he/she thanks God by blessing "*shehecheyanu*" שהחיינו (meaning "Who has kept us alive"). The blessing is recited at every joyous occasion in the Jewish life cycle, such that the gratefulness to God for anything we eat is inherent in the Jewish mental constitution. When my grandfather, a believing Jew, was on his dying bed, he was unable to avoid asking, like many other Jews, "where did I sin to God, to deserve the punishment?" At great odds is the Confucian "anthropocosmic vision" (as coined by Tu Weiming), namely, a vision that stresses the continuity of being, between human and cosmos. Thus, Confucianism is a language about humanity. A new fruit for a Confucian, signifies the shared work of co-creation of human beings, earth, and heaven. Sickness is first and foremost taken as an occasion for a communal responsibility for the needy. The mental constitution is all oriented at human-relatedness and responsibility. Hence, it is important to open by clearly stating that we deal here with two language games that must be clearly distinguished. If one wishes to discuss some important shared ideas, one must not overlook the important differences in advance.

My aim in the present chapter is to discuss the possibility of creating a fruitful dialogue between the two traditions, yet how can such a task be conducted? What methodology can we apply to systems that are essentially so different? One important aspect of a language game is its practice. In particular, there is great significance of practice in understanding a religious form of life (as Hilary Putnam stresses).[1] The significance of practice is due to its major role in human life, as well as to its explanatory and persuasive power. I therefore choose to focus on three points concerning the different practices of Confucianism and Judaism. Showing the uniqueness of both Jewish and Confucian practices will hopefully put us on firmer ground to start a dialogue.

The three themes set as the pivot of this discussion are the ultimate, the human community, and the exemplary person. The terms in which they are discussed in Confucianism and in Judaism are essentially different. In Confucianism, the general inclination is toward a partnership of human and *dao* 道 (the way). Hence, *unification* and *harmony* are essential motivations for action. The exemplary personality is the full realization of this harmony by means of *self-reflection*. In Judaism, the *halakah* הלכה (Jewish legal code) is given by God and, thus, while accepting some renewal, it cannot accept human beings as an equal creators. The inclination to *separation* and *disharmony* are primary motivations for action, and the exemplary person is *tested* by the One and can follow the way by successfully passing the test. These three tendencies are found in biblical stories as main Jewish motifs. Let us take a closer look at the three Jewish motifs, and then move on to the Confucian.

The Uniqueness of Traditions

In the story of man's creation and the Garden of Eden, we are called to depict the idea of the ultimate. God is presented as the creator by means of a power to separate day from night, earth from water, human from divine, and so on, and as a moral authority by being the only one who knows right from wrong. Although man is created in "the image of God" (Genesis 1:27), his creation forms a fracture in reality. Man is separate from the ultimate, commanded by Him, and, eventually, distanced from Eden by God. The human choice of eating the forbidden fruit in order to be more like God is punished. The very act of eating of it, however, is rewarded too, as knowing good and evil is the essential human ability for moral judgment, which is gained in the same event. A sinner as well as a knower of right and wrong, humanity is expelled from Eden, and distanced from its creator. Thus, the first story sets *separation* between different creatures, and moreover between creator and created, as the motive to enable life and progress.

Evicted from Eden, human beings were forced to overcome natural confines and organize communities, either agricultural or urban. The short story of the city of Babel and the attempt to build a tower, adds a new dimension to the perspective regarding separation between human and ultimate. The story establishes the Jewish perspective on human community (as related to the divine). While the unification of humanity is valued and is desirable (only when unified can the people of Israel receive the Torah. Deuteronomy 29:9; 33:3), God also demands of man to spread and fill the earth (Genesis 1:22, 28). The men of the generation unify not in order to take care of each other, but to build a tower "whose top may reach unto heaven," and thus to challenge God's greatness. The whole generation is punished by being scattered, and their language is baffled. As in the Garden of Eden, the punishment is a reward as well: we cannot consider ourselves human without the gift of plurality of languages, cultures, and traditions. In the story of Babel, God forces man to be more like man, instead of desiring to be like God. *Disharmony* in the human world is established as a necessary condition, as well as a motivation for action and progress.

Lastly, in the story of the *Akedah* עֲקֵדָה (the Binding of Isaac) we are introduced to the exemplary personality of the first patriarch, Abraham. Completely willing to leave his family and homeland (ibid. 12 1-9), Abraham follows the divine world-structure of separation as established in Eden. His willingness to give up his son according to God's demand (ibid. 22 1-10), expresses absolute compliance with the divine rule of disharmony as established in the story of Babel. When he is absolutely subdued and follows the command, we discover that the whole story was a test (ibid. 22:16). Abraham's reward is to be blessed with descendants and become the patriarch of Judaism. *Test* is the third motif I offer in the Jewish picture, and from the perspective of human life, especially with a stress on human practice; I understand it to be the hinge. The test is given to man in Eden by the two forbidden trees, and man fails it by responding with a lack of trust. The test is presented again in Babel, this time through the community of man forced to build its home in cooperation, yet never to reach heaven, never even to conceive of a possibility of something that can be as great as God, and again man fails. Abraham is the first to respond properly to the riddle posed by God — *disharmony, separation*, and living an ongoing *test*. He is the first one to understand that to be Jewish is to understand properly the meaning of the riddle "give all you have and get all you can have in a single act" as a test incessantly given by God to man, and relentlessly to be practiced.

The three themes of the ultimate, the human community, and the exemplary person are represented in Confucianism in a terminology that is completely different from the Jewish approach. As opposed to a *test* one is given by God, it can be conceived of as a *mystery* one deciphers step by step. The Confucian ideas offer a view of an ultimate as a power for *unification*, of a community based on *harmony*, and of a person who is morally measured by means of *self-reflexivity*. Going back to the origins of the ideas in classical Confucianism, we realize that the ultimate is presented in *Zhongyong* as sincerity (*cheng* 诚). The virtue of sincerity is presented as a heavenly perfection that is also "mundane." We read in the text: "Sincerity is the Way of Heaven. Making oneself sincere is the Way of Man." (2.20). Later on, in Song times (960–1279 CE), it is explained in terms of the Great Ultimate (*Taiji* 太极) as "the origin of the myriad things." Yet, the Great Ultimate is also no other than "all virtues and the highest good" (*Yulei* 11.118.). In this way, the text presents its reader with a spirit of *unification* of the human with the ultimate as a creative force in the tradition.

Regarding the proper way to run a community, the Confucian tradition extends the meaning of the rules of propriety ("rites", *li* 礼) as those who harmonize the community. In *Analects* we read:

> Do not look unless it is in accordance with (propriety) *li*; do not
> listen unless it is in accordance with *li*; do not speak unless it is in
> accordance with *li*; do not move unless it is in accordance with *li*.
> (12:1)[2]

The rules of propriety, created by human beings turn to function as a
cosmic order (or pattern, *li* 理). Thus, by means of *li* and its extension, the
text presents *harmony* as a necessary spur in human social organization.
Every action is seen as having an order that, if followed (rather than
imposed), makes the action what it is.

As for the sage as the exemplary personality, the Confucian understanding is achieved by extending the notion using singleness of mind
brought about by means of reflexivity and self-cultivation. There is no
authority to guide us as "it is not the way that broadens man, it is man who
broadens the way" (*Lunyu* 15:28). Broadening the way is essentially what
Confucian humanism and its spirituality are about. Our capability to
broaden the ultimate (as the way) is also our responsibility as human
beings. The self-reflexivity of the sage discloses a view of life as a *mystery*
that mirrors one's life but is not given from outside, which is to be deci-
phered step by step as the whole picture is never given, and can only be
approximated and approached by reproducing it in one's own practice. This
practice is echoed in Confucian texts.

Before addressing the possibility for dialogue and the shared grounds for
it, one cannot ignore the obvious gap between Jewish monotheistic and
Confucian non-theistic views. René Goldman, one of the few scholars
engaged in Jewish and Confucian thought from a comparative perspective,
reminds us that:

> There is a difference between the primary orientation of Confucian
> humanism and that of Judaic humanism: the former ultimately
> binds the self to family and society, and the latter to God.[3]

How and Why, then, a Dialogue Can be Created?

If the differences are so immense, why do we connect Confucianism and
Judaism, and where do they meet? We deal with the relatedness between
religious texts and practices under the presupposition that religion is
people's lives. This can be demonstrated, so I believe, by any choice of
traditions. A choice of more than a single tradition can contribute to a
perspective that is more universal, and thus has a better argumentative
power. The choice of Confucianism and Judaism embodies a personal
perspective on my side. Being Jewish by origin and Confucian by education has made me at certain times puzzled regarding issues of transcendence,

world harmony, and human predisposition. An initial study of Judaism and Confucianism shows, as we have already seen, that the two teachings that I consider my two spiritual springs of knowledge are quite contrary regarding these issues. The language of Judaism is about one God, transcendent, omnipotent, untouchable, distinct, and perfect. Confucian language is about humanity, human virtues, moral perfection, and personality, while transcendence has an altogether different sense (in fact, so different that some scholars claim it is non-existent).[4] When Judaism describes the world, there is a compelling sense of disharmony, even a rupture; Confucianism offers a picture of an "organismic whole" (as coined by Mote), and of being as harmonious continuity (in Tu's terminology).[5] Judaism takes the perspective that human nature has bad in it (*yetzer hara* יצר הרע), and defines human nature in a dualistic way, as a compound of conflicting tendencies formed in creation, realized from youth in a desire for bad. Early Confucian thought basically defines human nature in a monistic way as a single-minded entity, either in the Mencian line as a good nature to preserve and improve, or, even in the Xunzian case, as a heaven-endowed nature given to us for the work of improvement.[6]

I was, therefore, surprised to realize that the disagreement between the two traditions on issues of such significance did not bring about conflicting attitudes regarding the human way, practice, morality, and learning. In fact, I had a sense that both shared a vision of a humanistic way with a special emphasis on learning as a religious practice. It took me some time to realize that the multiplicity of perspectives regarding the "big," more theoretical presuppositions produced in my mind a dialogue of traditions, in which my birth tradition was revealed as helpful for better contemplating aspects of Confucianism discovered in my research. Not only that, Confucianism itself gives its learner the advice that to learn the way one needs first to be dedicated to the root. The Confucian *Analects* tells us that the exemplary person devotes his efforts to the roots, for once the roots are established, the way emerges; and that being filial and respectful to one's ancestors is the root (*Lunyu* 1:2). The *Great Learning* (*Daxue* 大学) develops the discussion on the order of things as their having roots (*ben* 本) and branches (*mo* 末). Knowing the root (*zhiben* 知本) is the knowledge of first and last, which leads closer to Confucian knowledge (*Daxue*, commentary 4; 5.1-2). One understanding of the root may be that it includes the person, and what a person brings before developing "branches," which are other beings, the community, and the state. Zhu Xi (1130–1200 CE), commented extensively on the order of things, and on "the root" as what is first. The *Doctrine of the Mean* (*Zhongyong* 中庸) elaborates on the root as the world's equilibrium, which brings about the universal way of harmony (I.4). Confucianism urges its learners to better know their own roots, for the sake of understanding *dao*.

In all these senses, my roots are in Judaism.

Hence, I feel that I have to use "the roots," my roots, to study Confucianism. Being puzzled at first can be an insightful start for realizing that the "contradictory" presuppositions of Judaism and Confucianism are helpful and intriguing, and when put together they expand the basis for the moral spirit and its call for pluralism. Eventually, I found the two traditions to be two balancing aspects of thought. The perspective we may gain from this type of work is, thus, more universal and more personal at the same time; it is more universal, as it brings together two remote traditions from the perspective of shared ideas, such that each can be understood by reflecting on the other. The bonding together is, however, obviously a very personal bonding. Each reader is welcome to make applications to traditions that are closer to her or his own heart. It will be more fruitful by far to see the present choice as a suggestion, than to assume that I intend to make here a claim about an inner relatedness between Judaism and Confucianism. The latter is not the purpose of this work; a better understanding is, so is dialogue.

What Type of Dialogue?

We may aim at placing Confucianism and Judaism in global philosophical and religious contexts. There is no inherent relation between Confucianism and Judaism, and I have no wish to suggest a relation of this kind. However, *because* of the self-sufficiency of both Confucianism and Judaism, it should be possible to have the traditions' messages *in discourse* with other cultures, intellectual viewpoints, and religious traditions. Jewish ideas introduce a challenge to Confucianism in the spiritual realm; Confucianism challenges the human responsibility in Judaism. Both Confucianism and Judaism encourage learning through dialogue. Both are well familiar with learning in small groups, with a teacher challenging and the students suggesting responses, the students posing questions and the teacher replies. Even the expression used in both traditions to questioning each other as "posing a difficulty" is similar in the traditions (*kushiya* קושיה in Hebrew meaning "asking" comes from the root ק.ש.י which signifies "difficulty", in Chinese *Nanshuo* 难说 has the same denotation.)

Confucianism and Judaism, like other religious traditions, are about human life, and living is being related to other human beings, to texts, to ideas, and, most importantly, to a totality of being. This totality is frequently considered "religious," and is sometimes seen as an aspect of life that is remote from the daily, belongs with transcendence, and is related to a reality that is not part of human partial existence. The great Jewish philosopher Martin Buber expresses an intuitive sentiment toward the power to bring the religious back into human life and practice, rather than segregating it to a remote realm:

In my earlier years, the 'religious' was for me the exception. There were hours that were taken out of the course of things. From somewhere or other the firm crust of everyday was pierced ... 'Religious experience' was the experience of an otherness that did not fit into the context of life ...

Since then I have given up the 'religious,' which is nothing but the exception, extraction, exaltation, ecstasy; or it has given me up. I possess nothing but the everyday, out of which I am never taken. The mystery is no longer disclosed ...

I do not know much more. If that is religion then it is just *everything*, simply all that is lived in its possibility of dialogue.[7]

According to Buber, a dialogue enables one to give up "religion" as a distinct and remote spiritual discourse and practice, and to realize that religion is life, or "everything." "Everything" is described as any given in the world that can be put into dialogue. A dialogue, in his view, has life of its own, and this life is based on human ability and will, not on divine command.

Buber goes on, suggesting:

And how could the life of dialogue be demanded? There is no ordering of dialogue. It is not that you are to answer but that you *are able.*

You are really able. The life of dialogue is no privilege of intellectual activity like dialectic. It does not begin in the upper story of humanity. It begins no higher than where humanity begins.[8]

A dialogue is in everyone's ability and is possible for everyone; it is not a demand, but an existent aspect of one's life that can either be realized or denied. In Buber's view, a dialogue is a true relatedness that can be expressed in the interaction between one and another, and between the individual and the ultimate. This dialogue can be realized through texts, yet neither words nor a cognitive process are demanded; rather, it is an embodiment of feelings, thoughts, and practices. This embodiment is life as dialogue, and this is the uniqueness of religion being life. In his writings, Buber discourses with Chinese philosophies (in particular with Daoism), which he sees as suggesting the world to human beings as a *task*. He writes:

But — and this is where all great Asiatic religions and ideologies meet — the unified world must not only be conceived, it must be realized. It is not merely given to man, it is given to him as a task; he is charged with making the true world an actual world.[9]

Learning is at least one way in which the task is pursued by human beings, in both Confucianism and Judaism. The religious significance of learning is expressed in dialogues among learners, between reader and text, and between human and ultimate. Learning through dialogue is a commitment of both Confucianism and Judaism. Therefore, a dialogue between the Confucian and Jewish traditions can be a fruitful way to broaden our understanding of the various senses of being religious. However, while inter-religious dialogues in general enjoy growth and burgeoning in contemporary times, as world thinkers open themselves to ways of life previously unknown to them, a dialogue between Confucianism and Judaism is, in important senses, yet non-existent.

When Friedrich Heiler discusses the idea of inter-religious dialogue, he assumes that the ultimate reason for dialogue is improving relations among adherents of different traditions. Heiler's view is well represented by Eric Sharpre's perspective, following the "liberal" fathers of comparative religion like C. P. Tiele, Max Muller, J. G. Frazer, and P. D. Chantepie de la Sausaye.[10] Heiler puts this spirit into words:

> If the student of comparative religion, it may be asked, does not hold the key to better understanding between Christians and Hindus, Muslims and Jews, what can be the purpose of all the effort he has put into his studies?[11]

While the immediate necessity for dialogue between Muslims and Jews is quite obvious to any sober mind, not so apparent is the necessity for dialogue between Confucians and Jews. The latter dialogue can indirectly contribute to the former, but what may one directly gain from it?

Comparative studies of Confucianism and Judaism originated in the West from comparative studies of Confucianism and Christianity. Max Weber's *The Religion of China: Confucianism and Taoism* emphasized the economic aspect; Julia Ching took a comprehensive approach in her work *Confucianism and Christianity*, and so did William Theodore de Bary in *The Trouble with Confucianism*.[12] Closest in spirit to the present attitude, and more influential on it, are works from recent years that deal directly with dialogue between the Confucian tradition and monotheistic traditions, especially Christianity. This type of work is done mainly by contemporary scholars of "Boston Confucianism," including Tu Weiming, Robert Cumming Neville, and, especially, John Berthrong in *All Under Heaven — Transforming Paradigms in Confucian–Christian Dialogue*.[13]

The Confucian–Christian dialogue, unlike Confucian–Jewish dialogue, "is well begun" as John Berthrong attests in *All Under Heaven*. Berthrong represents those who are particularly committed to Confucian–Christian dialogue, like Mou Tsung-san, Liu Shu-hsien, Cheng Chung-ying, and Tu Weiming.[14] In his book, he suggests three reasons for dialogue: one, encouraging pluralism; two, the ability of religious dialogue to bring peace among religions, which may lead to peace among nations; and three, the possibility of a renewal of past civilizations through dialogue.[15] While the first two reasons apply exclusively to the members of the traditions involved in dialogue, reviving human history through mutual learning of its sources is in the interest of any human being — to broaden perspective, and to adopt yet one more technique to deal with daily conflicts.

In the conclusion to his book, Berthrong mentions three different kinds of dialogue. First, is an actual engagement in inter-faith dialogue. This kind of dialogue "will cause people to change their minds and seek new ways of talking together to explore ultimate life virtues." Second, is a conversation among theologians about "what can be received from these explorations." Critical correlation will need to occur between the etic and emic dialogues for them to succeed.[16] These two kinds of dialogue are certainly non-existent when we refer to Confucian–Jewish dialogue. The last arena of dialogue, according to Berthrong, is the one that is also relevant to the present study. It is what Berthrong calls "dialogue of the heart." He explains:

> While cooperation in terms of community life and explorations of meaning and truth are noble experiments, no religious dialogue is complete until the participants respond to the callings of the meditative heart ... The ability to speak from heart to heart relies on trust, understanding and the translation of the hopes and aspirations from one culture to another.[17]

Berthrong believes that the dialogue of the heart can only come at the end of the process, and concludes with the optimistic note that the Confucian–Christian dialogue is well begun. I have to open this book with the awareness that Confucian–Jewish dialogue has not yet begun, at least not in the first and second senses described above. And yet, I wish to be able to start a "dialogue of the heart," with the hope that it will contribute to the establishment of communities of practitioners and engaged theologians.

When I borrow Berthrong's notion of a dialogue of the heart, I cling to the belief that in the heart, in the case of Confucianism and Judaism, there is a way in which the dialogue is existent, even if not yet developed to its mature, full sense. I want to briefly address what "heart" refers to in Chinese and in Hebrew. René Goldman reminds us of the special feature regarding the heart in the traditions of Confucianism and Judaism, and the languages of Chinese and Hebrew. The Chinese word *xin* 心, like its Hebrew counterpart *lev* לב and *levav* לבב, represents the bodily organ, as well as the seat of emotion and of thought, and both terms translate as "heart" and "mind." In Judaism and in Confucianism, study calls for intellectual–ethical growth and emotional–moral maturation in one process.[18] In Confucianism, the heart "knows." Mencius refers to it as the "great body" (*dati* 大体), as opposed to the "small body" (*xiaoti* 小体). In the *Great Learning*, the rectification of the heart (*xinzheng* 心正) is the basis for "cultivation of the person." Later on, Wang

Yang-ming (1472–1529 CE) unifies knowledge and action in the heart as "innate knowledge" (*liangzhi* 良知). In the Bible, the heart is mentioned 827 times. In Genesis, we read that "man's heart is evil" and that "Jacob's heart fainted;" in Exodus, God "hardens Pharaoh's heart," then God speaks to the "wise hearted;" in Leviticus, God gives as punishment the "sorrow of the heart" so that "the heart be humbled." The contexts vary widely. The *Talmud* continues the references and uses the Aramaic *libba*, adding to the physical perspective of the heart, the stomach, thorax, chest, and mind.

Because of the special sensitivity of the role of the heart in the embodiment of thought, in addition to its being the location of emotion, in the particular context of Confucianism and Judaism, the heart can serve as a starting point for a fruitful "dialogue of the heart," which is waiting to come to life, and then to gain wished-for maturity.

I believe that by now we are ready to join Friedrich Heiler in his hope that the justification for dialogue of religions is "to improve relations between the adherents of different religious traditions."[19] As more and more studies are done regarding religious dialogue, with the aim of learning from our differences, more can be done with Confucianism and Judaism. In addition to opening a new channel for inter-religious dialogue, we may seek a method for understanding religion — either one's own or a foreign one by means of comparative study. Nevertheless, there is a growing interest in the intellectual history of world traditions, we find more and more people involved in a certain religious spirituality and wishing to know about other spiritualities, many students who just started their studies of philosophy, religion or East Asian cultures, all raise the same question of reaching a more peaceful solution for the materializing world.

The type of dialogue I believe we may create emerges from Martin Buber's suggestion regarding religion:

> If that is religion, then it is just *everything*, simply all that is lived in its possibility of dialogue.[20]

The walk that we may now begin, which connects Confucianism and Judaism is not bound to a tradition, to a place, or to a time; it is first and foremost a stride of every human being, a journey of every mind. The cognitive structure of religious intellect is shared by diverse traditions and, when acting in this framework, this intellect calls for a form of thought that is expressed in a riddle, whose response is in human practices. Deciphering the riddle can be a helpful device for a person who approaches the form of life from the outside, as it gives a clue to "inside" views. Each tradition reflects, a specific riddle distinguishes the uniqueness of the views of a given form of life. Every form of life has its own riddle. Seeing the riddle is a possible first step in a response to the challenge for the human to broaden the way.

Notes

1 Hilary Putnam, *Renewing Philosophy.* Cambridge: Harvard University Press, 1990, p. 135; *Pragmatism*, Oxford: Basil Blackwell, 1995, pp. 49–52.

2 In general, references to *Lunyu* use D.C. Lau. *Confucius–The Analects.* London: Penguin Books, 1979. In this case, I chose to use "li" to stress the point.

3 René Goldman, "Moral Leadership in Society: Some Parallels Between the Confucian 'Noble Man' and the Jewish *Zaddik*," *Philosophy East and West*, Vol. 45.3, July 1995, pp. 329–365. The quotation is on p. 354.

4 For example, David Hall and Roger Ames completely deny the transcendence of Confucius. See the discussion in Robert Cummings Neville. *Boston Confucianism–Portable Tradition in the Late Modern World,* New York: SUNY, 2000, pp. 147–165.

5 I adhere to the views of Tu's "continuity of being," Needham's "Organism," Mote's "organismic whole," Graham's "correlative thinking," and Mou's "immanent transcendence," which I believe fit the Confucian perspective, as demonstrated hereafter. Michael Puett criticizes these traditional views, and disputes the view of a "Chinese" vision as harmonious in his book *To Become A God* (see *To Become a God,* Cambridge: Harvard University Press, 2002, pp. 14–26). While Puett deals with Chinese religious thought from a historical perspective, my attitude focuses on Confucianism as a specific *contribution* to Chinese religious thought. In this sense the perspective of continuity by means of Confucianism's human-oriented vision makes the views not necessarily contradictory.

6 See the discussion in Zhang Ping, *Bridging Between the Actual and the Ideal in Early Rabbinical and Confucian Literature.* Ph.D. dissertation, Tel Aviv University, 1999, pp. 72–80.

7 Martin Buber, "Dialogue," *The Martin Buber Reader, Essential Writings/Edited* by Asher D. Biemann, New York: Palgrave Macmillan, 2002, p. 193.

8 Buber, ibid., p. 196.

9 Martin Buber, "The Spirit of the Orient and Judaism," In Nahum N. Glatzer (ed.) *On Judaism*, New York: Schocken Books, 1967, p. 60.

10 See Eric J. Sharpre, "Toward a Dialogue of Religions?" in *Comparative Religion – A History,* La Salle: Open Court, 1975, pp. 251–266.

11 Ibid., p. 251.

12 Max Weber, *The Religion of China: Confucianism and Taoism*, trans. and ed. by H.H. Gerth. Glencoe: The Free Press, 1951; Julia Ching, *Confucianism and Christianity: a Comparative Study*, Tokyo: Kodansha International, 1977; William Theodore de Bary, *The Trouble with Confucianism*, Cambridge: Harvard University Press: 1991.

13 John Berthrong, *All Under Heaven — Transforming Paradigms in Confucian Christian Dialogue*, New York: SUNY Press, 1994, p. 187.

14 Berthrong, op cit., see discussion on pp. 43–65.

15 Ibid., pp. 13–15.

16 By "etic" I refer to the aspects of "shared ideas" and traditions having linguistic or behavioral characteristics considered interculturally without regard to their structural significance; as opposed to "emic," which is the inner significance of ideas and the non-translatability of religious languages among traditions, relating to, or involving analysis of linguistic or behavioral phenomena in terms of the internal structure or function (See Berthrong, op cit., p. 186).

17 Berthrong, p. 187.

18 Goldman, op. cit., see especially p. 346.

19 Sharpre, op cit., p. 250.

20 Martin Buber, "Dialogue," 2002, p. 193.

6

JUDAISM AND ITS REFERENTIAL VALUE TO THE CULTURAL RECONSTRUCTION OF MODERN CHINA

Fu Youde

The Enlightenment and modernization, products of the West, have been material and social hurricanes that have swept over the majority of peoples in the world and affected their cultural and spiritual traditions. With the challenge of modernization, no civilization, old or new, can escape the tensions between tradition and modernization. In the last two centuries, China has faced periods of reform and revolution, all of which have been related to the conflict between modernity and tradition. Chinese, Arabs, Indians, Mexicans, and Jews, it seems to me that the latter have been the most successful in managing the challenge of modernity. After a century of effort and uneven progress, the Chinese people have now embarked on a sure way to a prosperous economy: material modernization through a market economy. In contrast to the Chinese, the Jewish people have modernized themselves materially, living modern lives in Western countries on one hand, and maintaining a cultural identity, namely Jewishness, on the other.[1] Judaism, and the unique way Jews have blended modernity and tradition, provides an example for China of how to find the lost soul of its people.

Unlike the Jews, who are aware of their cultural identity and their Jewishness, from the perspective of a Chinese philosopher it appears that the Chinese people are still perplexed as to their cultural identity. Most Chinese do not know what their cultural identity consists of and how to keep it. In short, they have lost what it means to be "Chinese" and are, to some degree at the present time, culturally soulless. Over the last century, there have been a variety of opinions and theories concerning Chinese spiritual identity; these include "Overall Westernization" (全盘西化), "the quintessence of Chinese Tradition" (国粹主义), "Chinese Value as root and Western Science as Branch" (中体西用), "Western Culture as root and Chinese tradition as Branch"(西体中用), and Neo-Confucianism and Neo-Taoism.

I have no intention of rehashing the history of Chinese spiritual identity in this chapter. What I am trying to do is, by historical analysis and comparison of Judaism and Confucianism, identify the value of the Jewish Reform movement and the process of modernization that it brought in its wake, then make some comparisons between this and the current cultural reconstruction in modern China. I shall briefly describe the movement of Jewish Reform, analyze its outcome and significances to Chinese cultural reconstruction, and, finally, try to demonstrate why the success of Jewish religious reform and modernization can be applied to China today.

The Reform of Judaism and its Outcome

The theory of Jewish reform was rooted in the ideas of historical evolutionism upheld by Abraham Geiger (1810–74), Bachman Rocha (1785–1840), Sammuel Holdheim (1806–60), and, later, an American reformer Isaac Mayer Weis (1819–1900) and others. To varying degrees influenced by philosophers such as Hegel and Giovanni Battista Vico, the reformers thought that history was a process of evolution and expressed itself in different ways in various historical phases. They saw the Jewish tradition, which was classed as the manifestations of the Absolute Spirit, as something that needed to adjust itself to the changing of society. Judaism would have to adapt itself to the changing times.[2] As Geiger stated, Judaism was a living and changing system of faith. It shaped its form within history and, as a religious tradition, it involved its followers within an evermoving process. Judaism was divided into different forms with distinct characteristics in different historical stages. This theory was opposite to that of the traditionalist Jews, who regarded the Torah as both Mosaic Law and, to a less defined extent, Rabbinic Tradition, beyond history and timeless, therefore eternal and unchangeable. For the religious traditionalists, it was the Torah that influenced time and society, not the reverse.

The reformers changed mainly the rituals of synagogue worship and folk practices. They discarded Hebrew language in rituals and, instead, used German, introduced equality for the sexes into synagogues, and abandoned or altered numerous traditions. The most significant outcome of the Reform Movement was the split of traditional Judaism into three main denominations: (1) Reform Judaism, which crossed over the divide of traditional Judaism, and emerged as an independent denomination after a fierce struggle of nearly five decades; (2) Orthodox Judaism, the structures and people that remained dedicated to an intact tradition of laws and rituals and stood by them even as the reformers moved out. This includes Hasidim and Traditional Orthodoxy, Modern, and Neo-Orthodox groups, and some elements of the third category — Conservative Judaism. Orthodox Judaism is characterized by a mixture of rigid observance to the tradition of Jewish law, tradition, and a sense of historical romanticism; and (3) Conservative Judaism, which maintained the spirit of the historical reform school in Germany in the nineteenth century, but did not go to the extremes of the Reform Movement. Conservative Judaism formerly appeared in the United States of America. It upheld the principles of a reform of Judaism and adjusted outdated Jewish ideas and rituals with a progressive outlook, but adopted conservative attitudes and kept more tradition in synagogue services and religious tradition. Both Reform and Conservative Judaism belong to Liberal or Progressive Judaism, whose followers make up 72 per cent of the American Jewish population.[3] Apart from the three main denominations, another smaller denomination is Reconstructionism, which was founded by Mordechai Kaplan in the 1920s. It considers Judaism as a civilization with the concept of God being a force made for the purpose of "salvation." It is the newest movement of Judaism, with a radical theory combined with more conservative practice, and has impacted the Jewish world mainly by its philosophy.

Now to turn to the aims of Jewish Reform Movement and whether it was successful from a historical perspective.

The Reform Movement in the nineteenth century had a twofold task, which was advanced by Moses Mendelssohn (1729–86) when he defined the goals of *haskalah* (Jewish Enlightenment) in his work *Jerusalem*:

> [The Jew] sought to break down the ghetto barriers and transform the Jew into a European, who, at the same time, would retain his Jewishness. Accordingly, the Jew was to be integrated into Western culture and trained to live in two milieux, the worldly and the Jewish, thereby assuming dual cultural responsibility.[4]

In reality, two centuries since the beginning of Reform in the nineteenth century, we can now assert that the objectives of the Reform Movement have been attained in the main and it actually succeeded in general, which can be justified by the following facts.

Above all, most European and American Jews have modernized themselves by integrating into the West in many ways, especially in science and politics. Jews have been leaders in science, academia, and business, and have been an eminent political force in many countries apart from Israel. According to the *Political Graveyard*, a website about US political history and cemeteries, 138,150 Jewish politicians, both living and dead, are listed. Some Jews have become prime ministers or cabinet ministers in Britain, France, Australia, and other great countries. Furthermore, even Jewish households and family life have been changed and modernized tremendously, and Jewish children are some of the best educated children in the modern world.

However, despite much assimilation, it is still a fact that traditional and ritual dimensions of Judaism play a very important role in Jewish life. Take

American Jewry as an example. In light of the demographical survey of the United Jewish Community in 2002, the population of American Jews is 5.2 million, and around 56 per cent of these are registered in synagogues and participate in regular religious services.[5] Religious Jews spend Shabbat and other holidays and festivals in accordance with the Jewish religion; and a good number of irreligious Jews celebrate Jewish holidays too. It is unnecessary to enumerate examples to illustrate the spirituality and religiousness of the Jewish, as it is well known in the West that the Jews are a religious people and most of them find their identity in Judaism as a way of life.

Now I would like, from a Chinese perspective, to make some generalizations about the Jewish Reform Movement and its outcome as follows. First, tradition and modernity are not diametrically opposite to each other and modern Jews may find identity from tradition. Modernity is the manifestation of human reason, which creates modern science, technology, and industrialization necessary to human material life and promotes human wellbeing. However, humans also live moral and spiritual lives for which science and technology do not provide answers; these answers are provided by religions. For a people like the Jews with long history and rich culture, tradition should not be discarded. What we can do is innovate and reform, as has taken place in Judaism since the nineteenth century. A majority of modernized Jews, of whatever denomination, or however they have perceived their own Jewishness, have maintained tradition to some extent and found their identity from within their own perceptions of what it means to be a Jew.

Second, modernity can be grafted on the stem of tradition. A Jew can be a scientist and, at the same time, a religious person who follows Mosaic Law, goes to the synagogue on Shabbat, celebrates Jewish festivals and lives a religious life. Though not all successful Jews are religious, a good number of religious Jews have shown that traditional values and modern life can coexist without conflict. As a matter of fact, they can be complementary and beneficial to each other.

Third, tradition must be reformed. Tradition is not to be reserved without condition. The purpose of keeping tradition is to adapt itself to change in order to serve the people properly. Tradition without change cannot be the way of life of people in a vibrant society. If a tradition does not fit the altered society, it should be changed. If Judaism did not reform itself, it could not have been the guiding force for the modern Jewish community. It seems to me that Liberal Judaism can nowadays play an important role in Jewish spiritual and moral life for the majority of the Jews, mainly because of the Reform Movement initiated in the nineteenth century. Even Orthodox Jews have changed tradition to some degree in the direction of modernity.

Fourth, to reform is not to abandon tradition. The Jewish reform was in the frame of Judaism, rather than beyond it. In other words, to reform is to critically inherit tradition, not to give it up. This is reflected in a declaration by the Central Conference of American Rabbis in 1999:

> Throughout our history, we Jews have remained firmly rooted in Jewish tradition, even as we have learned much from our encounters with other cultures. The great contribution of Reform Judaism is that it has enabled the Jewish people to introduce innovation while preserving tradition, to embrace diversity while asserting commonality. ... This Statement of Principles affirms the central tenets of Judaism – God, Torah and Israel – even as it acknowledges the diversity of Reform Jewish beliefs and practices.[6]

Whereas the attitude of Zionism, dietary law and other precepts were revised and changed, the basic beliefs and principles of Judaism were not changed.

Finally, religion is irreplaceable in maintaining a nation's spirit or identity. Faced with a powerful Christian culture that has a strong missionary tendency, any non-Western people, if they intend to resist Western impact and be free from the fate of assimilation, have to strengthen and develop their religion in order to attract the masses and make it the soul or spirit of their people. Jewish people would have lost their soul and identity without Judaism. If ancient Judaism shapes ancient Israel, modern Judaism forms the Jewishness or identity of the modern Jews.

In short, the Jewish people in the Diaspora reacted against the challenges of modernity by choosing the middle path between tradition and modernity and have succeeded to a great degree. The Jewish way of coping with the relation between modernity and tradition points to a way of coping for other peoples with a similar social and cultural background.

The Referential Values of Jewish Reform to the Construction of Chinese Culture

> One Chinese proverb says, 'A stone from another mountain may also be made into a good jade.' That is especially true when it comes to the referential values of the reform of Judaism to the reconstruction of Chinese culture. The contemporary Chinese people can benefit a lot from the experiences of Jewish reform.

As the Jewish experience has demonstrated that tradition and modernization are reconcilable, the appropriate attitude for Chinese people in facing the same problems should be one of "both ... and" instead of "either ... or." That is to say, on one hand, it is improper to westernize by embracing foreign cultures without reserving tradition, on the other hand, the attitude of nationalism, characterized by sticking to the tradition stubbornly and excluding foreign cultures blindly, is not appropriate either. The wise choice should be accepting modernity while giving consideration to traditional values.

76

As Jewish people have succeeded in transplanting modern science, technology, and industry on to the basis of Judaism, it is advisable that Chinese people make an attempt to make use of Western science and technology on the basis of Chinese traditional values. Sciences, as universally useful truths, have no borders or boundaries. Although having originated and developed in Europe and North America, modern science does not exclusively belong to the West. It is one part of the civilization of all humanity in the world. History has shown that Chinese traditional culture failed to come up with a systematical science, not to say modern technology, though it included some scientific elements and factors. I cannot see any possibility or necessity in "developing" or tracing the origin of modern technology in Chinese tradition as some scholars have attempted.[7] One possibility might be learning from the Jewish attitude, that is, to take the existing modern technology from the West, and employ it in modernization in China. In this case, philosophers should avoid the consumption of their brains and let the scientists introduce and innovate bravely. As to the scholars of humanities, they have their own mission, that is, to reform and reconstitute the traditional creatively, set up spiritual values for Chinese people, and develop this into the soul of Chinese people. As the success of the Jewish experience lies in the reform of their tradition, we Chinese people can reform our traditional culture.

In dealing with values and cultural spirits, we should not take the attitude of "bring everything here," instead, we should emphasize reform and reconstruction. Reform of tradition is an approach of both preserving and discarding. Similar to the reform of Judaism, Chinese reform and reconstruction can be carried out on the basis of Chinese traditions, and "setting up a brand new oven after damaging everything." We should differentiate and conserve the essence of our traditions that is in accordance with the spirit of the times and humanity, while discarding the dross that is outdated in contemporary times. Simultaneously, we should open our minds, absorb and assimilate the universally excellent achievements in both Eastern and Western cultures. On that basis, we can set up new cultures and new spiritual structures that function as the soul of Chinese people.

Although the Judaic reform in nineteenth century Germany led to divisions of Judaism, none of the denominations has – from its own perspective – left Judaism entirely. Similarly, with the advent of the May Fourth Movement (1917–21), the Chinese academia split into several sects in facing the problem of Chinese tradition and Western civilization, such as the school of "Overall Westernization" represented by Chen Duxiu (陈独秀), Hu Shi (胡适), the school of "Chinese Value as Root and Western Science as Branch" with Zhang Zhidong (张之洞) as its representative, the School of "Quintessence of Chinese Tradition" represented by Zhang Taiyan (章太炎), Liu Shipei (刘师培), Ma Xulun (马叙伦) and others, and the post-Cultural Revolution school of "Western Culture as Root and Chinese Tradition as Branch" led by Li Zehou (李泽厚). The latter proposed to make use of

Western science and values as the backbone while preserving some Chinese traditions, which can be called "Quasi-Overall Westernization." With the experiences of Jewish reform in mind, we can say that theories of Overall Westernization and Quasi-Overall Westernization are expendable, as their principal orientation is negation of tradition and neglect of the succession of national spirit. The school of Quintessence of Chinese Tradition refuses to follow the mainstream of modernization, by sticking stubbornly to traditions without differentiation; hence, their approach is also expendable. The contrast between the school of Westernization and the school of Quintessence of Chinese Tradition is comparable with Jews converting to Christianity as opposed to those who remained Orthodox Jews within the Reform Movement. The former are rebels of their tradition, while the latter are its defendants. One of the fruits of Judaic reform is the successful restraint of Jewish conversion to Christianity.

Although still an independent group of religion, the Orthodox Jew is a minority (21 per cent of the religious Jews in the US). Thus, among the above options, we can see the thought of the school of Chinese Value as Root and Western Science as Branch is more practicable in the reform and reconstruction of Chinese culture today. It is comparable with Liberal Judaism, which includes the majority of Jews who belong to the Reform and Conservative movements.

However, with regards to the alternative Chinese Value as Root and Western Science as Branch, I propose this is quite different from the school with same name in the late Qing dynasty, represented by Zhang Zhidong. Their practice was to accept the traditional Chinese system of values unswervingly, while introducing Western technology. By *ti* (体), they meant the Confucianism of the Song and Ming Dynasties, and *yong* (用) referred to making use of Western science and technology. In their thought, *ti* contained the meaning of "fundamental" and "principal," while *yong* was instrumental, secondary, and complementary. In terms of their purpose, they did not transcend what Wei Yuan (魏源) proposed "learning from the strengths of the West to resist the West." They did not realize the changes of the times and, hence, failed to realize that *ti* should also be adaptable to the changes of the times. *Ti* is closely related to Chinese tradition, especially the Confucian tradition, but it should be the tradition reformed according to the spirit of the times and reconstructed on the basis of absorption of the cultural essences of both the East and the West, not the unchangeable old convention. I think *ti* in this sense is applicable to the *yong* of science and technology and is capable of meeting the needs of Chinese people, and, hence, can become the spiritual backbone and cultural identity, and function in the settlement of life of Chinese people.[8]

As to the differences between Chinese people and Jews, I propose two points: first, Judaism is a successive tradition without any breaks while the Chinese tradition is not; second, Jewish tradition is typically religious, while the Chinese tradition is not. The two differences mean that the reconstruction of Chinese culture should not be completely the same as the reform of Judaism.

The reform of a continuous tradition such as Judaism requires that innovation and reconstitution take place under a banner of historical evolution. The reformers differentiated and discarded the decadent and outdated doctrines, rituals, and customs, while choosing and reserving the factors that were adaptable to requirements of the times. In fact, the Reform and Conservative Movements within Judaism both adopted this approach; only the Orthodox elements rejected it. But this is not practical for the building of Chinese culture, as our tradition was broken in mainland China with the advent of the May Fourth Movement in the early twentieth century. Nowadays, the majority of Chinese know little about the traditional values, except for some professional philosophers and scholars. The traditional values were deprived of their carrier — people. Hence, the priority of contemporary Chinese culture building should not be innovation, as it was in the Jewish Reform Movement. The first mission should be the link or connection with tradition, that is, we should go back to where the tradition was broken, and bridge the gap between tradition and the present culture. Only after that can we take the task of innovation and reconstruction.

However, the linear quality of time means that history will never be replayed and we will never travel back to the past in terms of time. So, the sequence of connection to and innovation of the tradition is not in the sense of time but of logic. It is not practical to spend ten or more years recovering the tradition before reconstruction of the tradition and origination of a new culture in later years. In time, connection and innovation happen simultaneously. That is, understanding and connection of the tradition coincide with its reform and reconstitution. The combination of connection and innovation is a twofold mission, which is much more complicated and difficult than the innovation of Judaism. That should not be neglected in the process of building contemporary Chinese culture.

The second difference between Chinese and Jewish cultures is of great importance. The Jewish tradition is a religious one. It consists of not only beliefs, rituals and customs, but also organizations and believers. That is to say, Judaism is, amongst other things, an institutional religion. An ideology as a belief without organization or believers can only be a philosophical system, which is only a rational pursuit of a few people and, hence, very limited in its influence. With believers and organizations such as churches, the belief of a religion is deeply set in every believer's mind and is performed in daily life and specific actions. So, religion is much more acceptable for the masses than philosophy. At present, 80 per cent of the world population believes in certain religions and they regard their own religious beliefs as their cultural identity and spiritual settlement. That is what Judaism is to the Jews. Undoubtedly, the Chinese tradition included some religions, such as Buddhism and Taoism. But the disciples of Buddhism and Taoism are only a minority of the population in mainland China. Moreover, the two religions seem too passive and *Chu Shi* (escaping from the physical world) to become popular among most people. The factual mainstream of Chinese tradition is Confucianism. But Confucianism is not deemed as a religion in the minds of many Chinese people. Ideologically, pre-Qin Confucianism is much more religious in its thought concerning Heaven. But the Confucianism of the Song and Ming dynasties paid less attention to Heaven, and, instead, humanity became the active subject, whose main pursuit is the instruction of rite and self-cultivation. That undermined the religious characteristic of Confucianism. Functionally, however, Confucianism was a religion, an institutional religion consisting of beliefs (concepts of Heaven and man, nature and providence, for example), customs, and organizations. Ever since the "exclusive acceptation of Confucianism and discarding a hundred thought schools" during the reign of Emperor Wu of the Western Han dynasty, Confucianism was combined with the monarchal system and became the state religion. Since the Sui dynasty, with the promotion of the system of Ke Ju (a system of selecting governmental officials by examinations in ancient China), Confucianism became the national religion that attracted followers from extensive fields and was integrated with its contemporary bureaucratic systems as one. That condition continued until the late Qing dynasty. Undoubtedly, Confucianism functioned as the national identity and national soul in Chinese history, and as the destination of spiritual pursuit and guidelines of daily life for Chinese people. Considering the Jewish experiences, Chinese people should re-establish Confucianism and make it their belief and cultural identity. That has become the most important mission in the contemporary cultural building in China. To be exact, we should go back to the period of the May Fourth Movement and connect contemporary attitudes to tradition, Confucian tradition in particular. Through critical processes and creative transmission, we should try to make Confucianism a religion with doctrines, rituals, organizations, and believers.

The American Jewish scholar Joseph R. Levenson thought that Confucianism had been laid in the museum of history with the end of monarchy in China, and it would never recover and become a living religion.[9] He surely noticed the characteristic of unity of traditional Confucianism and the feudalist bureaucracy. But he forgot that Confucianism was not always the official religion, for example, during the period of time between Confucius and Dong Zhongshu in the Han Dynasty. So it will not necessarily be the official religion in the future. He did not understand that ideology is somehow independent and it can detach from its former subject and adjust to new carriers. My point is that after the collapse of the feudal bureaucracies, the carrier of Confucianism shifted from government officials and scholars to the common people. China has a population of 1.3 billion persons who, just as the people of most other countries and religions on the Earth, are thirsty for religious pursuit and spiritual guidance, which is required by human nature. That is, the fertile ground in which Confucianism can take root, sprout, and flourish. Hence, in the process of building contemporary Chinese culture, the mission of scholars should not only be to connect the tradition, set up new tenets, and extend the "intellectual course" of Confucian thoughts, but also to decentralize Confucian religion, transmit Confucian doctrines to the masses, and develop Confucian disciples of them, hence making Confucian beliefs and values practical guidelines of life for the populace. Only then can we proudly say that the Chinese people can not only realize the material modernization but also develop their unique identity and national soul, and, hence, become a real and dignified member of the World.

Notes

1 I know that a good number of people disagree with me and view enlightened Jews as having left their religion but, from my perspective and to my understanding, it seems that an essential culture and identity has been preserved by the modern Jews.

2 David Rudavsky, *Modern Jewish Religious Movements: A History of Emancipation and Adjustment*, New York: Behrman House, Inc., 1967, pp. 171–172, 177–188.

3 National Jewish Population Survey 2000–01, Introduction, p. 2.

4 Rudavsky, op cit., p. 73.

5 National Jewish Population Survey 2000–01, op cit.

6 *A Statement of Principles for Reform Judaism*, adopted at the 1999 Pittsburgh Convention Central Conference of American Rabbis, May 1999, p. 1

7 Mou Zongsan, an outstanding representative of Contemporary Neo-Confucianism, holds the view that the Confucian study of Sageliness Within, Xin and Xing cannot serve as the metaphysical basis of democracy and science. Thus, he proposed Self-Negation of Conscience and develops an indirect way of Kingliness Without for democracy and science. He also thinks that religion can only solve settlement of personal life, but not that of a nation. He failed to realize that an ideology or religion can act as a national spirit.

8 I agree with Dr. Chen Ming, chief editor of *Yuan Dao* on his cultural conservative standpoint and his proposal of reconstruction of Confucianism. However, in his thought I can only see the exclusive emphasis of *Yuan Dao* or searching for *Dao* without *Ti* or any specific affirmation of the tradition. I emphasize the positive elements of traditional Confucianism, such as the thought of Heaven, the moral principles such as *Ren, Yi, Li, Zhi* and *Xin*, and the secular ethics such as *Wen, Liang, Gong, Jian*, and *Rang*. Assimilation of the excellent achievement of cultures home and abroad will lead to a new Confucianism which should be the *Ti* of Chinese culture. The overall structure of contemporary Chinese ideology can be set up by the combination of the *Ti* of the new Confucianism and the *Yong* of democracy and science.

9 Levenson, *Confucian China and its Modern Fate*, China Social Sciences Press, 2000, pp. 334–343.

7

RETHINKING THE NANJING MASSACRE AND ITS CONNECTION WITH THE HOLOCAUST

Zhang Qianhong and Jerry Gotel

The "Holocaust" is the term that is usually used to describe the persecution and annihilation of European Jewry by Nazi Germany and its collaborators between 1939 and 1945. In fact, the very dating of the Holocaust is open to debate. Were one to agree with those Functionalist historians who argue that the decision to kill the Jews of Europe was reached in stages and was not intended from the beginning, then one could make out a good case for the Holocaust beginning in 1941. On the other hand, if one accepts the argument of the Intentionalists, that Hitler planned from the very beginning of his reign the destruction of Europe's Jews and that he just waited for favorable circumstances in which to implement his intention of finally solving the problem of Europe's Jewish population, then one could date the Holocaust from 1933, if not earlier. Although there was no Japanese equivalent to the "final solution" for the Chinese people, Japanese policies of persecution were the result of planned and systematic decisions taken over a period of time. The Japanese government intended to wipe out everyone in certain regions of China. One example of this was the "three-all" policy (loot all, kill all, burn all) practiced in Northern China, where Communist Chinese guerrillas had fought the Japanese furiously and effectively. Japan had entered China as a result of the September 18 Incident in 1931, and did not stop its incursion until the US dropped the atomic bombs on Japanese soil in August 1945. About 30 million Chinese people died as a direct result of Japanese action during the Japanese occupation. The Nanjing Massacre is the most noted historic example of Japanese crimes against humanity.

Chinese students are in increasing numbers beginning to study the Holocaust and make comparisons between it and the events in China between 1937 and 1945. In conferences on the Holocaust that are increasingly beginning to take place in China, the remark is often heard from Chinese that China also experienced the Holocaust. What we would like to do in this chapter is set out ways in which we can best compare and contrast these two historical events. Holocaust studies is a relatively new area of interest in China and it would be helpful to point out certain guidelines that might help in avoiding the pitfalls into which many students of the period fall.

At the root of the Nazi persecution of the Jews was a vicious unrelenting racial doctrine, which portrayed the Jews not only as sub-humans, but also as a direct threat to the physical and moral existence of the German people. Did such a racial doctrine lie behind Japanese policies in China? Is it legitimate to see the Nanjing Massacre as a holocaust perpetrated by the Japanese on an inferior Chinese people?

In the 1920s, Nanjing had a population of only 250,000. The Chinese Nationalist Government moved the capital of China from Peking to Nanjing in 1928. By the 1930s, the city was populated with over 1 million residents. This was a result of Japanese occupation and the countless refugees fleeing to southern cities from Manchuria and other areas. In December 1937, the Japanese army stormed Nanjing. The city fell on 13 December of that year. Over the following six weeks, the Japanese military forces committed mass executions, wanton killings, and looting. More than 300,000 people were killed — their only crime was that they were Chinese.

This forgotten Holocaust is often referred to as "The Rape of Nanjing," because approximately 20,000 women ranging in age from 9 to 70 were brutally raped. The Nanjing Massacre or the Rape of Nanjing became the most important symbol of Japanese militarism during the Second World War in East Asia. But is it legitimate to use the word "holocaust" in this context? The word comes from the Greek translation of the Hebrew Bible and specifically refers to a particular sacrifice, which was to be completely consumed by fire on the altar. People did not at first refer to the destruction of the Jews of Europe as a holocaust. It was only in the 1950s and 1960s that the word was increasingly used by the public and professional historians. Indeed, many people objected to the term, arguing that it was offensive to suggest that Jews needed to be sacrificed or that there was anything holy about such slaughter. There were other words in use as well. *Shoah*, used often by Israelis, is the Hebrew word used by the Prophet Isaiah to denote total destruction. Orthodox Jews tended to use the word *Churban*, which is the traditional word used by rabbis to refer to the destruction of both Temples, and which has become the paradigmatic term to describe great catastrophe in rabbinical writings and discourse.

As can be noted from the above definitions, it would be inappropriate to refer to the Nanjing Massacre as a holocaust. The total physical annihilation of the Nanjing population as a prelude to the total destruction of the Chinese people was never envisaged by the Japanese political leadership. To be sure, the Japanese military (supported by Tokyo) were not averse to using brutal and inhumane methods to terrorize and beat into submission a

Chinese population that vastly outnumbered them. But to infer from this that the Japanese intended the total physical elimination of the Chinese population is both absurd and inaccurate. That the Japanese would reduce the Chinese people to a slave people to be exploited and humiliated in the same way as the Germans were doing to the Slavs cannot be disputed. However, this is not, and was not intended by the Japanese to be, a total physical destruction of the Chinese people because they posed some existential threat to a superior Japanese race. In addition, the religious implications latent in the word holocaust are entirely missing in the Chinese context, and specifically in the Nanjing Massacre.

Memory is another useful area that Chinese students need to bear in mind when studying this period. The genocide committed against both Chinese and Jewish peoples during the Second World War, and it must be noted the war began for the Chinese in 1937 and it can be argued for the Jews in 1933, has raised thorny issues of memory. In the first 16 years that followed the Second World War, until the Eichmann trial in Israel in 1961, which proved to be a historic watershed, the Holocaust was not at the forefront of Jewish life. To be sure, there was a steady stream of books coming out by survivors and historians and, from time to time, court proceedings in various countries would hit the headlines, but this, if anything, proved that the Jewish world was getting on with the business of adapting to a world where East European Jewry no longer existed and where the greatly diminished Western Jewish population centers were painstakingly re-establishing their communities. This was mainly because the survivors (and the families of the victims) needed distance before they were able to remember such painful events. However, there is a second reason for their silence. After the war, the European public was not very eager to hear of past Jewish sufferings. Europeans had their own losses and painful war memories, particularly at the higher levels of society. This is not only true for Germany but also for all other occupied countries as well. The public wanted to get the unpleasant period behind them and it was not socially acceptable for surviving Jews to talk about the Holocaust. This was also the height of the Cold War when the West felt threatened by the Soviet Union and believed it needed a re-armed Germany as the first defense line against a feared Soviet invasion. To be constantly reminded of their shameful past by parading their leadership in front of the courts was not deemed to be the best way to gain the allegiance and devotion of the German people to the Western cause.

Beginning in the 1960s, the number of books on the Holocaust began to appear in astonishing numbers throughout the US, Israel, and Europe. This renewed interest led to the establishment in the 1970s of Holocaust Studies in academia, with the result that the Holocaust has become one of the most researched and studied periods in history. More and more people have realized the international influences and implications of the Holocaust. As Professor Yehuda Bauer said:

The Holocaust has become a world issue. It has had an enduring impact on contemporary civilizations and continues to shape, at least indirectly, the fate of nations. In order for its impact to affect mutual understanding, worldwide peace and related activities, and full-scale opposition to genocidal events, we all have to rethink exactly what happened then.[1]

The Nanjing Massacre was followed by a much longer silence than that of the Holocaust. Most foreigners, including highly educated adults, have never been told about the events that happened in Nanjing. One of the authors of this chapter, Zhang Qianhong, conducted an informal inquiry among the 22 members who attended the International Winter Seminar for Holocaust Educators, organized by Yad Vashem, in Jerusalem in January 2005. Fourteen of them knew nothing about the Nanjing Massacre. Five persons got the information from Iris Chang's book entitled *The Rape of Nanking* (1997), and three persons heard about the Nanjing Massacre on the internet, the BBC, or VOA news. What is even more shocking is that many Chinese people are very limited in their knowledge of the Massacre in Nanjing. Zhang asked university students who study natural science in Kaifeng: "Do you know of the Nanjing Massacre?" They answered: "Surely, yes, of course." They were then asked further: "When did the Nanjing Massacre take place, what was the reason for it and what were the consequences?" The answers from most of the students were: "I don't know exactly." It transpires that students studying the social sciences usually know a bit more than the students of the natural sciences, but their knowledge is still very superficial. If you ask those with little educational background, most of them will say: "I do not know of the Nanjing Massacre at all." If we argue that peasants cannot be considered the social mainstream in some Western countries, then the situation is definitely different in China, where the peasants account for nearly 80 per cent of the national population. Because of the above mentioned situation, this chapter focuses on the following questions: why has the Nanjing Massacre been all but forgotten? What are the reasons this atrocity has not had the attention it deserves both at home and abroad?

"Saving Face" is an Important Element in Traditional Chinese Society

There are many ways to explain the long silence of the Chinese people concerning the Nanjing Massacre, but we think the first factor to be considered should be the deep cultural sense of a loss of face. Avoiding loss of face is a tradition rooted in more than 2,000 years of Chinese history. According to Chinese values, "face" incorporates "dignity," "personality," and the notion of a very high moral standard. Losing face then brings enormous shame. In ancient Chinese history, many people chose death over losing face. The most obvious manifestation of this culture in daily life is embedded in a common proverb: "The skeleton in the closet does not spread." Applied to the whole country, this means that the humiliation should not be expanded widely, but rather will remain as private as possible. Even in modern China, the sense of "face" is still ingrained.

Throughout Chinese history wars occurred frequently, but the Nanjing Massacre stands apart from all other events. It was the most enormous spiritual insult to the Chinese people. This kind of affront is difficult to describe in any language. In Chinese culture, if a husband, or a father, is unable to protect his own wife or daughters in order to avoid such a ferocious insult, this would be considered his biggest shame. In Nanjing, the Japanese violated Chinese motherland and tens of thousands of women were mass-raped on the avenue, in full view of the public. The Japanese soldiers would rape pregnant women and cut open their bellies, take out the fetus and play with it as if it were a football. They even forced fathers to rape daughters, and sons to rape mothers. People who objected were killed instantly. They gang-raped women up to 20 times a day. When these women returned, they either fell into a state of depression or committed suicide out of shame.[2]

Another cause that made the Chinese people feel deeply about losing face was the mood of superiority of the Japanese race. Two main excuses were used by the Nazis to launch the "final solution." One was the theory of racial superiority; the other was the need to capture more living space. These two excuses were also used by the Japanese in their invasion of China. China and Japan are close neighbors, separated only by a strip of water. The two countries had maintained cordial ties for over 1,000 years. That such a small country with a population less than a quarter that of the Chinese could, in the timespan of eight decades, transform its society totally, enter the modern industrial world, and defeat a major European power in a war was cause enough for reflection on the part of China's political and intellectual elite. That this power now threatened the very political and physical existence of the Chinese state gave rise to the deepest sense of shame and humiliation.

But how valid is such a comparison? The argument for *lebensraum*, or in the German case the Drang Nach Osten, does not quite fit the circumstances in which the Japanese found themselves. Germany had abundant natural resources and a sophisticated chemical industry to bolster its claim as a major power in European affairs. Japan had no such natural resources and if it was to play a dominant role in Asian affairs, so the argument goes, it needed in the first instance the rich natural resources of Manchuria. This argument was then extended to include China, which was rife with internal dissent and incapable of defending itself against a determined adversary.

There are also difficulties in the racial argument. Can one equate Nazi racial attitudes towards the Jews with those of the Japanese towards the Chinese? Here we can also touch on the experience of the Jews, who lived in Europe for more than 2,000 years, as "close neighbors" of Europeans, but have only rarely been considered as "good friends" because Christian teaching saw the Jews as killers of Jesus. Even in periods where Jews had a good life, they were always the "other" and their situation was often tenuous. Christians had accepted the Jewish Bible as their own holy book but they did not admire the Jews for this, on the contrary they said that the Jews did not understand their own holy book and even had falsified it! Hitler was the most extreme, but logical, result of this hostility. He wanted to exterminate not only all Jews, but also all remnants of Jewish culture and civilization. Here is a difference between the Nazis and the Japanese. When the Nazis came to power, one of their first acts was the public ceremony of burning all Jewish books in Berlin in 1933. Such a thing was unthinkable in Japan — what would they have burned? Confucius, who was always venerated in Japan as well? *Sutra of the Heart* had been brought to Japan by Buddhist monks who spent years in Chinese Buddhist monasteries during the Tang Dynasty. It is indeed difficult to understand Japanese inhumanity towards the Chinese because Japan never abandoned that much of its culture, its religions, its writing, its architecture, even the layout of its imperial cities came from China. The friendly familiarity between China and Japan during the great Tang and Heian dynasties, the admiration for, and precise knowledge of, Chinese culture in the Japanese upper classes during this period has no parallel in Jewish–Christian history. A member of the Japanese court, ladies included, had to be able to recite the great Chinese poetry of the Tang by heart, and in faultless Chinese language! In turn, Chinese emperors of the Tang kept sending precious presents to the Imperial court of Nara where they are still kept as Japan's greatest national treasures to this very day! What is unbelievable is that the same Japanese committed these horrific crimes against Chinese people.

After the Meiji Restoration, Japan embarked on a path of militarism and invaded China many times. In 1874, Japanese forces invaded Taiwan. This was followed by the Sino–Japanese War (1894–95), the Jinan Incident (1928), and the September 18 Incident (1931). Finally, on 7 July 1937, Japan started its large-scale invasion in order to seize more territory and expand the Japanese emperor's domain. Access to Chinese goods allowed them to supplement both the Japanese resources and their markets, which were seriously insufficient. Japanese militarism was unique in its unceasing outward expansion. Their expansion was fueled by their theory of racial superiority. The Japanese educated their soldiers to believe that Japan was the best race in the world and that they, therefore, had the absolute responsibility to rule Asia. The Japanese war criminal, Yamaoka Shigeru described his military education stating:

At that time we harbored an ingrained sense of superiority of the Japanese race, and we adopted a condescending attitude towards the races. We also had a kind of cruel Bushido spirit, which considered killing a heroic act. Furthermore, from the extremism of worshipping the emperor came an inhumane ideology, which was to submit to the strong and powerful, and force into submission anyone weak or not powerful? It was precisely because we had this ideology that we viewed a war of invasion as a war of righteousness, committing cruel and inhumane acts as if they were nothing at all.[3]

Nevertheless, this sense of Japanese racial superiority cannot be compared with that of the Germans for the reasons given above.

As we know, the Chinese people have a strong cultural pride that is rooted in the notion that a few centuries earlier China was the largest, strongest, and wealthiest country in the world. Because of this, China cultivated the most cultured people in the world. They believed the ancient Chinese taught the Japanese how to read and write, and that Chinese culture nourished the Japanese civilization. But the Japanese used derogatory terms to describe the Chinese and in turn repaid China with some of the ugliest behavior. Consequently, Japanese racial discrimination has seriously harmed Chinese self-respect and thought. There is a tendency in Chinese culture to move past events too difficult to remember. One Chinese proverb says: "Do not uncover people's scabs!" Perry Link, a sinologist at Princeton University stated:

In 1937 something so grossly ugly and humiliating as the Nanjing Massacre seemed to Chinese sensibility so profoundly wrong – especially when suffered at the hands of the lesser-cultivated Japanese – that we believe, in a sense it deserved only to be ignored.[4]

For a long time, many people raised the question: why did the Chinese government not claim any compensation from the Japanese government? Many explanations were proposed. The Chinese government was considered too weak. China was in a civil war situation and was planning a post-war maintenance of Japanese trade. The cold war atmosphere was also raised. At that time, the US feared Communist China and believed it needed Japan as a military ally. The US, therefore, lent support to Japan over China. We believe that, in addition to all these factors, China failed to demand any compensation in order to uphold national and cultural dignity in order to save face.

Superficial Education and National Humiliation

Before getting involved in the question of Holocaust education, what we want to discuss here is a point of difference of historical consciousness between the traditional Chinese and that of the Jews. This will help us to understand the two peoples' different attitudes towards education intended to counter national humiliation. During their feudal society, the Chinese had formed one kind of historical idea. They regarded only emperors, ministers, and military leaders as the main functionaries of national history. Official history books and documents from different dynasties contain complete accounts of powerful personages and magnificent history, but neglect the history of the ordinary populace. They recorded only the great people's kind behavior and their good qualities, but sadly neglected to note their bad behavior and shocking actions. The Chinese could not divest themselves of this kind of latent idea: that all good people should always be good, and all unprincipled people should always be bad. This is very obvious in official historiography and there is nothing comparable with the systematic and severe moral critique of corrupt and criminal leaders than can be found in the historic books of the Jewish Bible.

Perry Link also touched upon this issue when he said, "There is a tendency in Chinese culture – observable contexts – to blur the line between what is and what ought to be, by obliterating things that ought not to have happened."[5] Chinese people can truly learn from the Jews. The Jewish people think that good and evil can coexist. People must be able to separate the good from the evil. Historical heroes, on the one hand, have great merits and admirable moral excellence, but, on the other hand, they also seem to be unable to avoid the average person's demerits and natural weaknesses.

Those who compiled biblical stories and wrote the "Holy Bible" highly valued Samson's bravery and courage but, at the same time, also pointed out his violations of the Commandments. They proudly praised King Solomon's wisdom and spirit of heroism, but did not deny his envy of others and his framing of faithful and upright persons. According to the Hebrew Bible, King David was a great and outstanding figure. He was recorded in Jewish history as the real founder of the Israeli kingdom, but, nevertheless, he also displayed many human weaknesses of nature. He violated not only his own promise, but also committed adultery and intentionally harmed innocent persons.[6] In the ancient documents and materials left by the Israelis, there is a lot of information exposing the ruler's corruption and degeneration; this does not mean that ancient Israeli kings were worse than the rulers of other nations, but rather that the Jews emphasized great people's strengths and weakness simultaneously. This may be regarded as humane and profound Jewish wisdom.

In the Jewish tradition, great value is placed on historical memory and collective suffering. With the end of the Holocaust and the establishment of the State of Israel in 1948, an argument can be made that Holocaust survivors failed to receive sufficient recognition and empathy from both the government and society. What Israel needed most was determination for fighting against those who did not support them as a new nation, as well as deep and untiring commitment in building the infrastructure of a state capable of absorbing the psychologically and physically scarred victims of both the Holocaust and the refugees from the Arab countries. The self-image that Israel sought to portray to the world was that of a hardy cactus living in the desert: the Jews were a nation of fighters, not sheep that were to willingly be slaughtered by hostile neighbors. But even during the years when this thinking predominated amongst Israel's political and military elite, Holocaust education in Israel was not neglected or disparaged

On the 27th of Nisan 1953, the Israeli Knesset passed a law that provided for the commemoration of the Holocaust. It was honored at Yad Vashem by a solemn state ceremony at the Warsaw Ghetto Square, and was attended by many dignitaries. The President and the Prime Minister of the State of Israel always participated in the ceremony. Since its inception, Yad Vashem has been entrusted with documenting the history of the Jewish people during the Holocaust period, preserving memories and stories of the 6 million victims, imparting the legacy of the Holocaust for generations to come through its archives, libraries, schools, and museums, and to the recognition of the Righteous among the Nations. Yad Vashem also became a very successful international center for education, research, and Holocaust-related publications. The Central Database of the Shoah Victims' Names contains 3 million names of Holocaust victims. It went online in November 2004. One of the aims is to provide a national focus for educating subsequent generations about the Holocaust and the continued relevance of the lessons that may be learned from it.

Another example was the Eichmann trial. Karl Adolf Eichmann was head of the so-called Department for Jewish Affairs in the Gestapo from 1941 to 1945 and was chief of operations in the deportation of millions of Jews to the various extermination camps. After the war, he fled to Argentina and lived under the assumed name of Ricardo Klement for ten years. He was found by Israeli Mossad agents in 1960. They subsequently took him to Jerusalem to stand trial. The Eichmann trial lasted from 2 April to 14 August 1961. Eichmann was sentenced to death and was executed in Ramleh Prison on 31 May 1962. The Eichmann trial became a significant worldwide event, not only because a criminal was brought to justice, but also because it served as the beginning of Holocaust education for the world. It unified Israel as a nation.[7]

In China, education of national humiliation began to grow in the 1980s. The Nanjing Massacre Memorial Hall was built in 1985 and enlarged to its present size of 28,000 square meters in 1995. Recently, Nanjing's local government has decided to expand the scale of the existing Nanjing Memorial Hall and build a World Peace Square and a park nearby. The move is designed to mark the sixtieth anniversary of the victory of the World War against fascism. Every year, on the anniversary of the victory of the war against Japan, the Chinese media organizes a number of relevant news reports and articles. Textbooks also contain special content for the education of students.

However, it is not sufficient to affirm Chinese nationalism and the war of resistance against Japanese aggression through educational means alone. We also need a National Day of Remembering. According to a survey by the Nanjing Normal University's institute on the Nanjing Massacre, and based on replies to 973 questionnaires, 54.1 per cent of the college students in Nanjing City had never been to the Nanjing Massacre Memorial Hall.[8] Many young Chinese avidly celebrate Christmas Day, All Saints' Day, and Valentine's Day, but do not know which day we should set aside for the remembrance of our own people and our own country. One incredible example of such historic insensitivity is the use or non-use made of the "July 7 Incident of 1937," the day that the Japanese invaded China. Over the years, this day has become the official examination day for higher education. Hundreds and thousands of young people are busy sitting examinations that decide their destinies, and, unfortunately, they have no time to consider the day's historical significance. Since 2004, the Chinese Government advanced the date of the college entrance examination to June, but this change was based on weather conditions. Admittedly, it is very hot in July, but this decision to change the date of the examinations was not a recognition or commemoration of the day's historical significance.

Until now, China has failed to designate a National Humiliation Day. Recently, many Chinese intellectuals have voiced their opinion to choose a date that can more effectively remind its citizens of the humiliation. Some lawmakers proposed 7 July or 18 September as appropriate dates. It should not be forgotten that Japan's invasion caused the most devastating trauma to the Chinese people, a fact that the Chinese people can hardly forget. We are optimistic that this new legislation will be issued soon. Some overseas sinologists also have expressed some penetrating observations concerning China's national humiliation education. Commenting about the Chinese reticence, in comparison with the Jewish memorialization of the Holocaust and the Japanese commemoration of the destruction of Hiroshima and Nagasaki, Lestz wrote:

> It is as though Chinese memories of the war have been rocketed into a barely accessible psychic outer space where they occasionally can be referred to, generally in a highly polemical or emotionally exaggerated way, but usually ignored. China's collective war memories are a bit like a photo album: they are stored away in the attic. On occasion the pictures happen to be looked at and, of course, they evoke pain, rage and tears. But the fact is they are rarely taken out and examined such that over time these reactions become irrelevant or stereotyped emotional frisson.[9]

The Denial of the Nanjing Massacre from the Japanese Right-Wing

The denial of the Nanjing Massacre began in the early 1970s, even though the facts surrounding the Massacre were barely acknowledged by Japanese society. In 1972, the right-wing political forces in Japan began to grow in strength. Japanese denials of the Nanjing Massacre and their other brutalities in Asia have lasted until the present day. In 1990, Ishihara Shintaro, a leading member of Japan's Conservative Liberal Democratic Party and the author of best-selling books such as *The Japan That Can Say No*, told a *Playboy* magazine interviewer, "People say that the Japanese made a Holocaust there [in Nanjing], but that is not true. It is a story made up by the Chinese. It tarnishes the image of Japan, but it is a lie."[10] Naturally, this statement enraged scholars and journalists around the world. Kajiyama Seiroko, the Japanese chief cabinet secretary, outraged several Asian countries when he stated that the sex slaves and rape victims of the Japanese imperial army were not slaves at all but willingly engaged in prostitution. In January 1997, he proclaimed that the "comfort women" of the Japanese army were in it for the money and were no different from the Japanese prostitutes who worked legally in Japan at that time.[11]

Nevertheless, many Japanese today, the younger generation in particular, have come to acknowledge the tragedy of the Nanjing Massacre. Some Japanese citizens truly try their best to refute the recent denial of the Nanjing Massacre by Japanese right-wing groups. The revisionists cannot change history, but they continue to confuse many people who are ignorant of the facts. What Michael Berenbaum, the director of the US Holocaust Research Center said of Holocaust denial is also true of the Nanjing Massacre: "The denial of the Holocaust is nonsense; pernicious, foolish, an insult to memory, and an insult to history."

Ironically, one of the main deep-seated reasons for Japanese denial is identical to the Chinese reason for not wanting to remember: the fear of losing face. This fear is as deeply ingrained in Japanese as it is in Chinese culture, and it may belong at least partly to the great cultural heritage that China has given to Japan during the centuries. For a typical Japanese, admitting such a crime would mean intolerable shame, losing face and losing all pride in the alleged superiority of Japan. Psychologically, it is easier to deny the facts than to face the truth.

China's Research on the Nanjing Massacre Remains Largely Unknown in the West

For more than 30 years after the Second World War, China was still a country excluded from the international arena. China did not understand the World and the World did not understand China. At this time, Chinese scholars had already started academic research on the Nanjing Massacre. The earliest achievement was in 1960, when the History Department of Nanjing University organized students to carry out an investigation of the facts of the massacre and subsequently wrote a book entitled *The Japanese Militarism in the Nanking Massacre*. Since the 1980s, the scholars in Nanjing continue the collection of comprehensive material and carry out related research work. They have published some documents, materials, and research books. Since the end of the 1980s, along with recent historical discoveries, the study of the Nanjing Massacre has entered a more thorough and deeper stage. However, many academic papers appeared in Chinese, preventing them from reaching an international audience. Furthermore, most Chinese scholars were unable to talk with foreign academics due to language and other problems. This resulted in the inability of international academic circles to know of the findings of Chinese research. This accounts in large part for the poor lack of knowledge of the Nanjing Massacre on the part of foreign scholars and the general public.

Finally, Iris Chang, a Chinese American author, wrote an eloquent and powerful book *The Rape of Nanking*, which gave the first major full-length English-language account of the atrocity, and aroused international concern about the Nanjing Massacre for the very first time. It is to be hoped that Chang's research will stimulate further interest and research on the part of both Chinese and foreign scholars.

In conclusion, we feel that Chinese students can only gain in historical knowledge by making more comparisons and contrasts between the Chinese experience and the Jewish experience during the Second World War. There can be no question that the Japanese behavior in China was genocidal in nature. That it cannot be compared with the Holocaust is also beyond the dispute. The Holocaust was without precedent in human history. The destruction of an entire people by virtue of being born Jewish, its very specificity is a category beyond that which the Japanese planned for its occupation of China. By comparing how the two peoples commemorate and memorialize their tragedies, Chinese students will better understand the role of the individual in society and the responsibility that individuals must assume for their actions if China is to construct a healthier and more just society. Stalin once said that the "death of one man is a tragedy but the death of millions is only statistics." The danger of subsuming the individual in the mass, in the crowd, be it in military or political life, is perhaps the foremost lesson our students will absorb by studying these two human tragedies.

More than 60 years has gone by since the end of the Second World War, and the Cold War has now come to an end. Peace and development are the common wishes shared by most nations and peoples, despite the fact that various wars continue to rage in many parts of the world. The question of genocide, and the Holocaust is arguably the quintessential genocide, is very much on the current international agenda: to wit the vote by a US congressional committee to classify the Armenian slaughter by the Turks in the First World War as a genocide, Darfur, and the conference on genocide that was held in October in Montreal and attended by representatives of many countries and the United Nations. It is, therefore, both fitting and proper for China to make its contribution to this agenda by drawing upon the appropriate lessons from its own history.

This article was completed with the help of Dr. Salomon Wald from The Jewish People Policy Planning Institute, Jerusalem.

Notes

1 Yehuda Bauer, *Rethinking the Holocaust*, New Haven: Yale University, 2001, p. 260.
2 Laura Rivera, "The Forgotten Holocaust," see < www.remember.org/imagine/china.html >.
3 Yamaoka Shigeru, "My Experience: Accusing War of Invasion," see Feifei, Sabella and Liu (ed), *Nanjing 1937*, Armonk: M.E Sharpe, Inc., 2002, p. 40.
4 Ibid, chapter 14.
5 Ibid.
6 Book of Samuel, II, Chapter 11.
7 See Ahron Bregman, *A History of Israel*, New York: Macmillan, 2003, pp. 98–99.
8 *China Youth Daily*, December 13, 2004.
9 Michael Leszt, *War and Memory: The Chinese Holocaust*, in Vera Schwarcz, *The "Black Milk" of Historical Consciousness: Thinking about the Nanjing Massacre in Light of Jewish Memory*; also Feifei, Sabella and Liu, op. cit., p. 191.
10 Iris Chang, *The Rape of Nanking*, New York: Basicbooks, 1997, p. 201.
11 Chang, op cit., p. 204.

Part III

CHINESE PERCEPTIONS OF JEWS

8

A CHINESE PERSPECTIVE OF JUDAISM AND THE JEWISH PEOPLE

Fu Youde

The diplomatic relationship between China and Israel, which has developed new paradigms of communication exchange for both nations, was formally established in the spring of 1992. In the same year, I was given the chance to study at the Oxford Centre for Hebrew and Jewish Studies, and I began my new academic career, changing my focus from the History of Western Philosophy to Jewish Philosophy and Religion. In the past ten years, I have visited and studied academic institutions in Israel, Britain, and the US several times, getting in contact with different members of the Jewish faith. Through the contact with Jewish people, I have gained a new understanding of Jewish culture and its national characteristics. Indeed, everyone's behavior is individually particular, so it is difficult to draw a general conclusion from the individual behavior of the Jews I contacted. In addition, I am still in the primary stages of doing research on Jewish religion and philosophy, its past and present, which make it more difficult to get a general opinion. However, on the tenth anniversary of the establishment of the diplomatic relationship between China and Israel, as a Chinese scholar doing research on Jewish culture, it is still of significance to discuss some ideas that I have not considered thoroughly enough.

There is a Chinese saying: "to seek common grounds on major issues while reserving differences on minor ones;" that is to say, the essences amongst nations, peoples, cultures, and humans are the same, while the differences and distinctions are only individual and specific. In other words, sameness is dominant and primary, and difference is subdominant and unimportant. Therefore, Chinese are used to seeking common grounds when we are in the face of "between/among" issues, and we try to avoid, neglect, or hide the difference in order to achieve peaceful coexistence. In fact, the idea of seeking common grounds while reserving differences has become the way of Chinese thinking and the general principle for dealing with "between/among" issues. In comparison with Jews, on the issue of sameness and difference, the Jewish people hold that the latter is dominant and more important, while the former is unimportant. Thus, they do not seek common grounds but pay more attention to differences when they dealing with "between/among" issues. It seems that seeking differences has become a principle for Jewish people to follow intentionally or unconsciously when they treat and solve problems, or that habit is the second nature.

One of my personal experiences demonstrates this Jewish characteristic. In the winter of 1993 I met Sir Sternberg in London, an influential Jew, who had escaped from Hungary to Britain, and gone on to make great achievements in commercial and cultural fields, was conferred Sir by the British Queen and was received by Pope John Paul II. One day, Sternberg gave me a document, and expected my opinions. That document was the well-known *Declaration of Global Ethic*. At that time, the Parliament of World Religions held in Chicago, which Sternberg attended as a Jewish representative, had just concluded. I was very excited when I read the document, not only because of its emotional language and writing style, but also because its content and style of thinking really conformed to the Chinese idea of "seeking common grounds while reserving differences." Though I did not know the author or his background, I was convinced that on the basis of acknowledgement of differences between every religion and culture, to seek the basic universal ethical paradigms of all nations, to call on all human beings whether with beliefs or not to stop conflicts and sufferings, and to actualize the world order with benevolence, justice and peace, are in conformity with the majority of human beings. Also, I held a view that this document was even an evangel for Jews because their history was full of oppression, persecution, and slaughter, which directly resulted from religious conflicts. The ethic declaration advocates seeking common grounds while reserving differences, benevolence and peace, and calls upon mutual understanding and respect amongst every religion, so it must be warmly received by the Jewish people. Therefore, I wrote down my understanding about *Declaration* and expressed my positive opinion. To my surprise, Sir Sternberg did not show his approval or satisfaction. He dealt with my opinion seriously, and asked his secretary to print my manuscript, even without suggesting any changes to my misspellings and punctuation errors. He disagreed with my universalistic tendency about seeking common ground and pursuing peace. Sir Sternberg expressed his ideas to the effect that Jews and Judaism are different from other nations and religions; they do not expect common grounds, and what he approved of and accepted is merely the mutual understanding and respect amongst every religion advocated by *Declaration*. For him, the inherent differences between nations and religions are unchangeable, and should not be concealed by common grounds but must be understood and respected sufficiently. I thought that our views diverged greatly in that we placed different emphasis on the relationship between seeking common ground and reserving differences. Sternberg emphasized reserving differences, which is the basis to pursue mutual understanding and respect; while I, on the contrary, placed emphasis on seeking common grounds, the condition of reserving differences. I believed that only on the basis of fundamental common ethical principles is inter-religious dialogue carried out, and mutual understanding and respect attained. Without common principles it would be difficult for inter-religious dialogue, and then how can we talk about mutual understanding and respect? No doubt the attitude of Sternberg stands for some people in some ways. Nowadays, in a world with multicultural coexistence, we must acknowledge the diversity of every nation's religion and culture; otherwise, the result will be absolute universalism or even culture chauvinism. Yet I believe that accepting differences on the basis of affirming common grounds will be more helpful to inter-religious or inter-cultural dialogues and communications, making it less difficult to achieve understanding and reconciliation, and more beneficial to establish world order with benevolence, justice, and peace.

As a matter of fact, it is the Jewish tradition to seek and reserve differences. Hebrew scripture says that Abraham, the Jewish patriarch, came to Canaan from Babylon, rejected the popular polytheism there, and firmly raised the first banner of monotheism. The Jewish people still hold this banner highly. From Abraham, to Isaac, to Jacob and Moses, Israelites confirmed the concept of Chosen People, which asserted that Jews are the only people endowed with the *Torah* by God, the unique people chosen by God, and distinguished from all other nations. From ancient Temple times to medieval and modern times of severe anti-Semitism, Jewish people always adhered to their faith firmly. After 70 CE, Jews dispersed into a Diaspora all over the world, so they belonged to a permanent minority. Not only was its population small, but also its culture was submerged in the culture of the host countries, so it was not easy for Jews to retain their religious belief separately and keep their lifestyle different from others in such circumstances. Nevertheless, they successfully did so. Whether in the Hellenist and Roman empires, or in the kingdoms controlled by Islam or Christianity, Jewish people tried their utmost to defend their religion, refuse conversion, and retain their tradition and custom, for which they paid a high price and many lives were sacrificed. A Jewish historian must know the story about thousands of Jews martyred, Akib as a typical representative, and from this we can see the heavy price that Jews have paid. In the face of powerful nations, dominant religions and cultures, Jewish people have dared to say no, strived to retain and defend their own religious beliefs and customs, showing their intrinsic characteristic of seeking and reserving differences.

Expressing different ideas and prone to disputes in daily life are illustrations of the Jewish characteristic of seeking differences. There is a Jewish saying: "two Jews, three opinions." Generally, it might be argued that Jews usually have varied opinions without unanimous conclusions, and hold on to their own ideas without concession. Indeed, every nation and its people cannot fashion completely homogenous thinking and ideas like monolithic monuments of steel, thus, there are always disagreements and divergences between individuals and groups. The reasons Jewish people are so particular lie in that they are more apt at seeking differences, and they do not settle disagreements or unify respective views. Difference exists objectively, so it is seen as better to maintain differences and make life rich and colorful rather than draw unanimous conclusions. As is well known, Pentateuch was the oldest scripture of Judaism, which was the Book of Law revealed to Jews through Moses by God, with sacrosanct authority. After the Biblical period, Jews in the Diaspora compiled the oral law, the *Mishnah*, in so-doing paving a legal mechanism for adaptation to the conditions in which they now lived. Hereafter, rabbis began their commentaries on the Hebrew Bible and *Mishnah*, giving way to the *Talmud*, *Tosefta*, and *Midrash*, among which are many and varied explanations of the same issue. The *Talmud*'s style is to quote a paragraph of *Mishnah*, after which rabbis list a variety of different arguments about the text. For example, in *Mishnah* (2a) Barakoth quotes the text about when the *Shema* may be recited in the evening, and rabbis give different explanations for it in order to clarify the meanings of "from the time the priests came back home for dinner," "until the end of the first watch," "until midnight" and "until dawn". There is no consensus, and rabbis only discussed their ideas. Again, Kiddushin quotes the different ideas between Hillel and Shammai about how to find and acquire a wife and how she acquires her freedom, and gives many interpretations. Such cases can be found everywhere in the *Talmud*. There is no absolute authority or general idea that everybody must follow, so Jews can adjust themselves flexibly in daily life without an imposed unified principle. This does not mean Jewish people cannot reach general agreement in any circumstances, but they are more prone to have different ideas than other peoples.

If Jewish people can be called a nation seeking differences, the Chinese are a nation preferring common grounds. No doubt there are often disagreements and divergences amongst Chinese; however, the attitude toward differences between Chinese people is greatly distinguished from that of Jewish people. From ancient times, Chinese people have thought it natural to unify thoughts and opinions, but regard disagreements as unnatural. Therefore, when different ideas appear, we Chinese do not follow them naturally but try to reach a consensus in a certain way. Can this statement be applied to all Chinese? Does it seem that disagreements are absolutely bad? A Chinese saying states "harmony is most valuable," and harmony is on the basis of identity, so seeking common grounds has its own good points. As a way of thinking, people who seek common grounds like to find general characteristics from diversified specific things, from specific to general, and in social life they are more lenient, generous, and easier to be approved by others.

During centuries of dispersion, the Jews of the Diaspora have still been able to retain their own belief and lifestyle, and exist as a unified nation, so for many people, these facts can really demonstrate that they are a people with a strong cohesive force, with one heart and one mind. In fact, this is just one aspect of the issue, and Jews can be united closely together at the moment of national crisis under attack from outside powers. On the other hand, there are endless disputes amongst Jews. Not to mention the narration that the other sons of Jacob threw their brother Joseph into a pit and sold him to an Egyptian trader, nor the conflicts amongst Sadducees, Pharisees, and the Zealots in the first century, there are different denominations and strife amongst modern Jews. In the early nineteenth century, with the influences of political emancipation and enlightenment movements, some Jews realized the crisis of Judaism and launched Jewish reform in Germany. In the beginning, Reform Judaism was split from Traditional Judaism and divided the original unified Judaism into two parts—Orthodox Judaism and Reform Judaism. Later, Conservative Judaism came into being, between the former two denominations. In the 1920s, Reconstructionism was founded in the US. Furthermore, there are several sects in one denomination, for instance, Orthodox Judaism includes Hasidim and Neo-Orthodox, and so on. Amongst Jews, there are not only different denominations, but also hostilities between various groups. Once, I met a follower of Liberal Judaism, and he told me that he could not bear "those outdated Orthodoxy Jews," and he knew of the hostility between Orthodox Judaism and Liberal Judaism and Reform Judaism. He mentioned that they are destroyers of Judaism in the eyes of the Orthodox, and they are worse than Christians. Therefore, besides social historical reasons, we can see that the characteristic of seeking differences is also closely linked with the split in Judaism and conflicts between each other. As it allows disagreements and different ideas to exist, there will appear different opinions in response to challenges, and the valid existence of different ideas will naturally develop into different denominations. More recently, we talk about deep-rooted bad habits of Chinese people being internecine struggle. In fact, this is not Chinese "patent," and many nations are the same as the Chinese, with the exception of Jewish people who seem to be extremely cohesive at first glance.

Seeking differences is a way of thinking, and people always trying to find the differences and divergences between things are more apt to create something original and unconventional, which is the characteristic of creative spirit owned by thinkers and scientists. In Jewish history, there have been world-class great thinkers such as Spinoza, Marx, Hasserl, Wittgenstein, Freud, Bergson, Buber, and Husserl. In the last century alone, there have been more than 120 Jews who won the Nobel Prize. Though the success of these outstanding people is attributed to many factors, the way of thinking to seek differences is no doubt of great importance.

Seeking differences is also a natural tendency. Leibniz's conviction that there could never be two identical leaves indicates that difference is absolute but identity is relative. Therefore, seeking differences is forever endless. The inclination to seek differences is to continuously discover the differences between everything, to ceaselessly probe without stopping on a definite spot. From Babylonian Exile in 586 BCE to the foundation of Second Temple, from the destruction of the Temple by the Roman Empire in 70 CE and the beginning of Jewish Diaspora to the foundation of Israel in 1948, from biblical Hebrew to Ladino and Yiddish in Diaspora to modern Hebrew as the official language of Israel, Jewish people have left footprints clearly in history, revealing their particular spirit of seeking differences, creating and constantly enterprising.

The Jewish people are a nation with a long history and profound culture, also being multicultural in its Diaspora. Therefore, its characteristics cannot be summarized simply as those of seeking differences. The ideas discussed above are but a shallow understanding of Jewish people, from the viewpoint of a Chinese individual who grew up under the influence of a culture that seeks common ground.

9

ISRAEL AND THE JEWISH PEOPLE IN CHINESE CYBERSPACE SINCE 2002

Zhang Ping

Background

In the year 2002, a dramatic change occurred in Chinese cyberspace concerning the Chinese understanding of Israel and the Jewish people. Described by some people as a language revolution, the change involved a re-examination of the history of the Jewish people, especially that of the State of Israel, discussions about the true situation of Palestinians and terrorism and the relationship between the Chinese people and the Jewish people. Empowered by a relative freedom of expression and information access on the internet, a large number of Chinese websurfers challenged the anti-Zionist tradition in Communist China and rephrased their expressions regarding Zionism, the State of Israel, the Jewish people, etc. While traditional pro-Palestinian voices are still the mainstream in Chinese official media, pro-Israeli activities in Chinese cyberspace in 2002 radically changed the whole picture and made pro-Israeli expressions a common fact in the Chinese virtual world.[1]

After 2002, the situation in Israel gradually calmed down. The topic of the Israel–Palestinian conflict became less prominent on the Chinese internet. Fewer discussions were held in popular Chinese webforums. Postings on the issue were far less popular than in 2002. Many Chinese news websites even removed the issue from their main page headlines. Nevertheless, the pro-Israeli trend that was formed in 2002 not only survived, but also expanded and deepened its influence. This influence can be observed in three major developments: (1) more Chinese personal websites dedicated to the subject of Israel or the Jewish people have been constructed, and most of them take a clear pro-Israeli stance or "objective" stance, which is a moderated expression of the pro-Israeli stand in the Chinese language; (2) Chinese academic institutions joined the trend and built their own Jewish

103

culture or history-related websites; and (3) official or semi-official websites were built both by Chinese and Israeli organizations.

The Three Major Developments

Personal Websites

By 2002, there were only four active Chinese personal websites, all of them with clear pro-Israeli or objective stands.[2] Among the four, two of them disappeared. *I Love Israel*, the most outspoken pro-Israeli website, was closed in 2004 for technical reasons, according to the webmaster. *In-Depth Reports on Israel*, the Chinese Christian website, closed in 2005, after having stopped updates for some two years. The other two websites, *Approaching Israel*[3] and *Canaan Forum*,[4] managed to survive, gained considerable enrichment and merged again in 2003. The *Approaching Israel* website changed its webserver several times and kept updating from time to time. It is still the most comprehensive introduction to Jewish culture and history that one can find on the Chinese internet. The *Canaan Forum*, which now serves as the discussion forum of *Approaching Israel*, contained 3,000 postings by September, 2005. It is without a doubt the largest Chinese online database on the Jewish people and Israel, and apparently will remain so in the foreseeable future, for the forum is still being updated on an almost daily basis.

Since 2002, four new Chinese personal websites on the Jewish people and Israel have been constructed.[5]

(1) *Jewish Net*.[6] The website contains more than 100 articles that are categorized in 13 categories, such as Judaism, Bible, Jewish Wisdom, Jewish News, Middle East issues, etc. In the category of Jewish Wisdom, the whole text of *Pirki Avoth*, basically my translation[7] with some revisions, can be found. The website also has its own forum with more than 100 and is updated frequently. The website has a clear pro-Israeli tendency, as the host openly declared himself an admirer of the Jewish people.[8]

(2) *Jewish Soul*.[9] Several hundred articles are arranged in seven categories, such as Jewish History, Judaism, and Israel. The last update was in April 2005. There is no information about who is managing this website. It does not contain any anti-Semitic or anti-Israeli articles.

(3) *Exploring Jewish World*.[10] The newly constructed Chinese Christian website about Judaism and Jewish life is an outspoken pro-Israeli database. The creator clearly stated that his purpose for constructing the site was "to promote the Chinese Christians' objective understanding of the Jewish people," and "to rectify the prejudice against Jews." He also declared that all the materials in the website should be used for a positive understanding of the Jewish people and should not be used for anti-Semitic or anti-Israeli purposes. The website is only partially built, with only four of its seven

categories completed, but it has some wonderful articles about Jewish holidays with beautiful pictures.

(4) *Baidu's Israeli Bar*.[11] The website is a discussion group located in one of the most popular Chinese search engines, Baidu. Originally a forum with a moderate pro-Israeli tendency, the bar quickly became a battlefield between pro-Israeli surfers and anti-Semitic ones. The only things that can now be seen are the curses and dirty words exchanged between the two sides. Despite this, the forum is still updated on a daily basis.

Among the above mentioned personal websites, only *Approaching Israel* and *Canaan Forum* have any academic quality. The other sites exemplify ordinary Chinese people's understandings and opinions of the Jewish people and Israel.

Academic Institutions

In 2004, two of the Chinese academic institutes on Jewish studies completed the construction of their own websites. The website of the Center of Jewish Studies Shanghai[12] and that of the Center for Judaic and Inter-Religious Studies Shandong University[13] Both bear many similarities in the structure of the websites and their contents. Both of them have news and information about their institutions and scholars, reports about their academic activities, lists of their publications or undergoing research projects, and a small collection of papers (on China–Israeli relationship in Shanghai's website and on Judaism and comparison in Shandong). It seems that both institutions update their websites regularly.

The construction of these two websites should be viewed as a good start to what the Chinese academic community may contribute to the Chinese understanding of the Jewish people and Israel in Chinese cyberspace. Of course much more work still has to be done in this area.

Official or Semi-Official Websites

In 2002, various governmental or non-governmental organizations constructed websites on the Jewish people and Israel, showing that these topics were both interesting and important to their organizations.

(1) *The Official Website of the Israeli Embassy in Beijing*.[14] As a regular embassy website, this website has typical contents such as the information of various departments of the Embassy, visa application procedures, etc. The website, however, also contains other material on Israel and the Middle East. In the section titled "Israel and the Middle East," the Israeli government's opinions on critical issues such as the peace process, Palestinian terrorism, Palestinian refugees, etc., were displayed in cyberspace for the first time. The FAQs of this section were posted on many Chinese forums and apparently served the interest of pro-Israeli activists.

(3) *Sights of True Israel*.[15] The website belongs to the news center of Sina, one of China's largest Chinese-language internet portals. China's official news center established this section on Israel as an exception. Apparently, it started after a trip by Sina's reporters to Israel. The website is full of praise and compliments about the state of Israel and the Jewish people. One can hardly find any condemnation of Israeli acts in the territories or one-sided sympathy towards Palestinians, the regular contents in other large Chinese internet portals or official news websites. Instead, the first thing on the main page is the link to a book titled *Why the Jewish People Are Excellent*. In an article about the first Middle East war, the Arab countries' military action was defined as an "invasion," and Israelis were described as defenders.[16] Such expressions have rarely been seen in Chinese media over the last 50 years. The website is the first one with a positive image of Israel in large Chinese webportals and its influence is probably larger than any other similar website.

(3) *Palestine Information Website*.[17] It is not clear if this is the Chinese web-site of the International Solidarity Movement (ISM). Nevertheless, there is an apparent connection between the two. The Taiwanese webmasters of the web-site declared that the website was built in memory of Rachel Corrie, the ISM activist who was killed in the territories in an accident, and their purpose is to arouse people's attention to the movement.[18] Built in 2003, the website cur-rently contains dozens of articles, most of them translated from English, that blame Israel for almost everything it did or did not do. Although this point of view is seen frequently in Chinese cyberspace, this is the first Chinese website dedicated entirely to this cause.[19]

Three Prominent Incidents Concerning Jewish People or Israel in Chinese Cyberspace Since 2002

As I indicated above, there have been some important developments of websites concerning Israel and the Jewish people since 2002. With due respect to these efforts, the influence of these websites is rather limited as the number of visitors to these sites is relatively small. For a website that is dedicated to a specific subject such as Israel or Judaism, it is unlikely to attract as many visitors as the general forums. Thus, the importance of the postings relating to Israel and the Jewish people should not be overlooked.

In 2002, pro-Israeli voices were still new to Chinese ears. Any outspoken pro-Israeli posting easily stirred up a fierce argument in any Chinese web-forum and immediately became the main page title of the day. Pro-Israeli webwriters like Suoluomen or Liuxingyu gained quick fame by simply posting their series of pro-Israeli articles.[20]

After 2002, arguments of this sort practically vanished. Pro-Israeli voices became common in Chinese cyberspace and nobody was keen to argue about it or even to look at it anymore. The situation in Israel has calmed down, webmasters preferred to preserve their main page space for some hotter topics. Nevertheless, several incidents happened in these several years and webpostings about them did stir up a lot of interest and became popular topics for a short period. Among them, three prominent incidents are worth our attention and are discussed here.

Did Jewish People Start the Opium War?

Around 1997, when Hong Kong became the focus of the media around the world, an English webposting titled "Hong Kong and the Sassoon Opium Wars" started to appear on English websites. With apparent signs of neo-Nazism and anti-Semitism, the article stated the following:

> When the 99 year British lease on Hong Kong's New Territories expired, the Crown of the City of London's Colony was ceded to China. Of hundreds of newspaper stories and TV reports that covered this event, not one revealed how England first gained control of Hong Kong! The truth lies buried in the family line of David Sassoon, "The Rothschilds of The Far East," and their monopoly over the opium trade. Britain won Hong Kong by launching the Opium Wars to give the Sassoons exclusive rights to drug an entire nation!

Picking up the anti-Semitic propaganda of the Japanese puppet government at Nanjing in 1943,[21] the purpose of the article is obvious. The neo-Nazis tried to use the opportunity of Hong Kong's return to China to sell their anti-Semitic ideas to the Chinese people. Although the article was frequently posted on the internet in English,[22] it was not translated into Chinese until the beginning of 2004. A posting titled "David Sassoon, the Jew and the Opium War" was posted on *Tianya Club*, one of the most popular Chinese forums, in February 2004.[23] The article is basically a translation of the English one, but the word Jew was added to the name of David Sassoon wherever it appeared, in order to remind people that it was the Jews who sparked the invasion.

One week later, a posting titled "True or False? Did Jewish People start the Opium War?" was posted on the *Canaan Forum*.[24] Based on two books about the Sassoon family,[25] the posting convincingly showed that the neo-Nazi's article was a complete lie. According to the author Taishixiong, the Sassoon family was not in the Opium trade before the Opium War, and the family members were not British citizens until 1853, some 13 years after the wars. The conclusion was that "now it's clear to us that the Sassoon family did not take part in the opium smuggling trade to China before the Opium War, neither did they motivate the war." The posting became a hit on Chinese webforums and the neo-Nazi propaganda was killed before it really took shape in Chinese cyberspace.

ZHANG PING

Mr. Nuowei Returned From Israel

In 2002, Nuowei was a well-known pro-Israeli writer in Chinese cyberspace. Based on his research of UN documents, his *My Supplement on America and the Establishment of the State of Israel* clarified that UN Resolution 181 and the establishment of the State of Israel were not a conspiracy of the US, a theory that had been dominating opinion in Chinese media for the previous 50 years.[26] His other postings criticized Arab regimes in the Middle East for their uncivilized behavior. His articles can be found on many Chinese webforums.

In September 2003, Nuowei traveled in Israel for five days with great enthusiasm at the beginning, but returned as a completely changed person with strong hostility against Israel. His trip went wrong from the very beginning. In Turkey, he met a young Israeli couple who, according to Nuowei, distanced themselves from this enthusiastic Chinese tourist. At the border control in Ben Gurion Airport, he was questioned for a long time. When he realized that he and another Chinese tourist were actually the only ones left at the border, he believed that it was racial discrimination against Chinese people. Things did not improve after entering Israel. He did not know about the Day of Atonement and complained that nobody told him. As a result, the checkpoint that he intended to pass was closed and he had to climb a fence in order to enter the West Bank. In Jericho, his camera was confiscated by an Israeli soldier for taking a picture of a checkpoint. Moreover, everything he believed about Israel and the Jews was reversed. Jewish people were indifferent and selfish, only cared about themselves. Even on the streets, he felt that "people look at you as if you are a potential enemy." At the same time, he felt that Palestinians treated him in a much warmer and friendlier way. In short, he declared that he had completely changed his viewpoints about Israel and Jewish people and thought that Israel was just "another South Africa." He posted his changed opinions and part of his travel notes on some popular Chinese forums and said that when he finished scanning his 20 films, he was going to publish his completed travel notes, which would obviously be anti-Israeli.

In October 2003, Nuowei was invited by *Canaan Forum* to join a discussion about his recent postings on Israel. During the discussion, Jeremiah and Tiago shared their experiences in Israel claiming that Nuowei's impression of the state in merely five days was one-sided and his conclusion was reached too hastily. They both stressed that the few Israelis whom Nuowei had met should not be taken as an example for the whole state. In the same way, it was wrong for him to assume that all Palestinians are friendly. In a response, Nuowei to some extent modified his impression, by recalling friendly Israelis that he had met and the hostility from some Palestinians. However, he maintained his opinions that the tension between Israelis and Palestinians was a direct result of the Israeli government discriminating against local Arabs.

Almost two years have passed since that discussion, and Nuowei has not published additional travel notes on his trip to Israel.

A Contract With a No Sex Promise

Towards the end of 2003, many of the Western newspapers and websites reported a story based on the words of Rafi Yaffe, the Israeli police spokesman. According to the story, "an Israeli company has required thousands of Chinese workers to sign a contract promising not to have sex with Israelis or to try to convert them." The contract also forbids the workers "from engaging in any religious or political activity." Moreover, the report quoted the spokesman saying that "there was nothing illegal about the requirement and no investigation had been opened against the company."[27]

The news was almost immediately translated into Chinese and became the headline on almost every large Chinese news website. Some of the stories added a comparison between the contract and the Nuremberg Laws of the Nazi Germany and an interview with Tel Aviv's Chinese Embassy spokesperson, who said that the embassy was looking into the matter. The news stirred up angry uproar on Chinese webforums. One comment called for, "collecting all the disgusting things that the Israelis did and making them widely known."[28]

Until now, the story has not been fully explained. The Israeli government never confirmed the report. There were no additional details of the story, no company name, no workers' names, no dates, etc. Nobody really saw the text of the contract and nobody knows the source of the contract. However, it was common practice for Israeli companies to use the same contract as Chinese companies. It is possible that the no sex, religious worship, or political activity requirements were taken directly from traditional communist regulations initially written for Chinese people who traveled abroad. The best arguments that the pro-Israeli side could provide, including an unofficial four-point response from an Israeli Foreign Ministry official through a private channel, was that the company's behavior did not represent the state of Israel or Israeli people.[29]

Conclusions

Since 2002, there has been an overall growth of the positive image of Israel and the Jewish people in Chinese cyberspace. Although the stormy pro-Israeli "language revolution" in 2002 did not continue and the issue of the Israel–Palestine conflict has moved out of center focus, more Chinese websites were built and dedicated to the Jewish people outnumbering those that were shut down. At the same time, with the involvement of the various institutes in building Jewish people- and Israel-related websites, the quality of the relevant websites and their variety were improved to some extent.

Moreover, those with a pro-Israeli or an objective stand have somehow formed an unofficial front and have taken the responsibility of confronting various ideas or comments that might cause damage to the image of Israel or the Jewish people in Chinese cyberspace. In *Canaan Forum*, for example, active members of the forum, in many cases, responded to new events that might cause damage. Their responses spread to other Chinese forums in the form of webpostings, and defended the positive image of Israel and the Jewish people. While the extent of their success is varied and difficult to measure, their efforts are apparent.

Standing as an opposition to the mainstream Chinese media, which usually expresses one-sided sympathy to Palestinians, pro-Israeli voices have survived and developed mainly because of the new reality of freedom of speech, which was enabled by the technical features of the internet.[30] Nevertheless, these features cause problems as well. As it is much easier to express themselves in cyberspace than in traditional media, many of the Chinese websurfers tend to be independent rather than to belong to a certain community. The personal Israel- or Jewish people-related Chinese websites, which are run by a handful of active surfers, do not have much communication between them and do not act in a coordinated way. Therefore, the websites often do not have their own style and their collection of the articles is but a repetition of other similar websites. Thus, most of them have few visitors and the webmaster quickly loses interest in updates. This is, to some extent, the main cause of the failure and the shutdown of some Israel- or Jewish people-related websites, such as *I Love Israel*.

There is also no apparent connection between the institutional websites and the personal ones. The Israeli Embassy's website, for example, has only one link to the Sina's *Sights of True Israel* and ignores all the others. The two academic websites completely ignore the existence of the personal websites and vice versa, with probably the only exception being *Approaching Israel*, which has the links to some of the personal and institutional websites. The various websites also do not act in an interactive way. The Israeli Embassy's website, for example, does not pay attention to what is happening concerning Israel and the Jewish people in Chinese cyberspace and does not react to incidents such as the "no sex" contract of the Chinese workers in Israel.

The ease of expression in cyberspace has also permanently changed the traditional factors that created the image of the Jewish people and Israel in China. There were basically three factors that created the image of the Jewish people in China: the superiority of the Jewish people, the similarity between Chinese people and Jewish people, and the connection between Jewish people and the dominating Western powers. The superiority of the Jewish people basically includes the achievement of modern Jewish intellectuals and the fortunes that Jewish businessmen have made, namely, the Jewish wisdom in a positive sense and Jewish cunning and frugality in a negative sense. The similarities include two nations' long history, ancient traditions, the values that they both honor, etc. The combination of the superiority in its positive sense and the similarities, has given many Chinese people, including many Chinese intellectuals, a positive sense of the Jewish people. The connection between the Jewish people and the dominating Western powers is a more complicated factor. There has been a belief from time to time that Jewish people are the most powerful people among the Western powers, for example, in America. This belief has produced both a positive and a negative image of the Jewish people. In a positive sense, the dominating power of the Jewish people is considered one of the achievements of their wisdom. In the negative sense, the domination turns the Jewish people into imperialists and connects with imperialism conspiracy around the world.

The image of the state of Israel in China is, however, created by some other factors. There are three basic factors: the miserable fate of the Jewish people as a stateless people, the connection between Israel and the Western powers, especially America, and the Israel–Arab conflict. Early Chinese sympathy toward Zionism, including Sun Yatsen's letter to N.E.B. Ezra in 1920 and the Chinese communists' newspaper editorials on the first Middle East war around 1948, is basically based on the first factor, including Chinese identification of themselves as an oppressed nation in modern history. The second factor includes the long-standing Chinese myth of the establishment of Israel as an American conspiracy and the viewpoint of Israel as America's "running dog." The third factor includes the misery of the Palestinians as the victims of the conflict, the Chinese friendship with Arab countries, and the feeling of the Chinese Muslim community. In the past 50 years of Communist China, a combination of the second and third factors has dominated the image of Israel in a very negative sense. At the same time, the first factor has been long forgotten and the traditional image of the Jewish people was ridiculously separated from the image of their state, Israel.

In 2002, pro-Israeli surfers in Chinese cyberspace tried to reshuffle the combination of the factors in order to create positive images both for the Jewish people and for Israel. They tried to merge the image of the Jewish people with the image of Israel, to recall the misery of the Jewish people before 1948 as a justified cause for the establishment of the state, to disconnect UN Resolution 181 from the role of America in its passage, and to devictimize Palestinians both politically and economically. Moreover, they introduced a new factor into the issue: the Sino–Israeli relationship. They praised Israel for its recognition of the PRC in 1950, the first among the Middle East countries, its rejection of establishing an official relationship with Taiwan, its arms sale to China, and the gratitude that it showed for the Jewish refugees who found shelter in Shanghai during the Second World War. They appreciated the compensations that the

National Insurance Institute of Israel (NII) paid to Chinese victims of Palestinian terrorism and their family members, in contrary to the indifference of the Palestinian Authority. The new factor perfectly met the nationalism trend among the Chinese youngsters and, to some extent, offset the misery of Palestinians as a factor in the Israeli image in Chinese cyberspace.

In 2002, this new factor was explored basically in a national sense, i.e. how China was treated by the state of Israel or how Chinese people were treated by Israel or the Jewish people. This factor has quickly become a focus almost everywhere a dispute erupts on Israel or the Jewish people. Instead of arguing how justified the Israeli action is, the point of disagreement is usually how Israel treated China or Chinese people. Since 2002, two new dimensions, a historical dimension and a personal dimension, were added to this factor. In the three incidents that we discussed above, the Opium War argument is related to the first dimension and Nuowei's case is related to the second. Because there were not many encounters between Chinese people and Jewish people in history, the importance of the historical dimension is relatively limited. The personal dimension is, however, an evergrowing element and increasingly important. With the help of easy webposting technology, a traveler like Nuowei can easily publish his personal impression of Israel without even really writing an article. This kind of impression is mostly a result of spontaneous events and is difficult to predict, but with the assistance of the internet, its influence could be great and very damaging in some cases. Since China awarded Israel the Approved Destination Status, more Chinese tourists are expected to travel to Israel. With webposting and blogging, more personal travel notes are expected to appear and add their contribution, positively or negatively, to the factor of Sino–Israel in the image of Israel in Chinese virtual and actual space.

In spite of the problems that the internet might cause, the Chinese pro-Israeli surfers are still benefiting from the freedom of expression that the virtual space provides and are doing things that they cannot accomplish in the real world. One of the best examples is the case of the Chinese character "You" (犹) in the word *Youtai* (犹太), meaning Jewish. Considering foreigners and minorities as barbarians, many Chinese words for their names had the characters with the radical of dog as the way of expressing Chinese cultural superiority. There is no evidence that shows that the translators of the Bible used this character for discrimination or that the word *Youtai* was used in a negative meaning because of this character. After the establishment of the Republic of China, all characters with the radical in the names of foreign nations or Chinese minorities were abolished following Sun Yat-sen's guideline, except for the character *You* in *Youtai*. As a result, *Youtai* became the only Chinese word for nations with a radical of dog. From 2003, the Taiwan Peacetime Foundation has been trying to change the character into the *You* (尤) without the radical of dog. The Presidential Office's

Human Rights Consulting Committee, however, rejected their petition to the Taiwanese president.

While the argument about the character in printed literature is still going on, some Chinese websurfers are too impatient to wait. After all, webpostings do not need an editor's approval and do not have to take any responsibility. Thus, many of them simply started using the *Youtai*, without the radical of dog, in their postings. Some of them might have done it by mistake, but some of them did it intentionally. A Chinese surfer with an alias of ok214 re-posted his posting and replaced all the *Youtai* with the non-dog character. In a brief note at the end of the posting, he promised that he would never use the *Youtai* with the dog radical again.[31] Today, a simple search for the compound *Youtai* without the dog radical in Google can turn up as many as 24,400 results. After filtering irrelevant results, such as the news about the case or occasional combination of the two characters for other meanings, there are still thousands of relevant results. Among them we can find the website of the Egyptian Embassy in Beijing, though the contents of the page are absolutely against Israel, they did drop the dog radical from the word *Youtai*.[32] Another interesting case can be found in the question and answer section of the Islamic Republic of Iran Broadcasting (IRIB) Chinese website. Xiao Lin, a Chinese listener who asked a question about the relationship between Islam and other religions, used the non-dog *Youtai* in his question, while the answer given by the IRIB kept all the *Youtai* with dog radical.[33] The usage of non-dog *Youtai* in Chinese cyberspace shows that, to some extent, the pro-Israeli "language revolution" from 2002 is still going on in Chinese cyberspace.

The mainstream in Chinese media, including those in Chinese cyberspace, still has a one-sided sympathy for the Palestinians. Nevertheless, forces with pro-Israeli or an objective stand have survived since 2002 and their strength is steadily growing.

A Brief Summary of Israel- or Jewish-Related Chinese Blogs Over the Last Two Years

During the past two years, the understanding of Israel and the Jewish people in Chinese cyberspace has been largely expressed through personal experiences in various blogs, just in the way that I predicted two years ago. Not only have many Israel- or Jewish people-related blogs been created during these two years, but also a blog community that focuses on Middle East issues has been formed and has been very active. Moreover, blogs have largely replaced the role that discussion groups have played since 2002 in shaping the Jewish or Israeli image in Chinese cyberspace. While a handful of webforums are fighting for their survival with several regular participants, tens of such blogs have been active during these two years, have attracted tens of thousands of websurfers, brought tens, sometimes hundreds, of people into discussions that are usually full of excitement and verbally abusive expressions, and produced hundreds of articles. Many of them were re-posted around Chinese cyberspace and some of them have become popular postings in large Chinese forums.

These Israel- or Jewish people-related Chinese blogs can be divided into four groups: blogs of Chinese journalists who worked or are working in the Middle East; blogs of Chinese scholars who are either professionally or personally related to the subject; blogs of Chinese people living or traveling in Israel; and blogs of other people who find interest in the subject.

The first group is the largest among the four. Ma Xiaolin, the former Chinese journalist of Xinhua News Agency in the Gaza strip, who created the *Bolianshe*, the only Chinese blog community that attributes great importance to Middle East-related blogs, recruited a considerable number of Chinese journalists who were, or are, stationed in the region for the community. Hong Man, for example, the Xin Hua news agency journalist who is stationed in Ramallah, keeps her blog active and posts her reports every several days. Her blog covers subjects such as the life of the Palestinians in the Western Bank, Israel–Palestine conflicts, etc. Although official Chinese news reports still have a clear pro-Palestinian tone, the journalists' personal blogs show a certain distance from their official stand and usually adopt a more objective approach.

The second group is the most influential group. Most of scholars in the group stayed in Israel for a certain period and their basic approach to the Israel–Arab conflict is neutral or pro-Israeli. Some of the bloggers are leading scholars of Jewish studies in China, such as Yin Gang, an expert on modern Middle East history and a professor from CASS, and his colleague Zhong Zhiqing, an expert on modern Hebrew literature. The contents of these blogs are usually more profound, and cover a larger area such as, history, religion, culture, etc. Because of their reputation and knowledge, some of these blogs are very popular and have high hit rates. Yin Gang, for example, usually has thousands of hits and hundreds of talkbacks for a single article. The blogs of this group are updated less regularly than the first one, but some of them, including my own blog, are very active.

Bloggers in the third group are mainly Chinese students and Chinese people who have settled in Israel as a result of marriage to Israelis. This group usually concentrates on daily life in Israel, and their personal relationship with the Jewish people. Tang Danhong, a known Chinese poet and film-maker, dedicates her blog to her family life and trips in Israel. Fan Yuchen, probably the only Chinese who lives in a Jewish settlement in the West Bank, vividly depicts the life and viewpoints of Jewish settlers. Given the tiny size of the Chinese community in Israel, both the number of the blogs and the strength of their voice are remarkable.

The last group consists of people who have no concrete connection to Israel or the Jewish people, yet they show an unusual interest in the subject.

Usually, the content of this kind of blog is limited to the Arab–Israeli conflict, which is probably the only thing known to the general public in China. Some bloggers, however, show much more knowledge. Lu Han, for example, wrote about the *Talmud* in his blog.

In internet forums, the most important thing is what is said; while in blogs, the most important thing is who is speaking. This is the key difference between a blog and a discussion group or internet forum. This unique feature of blogs profoundly strengthens the personal dimension of the image of Israel in Chinese cyberspace. In blog discussions, bloggers' personal experience in the Middle East and their knowledge on the issues, are frequently mentioned in order to ascertain the credibility of their words. Unlike the situation in forums, where strange opinions attract more attention, in blogs people who stay(ed) in Israel have a stronger voice than those who do not. Generally speaking, these people know more about Israel, and the more truth is revealed, the more positive is the image of Israel and the Jewish people. To some extent, this new feature has enhanced the positive side of the Israeli image because most people who have stayed in Israel hold a more positive opinion than those who do not, unless their stay in Israel was terribly unpleasant.

Although the Israel- or Jewish people-related blogs have developed extremely fast over the past two years, their future is somehow uncertain. After the excitement of a new media is over, people start to ask the true meaning of blogs. Scholars may find out that it is a very time-consuming and academically worthless toy, while the average citizen may doubt if the handful of visitors are worth their efforts to keep the blogs active. Therefore, in the past year, we have seen less and less active blogs from scholars. The activities in Yin Gang's blog, for example, have almost completely stopped. Thus, we can say that, although the Israeli image in Chinese cyberspace has enjoyed positive growth over the past two years through blog activities, the future is quite uncertain.

Selected List of Chinese Language Blogs with Jewish/ Israeli-Related Themes.

Bian Yamin, *Biblical Studies*, < blog.51.ca/u-118312 >.
Cao Xin, *Cao Xin's Blog*, < caoxin.blshe.com >.
Chao Tianxiao, *My Canaan Notes*, < davidfoto.blogbus.com >.
Chen Shuangqing, *Chen Shuangqing's Blog*, < chenshuangqing.blshe.com >.
Chen Xiangan, *Chen Xiangan's Blog* < chenxiangan.blshe.com >.
Chen Yiyi, *Chen Yiyi's Blog*, < chenyiyi.blshe.com >.
Fan Yuchen, *Fan Yuchen's Blog*, < fanyuchen.blshe.com >.
Jane, *Life is a One-Way Street*, < home.51.com/home.php?user=adinahebrew >.
Jiang Guopeng, *Jiang Guopeng's Blog*, < jiangguopeng.blshe.com >.
Ju Zi, *Jushuobadao*, < www.juzisaloon.blogspot.com >.
Li Xuping, *Israel Lee's Blog*, < blog.voc.com.cn/sp1/lixuping >.
Liu Bo, *Liu Bo's Blog*, < liubo.blshe.com/ >.

Liu Suyun, *Liu Suyun's Blog*, < liusuyun.blshe.com/ >.
Lu Han, *Non Linear Mischief*, < liwei1.blshe.com/ >.
Ma Xiaolin, *New Garden of Mawangye*, < mawangye.blshe.com >.
Meng Zhenhua, *Meng Zhenhua's Blog*, < mengzhenhua.blshe.com >.
Shnefly, *Shnefly's Garden*, < blog.sina.com.cn/u/1245428180 >.
Sophy, *Footprints*, < sophyljw.spaces.live.com >.
Tang Danhong, *Tang Danhong's Blog*, < blog.chinesenewsnet.com/?author=1108 >.
Tea Nana, *Sing Alone*, < teanana.blog.sohu.com >.
Xue Qingguo, *Xue Qingguo's Blog* < xueqingguo.blshe.com >.
Yang Zi Lazar, *Love with Israel*, < lovewithisrael.spaces.live.com/default.aspx >.
Yin Gang, *Yin Gang's Blog*, < yingang.blshe.com >.
Yu Jingyi, *Nama*, < blog.sina.com.cn/u/1213578202 >.
Zhang Ping, *Zhang Ping's Blog*, < hangp.blshe.com >.
Zhong Cuihua, *Zhong Cuihua's Blog*, < blog.voc.com.cn/sp1/zhongcuihua >.
Zhong Zhiqing, *Zhong Zhiqing's Blog*, < zhongzhiqing.blshe.com >.
Zhou Yijun, *Dancing with Kebab*, < zhouyijun.blogbus.com >.

Notes

1 Zhang Ping, "Israel in Chinese Cyber Space," *Zmanim*, No. 85, 2004, pp. 15–23.
2 Ibid, pp. 17.
3 Meng Zhenhua, *Approaching Israel*, < israel.nease.net/main.htm > (accessed 30 August 2005).
4 *Canaan Forum*, < www.xici.net/Cul/b84677/board.asp > (accessed 30 August 2005).
5 See < zgytlm.hotbbs.cn/ >. The fifth website, Chinese *Alliance of Jewish People* was under construction at the end of September 2005.
6 Hu Liangming, *Jewish Net*, < www.jewcn.com/ > (accessed 30 August 2005).
7 Zhang Ping, *Avoth: the Wisdom of Our Fathers*, Beijing: CASS Press, 1996.
8 Huang Fugao, "An Interview with the Creator of Jewish Net," < www.jewcn.com/ShowArticle.asp?ArticleID=748 > (accessed 2 June 2006).
9 *Jewish Soul*, < www.ijews.com/ > (accessed 1 June 2006)
10 *Exploring Jewish World*, < www.explorejewish.net/index.htm > (accessed 3 June 2006).
11 *Baidu's Israeli Bar*, < post.baidu.com/ > (accessed 3 June 2006).
12 *The Center of Jewish Studies Shanghai*, < www.cjss.org.cn/index.htm > (accessed 25 August 2005).
13 *The Center for Judaic and Inter-Religious Studies Shandong University*, < www.cjs.sdu.edu.cn/home/index.htm > (accessed 25 August 2005).
14 *Israeli Embassy in Beijing*, < beijing.mfa.gov.il/mfm/web/main/missionhome.asp?LanguageID=77&Question2=&MissionID=87&MissionID > (accessed 30 August 2005).
15 *Sights of True Israel*, < news.sina.com.cn/z/israel/index.shtml > (accessed 30 August 2005)
16 I was unable to open the article in Sina, although the link still exists. A quotation of the article, however, can still be seen in a posting in *Canaan Forum*. See < www.xici.net/board/xici_doc_show.asp?id=V2nFfbQRfcnQVbQvfcjufCQEfcjtV2ZQAWQD&grp=105004 > (accessed 30 August 2005).
17 *Palestine Information Website*, < palinfo.habago.org/ > (accessed 30 August 2005).

18 *Statement*, < palinfo.habago.org/static_archives/about/ > (accessed 3 June 2006).
19 The most important anti-Israel website in Chinese is actually the website of the Islamic Republic of Iran Broadcasting (IRIB) Chinese service. It contains many articles with the opinions of the Iranian government on Middle East issues and serves as a source for many Chinese Islamic websites. The website, however, is not dedicated only to the anti-Israel purpose, therefore is not reviewed here.
20 Zhang Ping, "Israel in Chinese Cyber Space," *Zmanim*, No. 85, 2004, pp. 15–23.
21 *Nanjing Republican Daily*, 25 February 1943.
22 A quick search of the title in Google showed 172 results, some of them appear in prominent websites such as *China Daily*. See < bbs.chinadaily.com.cn/forumpost1. shtml?pid=301668 > , or *Amazon.com* see < www.amazon.com/exec/obidos/tg/ detail/-/1563525666/104-3889534-4198366?v=glance > (accessed 30 August 2005).
23 "David Sassoon, the Jew and the Opium War," < www.tianyaclub.com/New/ PublicForum/Content.asp?flag=0&id-Writer=0&Key=0&idArticle=6902&strItem=no05 > (accessed 20 August 2005).
24 Taishixiong, "True or False? Did Jewish People start the Opium War?" < www. xici.net/board/xici_doc_show.asp?id=V2dEfWQRfcnQVbQvfcjufCQDfXjRVDzD VbQt&grp=105004 > (accessed 30 August 2005).
25 Cecil Roth, *The Sassoon Dynasty*, London: Robert Hall Limited, 1941; Stanley Jackson, *The Sassoons*, New York: E. P. Dutton & Co. Inc., 1968.
26 Zhang Ping, "Israel in Chinese Cyber Space," *Zmanim*, No. 85, 2004, p. 19.
27 Conal Urquhart, "Chinese workers in Israel sign no-sex contract," < www.guardian. co.uk/israel/Story/0,2763,1112442,00.html > (accessed 3 June 2006).
28 Jeremiah, "On the no-sex contract," < www.xici.net/board/xici_doc_show.asp? id=V2ZEfCQRfcnQVbQvfcjufCQDfcHCfcjFfCQS&grp=105004 > (accessed 30 August 2005).
29 Ibid.
30 Zhang Ping, "Israel in Chinese Cyber Space," *Zmanim*, No. 85, 2004, pp. 22–23.
31 User ID ok214, "Great Jewish people," < club.dayoo.com/read.dy?b=viewpoint& i=281465&t=281465 > (accessed 3 June 2006).
32 *Egyptian Embassy in Beijing*, < www.embassy.org.cn/eg/palestinian/blst01.htm > (accessed 30 August 2005).
33 < www.irib.com/worldservice/chinese/wenhua/xinxiang/2005011301.htm > (accessed 3 June 2006).

10

THE INFLUENCE OF JEWISH LITERATURE IN CHINA

Fu Xiaowei and Wang Yi

In the early twentieth century (1920–28), some Yiddish writers such as David Pinski, Isaac Leib Peretz, Sholem Aleichem, and Sholem Asch began to appear in periodicals including *Xiaoshuo Yuebao* (*Stories Monthly*) and *Wenxue Zhoubao* (*Literary Weekly*). Chinese left-wing writers like Mao Dun and Lu Xun enthusiastically introduced Yiddish literature into China, mainly because they thought the realist style of writing and the language revolution in Yiddish literature could be a model for their popularizing vernacular Chinese writing.[1] However, the Chinese cultural focus was soon shifted from vernacular writing to the conflicts between the Communist Party and the Nationalist Party (KMT), and, correspondingly, Jewish writers began to fade from Chinese attention. Our recent search of the catalogue shows that the National Library of China only holds eight books entitled "You tai" (the Chinese characters for Jew or Jewish) and four books of Sholem Aleichem published from 1927 to 1979.

It was only in the late 1980s that floods of Jewish writers, or to be more precise, writers of Jewish origin, entered China and began to exert great influence on contemporary Chinese literary writing. Along with the "Jewish fever" of the book market in China since the 1990s, more than a hundred "Jewish writers" appeared in various lists of Jewish celebrities, such as Joseph Heller, Norman Mailer, J.D. Salinger and, of course, those Nobel Prize winners of Jewish origin, including Nelly Sachs (1966), Joseph Brodsky (1987 and Nadine Gordimer (1991), though many of them are not mentioned otherwise and quite a number of them, such as Thomas Mann, Milan Kundera, and Samuel Beckett, are actually not Jewish. However, most of them, including the renowned writers like Henri Bergson, Stefan Zweig, and Marcel Proust are not read or studied as Jewish writers. So the most influential and generally acknowledged "Jewish writers" – not only because of their Jewish identity but also because of the Jewishness in their works – to Chinese readers, according to our survey, are Franz Kafka, Isaac Bashevis Singer, Saul Bellow, Bernard Malamud, Philip Roth, Sholem

Aleichem, Isaac Babel, Cynthia Ozick, and Shmuel Yosef Agnon. Therefore, our aim in this chapter is to study the critical reception of these writers and their influence in Chinese literary circles as well as the cases of Bellow, Kafka, and Singer.

Saul Bellow

The Best American Jewish Writer

If Saul Bellow is regarded the man among contemporary American writers receiving most critical attention, he has been, correspondingly, one of the most favored Western writers in Chinese critical and translation circles. The introduction of Bellow in China was Lu Fan's article "*Humboldt's Gift* and its Author Saul Bellow," and the translation of his two novels *Seize the Day* and *Humboldt's Gift* in 1981. From the 1990s, Saul Bellow study became the focus of Chinese foreign literature critics, perhaps mainly because of his rising status in the English critical world. Our survey on China National Knowledge Infrastructure (CNKI) – the most author-itative, comprehensive Chinese knowledge-based information resources of articles issued in various Chinese periodicals – shows that there are more than 110 articles on Saul Bellow, from 1979 to August 2007. It may serve as a kind of proof that Saul Bellow's status in Chinese critical circles is much higher than that of I. B. Singer (more than 60 articles) and Malamud (35 articles).

Bellow study seems to have attracted more attention in the beginning of the twenty-first century. In 2002, the Hebei Education Publishing House issued a 14-volume *Collected Works of Saul Bellow*, which covers almost all his works except dramas. Zhejiang Literature & Art Publishing House issued two selected collections of his stories in 2003. In 2004, Yilin Press published his last novel, *Ravelstein*; and so far two monographs on Bellow have been published, a biographical work and an English dissertation enti-tled *Female Representation in Bellow*.

Generally speaking, the major concerns of Bellow critics in China are discussions of the individual pursuit of one's own value, the meaning of life, family relationships and so on, while less emphasis is placed on the Jewish cultural elements. Up to now, we have only found three articles dealing with the Jewish background and features in his works. One scholar has pointed out that Bellow's works have a strong Jewish dimension, from the Yiddish expressions to the description of families and clan relations; therefore, the lack of study of this feature of Bellow would constitute an obstacle to a comprehensive understanding of his works. Yet it is, in our view, still a tough job for a Chinese Bellow critic, raised in a culture without Biblical tradition and with little or no access to Jewish religion or cultural tradition.

119

An Intellectual Writer Unlikely to Have a Vogue

Though regarded as "the backbone of 20th-century American literature," and held in high esteem in Chinese critical circles, Bellow has rarely enjoyed much public appeal. An investigation by Xinhuanet right after Bellow's death shows that Bellow's works do not sell well in China; e.g. the Wang-fujing Bookstore in Beijing only sold fewer than 50 copies of *Ravelstein* and *More Die of Heartbreak* in nearly a year; and half of the 3,000 sets of *The Collected Works of Saul Bellow* issued in 2002 still lie in stock.

After Saul Bellow died in April 2005, there appeared a small "Bellow Fever" in critical circles. Save for the commemorative essays in various journals, a number of newspapers interviewed some Chinese writers to share their opinions about Bellow and his influence in China. Unexpectedly, these writers' responses are quite different from those of the critics. Yu Hua, one of the most influential writers now in China and the one who claimed to be of the generation "brought up by foreign literature," said: "Saul Bellow is a writer whom I read long ago, but never got time to read again. I don't think he has exerted great influence on Chinese writers. Actually, I seldom heard my colleagues talk about him."[2] An article in *the International Herald Tribune* reviewed the impact Bellow had on young people in the 1980s:

> I am now not sure how many of his novels were in vogue at that period. It seems these book names are linked with him: *Seize the Day* and *The Dangling Man*. It was about 1982, and from the names one can imagine that they are about the dull and dissipated life of some youth. It could not get a ready response among a generation full of vigor and vitality. They felt it better to read Singer or Malamud, because at least they two could tell some interesting or meaningful stories.

He Xiaozhu, the poet and novelist, after making a comparison of Singer, Kafka, and Bellow, frankly expressed his preference of the other two to Bellow.[3]

And Sun Ganlu, an avant-garde once well known in the 1980s, simply ascribed Bellow's unpopularity to Chinese readers' reading comprehension. "Perhaps it is because of his Western intellectual experience, or his description of the urban life. Few Chinese can experience the spiritual alienation and predicament of his characters."[4] But Li Geng and Chen Cun attributed Bellow's little influence to his intellectual writing style. Chen called Bellow "a walking encyclopedia" and said: "His novels are for intellectuals. To read his stories, you have to be a man of great learning. Otherwise, you will find it hard to continue."[5] Li thought that Bellow's representative novel *Humboldt's Gift* was filled with various citations, great names and thoughts, with the protagonist wandering among politics, economics, logic, law, linguistics, philosophy, and so forth. But what he reveals is the vacuity and vanity that knowledge brings to man. Li claimed that, in a time when almost all Chinese believed that "knowledge is power," nobody really could have finished reading "this *Humboldt's Gift*." And he assumed that it would take an unconscionable time for Bellow to be understood in China.[6]

To sum up, if there has ever been a so-called Bellow fever in China, it is among foreign literature critics. He has, strictly speaking, not been popular among Chinese readers, especially writers.

Franz Kafka

Spiritual Mentor of Post-Cultural Revolution Youth

Among the writers of Jewish origin, Kafka is perhaps the most influential in China. The reception and influence of this writer from Prague might be an interesting case for study, leading, perhaps, to a better understanding of the modernist trend in the Chinese cultural and political context. The international "Kafka fad" never caught on in China before the early 1980s, though the name of Kafka was already mentioned in Chinese literary circles in the 1930s and 1940s, and then four of his short stories were translated with extremely limited circulation in the early 1960s for the purpose of criticizing decadent bourgeois culture. But in 1979–82, when the authorities loosened their grip on literature and art, Kafka's writings, together with a large number of other Western books, were then introduced into Chinese. Soon after "The Metamorphosis" was published in *Shijie Wenxue* (*World Literature*) in early 1979 with a short commentary, Kafka's name began to appear in various literary magazines and journals. By the end of 1981, Qian Mansu wrote an enthusiastic essay entitled "Kafka arrives in China," announcing that Kafka, after traveling in other parts of the world for more than a half century, had finally settled down in China.[7]

Belated as it was, Kafka, this time as a representative of Western modernist writers, was enthusiastically welcomed by Chinese readers and critics alike. Kafka's writings opened the eyes of Chinese young writers, who would say to themselves: "So fiction can be written in this way!" In the early 1980s, the word Kafka was, according to He Xiaozhu, a sort of contact signal or a synonym of modern Western literature. "Do you read Kafka?" "Yes." "Ok. We are friends."[8] Two decades later, when scholars summarized the foreign impact in the Chinese literary world, Kafka was named "the spiritual mentor of the post-Cultural Revolution."[9]

Yu Hua, once "the banner man of the Chinese avant-gardes," described how he was greatly shaken when he first read the Chinese version of *The Country Doctor*. "I was shocked." He said, "He turned into a heap of rubbish the set of writing principles I had built up in the past three years." He particularly marveled at Kafka's free style: "When he wants the horse to appear, it is there; when he wants it to disappear, it is not there. He does not set any background."[10] And then in Yu's first published story "Leaving Home at Eighteen" in 1987, the sudden appearing and disappearing horse in *The Country Doctor* became the sudden appearances of the truck, the tractors, and then the farmers stealing apples. Some say it is Kafka's cold and sharp style, his direct way of stabbing the sore spots of human beings that brought up Yu's detachment in describing bloody scenes. A number of his novels and stories issued from 1987 to the early 1990s such as *The Past and The Punishments*, "Worldly Affairs Are Just Like Smoke," "A Lover Story," and so on, are modeled on Kafka. And of course, we can find quite a number of Kafkaesque stories among other writers like Mo Yan, Ge Fei, Zong Pu, and Bei Cun, just to name a few.

"The Metamorphosis" and its Chinese Copies

"The Metamorphosis" is, in the eyes of many Chinese readers, the most typical of Kafka's stories. Among the 372 articles dedicated to him in the CNKI, the most frequently studied work is "The Metamorphosis." And when talking about Chinese writers' imitation of Kafka, it is also the most frequently quoted one. For instance, in Zong Pu's story "Who Am I?" the fantastic plot of a man turning into a snake obviously echoes Gregor's metamorphosing into a beetle, and Mo Yan's "Humorous and Interest" also reflects its Gregor shadow.

Perhaps the case of Can Xue, the "Chinese Kafka," is more typical. She not only presents the reader with a bizarre world, in which deformed characters act out preposterous events in a nightmarish atmosphere, following the model of "The Metamorphosis," but also copies some details from it:

> "He is my younger brother. He got a mole's tail and coat overnight." *Skylight*
> "The old man's voice squeaked out of his teeth. I turned around and found him a mouse. I remember he was not a mouse before, but this mouse in the corner is certainly he." *The Instant the Cuckoo Cries.*

These metamorphosed personae, no matter whether moles or mouse, remind us of the giant beetle. But Can Xue's obsession with Kafka does not stop here. There is an element of Kafkaesque style in almost all her works and her monograph *The Castle of Spirit: Understanding Kafka* (1999), is a unique contribution to the Chinese study of Kafka.

The Study of his Modernist and Jewish Features

It is generally acknowledge that "Kafka's contribution to the 20th century world literature lies not only in the description of a lonely individual's dread, perplexity and struggle in a strange hostile world, but also in his establishment of a totally new expression for 20th century literature."[11] Given his unquestioned high status, three newly issued provincial textbooks for high school students have included three of Kafka's stories respectively: "A Dream," "The Hungry Artist," and "The Metamorphosis." Three other Jewish writers, Bellow, Singer, and Malamud, each have only one short story included in the reading material for high-school students, still a sign of honor and approval from the authorities.

Critics in the 1980s generally took Kafka as an originator of expressionist writing, and mainly discussed the theme of alienation in his works. It happened that during that time the notion of alienation, known to the Chinese as *Yihua*, was a heated topic in Chinese intellectual circles. According to a survey, over 400 articles between 1979 and 1984 were published debating the issue of alienation.[12] However, since the 1990s, critics have begun to apply various new approaches to the interpretation of Kafka's oeuvre: allegorical, psychoanalytic, narrative, Marxian, deconstructive, and so on. On the other hand, the Chinese writers borrowed his way of melting into one the techniques of the absurd, deformation, paradox, dream and exaggeration, to describe an irrational world. They followed Kafka's narration of events, his portrayal of characters, and his depiction of scenes, believing that these seemingly absurd happenings and deformed images may be reorganized in the reader's mind to form a complete picture of a nightmarish world.

As in the case of Bellow, Kafka's Jewish identity was for a long time neglected. But things began to change in the late 1990s, after the issue of the Chinese translation of Max Brod's biography of Kafka, which offers "some extremely important information for us to have a stereoscopic understanding of Kafka, and confirms the Jewish complex in his thinking and writing." There are at least six articles discussing the Jewish element in his works and the monograph entitled *Toward Cultural Poetics: Studies in American Jewish Fiction* (2004) also mentions Kafka's Jewishness.[13]

Isaac Bashevis Singer

The perception and influence of Singer in China makes a striking contrast to Kafka in several aspects. Compared with Kafka's overnight success and then lasting leadership in Chinese literary circles, Singer's stories have witnessed a progression from initial blind worship to prompt cooling, and then a new favor amongst Chinese readers. Up until now, the new "Singer fad" has been quietly increasing without any critical promotion. The rise and subside of the two Jewish writers in Chinese literary circles is quite in conformity with the process of Chinese New Period Literary Development.

When the news that Singer had won the 1978 Nobel Prize for Literature came to China it immediately attracted the attention of the resumed and newly started literary magazines and journals. And this happened to be

China's first complete opening to the outside world in decades. Singer's works blew a whirlwind into literary life at a time when all were yearning for a revitalization of literature and curious about the mystery of Nobel Prize.

And the year 1979 in the Chinese foreign literary world can be called an I. B. Singer Year. In January, the magazine *Du Shu/Reading* issued Mei Shaowu's "The 1979 Nobel Prize Winner Isaac Bashevis Singer" and Feng Yidai's "Kazin on I. B. Singer." Subsequently, almost all foreign literary magazines like *World Literature, Foreign Arts and Literature, Yilin* (Translations), and so on, issued articles about Singer or translations of his novels and stories. And in October, the Shanghai Yiwen Publishing House issued *The Magician of Lublin*. In September 1980, the Foreign Literature Publishing House issued *The Collection of Singer's Short Stories*, translated by a dozen famous translators, and this pushed the first wave of the Singer fad to a climax with 90,000 copies quickly sold out.

He Xiaozhu, the poet and novelist, recalled that he was so fond of Singer's stories that he had even thought of pocketing the book borrowed from the library and had complained about why Singer's book was not reprinted for a long time. And Su Tong, the famous writer, wrote in one of his essays on *The Magician of Lublin* that the first scene of world literature he saw was Singer's "Spinoza of Market Street" and said, "I have long been infatuated with the Jewish feature in Singer's stories." And "the great sensation in Chinese book market world," according to Dr. Lu Jiande, the assistant director of the Institute of Foreign Literature of the Chinese Academy of Social Sciences (CASS), "probably started from Singer."[14]

Though the modernist writers soon replaced the Singer fad, the fad took the lead in opening the window for young literary fans to a wider vision and let a large group of young writers learn some invaluable rules of literary creation. Among them are those renowned both in and outside China, such as Yu Hua, Alai, and Su Tong, who once followed modernist writing and again turned back to Singer and to major nineteenth century writers.

The Second Singer Fad and the New Direction of the Chinese Letters

It is worth noting that it was not those young readers' original idea, but rather literary fashion that led them to become estranged from Singer. He Xiaozhu recalled that he had been strongly fond of Singer's works, but one day a young writer asked him to get all the nineteenth century classic novels off his bookshelves, saying these were all rubbish and the real pure literary works were "modernist" novels. He, 20 years old at the time, began to read abstruse Kafka and other modernist writers and force himself to "look at the world around with a Kafkaesque vision." Ten years later, He said, when

124

he and other young writers came to realize that the imitation of modernist techniques had led them into a dead end, Singer's stories became one of the channels leading them out of Kafka's "castle."[15] And Lu Yang, the writer and professor, shared a similar experience. "I still don't know why there was a time when I did not like telling stories," he wrote:

> especially when I thought I was doing serious writing. I often tried not to get involved in storytelling, and did not like others treating storytelling as the core of a novel, either. I tried intentionally to destroy the completeness and coherence of a story. ... Though I once drifted away from storytelling, my interest in it has hidden deep in my mind. ... Singer said what could finally survive was stories. Now I come to see that he is right. He has spoken the truth that only a master knows.[16]

Another avant-garde writer, Bei Cun, decided to turn away from Kafka in the mid-1990s.

> Finally, one day, when I found that I was merely chewing bits falling from the slits of Kafka's teeth, I decided to change. I found I had been doing a meaningless job. Though I could apply the skills learnt from those modernist masters to write one after another complex and skillful modernist novels without difficulty, it was as good as playing with fire.[17]

Bei also admitted his love of Singer's stories and was very happy to be called "the author that resembles Singer most in style."

And Yu Hua, who built up his literary status with his modernist techniques, also changed his style from avant-garde to more of a traditional style after the 1990s. He came to agree with Singer in the early 1990s that "The first position of a writer is to create something attractive to the readers. The reason many readers are disappearing is because writers are not able to write good stories, they scare them away with modernism."[18] The result is that several of his novels, like *To Live* and *Chronicle of a Blood Merchant*, were among the most influential books in China. And the hero of his recent novel, *Brothers*, can be seen as a typical Chinese Yasha Mazur, the protagonist of *the Magician of Lublin*.

The phenomenon that Singer was replaced by Kafka shortly after a temporary fad, and was once regarded as an outdated writer is actually the inevitable outcome of the pouring of the modernist wave into China. And the fact that writers are turning from Kafka to Singer is, according to some critics, the sign of Chinese writers – especially the avant-gardes – extricating themselves from the unconscious state of learning and imitation to become mature.

Gimpel the Fool and the Fool Fad

Just as "The Metamorphosis" led to a number of metamorphosis works, Singer's famous story "Gimpel the Fool" also exerted a great influence on the forming of the "Fool fad" in China. In the preface of his *Warm Trip*, a collection of his favorite foreign short stories, Yu Hua paid high tribute to "Gimpel the Fool," calling it "a soul stirring masterpiece." "Gimpel's short life is fully exhibited in this short story. ... His whole life is illuminated by Singer's vivid depiction of several episodes."[19] In addition, Su Tong, Lu Yang, Bei Cun, He Xiaozhu, and other writers, have written some articles on or about this Singer story. These, together with the works imitative of it, make "Gimpel" one of the most popular stories in China.

For instance, two of Yu Hua's highly praised stories, "I Am As Timid As a Mouse" and "I Don't Have a Name of Mine," are claimed by some readers "to be directly super linked to Gimpel the Fool." And in the new century, the influence of this Singer story seems to be even greater among younger writers. Ji Chen's "Mo Renzhen the Actor" (in *Huacheng/Flower City*, no.4, 2004) portrays a Gimpel-like character and is also described by some Singer readers as "a Chinese copy of Gimpel the Fool." And the newly issued novel of Dongxi, *Confessions* (in *Shou Huo/Harvest*, no. 3 2005) is also said to be imitative of Singer's "Fool."

Alai, the young Tibetan writer who won the fifth Mao Dun Literature Prize,[20] was also deeply influenced by Singer. When the English version of his prize-winning novel *Red Poppies* (or a literal translation *The Dust Settles*) was issued in the United States, an American critic compared it directly with "Gimpel the Fool."

> *Red Poppies* is a deceptively simple novel. We get sentences such as 'I am an idiot' standing alone as paragraphs in *Red Poppies* just as we read 'I am Gimpel the Fool' in the very beginning of Singer's story. In both novels the fool/ idiot is a trickster character who takes the role of leading protagonist as well as a narrator who is often absurd – the unusual combination gives this story its peculiar yet intense flavor.[21]

And almost all these works imitating Singer's "Fool" are among Chinese readers' favorites.

Singer in the Eyes of Chinese Critics

Singer is, however, obviously one of the less important Jewish writers in the eyes of Chinese critics, not as good as Bellow and Roth, and critical essays on him and translations of his works are far fewer than those on Kafka and Bellow. Nevertheless, his Jewishness has been more frequently discussed than that of any other Jewish writers. Among the 60 or so articles, apart from a few interpretations from the perspectives of narratology, structuralism, etc., and some comparative studies of Singer and Chinese writers, most involve Jewish religious belief and customs in his works, albeit unconsciously linking the Jewish religious ideas with Christian doctrines.[22] And the Chinese study of Singer in the new century reflects a new trend of comparing Singer with Chinese national culture.

Other Jewish Writers in China

Sholem Aleichem: the Writer Who Loves his People

Sholem Aleichem might be the only Jewish writer who was among the first to be introduced into China and has enjoyed attention ever since by Chinese left-wing writers and by the authorities, as a writer of an oppressed and harmed people, or a master of Russian realist writing. Yet his Jewish identity and the Jewish features in his works have not been given enough emphasis and his influence on contemporary writers is limited.

Early in 1921, Mao Dun, Lu Xun, and other left-wing writers began to translate Aleichem's short stories and write comments on his writing, calling him "the forerunner of the new Jewish literature."[23] There still exists in the National Library of China a copy of the 1927 *Collection of Jewish Stories* (more than half are Aleichem's works), translated from Esperanto. Since the establishment of the New China in 1949, Sholem Aleichem has long been highly praised as "the writer of the people," "the greatest realist writer in modern Jewish literature," and, in 1959, the Chinese literary letters held a grand centennial celebration for him.

In 1979, Yao Yi'en, a famous Russian translator, in his article "Writers Should Learn to Love his People," made a brief introduction of Aleichem's works and his translation in China. But just as happened in the 1980s when Singer fad was swallowed by the modernist wave, Chinese readers soon forgot Sholem Aleichem before he really became known to the young generation. Up to 2005, apart from the translator Yao, who had been alone in the translation and introduction of Sholem Aleichem for more than 40 years, the Russian Yiddish writer seemed to have been totally forgotten by Chinese readers.

However, with the waning of the modernist wave in the new century, works of realist writers began to attract more readers' and writers' attention. Sholem Aleichem's works were reprinted in 2006, and the musical based on one of his stories, "Fiddler On The Roof" was performed in public for the first time in China. He seems to have become a Chinese favorite again.

Bernard Malamud, Philip Roth, and other American writers

In Chinese letters, the mention of "Jewish writers or American Jewish writers" usually means Saul Bellow, Singer, and Malamud. As one of the writers with a strong sense of Jewishness, Malamud's oft-quoted statement "Every man is a Jew" has been the focus of almost all the 35 articles on the CNKI. Six translations of his novels and short stories are in the China National Library. However, the attention Malamud has received from the critics and his influence on Chinese writers still cannot be put on a par with Kafka, Saul Bellow, and I. B. Singer.

Though Philip Roth is a prolific writer and has won quite a number of America's literary awards, he still enjoys a smaller readership than Bellow and Malamud here in China. Perhaps Chinese readers' acquaintance with him comes principally each November when, prior to the announcement of the Nobel Prize, his name would repeatedly appear in various literary magazines or websites. Probably, it is the American intellectual experience in his works that prevents him from getting a ready response from Chinese readers and this is, as mentioned above, also the case with Saul Bellow. Roth has 8 books translated into Chinese and 17 critical articles on the CNKI.

Other American Jewish writers such as Cynthia Ozik, Grace Paley, Stanley Elkin, Walter Abish, and Paul Auster are only known to some critics and graduate students of American Jewish literature. Among them, only Cynthia Ozik has got several of her short stories, including *The Shawl* translated and three critical articles, to date.

Whereas there exists a kind of unbelievable blind worship of the Nobel Prize in the Chinese literary world, some of the prizewinners of Jewish origin, such as Joseph Brodsky, Nadine Gordimer, and Harold Pinter, still did not win Chinese readers' favor, not to mention those winners before 1978, when the Chinese had no idea of this prize. The main reasons are: first, few translations; second, poor translation, as in the typical case of Isaac Babel (to be discussed below); third, those Nobel Prize winners have not received much attention from Western literary critics and Chinese translators and critics did not feel it so important to introduce them into China.

Israeli Literature: a Chapter in the Making

The introduction and study of Israeli literature in China is, to borrow a term from Ruth Wisse in *The Modern Jewish Canon*, "a chapter in the making." Our search shows that about 20 Israeli writers' works have been translated into Chinese with more than 20 publishing houses and about 40 translators involved in this endeavor, and a dozen critical essays have been dedicated to these writers since the establishment of Sino–Israeli diplomatic relations in 1992. This is a small number compared with Singer, who has got 50 translators here in China. And as to the scholarship devoted to Israeli literature in China and its influence on Chinese readers, this is still only a beginning. Discussions on blogs show that there is an increasing interest in

Israeli literature, but many readers feel that, with little background knowledge of this country, not to say the authors, they are badly in need of some introduction and analysis of the works before they read these novels or stories.

Means of Publicizing Jewish Literature and its Impact in China

Introduction by Critics

The dissemination of Jewish literature in China is, to a great extent, typical of the dissemination of other foreign literatures. There are mainly two paths to the reader: one is through professional translators and researchers, for the perception of foreign writers depends not only on the quality of translations but also on introductions and critical essays. The other is through Chinese writers, who often guide the common readers in a more vivid and direct way with their own experience.

Take Kafka as an example. Ye Tingfang, a senior scholar from CASS, has, since 1979, issued dozens of critical essays, collected and translated major works of foreign Kafka researchers of the past 70 years, published a very important book of foreign critical essays *On Kafka*, and invited a group of translators to publish *The Collected Works of Kafka*. Because of Ye's social status and influence, a large number of translators and researchers were attracted to the study of Kafka. One even claims: "Were it not for Ye Tingfang, the Chinese Kafka study would be unimaginable."

However, sometimes introduction led by translators and academics may not be the most effective way for a foreign writer to reach the Chinese reading public. Actually, from our investigation of literary magazines and the media, and our recent search on the internet, quite a number of readers started their reading of Kafka because their beloved Chinese writers repeatedly mentioned this writer from Prague.

Introduction Through Writers

A more effective way to introduce new foreign works may be through Chinese writers. The perception of the Russian writer Isaac Babel can serve as an example. A textual research shows that the first Babel story translated into Chinese was probably his "Road," which appeared in a 1946 magazine in Chongqing, the wartime capital of KMT during the Second World War. The translator chose this article probably because numbers of young people set out to the Liberation area to join the revolution led by the Communist Party, just like the hero in "Road."[24] But it seems to have aroused limited interest from readers, and then nearly half a century passed before Babel's second visit to China. In 1992 and 2003, two publishing houses each printed a version of

Red Cavalry and several of his other short stories. The sales of the two were low, partly because of the poor translations, partly because of the lack of publicity. Babel has not received enough attention in Chinese critical circles to date.

Wang Tianbing, a Chinese American who called himself a super fan of Isaac Babel, decided in the late 1990s to promote Babel in China. He adapted *Red Cavalry* for a film and worked together with Daizong, the best translator of Russian literary works now in China, to publish three of Babel's works. He also hosted two workshops on Babel in Beijing and a number of press conferences in Beijing, Shanghai, Suzhou, Shenzhen, and Xi'an, inviting famous writers, critics of Jewish literature in China and two well-known Babel critics, Carol Avins from the US and Eifram Sicher from Israel, to attend the meetings. Moreover, through conversations in writing with famous writers like Wang Meng, the former minister of the Department of Culture, and young writers like Ma Yueran, Babel began to attract the attention of Chinese reader. Finally, the new version of *Red Cavalry* was elected the second of the 2004 ten top literary books and set a record of four reprints within a month, with a sale of 28,000 so far. And the new translation of *1920 Diary* issued by the People's Literature Publishing House in 2005 also sells well. A small "Babel fever" with little concern from professional critics is now quietly spreading in China.

The adventure of the Polish writer Bruno Schulz may serve as a more convincing example to show the influence of writers. His stories made their first appearance in China in the no. 3, 1992 issue of *Waiguo Wenyi* (*Foreign Literature and Art*). Several years after this debut, he happened to become popular among common readers without any critical concern simply through a short essay of Yu Hua "Literature and Literary History," in which Yu extended I. B. Singer's comment on Schulz (cited from the brief introduction of the author on the *Foreign Literature and Art*). Yu took the author's life and stories as the main thread of this article to express his idea that: "Each reader writes his own literary history based on his own reading history." And then in the 1999 book *Warm Trip: My Favorite Ten Short Stories,* Yu included Schulz's "The Birds." Since then, some readers of Yu Hua and I. B. Singer began to read and talk about Schulz. They even forwarded the four stories in *Foreign Literature and Art* to the website and, in this way, Bruno Schulz came into the vision of Chinese readers.

Conclusion

In the recent Jewish fever in China, apart from the popular books on the secrets of Jews' success in business, which have, to a certain degree, led to a serious misreading of Jewish culture, many Chinese are coming to be acquainted with Jewish culture through Jewish writers. Su Tong's oft-quoted remark reflects a widely shared view: "If you want to get to know the Jews, but are handicapped by not knowing how, it might be a shortcut to read Singer's stories."[25] And this is quite true with other readers of Jewish writers. A man wrote in his blog, "Because I am so fascinated with I.B. Singer, now I think I have started to love Agnon."

The reason is quite simple. In China, the Jews are meeting a great civilization not shaped by Biblical religion. The Chinese can look at Jews with a mindset not conditioned by Christian mental baggage anchored in holy books. But the shortage of Jewish information or reference books and the pervasiveness of Christian culture have left a common misunderstanding of the two religions, which is more often embodied as an unconscious Christian interpretation of Jewish ideas. In addition, the Jewish idea or message in literary works is usually hidden deep, and is not easy for translators to understand and express correctly in Chinese. Some readers have already come to realize this and one reader on his blog said: "The novels and stories of I. B. Singer are full of a strong sense of Jewish culture. So you'd better get some knowledge of Jewish culture before you sit down to read his works. Otherwise, your reading pleasure will be interrupted by repeated consulting of the notes." And there are more examples of readers of Jewish literature who have turned into Judaic scholars. Xu Xin, one of the most prominent Chinese scholars of Judaism, said his career of Judaic study directly originated from his study of Bellow, Malamud, and Singer. A graduate student from Henan University told me that she was eager to read Jewish classics like *Talmud* right after she read some of Singer stories. And Wang Tianbing also became interested in Jewish culture because of his love of Babel and plans to introduce more works on Jewish history into China. Therefore, the role of Jewish literature in promoting Chinese understanding of Jews and Jewish culture cannot be overemphasized.

Notes

The authors are grateful to Prof. Carol Avins of the State University of New Jersey for her generous help in revising the English of this chapter.

1 The Chinese versions were mainly based on their Esperanto and/or Russian translation. See Yang Bo, "Chinese Letters' Introduction and Study of Yiddish Literature in the 1920s," *Journal of Literature and History (Wenshi Zazhi)*, 1999, issue 3.

2 Xia Yu, "Saul Bellow in the Eyes of Chinese Writers," *Southern Weekly (Nanfang Zhoumo)*, 4 April 2005.

3 Zhou Tao, "Writers and Translators Talk about Saul Bellow," *City Daily (Dushi Kuaibao)*, 13 April 2005. Available at < dskb.hangzhou.com.cn >.

4 Xia, ibid.

5 Zhou, ibid.

6 Liu Yu, "In Commemoration of Saul Bellow, the Great Master and his Influence in China," *International Herald Tribune (Guoji Xianqu Luntanbao)*, 19 April 2005, available at < www.sina.com.cn >.

7 See *World Books (Shijie Tushu)*, 1981, issue 12.

8 He Xiaozhu, "My 1980s' Reading," 17 June 2001. available at < www.poemlife.com >.
9 Liu Chuanyue, "The List of the 20th Century Chinese Literary Giants and the Most Influential Foreign Writers," < www.dadao.net/htm/culture/2000/1002/507. htm >.
10 Yu Hua and Yang Shaowu, "I feel at Home when I Set Down to Write," *Contemporary Writers Review (Dangdai Zuojia Pinglun)*, 1999, issue 1.
11 Yan Hui, "Dialogue Between Souls: Kafka and Can Xue," *Journal of Hainan Normal College (Hainan Shifan Xueyuan Xuebao)*, 2002, issue 6.
12 Fudan University Chinese Department, ed., *Debates on Literary Studies: Collected Materials*, Shanghai: Fudan University Press, 1986, pp. 199–213.
13 Liu Hongyi, *Toward Cultural Poetics: Studies in American Jewish Fiction*, Beijing: Beijing University Press, 2002, pp. 5–7.
14 Lu Jiande, *Preface to 'Gimpel the Fool': Collected Stories of Isaac Bashevis Singer*, Beijing: People's Literature Publishing House, 2006.
15 He, ibid.
16 Lu Yang, "Blue and White Porcelain," in his *Selected Works of Lu Yang*, available at < www.yifan.net/yihe/novels/cnovel.html >.
17 Bei Cun, "Entering into Storytelling," *East Sea (Dong Hai)*, 1995, 1.
18 Michael Standaert, "Interview with Yu Hua," 30 August 2003. available at < www.mclc.osu.edu >.
19 Yu Hua, *Warm Trip*, Beijing: New World Press, 1999, issue 9.
20 It is China's highest literature prize, named after the aforementioned great writer Mao Dun, awarded to the best Chinese novels every four years.
21 Kabir Mansingh Heimsath, "Flowers and Dust: Irony and Brilliance in Tibetan literature," available at < www.himalmag.com/2003/june/review.htm >
22 And this unintentional misinterpretation may have resulted from the confusion of Judaism and Christianity in his Chinese versions and the lack of basic knowledge of Jewish religion, a common phenomenon in China but not the concern of this chapter. Readers interested in this topic see my "Confusing Judaism and Christianity in Contemporary Chinese Letters," *Judaism* (Summer–Fall, 2006).
23 See Mao Dun, "Review of Sholem Aleichem," *The People's Daily (Mingguo Daily)*, 21 June 1921 and "Introduction of the New Jewish Literature," *Stories Monthly (Xiaoshuo Yuebao)*, 1921, issue 10.
24 Cited from Wang Tianbing's unpublished article "Isaac Babel's Trip to China." Email received, 1 September 2007.
25 Su Tong, "How to Joke with the World," *Selected Stories (Xiaoshuo Xuankan)*, 7, 2003, p. 48.

Part IV

JEWISH STUDIES AND LITERATURE

11

AUSTRALIAN JEWRY, ITS RELATIONS WITH CHINA AND THE FIRST STEPS IN JEWISH STUDIES

Sol Encel and Suzanne D. Rutland

In the preface of his recent edited study of the relations between China and Israel over the 50-year period of 1948–98, Jonathan Goldstein noted that there were eight major players, including two Jewish leaders from Australia: Isador Magid and Isi Leibler.[1] This paper explores the relationship between Australian Jewry and China, and analyzes the contribution made by Leibler and the World Jewish Congress to the development of Jewish connections with China over the decade of the 1980s. The Jewish Studies Colloquium held in Beijing in April 1992, which initially aimed at assisting in developing formal ties between Israel and China, ended up marking the end of the gradual movement towards formal diplomatic relations that ended with recognition in January 1992.

Migration to Australia

From the beginning of the twentieth century a small number of Jews migrated from China to Australia. After 1881, Russian Jews sought to escape from the growing persecution in Tsarist Russia, with some escaping from the pogroms via Siberia to Manchuria where they established communities such as Harbin and Tientsin (today Tianjin). A small number decided to move to Australia, which did not require a visa before 1914. As Brisbane was the first port of call, they disembarked there. Officials who did not understand Russian met every boat and asked to be shown a passport. One Jewish refugee, an ex-soldier of the Imperial Army, showed a colored theatre program and got away with it![2]

The new arrivals from China found the Anglo Judaism of the Brisbane Hebrew Congregation strange and formal, so they built their own synagogue known as the Deshon Street Shule, in South Brisbane in 1910. This area became known as "little Jerusalem" as one could hear Yiddish and Russian spoken everywhere, as well as smell "the titillating [sic] aroma of Jewish cooking."[3] For a short period, Yiddish culture flourished in Brisbane. Most of the Russian Jews were manual laborers. They formed a Jewish Workers' Association based on Bundist principles and established a Yiddish library. Efforts to set up a Yiddish theatre failed, and the Association petered out after 1918. After the Russian revolutions of 1917, there was a further wave of Jewish migrants from the Soviet Union into China and some found their way to Australia, usually with Brisbane again serving as the first port of call. A number of these immigrants came to play a pivotal role in the development of Australian Jewry, including Abraham Rabinovitch, the founding father of Moriah College, the largest Jewish day-school in Australia today. Born in Russia, Rabinovitch escaped the Tsarist army and joined his brother Zelig in Harbin, Manchuria. In 1914 or 1915, he traveled via Japan to Australia to join his older brother, Nachum (Nicholas) Meyer, who had settled in Brisbane in 1911, this trip being paid for by Zelig. After the First World War, he moved to Sydney where he became a successful businessman and a community philanthropist.

However, the most significant wave of Jewish migration from China occurred after the Second World War. Before the outbreak of war in 1939, 18,000 Jewish refugees from Germany and Austria had fled to Shanghai, and in 1940 a further 1,000 Polish Jews were sent there from Kobe, Japan. At the end of the war, the Chinese Nationalists demanded the expulsion of these stateless Jews, few of whom wished to return to Europe. It was hoped that Australia could take a significant proportion of these refugees, and in 1946 over 700 of them arrived in Australia. In February 1947, Alec Masel visited Shanghai at the request of Arthur Calwell, Australia's first Minister of Immigration, to investigate the situation and suggest suitable Jewish migrants for Australia. He compiled a list of 1,865 persons whom he recommended for favorable consideration. The Immigration Advisory Council approved this list in May 1947 and an immigration officer, L. A. Taylor, was dispatched to Shanghai to process the applications. The American Joint Distribution Committee representative in Shanghai, Charles Jordan, also visited Australia to facilitate this migration program.[4]

These optimistic developments ended as a result of a number of factors. After the war, there was an outcry from members of the general population against Jewish immigrants, who were portrayed with the typical negative Jewish stereotypes, long noses, ugly features, and foreign mannerisms. Thus, a cartoon published in the *Bulletin* when the *Hwa Lien* arrived in Darwin from China, showed Arthur Calwell, the Minister of Immigration welcoming the Jews as "The Ever-Obliging Sentry" with the following caption:

When the *Hwa Lien* berthed at Darwin nearly 500 'European' refugee immigrants swarmed along the wharf and overran the town.

They are a section of the more than 2000 European immigrants in Shanghai who have been granted permission to land in Australia.
'Halt! Who goes dere?'
'Anodder five hundred of your Jewish broteges.'
'Pass vriends. All's vell.'[5]

In addition, the Australian Consul-General in Shanghai, Osmond Carl William Fuhrman, wrote a highly unfavorable report opposing Jewish migration from Shanghai in July 1947.[6] Fuhrman claimed that the Jewish refugees in Shanghai were "an enigma,"[7] and were unsuitable as migrants for Australia, especially as some were involved in criminal activities in Shanghai including drug running and prostitution. There was no basis for these allegations, but Taylor endorsed Fuhrman's report and he was recalled to Canberra before any applications could be processed. Calwell agreed to resume issuing of landing permits in Shanghai in late 1947 but only 300 Jewish refugees were to be accepted over a period of 12 months.

In mid-1948, further pressure was exerted on the Australian government to permit more Jewish refugees from Shanghai to enter Australia. The Labor MHR, Leslie Haylen, who was chairman of the Immigration Advisory Council, visited Shanghai to assess the situation in person. He endorsed Fuhrman and Taylor's reports and in the course of his confidential summation wrote that "I am convinced after weary years of contact with the Jew that what humanity you can extend to him is not because he is a Jew but *despite* it."[8] On the basis of the information he had gathered, Haylen concluded that Australia "had little to gain from Shanghai migration" but that in order to counter publicity a quota of 300 should be introduced as "a necessary face saver."[9] This decision led Adolph C. Glassgold to write in December 1948 to Walter Brand:

I have to transmit to you some information which should by now not be shocking to any Jew, but which nevertheless still horrifies one ... The new Australian Consul in Shanghai said:
'We have never wanted these people in Australia and we still don't want them. We will issue a few visas to those who have relations there as a gesture.'[10]

In all, about 2,500 Jews migrated from Shanghai to Australia between 1945 and 1953. They included representatives from all three groups in China: the Sephardi Jews, the White Russians, and the European Jewish refugees from Nazism.

The majority of these migrants from China settled into Australian Jewish life, with many making a significant contribution to both the Jewish and general communities. They included Isador A. Magid who was born in Harbin and moved to Shanghai in 1940. After the creation of the state of

Israel, Moshe Yuval was appointed as the first Israeli representative and, in Shanghai, he was active issuing visas to those who wished to immigrate to Israel, although no formal relations were established with the new state. After Yuval's departure, Magid was appointed as honorary consul in May 1949 and he served in that position until his own departure in 1951. In October 1949, Mao Zedong established the People's Republic of China (PRC) and, although David Ben Gurion recognized the PRC in January 1950, there was no reciprocal recognition. Despite this, Magid continued with his work of issuing visas to Israel as well as transferring the assets of the Shanghai Jewish community to the Jewish state. By the time he left Shanghai in 1951 the majority of Jews had migrated to Israel and other countries and his replacement, Dr. Abish, only served for a few months, by which time there were only a few dozen elderly Jews remaining in Shanghai.[11] Magid settled in Melbourne with his family where he became a successful entrepreneur, building shopping centers. He was a strong supporter of the Australian Labor Party, a leader of the United Israel Appeal, and a generous donor to the Hebrew University of Jerusalem.

Another Melbourne Jewish leader of Russian background, Sam Moshinsky, was born in Shanghai and he remembers Shanghai as "a multicultural city full of excitement."[12] He arrived in Melbourne in 1951, and later became a successful accountant and senior partner of Pannell Kerr Forster, a leading international accounting firm, then from 1982 to 1989 served as a senior executive with the Pratt Viziboard Group, and from 1990, after retiring from full-time employment, became an independent business adviser. He also was very active within the Jewish community, becoming federal chairman of the United Israel Appeal in 1989, and serving as a member and later chairing the Board of the *Australian Jewish News*, the main Australian Jewish newspaper.[13]

In Sydney, one of the leading Australian business figures from China, is Harry Triguboff. Born in Darien, China, in March 1933, he grew up in Tientsin amongst the Russian Jewish community there. His father was a builder and he was exposed to the building trade as a child when he visited his father at worksites in Tientsin. In 1947, he moved to Australia to complete his secondary schooling at Scots College in Sydney, and then completed his university studies in textiles at Leeds University in England. After working for a period in textiles in Israel and South Africa, he returned to Sydney in 1960 and became an Australian citizen in 1961. He initially drove a taxi, then had a milk run before establishing Meriton Apartments in 1963 when he built his first block of flats. Since then, he has become Australia's largest home unit developer, building almost 50,000 residential dwellings, mainly townhouses and apartments, in the Sydney metropolitan area and on the Gold Coast of Queensland.[14] He has focused on building low-cost apartments, but this approach has not been without controversy. As Adam Shand wrote in 2004:

Billionaire property developer Harry Triguboff is one of Sydney's most controversial businessmen. His company Meriton Apartments has so transformed the city, it's given rise to the term "to Meritonize — describing the proliferation of nondescript apartment buildings that dot the cityscape.

In the 1990s, Triguboff turned his focus to the city's central business district, bringing in thousands of new residents and creating scores of property millionaires in the process. His latest development, the 78-storey World Square, due for completion this year, is among Sydney's tallest buildings and a community in its own right.

But not everyone's wild about Harry's impact on the cityscape. He fought former Sydney Lord Mayor Frank Sartor for years as council strived to improve the aesthetic quality of Meriton's buildings. As a result of pressure from council, Meriton now holds design competitions attracting the world's best architects to Sydney.[15]

In many ways larger than life, Harry Triguboff has contributed not only to Australian business development but has also been a generous supporter of many philanthropic causes. In 1990, he became a Member of the Order of Australia (AM) and, in 1999, received the Officer of the Order of Australian (AO).

Among the German, Austrian, and Polish Jewish refugees who fled to Shanghai a number of names stand out, particularly amongst Sydney Jewry. Polish-born Henry Roth was assisted in Lithuania by the Japanese consul, Shugiharu, and later found refuge in Shanghai as a young man. He was very proud of the fact that he managed to support himself in the ghetto by making and selling Yahrzeit candles — the Chinese were very impressed with candles that could burn for over 24 hours. After the war, he joined his sister in Sydney, started in the clothing business, and later went into property development in the beach suburb of Manly where he built a substantial shopping mall and other buildings. Gerda Brender arrived as a young girl with her parents from Austria, as refugees from Nazism. After the war, her family migrated to Sydney where she met and married Joseph Brender, who developed Katie's, a women's clothing chain with stores across Australia, with his partner Sam Moss. Recently, Gerda's papers as a stateless Jewish migrant were found in a marketplace in Shanghai and returned to her after a period of 60 years. Hans Mueller also arrived in Shanghai from Austria as a youth where he met his wife to be, Gertie, and followed her to Sydney after the war. They built up a successful men's clothing chain, Lowes Menswear, as well as being very active members of B'nai B'rith with Hans Mueller eventually becoming an international vice president. These are a few examples of Jews from China who successfully adjusted to life in Australia and made important contributions.

Australian Jewry and Southeast Asia/the Pacific Region

In the period of the 1950s and 1960s, the period when there were almost no contacts between China and either the Australian government or Israel, the Australian Jewish community was focused on absorbing the large number of Holocaust survivors and Shanghai refugees, most of whom arrived with nothing. However, as the community became more established in the 1970s, it began to be more aware of the needs of its neighbors in both the Pacific region and Southeast Asia. The first regional conference was held in Sydney in 1969, organized by the Executive Council of Australian Jewry, with the support of the World Jewish Congress, whose president, Dr. Nahum Goldmann, and executive director, Dr. Gerhard Riegner, also attended. This was Dr. Goldmann's first visit to Australia and his presence attracted significant media coverage.

An outcome of this conference was the formation of the Federation of Jewish Communities of Southeast Asia and the Far East, with the aim of strengthening the Jewish communities in the area to ensure their survival. A second conference was held in Hong Kong in 1972, but nothing positive eventuated from these early endeavors. In May 1975, the Federation was reformed as the Southeast Asia Bureau, established as a sub-section of the World Jewish Congress (WJC). Following this, Dr. Kurt Rathner, the director of the United Jewish Education Board in Melbourne was sent on a tour of the region to ascertain the educational needs of the Jewish communities. He recommended that the most positive contribution that Australian Jewry could make was to develop curriculum and provide educational materials for these communities. The WJC provided a small budget and, for seven years, Dr. Rathner serviced the needs of these communities, being replaced by Michael Cohen in 1984. Cohen served in the same position until 1991. Eileen Franklin succeeded him, filling the position in 1993 after which no further appointments were made.

Isi Leibler and World Jewish Congress

In 1978, Mr. Isi Leibler was elected for his first term as president of the ECAJ. He was to serve for four terms, during which period he was very active in regional affairs because of his business interests. Born in Antwerp, Belgium, in 1934, Isi migrated with his parents as a young boy to Melbourne in 1938. He had just completed an Honors thesis in political science at the University of Melbourne, when his father, a diamond merchant, died in 1958. Isi Leibler put his university studies aside to assist his mother in the diamond business and, in 1964, he became a silent partner in a travel agency, Astronaut Travel, which he subsequently developed into Jetset Travel. By the 1970s, Jetset had become the largest travel agency in the South-Pacific region and Leibler became interested in developing the Jewish communities there. Emerging from his involvement in Soviet Jewry, he became active in the World Jewish Congress, becoming vice-president and then, in 1991, co-chairman of the WJC Governors' Board.

By the late 1970s, Australian Jewry and the World Jewish Congress were beginning to recognize the growing importance of the Asia–Pacific region for world trade and economic development. Whilst the Asia–Pacific region contained a significant proportion of the world's population, there was no strong Jewish presence in the area. Most of the Asian countries did not have diplomatic relations with Israel and only understood the Arab–Israeli conflict from the Arab perspective.

As the newly elected ECAJ president, Isi Leibler felt that world Jewish leadership had largely neglected this important area. This was a task for Australian Jewry, which "though geographically isolated from the large mainstream Jewish communities in the Americas and Europe, is nevertheless better placed than those communities to play a role." As he stated forcefully: "Geographically, Australia is part of Asia."[16]

In May 1980, the ECAJ convened a conference in Hong Kong where the Australia/Pacific Jewish Association was formed, replacing the Southeast Asia Bureau. Its major goal was to provide educational, religious, and support services to the small Jewish communities in the region, thereby enhancing their Jewish life and strengthening Jewish identity there. In addition to its regular educational work, a major aim of the APJA was to instill a regional Jewish identity. Over the years of APJA activity, this was achieved by holding fairly regular conferences, both in the region and in Israel.

Asian Jewish Colloquia

In response to the growing importance of the whole region in world affairs, Leibler through the APJA also initiated the concept of Asian Jewish colloquia to sponsor a dialogue between Asian and Jewish academics and intellectuals. These colloquia had three main aims:

1. To develop a basic understanding in the region of World Jewry and Jewish concerns, especially the links, often misunderstood, between World Jewry and Israel;
2. To heighten the awareness of the Jewish contribution to civilization; and
3. To sensitize public opinion elites towards a balanced view of Israel and the Middle East and, in particular, the manner in which the needs of their developing societies can benefit from better relations with Israel.

These aims, which all had a political agenda, added to the original aim of the Federation to foster Jewish life in the communities of the region. The colloquia introduced the concept of a "dialogue of ideas" between Jewish and Asian intellectuals.

The first Asian Jewish colloquia, held in Singapore on 11–12 September 1984, centered around the theme of "Cultural Interaction: Old and New Societies — New States." Its proceedings were divided into four sessions dealing with identity and change, political theory, religion and law, and science and technology. Organized under the sponsorship of Professor Yoram Dinstein, rector of Tel Aviv University,[17] and Isi Leibler, with the World Jewish Congress, the conference enabled for the first time an encounter between scholars of Asia and those from Israel and the Jewish world to discuss ancient cultures and modern states. It attracted leading scholars, scientists, and intellectuals. In all, there were 30 scholars from 12 countries. Most of the participants from the regional conference that was convened immediately prior to the colloquium also participated, with a total of 11 Jewish communities[18] represented, making it a watershed event.

In his opening address, Dinstein told the academics and scientists that there were three "cultural gaps," which he hoped the conference would bridge: those between Jewish and Asian diasporas; between the State of Israel and modern nation states in Asia; and between science and the humanities. He also stressed that Israel and World Jewry had little knowledge or awareness of Asia, while Asia was ignorant of the relationship between Israel and World Jewry.[19]

The uniqueness of the occasion was highlighted at the closing social function when Australian Aura Levin sang Hebrew songs for the gathering and elderly Indian Jewish leader, Ezra Kolet[20] joined in with his violin, encouraging all present to join in. The *Australian Jewish Times* editor, summed up the occasion as follows:

> The sight of so many eminent Asian intellectuals singing in Hebrew and dancing the *hora*, arms around their Jewish colleagues, was for even the most cynical an emotional charge of never to be forgotten intensity, and an augury of future co-operation for mutual benefit.[21]

Despite the positive elements of the colloquium in Singapore, the organizers were faced with two major problems. The international media, apart from the Jewish press, ignored the conference so that there was no media coverage of the event and the organizers found it difficult to attract a number of first-rate scholars.[22] Despite these problems, it was decided that a second colloquium should be held in two years time.

The second colloquium was held in Hong Kong in March 1987. Convened again by Professor Dinstein and Leibler, with the World Jewish Congress, the theme was "The Jews and Asia: Old Identities and New Images." This second colloquium attracted a much higher caliber of academic presentations and participants included Sir Zelman Cowen, former Australian Governor-General, who opened the proceedings and former

Australian Prime Minister, Malcolm Fraser. In all, there were 30 academics from Asia and the Jewish world, and the colloquium received widespread media coverage. ECAJ president, Leslie Caplan, attended with conference as APJA president, with Isi Leibler as its chairman. In addition to World Jewish Congress funding, these first two colloquia were subsidized by the APJA and Jetset Travel.

Creating Jewish Connections with China

From the departure of the last Shanghai Jews in the early 1950s until the late 1970s, there were no official contacts between China and Jewry. During the early 1980s, Chairman Deng Xiaoping introduced economic reforms, including a new open-door policy, which aimed at modernization and transformation. As a result, China began to seek contacts with the wider world and this included clandestine military and commercial contacts with Israel.[23]

The Chinese government was particularly interested in developing its tourism industry as this would attract foreign currency. As executive director of Jetset Travel, Leibler was invited to visit China for the first time in 1981. Writing to Rabbi Israel Singer, executive director of the World Jewish Congress, before this visit, Leibler stated: "I have decided not to proceed with Jewish matters in Peking on this occasion. I will be going there purely in a travel sense."[24] During this visit, Leibler met with Tan Wen Zui, among many others. Editor of the International News Department of *People's Daily*, he advised Leibler that "patience was a virtue in China and he was happy that he (Leibler) was not pushing matters to a head."[25] Following this visit, Leibler wrote that "diplomatic relations with Israel is not on the agenda in the foreseeable future."[26]

A new phase began with the joint Sino–British Declaration in 1984, that Britain would return Hong Kong to Chinese sovereignty in 1997. As part of this agreement, China announced that: "according to the circumstances of each case, consular and other official missions of states having no formal diplomatic relations with the People's Republic of China may either be maintained or changed to semi-official missions."[27] The Israeli Foreign Ministry, headed by David Kimche, recognized this opportunity and, in May of that year, its deputy-director, Hanan Bar-On requested Reuven Merhav to investigate whether Hong Kong would be a good base to open up China both diplomatically and politically.

Merhav agreed to take on this mission and, whilst undertaking this study, he was instructed by his Ministry to meet with Isi Leibler. At that meeting, Leibler offered to act as a "surrogate" diplomat for the Israeli Ministry to Foreign Affairs, as at that time there was no official contact between China and Israel. Merhav stressed the importance of working "discretely and quietly" and proposed that Israel should sponsor young intellectuals to come to study in Hong Kong to prepare them for leadership positions. Leibler agreed to assist in this endeavor and provided a generous scholarship. Ruth Kahanoff, a graduate from the Department of East Asian Studies at Hebrew University who was working with the Foreign Ministry, was selected as the scholarship recipient and she arrived in Hong Kong later that year. When the two men parted, they promised to keep in touch and over the subsequent six years worked closely together.[28]

On the basis of Merhav's report, Israel decided to reactivate its consulate in Hong Kong and, in August 1985, Reuven Merhav assumed the position of consul-general, although in reality he enjoyed a rank equal to that of an ambassador.[29] In the subsequent three years, Merhav used Hong Kong as a base for developing relations with China, working closely with Li Chuwen who, in June 1983, had been appointed as deputy director of the Xinhua's (New China News Agency) Hong Kong office, the PRC's "unofficial" embassy in Hong Kong.[30]

In October 1985, Leibler undertook his second, and in many ways groundbreaking, visit to China, officially as the guest of the state-operated China International Travel Service (CITS), but unofficially to investigate the possibility of holding an Asian Jewish dialogue there. China's interest in acquiring foreign currency through the development of tourism coincided with Isi Leibler's activities, and this assisted him in his mission. A travel associate in Hong Kong with close links with Communist China, H. P. Kong, facilitated this trip. Before Leibler went, he met with Rabbi Singer in New York and obtained formal authorization to proceed on a WJC level, and he discussed the trip with John Bowen, Foreign Affairs liaison officer of the office of Prime Minister Bob Hawke. He also met with Merhav and informed him of his plans. Australian Jewish journalist, Sam Lipski who was vice-president of AIJA and a member of the APJA executive, accompanied him.

During this visit, Leibler and Lipski met with a range of different organizations, including a two-hour meeting with the CITS president, Wang er Kong. They also met with officials from the Chinese Bureau of Religious Affairs with the aim of establishing the groundwork for holding an Asian Jewish colloquium in China. Leibler later described this encounter as follows:

> I began with greetings from the World Jewish Congress, the Asia-Pacific Jewish Association, and the Executive Council for Australia Jewry. I confirmed that this was the first time the bureau had ever met with representatives of a Jewish organization. I made my standard presentation, noting the propitiousness of the time for establishing contact between China and the Jewish peoples.
>
> Both men were friendly but they were clearly nonplussed by the situation, which, for them was literally unprecedented.[31]

Isi Leibler had similar experiences with meeting other Chinese officials, as for many it was the first time that they had met with Jewish representatives. In discussing the concept of a colloquium in China, one official, Yao Renku expressed concerns about being misreported in the Western press and stressed that such an idea would be "quite a major step." He stated that while China had no problem dealing with Jews as individual citizens, there were concerns about dealing with "a Jewish group *qua* Jewish group." Both Leibler and Lipski stressed that various international Jewish organizations had been dealing with governments and non-government organizations around the world for 40 years. Only China remained as "the last great frontier."[32] They also met with Dr. Li Shenzhi, Director of the Institute of American Studies and vice-president of the Chinese Academy of Social Sciences, who had been a friend of H.P. Kong before 1949.

After this visit, Leibler continued to pursue these Chinese contacts. In January 1987, he wrote to Dr. Li Shenzhi about a Chinese scholar attending the Hong Kong Asia–Jewish Colloquium.[33] Through an invitation extended by Claudio Veliz, Professor of Sociology at La Trobe University in Melbourne, Dr. Li came to Melbourne at the beginning of March 1987 to lecture on Sino–American relations. Kong, himself, "coincidentally" arrived at the same time as did Merhav.[34] Past Prime Minister, Malcolm Fraser, met with Dr. Li, and later Leibler hosted a private dinner at his home for Dr. Li together with Merhav and Kong. Dr. Li discussed Israeli–Chinese relations. He was not optimistic about establishing diplomatic relations with Israel, but felt that opportunities for sponsoring Jewish Studies and Hebrew in China should be explored.[35] Merhav later commented that Dr. Li's comments made him realize that the humanities and social sciences were not the best avenue to open dialogue, as these academic areas could be suspect to the Chinese government, and that it was better to establish links with the scientific, technological, and engineering areas of academia. This was, indeed, the path Merhav pursued after his Australian visit, with significant success, as it appealed to Chinese pragmatism.[36]

Despite these meetings, nothing was finalized about a Chinese scholar attending the April 1987 symposium. However, at the last minute, Professor Sidney Shapiro, was sent. Known by his Chinese name, Sha Bo Li, Professor Shapiro was a Jewish lawyer from Brooklyn who enlisted at the start of the Second World War and was sent by the army to study Chinese, which he did first at Cornell University and later at Yale. After the war, he felt he could not return to being a New York lawyer, and made his way to Shanghai where he met a Chinese theatre critic and they decided to get married. They left Shanghai and settled in Beijing where they had two children and, in 1963, Shapiro became a Chinese citizen. During the Cultural Revolution, the family was separated, but after the upheavals they were reunited in Beijing. Shapiro worked as a translator of Chinese literature into English and became an adviser to the Chinese government. He attended the conference and presented a paper on the Jews of Kaifeng.

Leibler believed that Shapiro's participation in the March 1987 colloquium was a significant breakthrough and his presence attracted significant media coverage. Its success encouraged Leibler to continue his efforts to hold the third colloquium in Beijing. Shapiro agreed to be a member of the international steering committee.[37]

The 1992 Beijing Conference

In September 1988, before his departure from Hong Kong, Merhav was granted permission to visit the Chinese mainland for unofficial meetings in Beijing.[38] This visit paved the way for two Israeli academic missions to visit China in 1989 and, in February 1990, a CITS office was established in Tel Aviv and at the same time an Israeli Academic Mission was opened in Beijing, headed by Dr. Jospeh Shalhevet, an agriculturalist, with Ruth Kahanoff as its deputy-director, and Yoel Guillat, a career diplomat.[39] These developments appeared to increase the possibility of a Jewish Studies Symposium in Beijing.

After the Beijing massacre in 1989, Leibler expressed concern but still envisaged that there would be a substantial improvement of relations between China and Israel to enable the third Asian Jewish Colloquium to take place in Beijing.[40] He worked closely with Merhav, who was appointed Director-General of the Israeli Ministry of Foreign Affairs in 1989, and Stephen Solarz of the US. His prediction proved correct as a result of the radical changes on the international scene with Arafat's Geneva Declaration of December 1988 recognizing the two-state solution, the collapse of the Soviet Union, the first Gulf War, and the Madrid Conference, which inaugurated dialogue between Israel and the Arab States.[41]

In April 1990, Leibler undertook another visit to Beijing. He noted that after the Tiananmen Square incident, the Chinese were concerned that the US would revoke its Most Favored Nation status, severely affecting its trade. In his discussions with the Chinese, Leibler noted that "in this context, the influence of the Jewish lobby in the US gained added status and was raised by Chinese officials during his visit."[42]

The year of 1991 proved to be the crucial turning point in Sino–Israeli relations when "all the pieces of the puzzle fell into place."[43] Dr. E. Zev Sufott, a veteran Israeli diplomatic, joined the academic mission in Beijing in March 1991 when a Chinese delegation headed by Ambassador Han Xu, President of the Chinese People's Association for Friendship with Foreign Countries, visited Australia and met with Leibler in Melbourne. Han Xu again spoke extensively about Jewish influence in Washington and discussed the proposed Sino–Jewish Colloquium.

During the latter part of 1991, a number of important meetings took place between Chinese and Israeli representatives, including a meeting between the two country's foreign ministers in New York before a United Nations meeting, which was reported on for the first time in the Chinese press and a visit by the Israeli Defense Minister, Moshe Arens, to Beijing, which was also publicized.

As part of this changing diplomatic climate, in August 1991 the World Jewish Congress was invited by the China International Culture Exchange Center (CICEC) to organize a mission to Beijing. The CICEC was established in 1984 with direct authorization of Deng Xiaoping, and it was understood that this invitation was to conclude an agreement about the Beijing symposium. Sol Kanee of the World Jewish Congress and Dr. David Berstein, director of research of the Australian Institute of Jewish Affairs, accompanied Leibler and they spent five days in Beijing, meeting with the Australian and American ambassadors, the Israeli Academic Mission, and the CICEC. At the CICEC meetings, the details of the colloquium were discussed and agreed, including the fact that it would be a joint venture between the two organizations, it would be announced in the Chinese press and that a tour of China organized by the WJC would take place at the same time. They also met with the CITS, and its chairwoman, Madame Lu Fenyan, expressed a willingness to meet with Raphael Harlev, the president of El Al, and the head of the Chinese Civil Aviation Authority.[44] On the second last day, Cheng Siyuen, president of the CICEC, hosted a second banquet in the Great Hall of the People.

However, by far the most important meeting was with the Chinese Foreign Minister, Qian Qichen on 11 October 1991. Whilst it was initially indicated that this was a private meeting, they were informed that it could be publicized and official photos were taken. Leibler outlined the role of the World Jewish Congress and its role as the "parliament of World Jewry." He also raised the issue of the 1975 UN resolution, "Zionism is Racism," and expressed the hope that China would support its recision in the United Nations. Qian responded warmly, paying tribute to the two ancient civilizations and also expressing his sympathy for Jewish suffering during the Holocaust. He noted that he had met with three Israeli foreign ministers – Shimon Peres, Moshe Arens, and David Levy – regretted the fact that there were no formal diplomatic relations between the two countries but pointed out there were non-government offices in Tel Aviv and Beijing. He also noted China's interest to assist in the peace process. In regard to the United Nation's resolution he stated "we do not believe that the language of the resolution is consistent with the fact."[45] Subsequently, the mission also met with Wan Li, the chairman of the standing committee of the National People's Congress. These last two meetings were very significant and indicative of China's changing relations with Israel and the Jewish people.

Within a couple of months of the WJC Beijing mission, China established diplomatic relations with Israel on 24 January 1992, and India also subsequently extended full diplomatic recognition to Israel. From 6–8 April 1992, the Chinese Jewish colloquium was held in Beijing under the auspices of the World Jewish Congress and the China International Culture Exchange program,[46] with official endorsement from the Chinese government. Again, this was a watershed event, with Professor Dinstein and Leibler as key organizers, and 24 international Chinese and Jewish scholars participating. They included nine of the Jewish world's outstanding scholars and writers from both Israel and the Diaspora.[47] Leibler opened the colloquium, analyzing the parallels between Jewish and Chinese history, and Diaspora experience. A meeting was also held with the vice-premier, Wu Xueqian, who stressed the importance of a just peace in the Middle East and spoke of the importance of continuing China's economic development.[48] One of the participants, Professor Zwi Werblowsky of Hebrew University summed up the experience as follows: "for the first time Judaism has spoken for itself, about itself, in an unmediated dialogue with Asian culture."[49]

The three colloquia organized with the assistance of the WJC proved to be groundbreaking initiatives. They helped to foster academic exchange and to create a greater understanding of Jewish history, World Jewry, Jewish concerns and Jewish links with Israel in the region. Through the informal social links that are an important element of all conferences, they helped to change perceptions, create a better basis for understanding and so, as Michael Cohen stressed, create "a generally better acceptance of an international Jewish dimension in the thinking of elites throughout the South East Asian region."[50]

Re-Emergence of the Australian Connection

With the opening up of China to Western tourism, especially after 1992, a number of Australian Jews who had their roots in China went back to visit the places of their youth and sought to became part of those who chronicled the history of the Jews in China. In 2004, there was a major gathering in Tienstin in which Harry Triguboff and his daughter Orna participated. Professor Andrew Jakubowicz, a Professor of Sociology and an expert in multiculturalism, race relations, and action research at the University of Technology, Sydney, is particularly active in these endeavors. Professor Jakubowicz's parents had escaped from Lodz in central Poland to Shanghai and he was born in Sydney after the war. He grew up, very aware of this background and the influences of Chinese culture in his home. He has produced a multimedia interactive program, "The Menorah of Fang Bang Lu: Shanghai Modernity and the Jews of China," showing how Jews were part of the engagement between Western modernity and Chinese culture following his discovery of an old Menorah, a music box, in the Fang Bang Lu marketplace during his visit to Shanghai in November 2000.[51] In 2001–03, major exhibitions on Shanghai Jewry were held in both Melbourne and Sydney. The Sydney Jewish Museum's exhibition, called "Crossroads

Shanghai,"[52] effectively created the sense of Jewish life in Shanghai before, during and after the Second World War, and received a government grant to become a traveling exhibition with Jakubowicz as historical adviser from 2002 to 2003. A television program from the ABC religious affairs series, *Compass*, was produced based on this exhibition and the one entitled "Exit Shanghai" held at the same time at the National Maritime Museum in Sydney.[53] In July 2005, Professor Jakubowicz and Harbin-born, Sydney-based journalist, Mara Moustafine, who wrote her family's saga in China and Russia entitled *Secrets and Spies: the Harbin Files*,[54] both lectured at the summer program of the University of Shandong where Australian-born Dr. Avrum Ehrlich is a professor in Jewish philosophy.

Conclusion

As discussed above, a number of Jews from China have made substantial contributions to both the Australian general community and the Jewish community. This contribution can be seen when walking through the grounds of Moriah College's new campus opened in 1994, with major sponsors including Harry Triguboff, Henry Roth, and Gerda and Joseph Brender. Each of their stories represents hard work and perseverance in rebuilding their lives in Australia after leaving China. In addition, largely due to the efforts of Isi Leibler as president of the Executive Council of Australian Jewry working with the World Jewish Congress, Australian Jewry played its part in the events leading to the recognition of Israel and the opening up of China to Jewish Studies, with the holding of the first major Jewish Studies conference in Beijing in 1992.

Notes

1 Found in the preface of. J. Goldstein, (ed), *China and Israel, 1948–1998: a Fifty Year Retrospective* Westport: Praeger, 1999.
2 Solomon Stedman, "From Russia to Brisbane, 1913," *Australian Jewish Historical Society Journal*, vol. V, part 1, 1959, pp. 21–22.
3 Ibid., 27.
4 S.D. Rutland "Waiting Room Shanghai: Australian reactions to the Plight of the Jews in Shanghai After World War II," *Leo Baeck Year Book*, London: 1987, pp. 407–433.
5 *The Bulletin*, 22 January 1947.
6 Born in Melbourne to German parents, he was named Otto Carl Wilhelm Fuhrmann and he later Anglicized his name. He fought in the First World War when he reached the rank of Major General and, during the interwar years, he worked in key positions at Australia House in London, before embarking on a diplomatic career in the newly established Department of External Affairs. He served as consul-general in Shanghai from 1947 to 1949 when he was appointed as Australia's first minister to Israel.
7 "Legal and Consular Immigration. Migration from Shanghai," Memo for the Dept of Immigration, 22 July 1947, from Australian Legation, CA 18, Dept of

External Affairs, Corres. Files, Australian Archives Office, CRS A1068, Item 1C 47/31/15, p. 5.

8 L. Haylen's Report, 1948, p. 6, "Reports from Shanghai on Alien Immigration," CA51, Dept of Immigration, 1945–1974, Corres. Files, Australian Archives Office, CRS A434, Item 47/3/21.

9 Ibid., p. 9.

10 C. Glassgold to Walter Brand, 2 December 1948, Box E12, ECAJ Corres. Files, *Archive of Australian Judaica.*

11 Magid, Isador A., "'I Was There': the Viewpoint of an Honorary Israeli Consul in Shanghai, 1949–1951," in Goldstein, op. cit., p. 45.

12 See < www.cts01.hss.uts.edu.au/ShanghaiSite/menorahsplash/cat/child.html > (accessed 15 September 2005).

13 Suzanne D. Rutland, *Pages of History: A Century of the Australian Jewish Press,* Sydney: Australian Jewish Press, 1995, pp. 254–255.

14 "Harry Oscar Triguboff, AO," Program | Background Resource Paper | Speakers-bio | Presentations | Summaries | Media Contact Home » G.au » Bio » Harry Oscar Triguboff, accessed Thursday 15 September 2005.

15 Adam Shand, "Harry Triguboff: a man of property," Sunday, 14 March 2004, < mediacentre.ninemsn.com.au/mediacentre/about.aspx > , (accessed 15 September 2005).

16 Isi Leibler, "Report on the Asia-Pacific Region presented to the plenum of the World Jewish Congress, Jerusalem May 1991."

17 Other key academics on the committee included Professors Shlomo Avineri, Efraim Urbach, Shaul Friedlander, Zvi Werblowsky, Yehuda Elkana Yuval Neeman, and Aphraim Katzir.

18 The communities represented included India, Japan, South Korea, Singapore, Nepal, the Philippines, Thailand, Australia, Israel, Europe, and the US.

19 Press release, 17 September 1984, p.3, Vol 4, APJA, 792/20, Leibler Archive, Jerusalem.

20 Kolet was head of the Indian Jewish Council. He was a key figure in all the APJA gatherings. In 1980, Isi Leibler described as "the absolute life of the proceedings. He made everybody think that he was Peter Sellers masquerading as an Indian." Vol. 3, APJA, Leibler Archive, Jerusalem.

21 Susan Bures, "Australia sets pace for Asia Jewish Future – special report," *Australian Jewish Times,* 4 October 1984.

22 Isi Leibler, "Confidential Report on the Second Asian Jewish Colloquium, 23–24 March 1987."

23 Shichor, Yitzhak, "Hide and Seek: Sino–Israeli Relations in Perspective," *Israel Affairs,* vol. 1, no.2, Winter 1994, p. 74.

24 Letter to Professor Israel Singer, 13 March 1981, ASIA, Leibler Archives, Jerusalem.

25 "Report on visit to China, 29 March–5 April 1981," ASIA, Leibler Archives, Jerusalem.

26 Ibid., p.29.

27 R. Merhav and Y. Shichor, "The Hong Kong Connection in Sino–Israeli Relations," in Goldstein, op. cit. p. 97.

28 Tape recorded interview with Reuven Merhav, Jerusalem, 20 November 2000.

29 R. Merhav and Y. Shichor, op. cit., p. 98.

30 Ibid. p. 99.

31 Isi J. Leibler, "Report on Visit to Beijing, China, 20–24 October 1985." 54-page report.

32 Ibid.

33 Dr Li Shenzhi was vice-president of the Chinese Academy of Social Sciences and Director of the Institute of American Studies. He was a key adviser to the

government on anything to do with the US. As such, he was a senior deputy with access to Deng Xiaoping. He was very close to Zhou Enlai, Chinese Foreign Minister, had been his speech writer, and had survived the cultural revolution. Leibler Report, 1987, ASIA, Leibler Archive, Jerusalem.

34 Interview with Isi Leibler, 6 November 2000, Jerusalem.
35 Leibler correspondance, AISA, Leibler Archive, Jerusalem.
36 Interview with Reuven Merhav, Jerusalem, 20 November 2000.
37 Report on the Second Asian Jewish Colloquium, Hong Kong, 23–24 March 1987, p.16. AJHS Archive, Mandelbaum House, Sydney.
38 R. Merhav and Y. Shichor, op. cit., p. 100.
39 Ibid., p. 102.
40 Isi Leibler, President's Report, ECAJ Annual Conference, December 1989.
41 E. Zev Sufott, "The Crucial year 1991," in Goldstein, op. cit., pp. 111–116.
42 "Bridging the Gap: World Jewish Congress Mission to Beijing," October 1991, p.7, Archive of Australian Judaica, Fisher Library, University of Sydney.
43 Sufott, op. cit., p. 107.
44 Ibid., p. 13.
45 Ibid., pp. 19–22.
46 Leibler worked closely with Professor Cao Dapeng, deputy secretary-general of the China International Cultural Exchange Group. See IJL Personal File, 1992, Leibler Archive, Jerusalem.
47 The Jewish, Israeli participants were Professors Yoram Dinstein, Saul Friedlander, Rabbi Norman Lamm, Chaim Potok, Rabbi Shlomo Riskin, Professors Anita Shapira, David Sidorsky, and Zwi Werblowsky. The WJC group consisted of Isi Leibler, Israel Singer, Sol Kanee, Zalman Abramov, and Avi Becker, with former Israeli president, Yitzhak Navon also participating. Reuven Merhav, who had retired from his position as director-general of the Israeli Foreign Ministry was also present.
48 "Report on the First International Chinese-Jewish Colloquium," WJC, 6–8 April 1992, ECAJ Archive, Darlinghurst, Sydney.
49 Press Release, 16 March 1992, IJL Personal File, Leibler Archive, Jerusalem.
50 Michael Cohen, "The Asia-Pacific Region," ECAJ Annual Report, 1988.
51 Andrew Jakubowicz, "The Menorah of Fang Bang Lu: Shanghai Modernity and the Jews of China," < d05.cgpublisher.com/proposals/326/index_html > , (accessed 15 September 2005)
52 This was coordinated by a team consisting of Professor Andrew Jakubowicz, Alan Jacobs, Barry Luke and myself, and designed by Derek Freeman & Associates, See the website: < www.cts01.hss.uts.edu.au/ShanghaiSite/menorahsplash/cat/child.html > , (accessed 15 September 2005).
53 This was produced by Mark Edmonson and went to air on Sunday 27 October 2002. See ABC Home Radio Television News ... More Subjects, < www.abc.net.au/compass/s712283.htm > , (accessed 15 September 2005).
54 Mara Moustafine has been a journalist, intelligence analyst, diplomat, senior business executive and at present if the Director of Amnesty International Australia. She is fluent in both English and Russian, < www.jewishaustralia.com/books > , (accessed 25 September 2007).

12

THE DEVELOPING ROLE OF THE
HEBREW BIBLE IN MODERN CHINA

Yiyi Chen

One of the most important pillars of Jewish culture is the Hebrew Bible. No matter which camp of Judaism a modern Jew belongs to, or whether or not he or she considers him or herself a religious person, chances are the above statement will be accepted. In the mind of every Chinese that has some knowledge of the Jewish people, Albert Einstein, Karl Marx, and probably Sigmund Freud and Alan Greenspan are the typical caricatures of Jews. However, few know that the single shared book that all these four and probably all Jews must have read is the Hebrew Bible, or one of its translations into many of the world's languages. This fact also gives us a very telling glimpse into the knowledge of the Hebrew Bible among common Chinese today. If a group of typical Chinese were asked in which book characters such as "Adam," "Eve," or the concept "Noah's Ark" are depicted, for many, the answer "Bible" would come as a fast response; however, few would know that the "Bible" that contains these characters was written in the Hebrew Language, and even fewer would know that the main character of the Bible, "Jesus," according to them, was actually depicted in a different segment of the Bible that was written in another language.

However, this situation has improved very quickly during the last decade or so, especially among many of the college students in China. The change owes to an increase in the study of the Hebrew Bible on Chinese universities campuses. However, this new wave of study of the Bible is just a twenty-first century phase of over 200 years of the developing role of the Hebrew Bible in modern China. This article will trace this development from several aspects, with a focus on various translation efforts.

Historical Translations of the Hebrew Bible

Interesting enough, but not surprisingly, based on scholarly research, it was not the Jews who first introduced the Hebrew Bible to the Chinese.[1] It was the Christian missionaries.

The earliest mention of a Chinese translation of the Hebrew Bible is found on a stone stele dating back to 781 CE. The stele was excavated in the city of Xi'an in 1625. It was erected by Nestorian Christians, who started to settle in China's capital Changan, modern Xi'an, in 635 CE. Many (1,756) Chinese characters were found on the stele, together with 70 Syriac words. The literal translation of the stele's Chinese name is "the Memorial of the Propagation in China of the Luminous Religion from Daqin" (大秦景教流行中国碑, *Daqin* being the Chinese term for the Roman Empire). Among the characters on the stele, we find Chinese expressions such as "real canon" and "translating the Bible." So far, no preserved Bible translations of this period as mentioned in the stele have been found.[2]

Another recorded attempt to translate the Hebrew Bible for the Chinese was in the late thirteenth to early fourteenth century, by Father John of Montecorvino, who mentioned his effort in some of his letters written in Latin. However, the target language of the translation is not Chinese but Mongolian — the language of the ruling ethnic group in China during the Yuan Dynasty. This is yet another translation attempt that did not leave any preserved copies for us.

Perhaps the most famous translator whose works have been preserved is Jesuit Matteo Ricci, who lived in China during the sixteenth century. We have only his rendering of the Ten Commandments in Chinese, and this is the earliest Chinese translation from the Hebrew Bible of which we have a sample. There are many clues that point to the possible fact he only translated sections from the Bible that were considered useful for his missionary activities.

Since the days of Matteo Ricci, there have been more than twenty recorded attempts to translate the Hebrew section of the Bible into Chinese. Each effort is unique and has a story of its own. This article is not the place to dwell on the details of these efforts, which have already been dealt with in my previous writings. The following table summarizes these efforts (Table 1.1).

A glance at the table tells that almost all Hebrew Bible translation initiatives were conducted by Christian missionaries. Probably the only scholar in the long list of translators is Lü Zhenzhong of Yanjing University; yet he was also trained in Christian theology and an ordained pastor.[3] This does not by any means imply that translations by Christian missionaries of the Hebrew Bible are inferior quality; however, although many of these translations were of first-grade scholarly quality, there is an unavoidable tendency for these translations to reflect a Christian view of the books. To be objective, probably the majority of the texts in the Hebrew Bible would not be rendered differently in Chinese by either Christians or non-Christians; however, at places when theological matters do make a difference, the Christian background of the translator most likely would leave a trace, albeit perhaps subconsciously. For example, the word "almh" in Isaiah 7:14 was translated in these translations as "virgin," or a later

Table 1.1 Historical Attempts of Chinese Translations of the Hebrew Bible[a]

#	Date (C.E.)	Translation	Preserved	Chinese
1	781	Nestorian Stele	No	景教碑中提及 "翻经" 活动
2	Late 13th century to early 14th century	John of Montecorvino (Mogolian Translation)	No	《若望孟高维诺译本》：诗篇（蒙古文）
3	Late 16th century	Jesuit Matteo Ricci, leaflets containing a Chinese translation of the Ten Commandments	Yes	利玛窦译 "祖传天主十诫"
4	Late 18th century	Jesuit Louis de Poirot, almost all of the Hebrew Bible books	Never published, manuscript in Beitang Library, Beijing	贺清泰《古新圣经》，未印刷发行
5	1822	English Baptist missionary Joshua Marshman	Published	《马殊曼译本》
6	1823	Robert Morrison and W. C. Milne, both from London; full translation of the Hebrew Bible included, first published in Malacca in modern Malaysia	Published in Malacca, Malaysia	马礼逊《神天圣书》
7	1840	Walter Henry Medhurst, Charles Gutzlaff, E. C. Bridgman, John R. Morrison	Yes	麦都思、郭实腊、裨治文、马儒汉《旧遗诏书》
8	1854	Walter Henry Medhurst and sinologist James Legge, sacrificing accuracy for elegant Chinese	?	《委办译本》
9	1862	American protestant missionary E. C. Bridgman, loyal to original Hebrew	?	《裨治文译本》
10	1868	J. T. Goddard etc., both elegant and accurate	?	高德、罗尔悌、迪因修译《旧约全书》
11	1875	Jewish Episcopal Bishop S. I. J. Schereschewsky	Yes	施约瑟《北京官话旧约全书》
12	1892	De Ya's annotated translation	?	德雅《四史圣经译注》
13	1902	Jewish Episcopal Bishop S. I. J. Schereschewsky	Yes	施约瑟《二指版》
14	1905	Scotland Bible Society Griffith John	Yes	杨格非《旧约浅文理译本》（至雅歌）

Table 1.1 continued.

#	Date (C.E.)	Translation	Preserved	Chinese
15	1919	U. S. A. Presbyterian Church, C. W. Mateer; American Methodist Episcopal, Church G. Owen and S. Lewis; American Congregationalist C. Goodrich and China Inland Mission's F. W. Baller: Chinese Union Version	Yes	《文理和合本》《国语和合译本》
16	1926	Zheng Shoulin and Henry Ruck	Yes	郑寿麟、陆亨理合译《国语新旧库译本》[b]
17	1946	Wu Jingxiong	?	吴经熊《圣咏译义》
18	1955	Di Shouren	?	狄守仁《简易圣经读本》
19	1954 (started in 1935) 1st ed., 1968 with New Testament; 1992 first edition in Mainland China	Italian Franciscan Friar Gabriele Allegra translated directly from Hebrew	Yes	雷永明《思高圣经译本》之旧约部分完成出版
20	1970 (started in 1940)	Yanjing University scholar Lü Zhenzhong, based on original Hebrew	Yes	《吕振中译本》
21	1979, 1984, 1995 editions	United Bible Societies guided Taiwan effort, using Today's English Version as its blueprint; easy-to-follow style	Yes	《当代圣经》（《现代中文译本》）
22	1992	Lockman Foundation from California, based in Hong Kong, sponsored translation, not successful	Yes	《圣经新译本》（向导版）
23	1987 announced beginning of effort	*Commission for Chinese Bible Translation Cooperation* established to translate directly from *BHS* Hebrew texts	Not published yet	

[a]Table adapted from Y. Chen 2005, with modifications and updates. In the "preserved" column, a "?" mark denotes that the author is not aware of whether this version has been preserved, and does not have the resource to track the fact down. The author is also aware of several recent efforts translating the Hebrew Bible into Chinese. However, due to the relative obscurity of these translation efforts, they are not listed here. For comments on some of these efforts, please refer to Y. Chen 2007, p. 58, note 17.

[b]贾保罗 (R. P. Kramers), '最近之中文圣经译本", 载《圣经汉译论文集》, 贾保罗编, ' Hong Kong: Fuqiao publishing, 1965, pp. 29–37.

improved version of "young woman," instead of the probably more appropriate "chief queen."[4] This specific term in this verse has been discussed extensively due to its important role in Christianity theology. However, by rendering "virgin," or this English term's close equivalent in Chinese "处女" (*chunü*), the text delivers a crucially different connotation that was probably not intended by the Hebrew author(s) who composed this line of poetry over 2,500 years ago.[5]

Using the same line of argument, one would propose that a translator of Jewish descent who is a native speaker of the Hebrew language might produce a better translation, without any Christian influences. This argument is problematic due to the dynamic history of the Hebrew language itself. It is undeniable that a translator well immersed in Jewish culture would have many fewer difficulties in dealing with the Hebrew Bible's original text. One reason for this is that a well-educated Jew, according to the standards that existed before the modern era, should have extensive knowledge of the *Mishnah* and *Talmud*, which are both rabbinical discussions of Jewish law that all supposedly originated from, and are based on, the Hebrew Bible; the former is also regarded as the parallel oral tradition with the Hebrew Bible. In the above table, Jewish Episcopal Bishop S. I. J. Schereschewsky was such a person; born a Jew in Lithuania in 1831, he went to Germany to study for the rabbinate and there he converted to Christianity. By the age of 28, he had already finished his priesthood training in the US and was sent to China by the Episcopal Church. Due to his conversion, Schereschewsky's translation does not differ much from other Christian translations in terms of theological point of view. Nevertheless, his intimate knowledge of the Hebrew language and close collaboration with several native Chinese speakers during the translation process did help to produce one of the best accepted vernacular translations till this day.[6]

As today's biblical scholars understand, not only is the Hebrew language in the Hebrew Bible different from later periods such as Mishnaic Hebrew, but also the Israelite religions as reflected in the book are distinct from later period Judaism. Extensive research about ancient Palestine and the Ancient Near East in general, during the last century or so, played a crucial role in improving our understanding of the Hebrew Bible, thus resulting in better translations.[7]

Therefore, the new task for the last decade or so has been to introduce the vast amount of knowledge accumulated during the past century about the *Sitz im Leben* of the Hebrew Bible, in order to give the Chinese people a better understanding of the Hebrew Bible.

Modern Initiatives to Study and Translate the Hebrew Bible

Efforts by Christian missionaries during the last several centuries, especially the last two, have contributed tremendously to the understanding of the Hebrew Bible. After the establishment of communist China in 1949, the majority of the Chinese lost contact with the Hebrew Bible, or Bible in general, for political and ideological reasons. Since reform efforts started in China in 1978, three types of activities developed in chronological stages and played important roles in bringing knowledge of the Hebrew Bible to China and the Chinese people.

The first factor was the mutual exchange of visiting scholars and students between China and Western developed countries, where the Bible has a very crucial status in social and value systems. To be sure, the first several waves of Chinese exchange scholars and students were in fields that were not even remotely related to biblical studies. Yet these were the first groups of Chinese intellectuals who started to observe the big economic gap between developing China and the developed West. Besides the search for answers in advances in science and technology, they also started to pay attention to the ideology that drives Western societies. Since the mid-1980s, the study of Western philosophical classics has been amongst the most popular activities on university campuses. Hundreds of masterpieces in the field were translated into Chinese and published widely. Names such as Jean-Jacques Rousseau, Immanuel Kant, and Baruch de Spinoza, became very familiar to young Chinese intellectuals, especially those in the fields of study of social sciences and humanities. People reading these works will sooner or later encounter topics related to, or based on, the Hebrew Bible. Therefore, the opening of China to the World in the late 1970s and early 1980s renewed a link that had been broken for 40 years between Chinese and Western culture in general, and the Hebrew Bible in particular.

The second stage of reintroducing the Hebrew Bible to China was a gradual process. As a result of both China getting wealthier and its own policy towards foreigners visiting the country becoming more lenient, new waves of Christian missionaries started to set foot on the mainland from the mid- to late 1980s. Their activities drew growing interest in the Bible, either from their followers or non-Christians. Although the focus was on the Greek New Testament, with several books from the Hebrew Bible such as Psalms and Isaiah, the stories in the Hebrew Bible were naturally more attractive to the general Chinese public, who are raised in a culture more accustomed to storytelling. Despite tensions between these missionaries and the central government of China, they have become more and more active over the last 20 years. One of the main catalysts for the rapid increase in Christian missionaries' is embedded in China's own everincreasing social inequity during the last two decades of tremendous economic development. Spiritual needs of the common people have become more and more apparent while communism has never been a religious system; its rule in China has created a vacuum for people's religious need. Some naturally turned to Christianity, others to Buddhism or Daoism, for their spiritual aspirations.

The third type of activity that has played a contributing role in extending the knowledge of the Hebrew Bible to the Chinese is the development of

Jewish studies and, more directly, biblical studies scholarship, in many prestigious Chinese universities. China started a Hebrew language program as early as 1985 in Peking University.[8] During their time on campus, the dozen students of the first class received systematic exposure to Jewish cultural classics, amongst which the Hebrew Bible had an integral part. Professor Zhang Ping of Tel Aviv University, one of the prominent scholars comparing classic Chinese and Jewish philosophies, started his first exposure to Jewish culture in this class. The second class started in 1990, and by the time China and Israel established embassy level diplomatic relationship in 1992, these students were already fluent speakers of Modern Hebrew. Among their class material were famous passages from the Hebrew Bible, read and explained in the Hebrew language itself. Some of the students went to the US to pursue graduate-level training in biblical studies and related fields. This marks a new era of serious research about the Hebrew Bible in China.

Faculty members in several Chinese universities started the study of the Hebrew Bible as early as the early 1980s through their Western literature, history, and philosophy courses. Most prominently, Professor Zhu Weizhi (1905–99) from Nankai University, one of the scholars trained before communist China, started to recruit and advise graduate students in biblical literature. Among his protégés, Professor Liang Gong, now at Henan University, directs a center for biblical literature and has trained a few dozen graduate students who read the Hebrew and Greek Bible as a literary work.

The Hebrew Bible has also been approached as one component of Jewish culture, thus being studied in the Jewish studies programs at three universities. The earliest one is mentioned above, at Peking University, together with the Hebrew language program. The second one was the Jewish Culture Center established in Nanjing University by Professor Xu Xin, who was the translator and editor of the first Jewish Culture Encyclopedia in Chinese; his team is among the most active in Jewish studies in China. Prominent scholar Song Lihong is an expert in second to first century BCE Jewish history. Shandong University's Jewish Studies program has an emphasis on comparative religion, where the research of Professor Fu Youde focuses on the revival of Confucianism based on his analysis of the history of Judaism. Perhaps one of the most bold acts by Professor Fu was the hiring of Avrum Ehrlich, an Australian Jew who was trained at an early age in various schools of Talmudic studies in Israel, is an ordained rabbi, was once a combat medic in Israel's defense forces, and has a doctorate in leadership strategies of Hasidic masters from the University of Sydney, to work as a full professor at the university. The diverse and unique background of Professor Ehrlich has proven to be extremely beneficial to the students in their pursuit to understand the Jewish culture in general, and the Hebrew Bible in particular, especially the opportunity for the students to learn about the Hebrew Bible from a traditional Jewish culture's perspective with a modern Israeli Jewish touch.

Outside of mainland China, the most important center for the study of the Hebrew Bible is at the Chinese University of Hong Kong,[9] where Professor Archie Lee, trained at Edinburgh University in the 1970s in the study of the Hebrew Bible based on Ancient Near East context, has published extensively since the early 1980s on the hermeneutics of the Hebrew Bible from a crosscultural context perspective. Among his most recognized discussions, is the naming of the Hebrew God in various Asian cultures.[10] During the last decade, he has trained over ten graduate students with the most strenuous methodology according to Western standards. Besides by Lee himself, these students have also been taught by many of the established scholars from around the world in their respecting areas in the general Ancient Near East studies field, as well as in Palestinian and Hebrew studies. All these students are native Chinese speakers, and most are from mainland China. Many have started, or will soon start, teaching Hebrew Bible studies in universities all over mainland China. This fresh wave of scholars will eventually bring the standard of Chinese university students' understanding of the book to a significantly higher level in a much more widespread fashion.

Before leaving this topic, a mention of the contribution of the internet, information technology, and the role computing linguistics played in the translation effort of the Hebrew Bible is well in order. For example, Andi Wu of GrapeCity Inc. and Kirk Lowery of Westminster Hebrew Institute are collaborating to create "A Cantillation-Based Hebrew Tree Bank" (article presented at a Near Eastern Studies international conference at Peking University, June 2006) using computer modeling technologies. One of the main goals of such a tree bank is to facilitate group translators in their collaborative efforts to generate syntactically uniform Chinese sentences faithful to the syntax of the original Hebrew; the model, therefore, can be used to verify the Chinese translation in order to eliminate unavoidable human errors and inconsistencies between different translators, to maintain a homogeneous style in the Chinese version. *Wikipedia*'s English site has been selectively opened to Chinese internet users by the Chinese government since early 2007. The information contained there will benefit both Hebrew Bible scholars and students. Many top-level universities started to pay to subscribe to online scholar resources such as *JSTOR*, the humanities and social science scholarly journal archive. This will also benefit the Hebrew Bible scholars. Free online resources such as *Google Scholar* and *Google Books* are available for use within mainland China, although the connection is not stable; today it is already much better than before this technology was available, when scholars could not gain access to many important research resources without traveling abroad. *Wikipedia* technology also opened the door for a cross location real-time collaboration amongst scholars engaged in the Hebrew studies field. Relatively loosely edited weblogs (blogs), linked with more coordinated *Wiki*s have made a dynamically annotated Hebrew

Bible translation possible — a translation that can self-improve and grow organically based on the organic growth of the entire scholarly communities' knowledge of the Hebrew Bible.

Towards an Idealistic Paradigm in Improving the Understanding of the Hebrew Bible in China

The editor of this volume suggested that I list 10–20 major terms in the Hebrew Bible, and my suggestion of how they should be translated into Chinese, with brief explanations and justifications.[11] I do not think this chapter is an appropriate place for such an exercise for a couple of reasons. First, this is a chapter written in English. Besides the awkward and unnecessary (were the article written in Chinese) English transliteration and unavoidable translations and/or explanations of the involved Chinese (supposedly) equivalents of the Hebrew originals, raising such a list in the English language is actually assuming the readers, in order to take advantage of the information, must be knowledgeable in all three languages involved. This assumption by itself does not seems to be detrimental; however, if we borrow slightly the post-modern point of view, the act itself is proclaiming that the article is intended for a very limited number of readers who are privileged with in-depth knowledge of all three languages; the act itself can be easily labeled discriminating as it implies the dominant role of the English language in the discussion of Hebrew Bible's (Chinese or other non-Western languages) translation matters. The above-stated reason for avoiding such a suggested list reads like a word puzzle, but it does present a very important standpoint of the translation task, i.e. who should be the dominant decision-making cultural group when different choices present themselves in front of the translators — in this particular case, whether it should be the group who knows English well (thus, the English translations), or the group who speaks the actual target language.[12]

The second reason that I do not intend to list any specific Chinese translation suggestions is closely related to the first one stated above — I am fully aware of my training background, thus the limitation that comes with it. As a secular scholar who was trained in the general background of Ancient Near East and the cultural history of ancient Palestine, my point of view will inevitably be reflected in my translation choices, especially in those crucial terms that have theological implications and rendered differently based on the different understanding of the Israelite religion.[13]

I do not intend to apologize for my training background and my particular point of view in the above paragraph. As a matter of fact, any translation is full of personal choices, sometimes consciously, sometimes subconsciously. Sometimes, even a commentator of a translation takes up a stance with obvious biases. For example, when Eber commented on Schereschewsky's rendering of Genesis 17:10-11, the passage on circumcision, she stated:

Circumcision, which is included in God's covenant with Abraham (Genesis 17:10–11), presented a similar problem, but was handled differently. The term used for the Hebrew word was *geli* which may be defined as ritual cutting. In the translation, Abraham is told to circumcise, but the first part of verse 11, specifying what is to be cut, is omitted and the injunction to circumcise is simply repeated. Verse 14 is handled similarly. The omission was of no consequence to either missionaries or converts, and Schereschewsky's decision, based, no doubt, on avoiding embarrassing explanations, is perfectly understandable.[14]

Eber might be right in asserting that "the omission was of no consequence to either missionaries or converts;" she might also be correct in claiming that the omission "based, no doubt, on avoiding embarrassing explanations, is perfectly understandable." However, Eber's statements are based on the social context in China at the turn of the twentieth century. In other words, it is her assumption that the mention of the term "foreskin" then in China would be embarrassing. Even if this might be true,[15] it was only true then and there, i.e. in late nineteenth century and early twentieth century conservative China. Judging from some of the Western language translations of the Hebrew Bible in existence during the same period, the use, faithfully to the original Hebrew texts, of "foreskins," obviously did not embarrass the Western readers of the same era. We can probably safely assume that in today's China, this term will not raise many eyebrows if placed blatantly in the translated text, as the original Hebrew text did. Therefore, a translator's concern may disappear or at least diminish with the progress of time and the development of the receiving society.

This example is a reminder to us that, as modern day interpreters of the Hebrew Bible, we may need to be very cautious in one aspect of our efforts. We need to be conscious that in our translation(s) of the Hebrew Bible, by omitting information that we do know and understand, we are actually exercising the power of depriving the readers of the translation(s) the right to a very similar reading experience of the original Hebrew text. And who are we to have such a power to decide what to omit and what not to? When we exercise such power, we are no longer translating; we are interpreting the text with our own point of view. The readers who are eager to learn what the original texts want to tell them and what the cultural background behind the texts was, are left with a fragmented, if not tinted, piece of work to deal with at best.

Due to my understanding of my own limitation, as well as all scholars' limitations, whatever our backgrounds, Jewish, Christian, or secular, I prefer not to list translation suggestions in this article for specific terms in the Hebrew Bible. Instead, I would like to suggest the possibility of approaching a new translation paradigm based on general scholarship of the Hebrew Bible in today's China.

The first pitfall to avoid in a new translation initiative is the likelihood for the task to fall into the hands of one single methodology school, whether it is just a sect of Christianity, or Jewish studies scholars, or only secular scholars. Each school will bring its own strength, but inevitably its own limitations. Therefore, instead of a methodology monopoly, we might propose a paradigm of methodology mutual tolerance. In this paradigm, participating scholars are to respect each other's training and research background; both strength and weakness. Instead of a constant undercurrent fight of the ideology politics; all participants should channel their energy to collaborate on specific textual analysis tasks. This way, the team can consolidate and maximize what is otherwise each individual's very limited energy and time. Pooling the collective expertise is the only feasible method to guarantee the highest possible quality of the resulting product.

No translation of the Hebrew Bible can be considered as perpetually the best; it can only be the best at the time of its production, by the best collaboration of society's collective expertise. It is not hard to produce another "new" Chinese translation of the Hebrew Bible; it is hard to produce one that really represents today's best level of collective scholarship and understanding of the original texts, on an approaching ideology-free, though not necessarily religion-free, platform. If there is one ideology to be represented in the translation, it should be the same one as the original group of people who authored the Hebrew Bible. A new Chinese translation of the Hebrew Bible that reflects the point of views of one religion or another that bases their beliefs on the book is probably not as urgent in today's China as one that faithfully represents the religious view within the book.

Proponents of new translation efforts of the Hebrew Bible have different, albeit all glorious, reasons for their cause. Whatever the reasons are, one fact is undeniable — more and more Chinese are looking into one of the cornerstones of Western civilization, the Bible, both as a literary masterpiece, a cultural artifact, and a religious canon based on which thousands years of human history evolved, for inspirations to solve many social and spiritual problems in today's China after twenty years of tremendous economic development. The searching does not guarantee any meaningful result, but the process itself has already brought much improved mutual understanding between China and the West. The task can be better accomplished by a diversified group of philosophers, social scientists, theologians, politicians, and other cultural studies scholars.

As scholars of the Hebrew Bible, whichever background we are from, it is our primary task to first give the interested parties a faithfully translated text to work with. In this, we probably do not want to implant our own point of view; at least we should try. If the collaborative paradigm works, it might play a constructive part in the new stage of the developing role of the Hebrew Bible in modern China.

Notes

1 There are numerous discussions on the Kaifeng Jews (the earliest datable Jewish community that found their way in China), and many touched upon their scriptures, yet there is no mentioning that they ever attempted a translation of the Bible to Chinese for non-Jewish readers. In Jewish history, almost all attempts of translating the Hebrew Bible to another language by the Jewish people themselves were for their own usage; this is significantly different from Christians' Bible translation efforts. For the latest bibliographical information in a single volume on the Kaifeng Jews and their history, see: Donald D. Leslie, *Jews and Judaism in Traditional China: a Comprehensive Bibliography*, Sankt Augustin: Monumenta Serica Monograph, XLV, 1999.

2 Please refer to Y. Chen, 2005 for further bibliographical details. Based on the information found in a Nestorian Church canon Zunjing (尊经) discovered at Dunhuang (敦煌) in 1907–08, translated books by the Nestorians from the Hebrew Bible were Genesis, Exodus, the book of Psalms, the book of Zechariah, and the book of Hosea, among others.

3 "吕振中," *Wikipedia*, < *zh.wikipedia.org* > (accessed 31 August, 2007).

4 See Y. Chen 2007, p. 54. Detailed discussion on the rational of translating the term to "young woman" can be found in various publications, for example, in Dingbang Cai 2005. The translation of "chief queen" is proposed by Nicholas Wyatt 2005, p. 63, based partially on Ugaritic lexical evidence.

5 For additional bibliographical information, see *Anchor Bible Dictionary*'s entry "Virgin" etc. Ancient Israelites' concept of virginity was probably not very different from the general Ancient Near East; for a comprehensive discussion of this concept in the Ancient Near East in general from Assyriology perspective (and extensive bibliography), see Jerrold Cooper, "Virginity in Ancient Mesopotamia," *Rencontre Assyriologique Internationale 47*, pp. 91–112, 2002.

6 Extensive discussion about his work are to be found in I. Eber 1993 and 1999.

7 Y. Chen, 2007, discusses this point extensively.

8 Now, one can consult the article by Z. Meng and Y. Chen, 2007, for more detailed description of the Hebrew Studies program at Peking University.

9 Due to limited access to relevant high quality material and data about Taiwan's academic development of Hebrew Studies, the author regrets that he cannot cover this topic in this article.

10 See, for example, A. C. Lee, 2004 and references there.

11 The suggested terms are "YHWH, Elohim, Israel, Abraham, Isaac, Jacob, Hebrew, sin, commandment, law, ordnances, Shabbat, and so on;" based on personal email communications with Dr. A. Ehrlich.

12 A similar issue was raised by A. Lee (e.g. 2004) on various occasions; his major concern is not on the translators' knowledge of the English language, but whether a Christian translator's choices should weigh more when translators try to decide on ambiguous choices.

13 For in-depth discussion of this topic, see Y. Chen, 2006.

14 I. Eber, 1993, p. 228.

15 The social context then, based on some of the literatures of the time, was actually not that conservative at all. However, we do not want to dwell on this point due to its irrelevancy to this article.

MODERN HEBREW LITERATURE IN CHINA

Zhong Zhiqing

In China, many people begin to know Hebrew Literature from the Bible. In the view of Chinese people, the Bible is not only a religious work, but also of great literary value. An important source of Western civilization, the Bible has left us a series of "puzzles" to reckon with. Therefore, from the end of the 1970s, the Bible became a part of the course of Oriental Literary History taught at universities in China.

Generally, the Bible as literature taught in China can be classified into two main groups. One group changes the map of Bible according to literary genres, accordingly, the Bible was divided into tales and legends, e.g. the creation by God, the flood story; historical stories, e.g. the story of Joshua, the story of Samson; novels, e.g. Ruth; play, e.g. Job; and poems, e.g. Psalms, Songs of Songs, Lamentations, and so forth. The methodology they applied is similar to that of the new interpretations of Western literary and Biblical scholars since the 1970s, although at the very beginning "terms as literature was still relatively new," to some extent "as a voice crying in the wilderness."[1] The other group discusses the Bible as literature according to the traditional designation by Jews as *Torah* (Five Books of Moshe), *Nevim* (Prophets), and *Ketuvim* (Writings). Meanwhile, there are also some scholars who engage or try to engage in the programs of comparative culture, comparative philosophy, and comparative literature between these two ancient civilizations. However, it must be noted that the versions of the Bible on which they are mainly based were not translated from Hebrew, but from English, Greek, or Latin.

Modern Jewish literature was translated into Chinese starting from the May 4th Movement of 1919. Mao Dun and Hu Yuzhi, the pioneers of China's New Culture Movement which advocated fighting against classical Chinese ideology, translated Sholem Aleichem's writings from Yiddish into Chinese in the 1920s; in the 1930s, Tang Xuzhi translated Sholom Asch's *The God of Vengeance* from English into Chinese. As for Modern Hebrew literature, a few Hebrew poems were also published in the 1920s in *Xiaoshuo*

Yuebao, a monthly magazine for novels; however, a few decades after that scholars and translators did not pay any attention to Hebrew literature. Reasons for that are from language, ideology and esthetic interest, which are not my focus in this article.[2]

In the 1970s and 1980s, Taiwan published a number of Israeli works, including *A Collection of Contemporary Israeli Short Stories* (1971); short novels by Shai Agnon (translated by Wang Runhua and Zhu Biyun, in *A Collection of Nobel Writers*, 1983) and Aharon Appelfeld (translated by Lv Wenling, 1987). Almost at the same time, a short story by S. Y. Agnon was published in mainland China (translated by Qian Hongjia, 1981). Compared with literature from Russia, Europe, American, and other Oriental countries, there was almost no voice for Israeli literature until the beginning of the 1990s.

The establishment of the diplomatic relationship between China and Israel in 1992 broke the silence in translating Hebrew works. In the same year, three Hebrew titles in Chinese translation were published; namely, *An Anthology of Hebrew Short Stories,* edited by Xu Xin; Songs of Jerusalem: a Collection of Poetry by Yehuda Amichai, translated by Fu Hao; and *A Concise History of Modern Hebrew Literature* by Joseph Klausner, translated by Lu Peiyong. According to the statistics of the Institute from the Translation of Hebrew Literature in Israel:

> About 60 books of fiction have been published since 1992 and there are agreements for the publication of at least 15 new titles within the near future. The data base at the Institute for the Translation of Hebrew Literature records publication in Chinese of about 800 entries of Hebrew literature: short stories, poems, books for children etc. While the decade of 1986–96 saw the publication of 12 Hebrew books in Chinese translation, the last ten years have been much more fruitful with 48 titles published.[3]

Most of the Hebrew works were translated from English or other languages, and the academic circles sometimes muttered their disapproval of this phenomenon. No doubt, the most idealized way is to translate Hebrew Literature from the original. But is it impossible to reach this realm in China nowadays simply because there are very few people who are working in this field? Even the University students in Hebrew studies hardly have any background in general literature and Hebrew literature due to current teaching programs.

Actually, cultural, in particular literary, training is a basic requirement for a translator. "The most difficult thing in translation is not the language, but a different culture."[4] Such cultural difficulty comes in two parts: one is the ability of mastering another culture, which can help you to understand the original text; the other is the attainments of your maternal culture, which can make you see through the style, the mood, the emotion, the contextual meaning, the cultural heritage, the national spirit, etc., in an accurate way, to open a new channel of conversation and bridge between writers and readers. A good translator is requested not only to have a good training of foreign language, but also to have a sound academic foundation in literature, as well as translation experience. Most of the English translators of Hebrew literature are bilingual, or even have two mother tongues, which means that they were born in English-speaking countries and immigrated to Israel afterwards, or vice versa. Above all, they grew up with a Jewish cultural background. Their understanding of the Hebrew verse and their English expression are close to perfection. Although something is still lost while translating, the translation is definitely reliable and lucid. By comparison, it is extremely difficult for Chinese scholars and translators, who come from another maternal culture, to achieve the same level as the translators of Hebrew literature into other languages in Hebrew, literature, culture, and translation experience. Therefore, if those who translate Chinese from English had good training in literature, translation techniques, and ability to deal with the intricacies of culture, they would produce good translation works. Of course, if such translators have a chance to achieve a good command of Hebrew, it is as if the tiger has grown wings. On the other hand, however, a Hebrew learner in China perhaps has an advantage of understanding Hebrew context, though they should work very hard to enter that context. After all, language is just a tool; a good translator needs a diversity of cultural attainments and a lifetime of experience.

Translation of the History of Modern Hebrew Literature

Up to now, only two works on the history of modern Hebrew literature have been translated into Chinese. One is, as we have mentioned earlier, *A Concise History of Modern Hebrew Literature* by Joseph Klausner (1874–1958). This work was translated from Arabic. It shows a general map of modern Hebrew literature from Haskala to the early years of the statehood of Israel. The other is Gershon Shaked's English work *Modern Hebrew Fiction*, translated by Zhong Zhiqing. *Modern Hebrew Fiction* is an abridgement and translation of Shaked's Hebrew study *Hebrew Fiction 1880–1980 (Hasiporet ha 'ivtir 1880–1980*, Jerusalem: Keter and hakibutz Hameuchad, 1977–1999), which encompassed five volumes and was highly detailed and annotated. Shaked discusses internal literary developments in the tradition of Hebrew prose and the interaction between social processes and the writing. He focuses on the most notable writers and their best works.

Shaked's work is of higher academic value and ideological significance. As written in the editor's foreword, Shaked locates the relationship between the esthetic and the social–political, cultural, and historical contexts of Hebrew fiction. He pulls into view the ultimate intertext: the play between literature and life. More importantly, Shaked performs another function as well, one not usually required of literary historians, at least not those who write about the major Western traditions. He conveys those features of the canon of modern Hebrew fiction that qualify it to enter into the arena of contemporary cultural and literary study.[5]

As a translator of this intensive and significant work, I cannot help asking myself whether the common Chinese readers who have no Hebrew cultural background and sometimes confuse the definition of Jewish literature, Israeli literature, and Hebrew literature, could understand the intent of the author; it is equally questionable whether students of the Hebrew language, who, to my astonishment, even regard Kafka as an Israeli author, could follow the texts. These two groups of Hebrew readership are typical in China.

The Translation of Hebrew Fiction

The translation of modern Hebrew fiction is more impressive. At the introduction of Hebrew literature to China, the publishers and the people involved in this cultural distribution paid close attention to Hebrew classics. Early collections of Hebrew short stories both in Taiwan and in mainland China mainly included the writings of S. Y. Agnon, S. Yizhar, Haim Hazaz, Benjamin Tammuz, Moshe Shamir, Yehuda Amichai, etc. The mainland collections were distributed later than those in Taiwan, therefore mainland collections selected several world famous Hebrew authors who came onto the literary scene in 1960s such as Amos Oz and Aharon Appelfeld. After that, some literary magazines published special issues on Hebrew or Israeli Literature (*Cotemporary Foreign Literature*, vol. 2, 1991; *World Literature*, vol.6, 1994, etc.), and selected classical writers. For instance, *World Literature*, one of the best literary translation magazines in China, published a special issue on *Contemporary Israeli Literature* in 1994. This included "The Continuing Silence of a Poet" by A.B. Yehushua; "Where the Jackals Howl" by Amos Oz; "Momic," an excerpt from David Grossman's masterpiece *See Under: Love*; and some leading poets.

At the same time, a number of Hebrew novels and novellas were also translated into Chinese in succession, among them *Three Days and a Child* by A.B. Yehushua, translated by Chen Yiyi, 1993; *The Bridal Canopy* by S. Y. Agnon, translated by Xun Xin and Liu Hongyi, 1999; and *Past Continues* by Yaakov Shabtai, translated by Mai Lijuan and Xie Yong, 1995; amongst others.

In the years that followed, some publishers started to work on a series of Hebrew novels. In 1996, Yilin Press in Nanjing bought the copyrights for, and published, five books by Amos Oz: *Elsewhere Perhaps*, translated by Yao Yongcai, 1998; *My Michael*, translated by Zhong Zhiqing, 1998; *To Know A Woman*, translated by Fu Hao and Ke Yanbin, 1999; *Perfect Peace*, translated by Yao Yongqiang and Guo Hongtao, 1999; and *Fima*, translated by Fan Hongsheng, 2000. This was the first time a single Hebrew Israeli author was introduced on a large scale in China. Female writers Chi Li and Xu Kun gave positive understanding to Amos Oz's view of woman; Chi Li mentioned many times the influence of Amos Oz's poetic and concise language on her own writings.[6] Professor Ding Fan, a leading critic at Nanjing University, shows deep identification to Amos Oz and the culture he represented.[7] In 1999, *My Michael* received a national book prize in Foreign Literature in China; it was also the first Israeli book that won a prize in China. Later on, *My Michael* and *To Know A Woman* were reprinted and republished by Huang Guan Publishing House in Taiwan in 2004. Just before Amos Oz's first visit to China in 2007, these two novels were republished in mainland China by Yilin Press. Another Hebrew writer who was published by a Chinese publisher independently is Uri Orlev. Three of his novels, including *The Man From the Other Side*, translated by Yang Hengda and Yang Fan; *Lydia, Queen of Palestine*, translated by Yang Hengda and Yang Rong; and *The Island on Bird Street*, translated by Li Wenjun; were published by Hebei Children's Publishing House in 2000.

In cooperation with the Institute for the Translation of Hebrew Literature, Anhui Literature and Art Publishing House published a best Hebrew Fiction Series in 1998. It included Yosef Haim Brenner's *Breakdown and Bereavement*, translated by Luo Han and Meng Jian; David Vogel's *Married Life*, translated by Yang Dongxia and Yang Haihong; Yossel Birstein's *A Face in the Clouds*, translated by Liao Huixiang and Xiao Yaozhen; and Ruth Almog's *Tiny Coat*, translated by Diaso Haifeng and Wang Mingqian. Also supported by the Institute for the Translation of Hebrew Literature, in 2000, Baihuazhou Literature and Art Publishing House published a series of contemporary Israeli novels edited by Mr. Gao Qiufu, former deputy President of Xinhua News Agency. These four books are Yehoshua Kanaz *After the Holidays*, translated by Zhong Zhiqing; Birstein's *Collector*, translated by Sui Lijun; Yoram Kaniuk's *Aunt Shlomzion the Great*, translated by Shen Zhihong and Gao Sui; Aryeh Sivan's *Adonis*, translated by Dai Huikun and Xiaodai. This series of books were reprinted and also received the national book prize in Foreign Literature in China. In addition, China Social Sciences Publishing House published Ruth Almog's *Death in the Rain*, translated by Zhu Meihui; Orly Castel-Bloom's *Mina Liza*, translated by Yang Yugong; and Tammuz's *Minotaur*, translated by Zheng Yalan, in 1998. Presently Shanghai Yiwen Press is working on ten Hebrew classical books; four of them can be found in the market now. Among them there are Amos Oz's *Black Box*, translated by Zhong Zhiqing, 2004; S. Y. Agnon's *A Simple Story*, translated by Xu Chongliang, 2004; Meir Shalev's *Blue Mountain*, translated by Yu Haijiang and Zhangying, 2005; and David Grossman's *See Under: Love*, translated by Zhang Chong and Zhang Qiong, 2005. The publication of these series marks the fact that Hebrew literature in Chinese translation has become more and more systematic and scaled-up.

Special issues on Hebrew literature in periodicals are also well organized; for instance, *World Literature* published "The Younger Generation Israeli Writers" in 1999 and "The Holocaust Literature in Israel" in 2003, highlighting a specific literary imagination and literary group, together with a good review essay or introductive preface. Meanwhile, the editor's thought and motive to readers can also be found through People's Literature Publishing House's *The Scorch Land: A Selection of Modern Israeli Stories*, edited by Gao Qiufu, 1998; and Chinese Women's Press *The Mediterranean Rose: A Selection of Israeli Women Writers*.

At the same time, some publishers hoped to conquer the book market and started to import bestsellers. For instance, People's Literature Press bought the copyright for Zeruya Shalev's *Love Life* translated by Zhou Xiaoping, and the first print run will be 8,000 copies. However, it will take time to see whether the bestsellers in Israel and other European countries are appreciated by Chinese readers.

The Translation of Poetry

In contrast with Hebrew fiction, translation of poetry translation has been less frequent; however, the translations are of good quality. As mentioned before, *Song Of Jerusalem: The Selected Poems of Yehuda Amichai* translated by Fu Hao has influenced many younger generation Chinese poets. Almost ten years later, Hebei Educational Publishing House published two volumes of *A Selection of Yehuda Amichai's Poems*. The first Chinese collection of Hebrew poets was published by People's Literature Press, edited and translated by Gao Qiufu, including around 200 pieces of poems by 43 established Hebrew poets, such as Bialik, Gilboa, Alterman, and Amichai. In the meantime, some literary magazines published a large number of Hebrew poets such as Yehuda Amichai, Yona Wallah, Dalia Ravikovitch, Meir Weiseltier, etc. Chinese readers were deeply touched by Hebrew poetry's content and style.

Research

Hebrew literary study in China is still in its early stages. In the context of Chinese academics, Hebrew literature is regarded as "the literatures of small country and minor languages," or minorstream literature (*xiaoguo wenxue, xiao yuzhong wenxue*, 小国文学, 小语种文学), a special terminology for some regional literatures such as Arabic, Persian, or even Spanish literature; while English, American, and French literature are regarded as mainstream, Russian literature is still a controversial issue.[8] There are not so many people who are dedicated in this field. Starting in the early 1990s, Chinese scholars began to introduce Hebrew literature to China. Most of these scholars were translators, such as Xun Xin, Gao Qiufu, Lin Xianghua, Fu Hao, and later Zhong

Zhiqing. Xun Xin's *An Introduction of Modern Hebrew Literature, Israeli Literature in the Last Four Decades,* and Gao Qiufu, Fu Hao, and Zhong Zhiqing's preface to their selected works are basically translations, though they instilled some Chinese thinking while reading Hebrew Literature, which shows a different point of view from the Westerners.

A Study of Contemporary Israeli Authors by the present author, the first Chinese scholar awarded a Ph.D., from the Department of Hebrew Literature in Israel under the supervision of Professor Yigal Schwarz and Professor Andrew H. Plaks at Ben-Gurion University, is the first Chinese work on contemporary Israeli literature from pre-1948 to the present.

This work attempts to give a general map of Israeli literature over the last few decades. It includes eight chapters, investigating chronologically three generations of Israeli authors: "Sabra Writers and the Literature in the 1940s and 1950s," including the writings of Smilansky Yizhar, Moshe Shamir and other Sabra writers and poets; Shai Agnon and authors from the Diaspora; "New Wave Writers and the Literature in the 1960s and 1970s," including Amos Oz, Abraham B. Yehoshua, Yehoshua Kenaz, Yoram Kniuk, Yaakov Shabtai, Yehuda Amichai, Amalia Kahana-Carmon and female writers; "Younger Generation Writers and Literature in the 1980s and 1990s," including David Grossman, Meir Shalev and female writers, as well as a few Arabic authors in Israel.

Special concern is given to questions such as Holocaust literature within the context of nation-building, including the Eichmann Trial and its impact on Israeli Society; writings of native-born Israelis, such as Haim Guori and Hanoch Bartov; Holocaust survivors, such as Aharon Appelfeld, Ka-Tzetnik, and Ori Orlev; the Second Generation, such as Nava Semel, Savyon Liebrecht, etc.; the image of Arabs in Israeli literature; Israeli literature and religion, including some topics that mostly interest Chinese readers, such as religion in contemporary Israeli society, traditional religion motif, for instance the binding of Isaac, David and Goliath, the few against many in contemporary texts, image of God in contemporary writings; and the challenges of Israelis after the founding of the State; with authors including Smilansky, Yizhar, Tammutz, Yehoshua, Oz, and Grossman.

In October 2006, at the proposal of Professor Yigal Schwartz, the director for the Center of Jewish and Israeli Literature and Culture Studies at Ben-Gurion University, the Institute of Foreign Literature at Chinese Academy of Social Sciences (CASS), a leading research institution in China, co-organized with Ben-Gurion University a seminar of "Literature and National Awareness." A dozen Chinese and Israeli literary scholars were sitting together for the first time to discuss literary issues. This significant event might stimulate Chinese scholars and common readers to pay more attention to Hebrew literature and culture.

More excitingly, at the end of August 2007, Amos Oz, a leading Israeli writer, came to visit China, invited by the Institute of Foreign Literature at

CASS with the assistance of the Israeli Embassy in China. In addition to launching *A Tale of Love and Darkness* (translated by Zhong Zhiqing, Yilin Press, 2007), several lectures at CASS, Beijing University and elsewhere, cultural activities in Beijing and Shanghai, a seminar on the works of Amos Oz with more than 100 participants was held by the Institute of Foreign Literature at CASS. This is the first time such a seminar had been held in China, devoted to the writings of a single Hebrew writer. Three generations of Chinese writers such as Mo Yan, Yan Lianke, Xu Kun, Qiu Huadong, and Zhang Yueran attended it. Mo Yan, Yan Lianke, Xu Kun, and Qiu Huadong contributed a special understanding of Oz's *A Tale of Love and Darkness*, and *My Michael*, and Oz's image in China. Nilli Cohen, the director of the Institute for the Translation of Hebrew Literature talked about the reception of Amos Oz worldwide. Scholars like Chen Zhongyi, an expert in Spanish literature and the director of the Institute of Foreign Literature at CASS, Lu Jiande, an expert in English Literature, and Zhong Zhiqing, specializing in Hebrew literature presented a paper on Oz's *Fima*, *My Michael*, *Elsewhere Perhaps*, and *A Tale of Love and Darkness*. Gao Qiufu, a former president of the Xinhua News Agency and a forerunner in the cultural exchange between China and Israel, and Fu Hao, an expert in English literature and a translator of Israeli literature, talked about their contacts with Hebrew literature.

The literary characters of Amos Oz discussed during the seminar, such as Noga in *Elsewhere Perhaps*, Hanna in *My Michael*, Fima in *Fima* (*The Third Condition*), father, mother and the little child in *A Tale of Love and Darkness* lived provincial lives. However, they were revived and traveled to China through literary translation and discussion. That is why Amos Oz was deeply convinced that literature contains a certain magic, "the more local it is, the more universal it might become; the more provincial the story is, the more universal it might become." He also highly evaluated the work of translators, "the single most important invention in the history of human civilization is the translation." Only through translation, can modern Hebrew literature reach China and show the depth of another people and civilization.

Notes

1 Robert Alter, *The World of Biblical Literature*, New York: Basic Books, 1992, pp. iv–v.
2 Some Chinese scholars asked why almost no Israeli books were translated into Chinese after the founding of new China. For instance, Wang Xiangyuan. *Dongfang geguo wenxue zai zhongguo: yijie yu yanjiu shulun (Oriental Literatures in China: Translation and Research)*, Jiangxi: Renmin Publishing House, 2001. pp. 106–108.
3 Thanks to Mrs. Nilli Cohen, the director of the Institute for the Translation of Hebrew Literature, who provided such information on the Evening of Israeli Literature in China on 28 August 2006.

4 From a conversation with my second supervisor, Professor Andrew H. Plaks, who himself knows a dozen foreign languages and has translated Da Xue and Zhong Yong into Hebrew and English.
5 Editor's Foreword; Gershon Shaked, "Acknowledgments," In *Modern Hebrew Fiction*, Bloomington: Indiana University Press, 2000.
6 Chi Li "Juemiao de jianyue zhimei (The Perfect Beauty of his Terse Style)," in *Dongfang Wenhua Zhoukan (Oriental Culture Weekly)*. Vol. 8, 1998. Xun Kun "Yelusaleng, Yelusaleng (Jerusalem, Jerusalem)," in *Zhonghua Dushubao (Chinese Reader Weekly)*. March 24 1999.
7 Ding Fan, "Tupo Wenhua Goutong de Pingzhang (Bridging the Cultural Gap)," in *Zhonghua Dushubao (Chinese Reader Weekly)*. March 24 1999.
8 For further details, see the present author's paper "Reflections on the Study and Teaching of Modern Hebrew Literature in China," in *A Study of Oriental Literature*, Beijing University, 2007.

Part V

KAIFENG JEWISH DESCENDENTS

14

THE CONTEMPORARY CONDITION OF THE JEWISH DESCENDANTS OF KAIFENG

M. Avrum Ehrlich and Liang Pingan

In 1998, the 1,000th anniversary was marked of the immigration of Chinese Jews to Kaifeng, which was at the time, the imperial capital of ancient China. Despite decades of modern investigation and research, still nobody can offer any official materials or references concerning Judaism in Kaifeng during this period and the centuries that proceeded. Many questions remain unanswered relating to what exactly caused their disappearance as an intact community, how did they behave throughout the centuries and what were their worldviews and modes of thinking? How close was their relationship with the Han Chinese? What was the relationship of the Chinese authorities towards them before 1949 and the establishment of modern China?

In 998 CE, the first Xianping year of Zhenzong's reign of the Northern Song Dynasty, a group of what evidently were Jewish trading pioneers of the Silk Road entered Kaifeng, the imperial capital of China, and found there what later proved to be a "Promised Land."[1] They were met by an imperial delegation and by the Emperor, and were accepted as part of the Chinese nation. The Emperor issued an edict concerning the immigrants quoting Confucius: "what a great pleasure when you have friends visiting from a far place." He continued "stay in Bianliang (the ancient name of Kaifeng) and maintain your own customs."[2]

The Jews enjoyed a comfortable, influential, and highly assimilated life amongst the Chinese, separated in what may be referred to as an "orphan colony" from the mainstay of Jewish life in lands further westward.[3] Their form of worship seemed little different from the Chinese practice of Daoism, Buddhism, and Confucianism. The Jews were not recorded to have demonstrated threat or offense to the ruling philosophies of the various succeeding dynasties. They especially likened themselves with Confucianism.[4] As traders, they were not accompanied by a lot of women and took local wives, and, though their teachings and customs, survived for centuries;

ethnically they assimilated into the majority Han Chinese. Many theories exist about their influence and existence in Kaifeng. Some tell of important officials over several dynasties and even a chief of the army who were Jewish, others postulate that many Jews were, from the perspective of the Chinese, indistinguishable from the Muslims and therefore assimilated with them, or at least found in Islam a more convenient vehicle for preserving their identity, dietary habits, notions of monotheism, circumcision, prayers, and so forth. The kindness offered to this mini-community was relatively insignificant for the huge empire, which had also been gracious to many other foreign travelers, including a large number of Arabs and Muslims, and other minorities in China and from other Asian kingdoms. Quite a few of the emperors and their family members even donated the costs of building Buddhist monasteries and Taoist temples, as well as assisting in building the Jewish place of worship in Kaifeng.[5] They did so as earnest patrons and believers, especially as their doctrines were favorable to the ruling class and supporting various religions in a non-exclusive manner was not frowned upon, as it is amongst monotheistic religions.

In 1949, communism became the only official doctrine in China. By that time, the Jewish community had been left in a state of decline and severe poverty and problems, which has been described in detail in other places. That same year, Ai Dianyuan, a member of the historic Jewish community in the city of Kaifeng in Henan province, was sent as a communal representative to the Fifth Founding Celebration of the People's Republic of China. Apocryphal stories relate that at this meeting he met Party Chairman Mao Zedong, thus becoming the envy of his community for the rest of his life. Ai Dianyuan's presence, and his special dress and the request he submitted for recognition of his community as a national minority, had the opposite effect desired; instead of gaining sympathy or help from the echelons of government, he got a reaction that spurred a period of decay that has lasted till the present. Chairman Mao, who possessed a wide knowledge of Chinese culture and history, was surprised to learn that there was a community of Jews in China, and even more astonished that there was anything beyond his knowledge in Chinese history or culture. Mao Zedong had tried to demonstrate sensitivity to other religions and ethnicities, and ordered an investigation of the situation regarding Kaifeng Judaism. The findings of this inquiry were the deathknell of the community and made support of the community from any ranks of government taboo.[6]

Despite acknowledgement of their existence from the highest levels of government, Kaifeng's Jews have for decades repeatedly failed to receive official recognition at the local and central government levels as a minority group within China. The era of social and economic openness that began in the late 1970s created unprecedented opportunities for cooperation between Chinese and foreign Jews, as well as for local and international researchers to investigate Kaifeng's Jewish community. While great achievements have been made in the last three decades in the research of Chinese Jews in general, and Kaifeng Jews in particular, there still remains a great deal of unfinished work.

This chapter will explore the history of the politics of Kaifeng Jews in China since 1949, and explain why Chinese Judaism remains a sensitive topic even today. It will survey its development until the present and speculate on its future.

"There is no more Chinese Judaism," 1949–70s

In February 1955, six years after the Communist army liberated China, three officials from the state National Affairs Committee arrived in Kaifeng, then the capital of Henan Province, to investigate the Jewish community. Different from other visiting delegations in previous centuries, these officials were supported by all levels of the local administration. They visited all the major Jewish families in Kaifeng whose surnames were Ai, Shi, Gao, Jin, Li, Zhao, and Zhan; sinofications of the original seven Jewish clan's family names: Ezra, Shimon, Cohen, Gilbert, Levy, Joshua, and Jonathan. The officials listened to local Jewish legends and recorded communal history. Two weeks later, an official written report about Kaifeng Chinese Judaism was produced and with that the delegation returned to Beijing.

Upon their arrival in the capital, the three officials presented a detailed research report to their leader. They explained that the last Kaifeng synagogue was flooded by the Yellow River in 1842. At that time the local Jews fled with their neighbors, and the community lacked the wealth to reconstruct the synagogue. The last rabbi died in 1850 and, because no one in the remaining community could read Hebrew, all rituals were abandoned at that time. Based on this, Mao Zedong wrote the following response:

> According to Comrade Stalin's Theory of Nationality, there should be at least three elements to be a nationality: its own language; its own folk (religious) customs; and its own living area (i.e. the Tibetan and Uyghur Autonomous Regions in Tibet and Xinjiang). Since the Chinese Jews lost all the specialties and features mentioned above, they cannot still be taken as Jews.[7]

Liu Shaoqi, former President of the PRC signed the report: "Do as Chairman Mao orders." "I agree with the two leaders" was the instruction of Deng Xiaoping, the Party Secretary General. A document, which was the method at that time of issuing official policy, rather than the issuance of a specific law, was drafted concerning the status of modern Chinese Jews. The Kaifeng Jews were denied official minority status, and, as a result, they were considered completely assimilated into the local Chinese community. However, they still kept some special customs and traditions. On the eve of

Passover they baked *matzos* and painted their doorframes with lamb's blood. They never ate any pork similar to their Islamic neighbors, "Blue Cap Muslims were our nicknames."[8] However, unlike local Muslims, when the Kaifeng Jews were registered for national identities, local authorities designated them as part of the majority Han nationality. Some of the Kaifeng Jewish families even chose to be identified as Muslim, as both communities led similar lifestyles. Shortly following this, another official document was drafted, this time stating that "considering their historical background, traditions and customs, some special concerns should be offered to this special group." As a result, a ration ticket for half a kilogram of mutton was granted monthly to each Jewish "Han," a privilege only granted to Muslims during the decades of hunger from the 1950s–70s.[9] There were some instances where Chinese Jews had been permitted official identity as members of a "Jewish Nationality." Severe flooding in 1942, in the midst of the repressive Japanese occupation of China, had caused some Kaifeng Jews to migrate to rural areas. In the 1950s, authorities in these regions were not aware that the government had issued an official document which denied Jews their own nationality. As a result, some Jews were granted ID cards that read "Jewish Nationality." However, this mistake was quickly rectified and local officials who signed the documents were reprimanded.

The Influence of Chinese Foreign Relations on Kaifeng Jews and Arrival of Foreign Researchers, 1970s–1990

Today, the Jews of Kaifeng have become a magnet for the attention of many foreign Jews from the West, journalists, and historians. Packed in the luggage of these visitors is frequently the book *Chinese Jews*, published in 1942 by Canadian Anglican Bishop William White, who stayed in Kaifeng for more than 27 years during his mission. Such widespread attention has caused many Kaifeng Jews to maintain ties to their past, much of which may have otherwise been lost; the visiting foreign tours also served to awaken the interests of local Jews to their own unique past.

When foreign visitors first began to arrive in Kaifeng in the 1970s, the central, provincial, and local governments became concerned, as the Cultural Revolution was at its peak and no-one was looking for trouble. Kept apart from international society for almost a quarter of a century, the Chinese had grown accustomed to isolation from the international community. But through these new contacts, the local Jews learned that most foreign Jews led better lives. "To prevent anything unexpected from happening," the central government issued new documents reinforcing what was declared 20 years earlier. The local authorities kept close watch over the Chinese Jewish community and, at this time, Kaifeng Jews showed little desire to develop relations with their foreign coreligionists.

Further complicating relations between foreign and Chinese Jews, was the volatile situation in the Middle East and Chinese foreign policy. During the Middle East War in 1973, China supported the Arab states against the "Israeli invaders." At this time, Muslims comprised one-sixth of Kaifeng's urban population, and the Chinese government worried about potential disorder. The authorities were instructed to pay particular attention to any possible cooperation between "foreign Zionists" and Kaifeng Jews, which would damage the hopeful victory of China's Arabian brothers. Officials feared that Jewish tourism in Kaifeng, which at this time consisted of visitors from Eastern Europe due to the Cold War, would be viewed suspiciously by Arabian countries. Consequently, Jewish tourism to Kaifeng was tightly controlled. Fortunately, Kaifeng Jews had little concern for international affairs, and focused most of their attention on their own daily lives. Similarly, local Muslims attended mosque for regular prayers, rather than protests.

In 1978, after the end of the Cultural Revolution and the death of Chairman Mao, extreme-leftists in the Communist Party were expunged from all governmental organizations, and most Chinese officials moved their sights away from political struggles and towards the economic development encouraged by Deng Xiaoping, the new national patriarch. At the same time Sino–foreign relations warmed, and Jewish visitors from Western countries came to Kaifeng in increasing numbers. Several Jewish tycoons, like Saul Eisenburg, visited Beijing and met with central government officials. These foreigners were curious about the history of Chinese Jews. They were interested in nothing but the legends of the "Orphan Colony" in this mysterious oriental world. In response to this, Kong Xianyi, a well-known historian, a local Kaifeng high school teacher, and a member of Kaifeng Political Consultative Conference, an official organization consisting of well-known people of all professions, drafted a request titled "The Reconstruction of the Kaifeng Synagogue for the Purpose of Attracting Foreign Tourists." All members who attended the meeting were encouraged by his suggestions and took it as the best plan to help improve the local economy; unfortunately, this draft was destined for rejection by local authorities. At this time the reform period had just begun; "doing nothing, rather than taking risk" was the surest way for officials to remain in office.

While Chinese Jews were again denied official recognition, the new era of openness permitted Chinese researchers to begin a thorough investigation of the Kaifeng Jews. In the early 1970s, Wang Yisha, a historian and former curator of Kaifeng Municipal Museum, began to investigate Chinese Judaism. Taking advantage of his post, he studied numerous records and remains of Kaifeng Judaism in the museum's collection; he also made friends with many Kaifeng Jewish descendants. Wang conducted countless interviews, studied diaries, and established archives. He journeyed across China to cities where the Chinese Jews were scattered, with virtually no

179

funding to support his research; the limited museum budget was unable to assist him in any way.

Wang was the first local scholar on Kaifeng Judaism, and, as such, many foreign Jewish scholars and historians came to visit him. Unfortunately, he was forced to retire at age 50, which was rare in China unless someone has received official discredit. From then on, Wang spent all his time sorting out the files and materials he had collected over the years. He established the Kaifeng Research Institute on Ancient Jewish Culture in 1992 and was elected its standing president. In 1994, he published his first book, *The Spring and Autumn of Kaifeng Judaism*. He died of cancer in 1996, with the comfort that he lived to publish his first work, and with regret that he left his children nothing but his numerous files as a heritage and a burden.

In the 1980s, foreign researches also began to arrive in China to investigate Kaifeng Jews. In August 1985, Wendy Abraham, a young researcher from Stanford University, arrived in Kaifeng. She had longed to visit for many years, enchanted by the city's legends of Chinese Judaism. After settling into the Kaifeng Guesthouse, she immediately went to visit the local Jewish families, aching to validate what she had read in books. She was fascinated by Kaifeng, one of the few Chinese cities to maintain its pastoral views, characteristics, and traditional ideologies. Abraham's wishes had finally come true; her only regret was that, as a young foreigner, she was unable to understand Chinese people, just as the Chinese could not understand her.

Despite benign intentions, the presence of a foreign researcher caused alarm for local officials. On one occasion, Wendy Abraham met some local Jews at the Kaifeng Guesthouse and played a video-cassette about Jewish customs and lifestyles for them. She never imagined that a simple cultural introduction would cause the city Party Committee to go on high alert. Dozens of policemen, in plain clothes and uniforms, were distributed around the guesthouse. She was brought to the local Public Security Bureau and was kept in custody for several hours. The local Jewish audience was cautioned and required to offer a written report, which was held on file at the office of local Civilian Affairs. Wendy left Kaifeng, and did not return to the city for over 13 years.

The same summer that Abraham arrived in Kaifeng, Dr. Shlomo Shultz, an American Professor then teaching at the Beijing Foreign Languages Institute, traveled to Kaifeng with his wife. They met with Zhu Zhencheng, the then mayor of the city, and proposed a plan for reconstruction of the Kaifeng synagogue. Dr. Schultz explained that they could collect funds in America, and that such a project would, no doubt, attract foreign tourists and investments. The new mayor, who knew little about Kaifeng's Jewish background, was very excited about this presentation. He was anxious to jumpstart the local economy and hopeful that improvements would produce positive marks on his career; he offered the American couple a welcoming lunch in the company of local Foreign Affairs officials. But the higher authorities claimed that "the Reconstruction of Kaifeng Synagogue Equals the Revival of Chinese Judaism." Zhu was scared away from the plan and he disappeared from Dr. Shultz's sights forever.

Attempts at Cooperation and Establishment of Sino–Israeli Relations, 1989–early 1990s.

In August 1989, just after the turmoil that took place in the spring in Tiananmen Square in Beijing, two officials from the China International Friendship Association, an organization of the General Politics Bureau of the People's Liberation Army, journeyed to Kaifeng to research Kaifeng Judaism. Local officials viewed this visit as a real chance to revive all things cultural and historical relating to Judaism in Kaifeng. They knew these men were very high officials and had the power to influence change on the conservative and outdated policies, which were hindering the advancement of Kaifeng Jewish heritage. The two visiting officials explained the purpose of their visit as follows: they had received some information in New York that some Jewish business tycoons, who were dealing with relevant Chinese military industries, expressed their wishes to support and fund the reconstruction of the Kaifeng Synagogue. Because China has strict policies dealing with nationalities and religion, they put forward an unexpected proposal: as there were officially no more Jews or Judaism in Kaifeng, the synagogue would be used only as a museum attraction for global tourists. Also, a part of this plan was a proposal to build a memorial in the Hongkou District of Shanghai, the biggest city of China, where about 35,000 Jewish refugees found shelter during the Second World War.

Upon completing their research the two officials returned to Beijing, while local authorities in Kaifeng waited with great patience for a revolutionary moment that would change the existing stubborn doctrines regarding Kaifeng Jews. Two months later, a file from the Foreign Ministry and the China International Friendship Association, arrived at Kaifeng. The first paragraph still quoted from Mao Zedong's orders on Kaifeng Judaism. The second part indicated deeper worries, such as, "Any attempt to reconstruct Kaifeng Synagogue, even as a museum, will no doubt raise the suspicions and concerns of some Arab countries about our diplomacy." Again, the Kaifeng Jewish community had lost an opportunity to rebuild their synagogue.

In October 1990, more than a year after the events in Tiananmen Square in Beijing, China was still sanctioned by most Western powers and foreign trade and tourism were at a historic low. Still, a family tour group of about 62 people, headed by Maven Josephine, a distinguished American Jewish businessman, traveled to Kaifeng. The tour group consisted of Jews from America, Israel, and some other countries as well. Most important, was the presence of James Lilley, the American Ambassador to China at that time. The primary purpose of their trip was to hold a *bar* and *bat mitzvah* ceremony in the Judaic wing of the Kaifeng Municipal Museum, where some relics and remains of the Kaifeng synagogue were on display. This delegation was organized by a travel agency attached to the China Trust & Investment Corporation, headed by Rong Yi-ren, Vice President of the PRC. Vice President Rong personally arranged the tour for the Maven Josephine family, one of the wealthiest Jewish families in America. Having such strong bureaucratic support, from both America and China, they did not expect any obstacles to hinder their intentions.

The night before the ceremonies were scheduled, a serious meeting was held between the tour organizers and local officials. Representatives from the China Trust Travel Agency strongly urged that the ceremony be held on schedule, but the local party secretary, the mayor, and other major officials hesitated to grant permission. Two representatives of the Central Party Committee and State Council in China arrived at the meeting unannounced. At first, local officials did not understand who they were, and questioned their authority. The local party secretary argued, "Who are you? I think it should be me to decide yes or no since I'm still the boss of this city." The men replied, "It's true you are and will be the boss of this city after you accept my suggestion on this matter." Following this, the two representatives met privately with the local party secretary, and shortly after he announced that the Jewish ceremony could not be held at the local museum. Instead, the *bar* and *bat mitzvah* were held in a large meeting room in a hotel, and some Jewish antiques were brought on loan from the museum. The Maven Josephine family left Kaifeng with regret, queries, and frustration. None of them ever returned to Kaifeng, nor did their investments.

The 1990s saw China achieve unprecedented economic prosperity and receive a large influx of foreign visitors. This occurred nowhere more so than in the city of Shanghai, where in December 1991 a presentation titled "Remember Forever, Holocaust 1942–1945" was held. Sponsored by the Simon Wiesenthal Center and the Judaic and Israeli Center of China Peace and Development Institute, this was the first public event held in China to honor Jews. To lessen the sensitive nature of the meeting, a coin collecting display was held at the same time. Yang Fuchang, the Vice Foreign Minister of China and other senior officials from the ministry were present at the ceremony. Yang accepted a *menorah* from a representative of the Simon Wiesenthal Center and passed it to his secretary within seconds, as if it was a hot potato. Everything happened so quickly that journalists present did not even have the opportunity to take photos. Following the public ceremony was a meeting, also sponsored by the Simon Wiesenthal Center and the Judaic and Israeli Center of China Peace and Development Institute, which was closed to media coverage.

Events in China seemed to indicate that the country would establish diplomatic relations with Israel soon and that would be a good omen for Kaifeng. On 24 January 1992, the State of Israel and People's Republic of China met in Beijing and signed a diplomatic communiqué. Kaifeng applauded this new era, as it seemed the government was no longer worried that Kaifeng Judaism would negatively effect their international relations. In early March 1992, the Sino–Israeli diplomatic establishment encouraged a research delegation of six scholars from the China Social Science Academy, the top state academic organization, to go to Kaifeng to conduct research and write an academic report. Song Jian, the Minister of China Science and Technology, read the report. Intrigued by the topic, he traveled to Kaifeng, and suggested that another report be written and submitted to higher officials; the local authorities were required to make detailed measures of conduct. But up to now, most items relating to the development of Kaifeng Judaism were still at the stage of research. Anything seeming different from official ideology could be forbidden by any government level, no matter who was the advocate. This was one of the rare democratic symbols within the Chinese Communist Party

The Kaifeng Research Institute on Ancient Jewish Culture

Initially, many scholars who researched Kaifeng Jews did so quietly, so as not to disturb a sensitive political topic. But shortly after China established formal diplomatic relations with Israel, several impetuous Chinese scholars brought their exploration of Chinese Judaism from the underground onto the open stage. After decades of effort, the Kaifeng Research Institute on Ancient Jewish Culture finally received a permit from the local Party organization and registered legally. The institute was honored to have Zhang Jingxiang, a deputy mayor, serve as honorary vice president. This was not to imply that Zhang was a scholar on Judaism, but rather a traditional Chinese way of showing respect and lobbying for official support for the academy. In truth, without Zhang's dedicated support the institute might very well not have existed.

The Kaifeng Research Institute on Ancient Jewish Culture consists of the board, secretariat, liaison office, and construction office, which was responsible for the future construction of the Kaifeng Synagogue Museum. Most of the members are local historians, professors, and scholars who work at the Kaifeng Museum, and local officials who are keen on Jewish subjects. There is a conference room used for free study and regular exchange. Although the institute was legally founded, it was watched closely by government officials, and any carelessness would have caused a total collapse. The first president of the institute was Zhao Xiangru, a Jewish descendant of the Kaifeng Seven Clan and a professor at the China Social Sciences Academy. He was well known throughout the Jewish communities in both Beijing and abroad. Zhao was invited to visit Israel where he gave a speech on "the Present Situation of Kaifeng Jewish descendants." His presentation was not approved by the authorities and, as a result, the Central Government sent investigators in to Kaifeng. Officials had been looking for an excuse to close the Research Institute, and they saw this as a good opportunity. To avoid forced closure, the institute had to publicly announce that they did not authorize Zhao's speech and Zhao "resigned" soon after.

In late 1993, a Chinese Christian from Beijing made contact with the Jin family, descendants of the Jin Clan, the first of the seven clans of Kaifeng Jews through a local Kaifeng Christian who had heard about the Jewish descendents. Using his ties with a group of Christians from Finland who supported Jews returning to their roots and wishing to return to Israel, he encouraged them to apply for immigration papers to Israel and helped arrange financial support and other assistance from Finland to make this possible.

In early 1994, Jin Guangyuan and his family and two other Kaifeng Jews came to the decision that they would like to emigrate to Israel under the Israeli "right of return." They went to the Israeli Embassy in Beijing and were told they would not be recognized under this law unless Jin Guangyuan's status as a Jew was confirmed by the Chinese authorities. They went to the Chinese Foreign Affairs Office in Beijing and the office quickly processed the proof and furnished them with a document saying they were of the Jewish minority ethnic group. Upon returning to Kaifeng, the local police came to their home and informed them that this document was issued by mistake and should be returned. They were not able to find or reclaim the document. The two local notarization officials who issued documents to Jin Guangyuan and his family were fired.

The Finnish group, fearing that by indicating their intentions to go to Israel it may jeopardize or risk their chances, decided to bring them first to Finland for three months and from there process their application to immigrate to Israel. Whether or not this was an attempt to missionize the family or out of good will and desire to see their move proceed smoothly, is not clear.

After a series of complications, Jin Guangyuan and his family finally immigrated to Israel, becoming the first of the Kaifeng Jews to live in the Holy Land. Jin Guangyuan's daughter, Jin Wenjing or "Shalva" in Hebrew, was the first to formerly convert to orthodox Judaism in 2002, and, after years of study, the parents were formally converted to Judaism in 2005; Jin Guangyuan took the name "Shlomo." A celebratory marriage ceremony under a *Huppa,* according to Jewish law and custom, took place in Jerusalem, where the family continues to live. Shalva now studies East Asian studies at the Hebrew University in Jerusalem.

In 2006, Shlomo Jin returned to Kaifeng for a family visit and was able to regain his Chinese passport. He kept his visit relatively secret so as not to arouse the interest of the local police, and he was able to leave again and his immigration to Israel did not seem to cause alarm or trouble in Kaifeng.

Research on the subject of the Jews of Kaifeng conducted outside of the Kaifeng Institute also continued to come under official scrutiny. In the autumn of 1993, Xu Xiangqun, the only scholar of Judaism holding a major general rank in the General Staffs of PLA, traveled to Kaifeng, and, with the help of his crew, made a documentary on the Jewish history of the city. This was the first official project on Chinese Judaism and culture headed by the Chinese since 1948. Once completed, the documentary was aired on China Central TV. It focused most heavily on historical facts, giving detailed descriptions of Jewish relics and antiques. The program also discussed academic scholarship relating to the Jews of Kaifeng. After the program aired, Xu and his crew were criticized for breaking a prohibition on the coverage of Chinese Jews that had existed for decades. Similar to Wang Yisha, Xu was forced to rethink his actions, and embarrassingly retired early.

Wang Yisha was well known as a Hebrew scholar in China. His dismissal was yet another example that the authorities could punish anyone who worked within this politically sensitive field. However, in recent years some leeway has been made, proving that some freedom of scholarship does in fact exist in the field of Kaifeng Jewry.

From the late 1990s until the present, probably one of the most active proponents and spokespeople on behalf of the Jewish descendents of Kaifeng has been Professor Xu Xin. A scholar of American literature at the University of Nanking, Professor Xu Xin became interested in American Jewish writers and, during a stint at an American university, was a guest at a Jewish family's home and subsequently developed a greater insight into Jewish thought and practice. His wife, who ran a Chinese tour company, started organizing Jewish tours of China and Kaifeng became an important destination on this trip. Professor Xu Xin conducted and lectured about the Jewish communities of China, and especially about the history of the Jews of Kaifeng. He introduced the Jewish tourists he guided, which by now must number many thousands, to Jewish descendents in the city and, in this way, their identity as Jewish descendants was reinforced and a dialogue with American Jews formed. Professor Xu Xin wrote two books on the history of the Jews of Kaifeng, including stories and tales of how they arrived in China, which was published in the United States and enhanced his reputation as a scholar of the subject. He is widely sought to lead tour groups to the city and other Jewish related venues in China.

In 1999, Professor Xu Xin led a group of 12 Jews from Australia, Israel, and the US who lived in Beijing, for a *Shabbat* in Kaifeng. The journey was filmed and eventually produced as a documentary narrated by Leonard Nimoy entitled, *Minyan in Kaifeng: A Modern Journey to an Ancient Chinese Jewish Community*. The movie shows how they were hosted by the Kaifeng Jewish descendents and conducted a *Shabbat* dinner and services with them. The film airs the discussions that ensued about Jewish identity, including the questions, "Are they really Jewish?" and "what am I doing in an impoverished Chinese town with people who share none of my culture?"

One of the participants in the journey was Matt Trusch who argued on film that their interest in Judaism, however genuine it may or may not have appeared, was enough for a tolerant style of Judaism to welcome them as Jews even without formal conversion. The same Matt Trusch later became an orthodox Jew through the Chabad movement and remained in Shanghai to work with the Shanghai Jewish community and pursue business; today, he is more skeptical about their Jewish status and in favor of a rigorous conversion process.

On 14 July 2002, 12 Jewish descendants from Kaifeng traveled to Nanjing to attend a three-week workshop on Jewish history and culture, hosted by Professor Xu Xin. His success in the management of this political hot potato without repercussions indicated that he understood Chinese politics better than many of the scholars previously discussed. His secret was action without media attention, as Chinese authorities considered public exposure their greatest threat.

There is perhaps another reason. The Chinese authorities are unsure how to treat religion and religious history, though not part of their political worldview, it is recognized as something valuable to many people and perhaps valuable for social integration. The authorities tend to relegate such sensitive topics to university departments and academic frameworks, in the setting of a center for Jewish studies or among academic scholars of religion most topics can be studied and discussed freely without fear of political rapprochement. Several Kaifeng Jewish descendents have attended academic seminars on Jewish-related topics and are particularly free to do so outside of Kaifeng. Most recently, a group of descendents attended a summer school and studied Judaism on an academic level and within an academic framework at Shandong University's Center for Judaic and Inter-Religious Studies. This has, for now, proven to be a successful way for them to study Jewish history and culture, and gain some understanding of their personal history and Jewish identity within the structures set out by Chinese officialdom without causing alarm or political dissatisfaction.

Many of the Jewish tours led by Professor Xu Xin were introduced to the Shi family, one of the largest clans of Jewish descendents. Wendy Abrahams had interviewed the patriarch of the family a decade earlier. A young boy at the time, Shi Lei witnessed his grandfather welcome groups of foreign Jewish tourists into their home and, to the great surprise and probable admiration of the entire neighborhood, described his family's Jewish history. His father, Shi Xin Guang, continued to do this and as Shi Lei got older was also invited to talk to visiting groups and eventually began to conduct tours of the site of the Kaifeng synagogue, South Teaching Torah Lane, and the family gravesites, and other interesting locations in Kaifeng.

In the year 2000, a visiting US attorney, Irvin Berg, introduced Shi Lei to Rabbi Marvin Tokayer, a former rabbi in Japan who returned to take up a pulpit in Long Island, New York; Tokayer also conducted Jewish and kosher tours of China. Rabbi Tokayer offered to arrange a scholarship for Shi Lei to Bar Ilan University in Israel.

Though he wanted to be a tour guide, Shi Lei took up the offer and, with the help of members of Rabbi Tokayer's tour group who provided him with "pocket money," Shi Lei went to Israel in 2001 to do the one-year program including Hebrew ulpan, religious classes in the morning, and Jewish history in the afternoon. During his stay at Bar Ilan, he was interviewed by then *Jerusalem Post* reporter Michael Freund, who took an interest in him and helped Shi Lei continue his studies at the Machon Meir Yeshiva in Jerusalem; Shi Lei continued to study in Machon Meir for two years. Ironically, it was there that he met Matt Trusch, the same participant in the Minyan in Kaifeng. They were both rediscovering their religious heritage in Jerusalem.

Shi Lei learnt to speak fluent Hebrew and gained insight into Jewish life and traditions, but chose at the time not to formally convert to Judaism. He viewed himself as a Han Chinese and, though very proud of his Jewish ancestry, was not sure whether conversion was the right way. He returned to Kaifeng and slowly began to gain work as a tour guide, gained a tour guide license, and began taking more groups around China and Kaifeng. At present, he is probably the first and only tour guide from the descendants of the Jews of Kaifeng. In 2005, with the help of Michael Freund, he returned to Israel to try and gain Israeli citizenship based on the law of return, without the need to undergo formal conversion. This trial balloon was nearly successful and may have paved the way for other Jewish descendents to do the same; however, there was expression of concern from the Israeli Interior Ministry: what would stop the growing numbers of Chinese laborers working in Israel from claiming they were descendents of the Jews of Kaifeng and how could their claims be proved? The process was put on hold until a solution was found and Shi Lei returned to China.

In the year 2000, Noam Urbach, an Israeli student studying for his Masters degree at the Department of East Asia at Hebrew University arrived in Kaifeng to study Chinese language at Henan University. He remained in the city for four months, and made contact with the Jewish descendents. As a religious Jew, he was hesitant to recognize the legitimacy of their claims of Jewish descent and felt this may be more related to the tourist interest in them and their Jewish identity; almost as a self-fulfilling process, Jewish tourists excited at the prospect of meeting exotic Chinese Jews were met by individuals who for some force of history were willing and able to invent themselves in this image, out of the relics of a past history either real or fictitious, belonging to them and their ancestors or not.

Throughout his duration, however, Noam became more curious about the political tension surrounding their claims. The tension at the time was especially around the attempt to open a Kaifeng Jewish Museum that could also be used as a community center/synagogue for the descendents. This issue seemed to embody the entire question of their identity and desire to re-associate with Judaism. Noam eventually wrote his M.A. thesis on the Kaifeng Jewish community throughout the 1980s and 1990s, and filmed and interviewed the Jin family as preparing to immigrate to Israel, during their conversion process, and in their new lives in Jerusalem. Even though he observed the *Shabbat*, the Kaifeng Jewish descendents were not participating in any *Shabbat* or festival meals or activities at that time and only had an oral knowledge of their Jewish ancestry. The next time Noam returned to Kaifeng was in 2006 as a visiting researcher at Shandong University's Center for Judaic and Inter-Religious Studies.

Significant developments in the community transpired as a result of the assistance of a number of figures who had appeared in the interim, including a Hebrew teacher, a local Kaifeng descendent with a Jewish education, many tourists, travelers, teachers, and rabbis who began to interact with the community.

In 2002, an American-born Jew whose family immigrated to Israel, who we will call by the pseudonym "Naphtali," to protect his identity, arrived in Kaifeng. He was first accompanied, it has been told, by the same Chinese Christian man from Beijing who had made contact with the Jin family. He had visited the US and stayed at Naphtali's parent's home, and told them about the Kaifeng Jewish descendents and aroused an interest in Naphtali to work with them. They arrived together and the Christian friend introduced Naphtali to some of the members of the community. He later returned ostensibly as an English teacher at the local university and, after a period of time, started formerly instructing the Kaifeng Jewish descendents in Hebrew and gathering them for Friday night dinners and festival celebrations.

He rented an apartment, which was used as a community center and study hall. He helped consolidate the group and developed relations with the younger members. He helped arrange a number of scholarships for some of the members to go to Israel and made contact with several Israeli organizations who take an interest in Jews on the periphery, especially with Michael Freund's organization Shavei Israel, dedicated to help such groups return to their roots and to Israel.

There were concerns that Naphtali was a Christian missionary, or a messianic believer with an ethnic identity as a Jew but a Christian theology, whose intention was to bring these members into the Christian faith and then to Israel. There is still ambiguity about this subject. Members of the descendents had observed him entering or giving talks in churches and others said that he was indeed Christian. Nonetheless, he claims to be working for the return of the Kaifeng Jewish descendents to Jewish orthodoxy.

In 2004, the first author, Avrum Ehrlich, visited Kaifeng for the first time with the co-author Liang Pingan and conducted meetings with Jewish descendents, including Moshe Zhang, members of the Jin and Shi families. He also met the family of Wang Yisha to view the documents and research he had left and negotiated to purchase it from the family to be used for research and to be protected for posterity. In these meetings, close relations were developed between members of the community and arrangements were made to assist in educating some of the community's youth. At this time, the first author, together with members of the community, identified the areas of Jewish culture and tradition that would be necessary to perform so as to gradually bring the descendents into conformity with basic Jewish practices of Jews worldwide. This included learning Hebrew and ancient Hebrew literature, *shabbat* and festival gatherings, not eating pork, and preferring eating Muslim-slaughtered meat over others. A list of basic principles was drawn up and handed to Shi Lei, who was by now emerging as a de facto leader of the community. There was great sensitivity in ensuring that the principles by which the Kaifeng Jewish descendants would behave would be acceptable within Chinese law and the expectations of its citizens, and in reinforcing the descendant's Chinese patriotism. The author also met with Naphtali to understand more about his motives in working with the community.

On this trip, Professor Ehrlich met Jerry Gotel, who was a visiting scholar and lecturer of Holocaust Studies at Henan University, and introduced him to members of the community. He immediately became active in their support, provided them with funding for the running of their classroom, for heating in the winter and for food for *Shabbat* and festival dinners. He has brought several tour groups to visit Kaifeng to meet with the Jewish descendents, who offer several components of support.

In 2004, in coordination with Michael Freund, a *beit din* of rabbis including Rabbi Eliyahu Birnbaum and Rabbi Shlomo Riskin traveled to Kaifeng and visited the local Henan University's center on Holocaust and Jewish Studies, ostensibly as a legitimate reason to visit the city without drawing too much attention, and then met with the descendents in the hired study hall apartment. Naphtali organized a group of about 50 Jewish descendents to greet the delegation. They spoke to some of the descendents and danced, then returned to Beijing. Since that time, a number of descendents have been funded by Shavei Israel to attend seminaries and schools in Israel. The first group of four girls came to Israel and lived and studied in the religious village of Bat Ayin in the Gush Ezion region near Jerusalem, and the next group of two girls and a boy arrived in 2006.

Naphtali's contribution to the education and reconsolidation of a Kaifeng Jewish identity had been invaluable. Yet some of his work and personal interactions with other people visiting Kaifeng, including the author, were often unusual, having misguided ideas and perhaps paranoia, and some of his actions having detrimental consequences.

Doggedly protecting his turf, and sure of his unique ability to guide the Jewish descendants, he tried to manage and select the visitors coming to meet the Jewish descendants and suggested who they should not see. Fearful that he would withhold his support, those most dependent listened to him. Arguing that he was guiding them through political minefields, he in fact created his own political instruments. On one occasion in 2004, he advised them not to participate in a summer school in Jewish studies, which provided full scholarships, arguing this would bring too much attention. The possibility that he would lose his influence on them seemed to be the more likely reason. When finally they did participate, the fears that it would be dangerous for them proved baseless.

This behavior also stifled some of the local descendants who may have risen to the occasion and taken on leadership roles amongst their peers. The dynamic of a locally led rediscovery of roots, rather than a foreign imposed one, would be interpreted by Chinese officialdom as being more legitimate.

Naphtali insisted nothing should be written on the community at all. He argues that accounting for the last few years of activity would have repercussions, putting the Kaifeng Jewish descendants at risk. He writes that: "Whether the government knows about what is going on or not is irrelevant. The point is that you would provide them with the necessary evidence and proof that the government needs in order to crack down on the Kaifeng Jews." He believes that "it is possible for the government to crack down on them (they have done it before), and in the end it is the Kaifeng Jewish community who will suffer the consequences ... they are the ones who will suffer police harassment, abuse, and imprisonment."

He claims that any documenting of events would "endanger my life, and those associated with me. And if anything occurs as a result of this information you are going to be held personally accountable for your actions." He continues to write:

> By publishing information about the current activities you are jeopardizing the highly fragile attempts to help the Kaifeng Jews return to Israel, unless of course that is your intention." You can choose to do what is right for the Kaifeng community or not ... in the end you will have to carry the responsibility and repercussions of your choice.

The counter position, of course, is that the clear documentation of events is an academic right and the right of others to understand the circumstances surrounding the difficulties of this nascent Jewish group. The wider Jewish world, other religious institutions, and government and international bodies are curious to know more about them, communicate with them, and extend them assistance and support. Censoring information about their revival and hiding it would be a disservice, detrimental and academically derelict. Their documented existence is their best protection. Documenting the developments in Kaifeng is proof and picture of the situation and makes it difficult to expunge. It ensures the progress made cannot easily be reversed or quashed or denied in the current open door and more transparent environment of contemporary China. China's policy of openness guarantees the rights of ethnic minorities and of religious faith and basic human rights as long as they live within the rule of law. It would be very unlikely for there to be a clampdown on the community in that environment. The diplomatic constellation with the Arab and Muslim world would not benefit from it, nor would relations with Western countries. Relations with the state of Israel and the Jewish world would be turned on to high alert. But most importantly, China is concerned for ensuring ethnic diversity for its own reasoning and interests, more than for concern for Western opinion. The Chinese have shown great consideration for ethnic identity and their concerns are not so much with the identity and practice of the descendants as Jews, so much as the political and diplomatic repercussions, which seem to be inconsequential today. Apart from perceived insult or challenge to its authority, government officials would likely be pleased to see a peaceful and harmonious emergence of a Jewish Chinese ethnic minority.

After a two-year stay in Kaifeng, Naphtali's visa was eventually invalidated, the reason given by the authorities was that he was no longer officially employed by the university. Most likely the authorities were concerned about his activities on two fronts: the first was their claim that he was teaching and encouraging religious activities; the second that he was doing so as a foreigner. Religious activities amongst Chinese citizens are tolerated by the Chinese authorities, but perceived missionary activity by foreigners is strongly opposed and perceived as an offense to Chinese pride and sovereignty, and as the descendents are not recognized as Jews, his activities were likely interpreted to be missionary.

He returned to Kaifeng in 2006 and stayed a month, before again having his visa invalidated and being forced to leave. He continued to work on behalf of Kaifeng Jewish descendents and it has been said continues to make short trips to the city.

Throughout this period, one of the local spokespeople of the Kaifeng Jewish descendents was a man called Moshe Zhang. He was "discovered" and identified as a Jewish descendent by Wang Yisha. He used to live on Liu Family Lane, which was close to South Teaching Torah Lane, the small street where the Jewish descendents lived. Though a Muslim by upbringing, he quickly re-identified as a Jew and became a popular station for visiting Jewish groups seeking to meet a Chinese Jew. Over the years, Moshe Zhang collected an extraordinarily large collection of business cards from visiting Jewish dignitaries, senators, tycoons, business people, professionals, movie-makers, and artists. He started to gather some parts of the community in his home, and set up a small exhibition on the Jews of Kaifeng. He used to welcome guests wearing a blue yarmulke and adopted as many Jewish customs as he knew how. He was appointed to the Kaifeng City Council; however, many members of the Kaifeng community disliked him and refused to come to his home or participate in the events he organized. They claimed he was not a Jewish descendent and that he was pretending and becoming rich by representing them. In 2004, the community seemed split between two groups of descendents: those that supported Moshe Zhang and those that did not.

It was said by one of the elderly ladies whose husband had been a Jewish descendent, and who still lived in South Teaching Torah Lane, that Moshe Zhang had tricked Wang Yisha into thinking he was a descendent. According to her, he had lived in the area and knew a lot of the history and the descendents, had observed many foreigners coming to visit, and had hoped to take advantage of this. She claimed that the older descendents and people who lived in the area knew this. She explained that Moshe Zhang had won the affection of Wang Yisha by helping him find a new wife after his wife had died, and that Wang Yisha had endorsed him as a descendent.

Some of the descendents claim Moshe was an agent placed inside the circle of the Kaifeng Jewish Community by the PSB (Public Security Bureau). They claim he continually informed the security branches on the activities of the community and the people that visited. Some descendents describe him as self-serving, having cheated the community and brought it into disgrace by begging foreign tourists for money.

Since 2005, Moshe Zhang has been removed from his position on the Kaifeng City Council and is not allowed to meet any foreign Jewish tourists or tour groups. He is seen to be completely outside the community; however, a number of friends claiming to be Jewish descendents remain loyal to him. With the removal of Moshe Zhang and the exit of Naphtali from Kaifeng, a leadership vacuum developed. There was sufficient interest in Jewish identity; however, no-one was ready to step in.

In 2005, when he returned from Israel, Shi Lei started teaching the younger descendents Hebrew and English in the apartment belonging to his now-deceased grandfather. He holds weekly classes with about ten students between 7 and 23 years old attending, more would attend but the apartment is too small. He holds *Shabbat* and festival meals at a Muslim restaurant and pays for this out of the donations he receives from Jewish tourists. He has sent a number of students to attend summer school in Jewish Studies at the Center of Judaic and Inter-Religious Studies and has maintained contacts with the first author. He hosts and guides several Jewish groups a month and introduces them to the community members, which serves to reinforce their identity, to provide the opportunity to teach and learn, and also the tour groups and their leaders, including Rabbi Tokayer and Jerry Gotel, encourage the travelers to donate to the community as they do themselves.

The economic outlook of the Kaifeng Jewish descendents is not bright. All are very poor. Though most of the youth are now attending universities, there are no businesses or wealthy members to support the others. Discussion about suitable industries from Jewish religious clothing, coats, hats and *kippot*, have had some outcomes. Hopes that one day the old site of the Kaifeng synagogue would be purchased from the government and the synagogue rebuilt are unlikely as the site is used as a hospital. Thoughts of buying a Hutong courtyard and turning it into a high-end guesthouse for Jewish and other tourists to Kaifeng, raised excitement amongst community members as this would provide many with jobs and an opportunity to meet interesting foreign guests while learning from them and satisfying their curiosity about the history of Chinese Judaism. This would invariably provide the base for a community center and museum, and place to study and develop the community. The people involved are still seeking a donor for this project.

Visiting Jewish tourists are encouraged by their tour guides to donate to the community. There is now a regulated system of accepting money. One of the descendents accepts the money, counts it and gives it to Shi Lei's father, Shi Xin Juang who records it in a booklet. The booklet is open to be viewed by any member of the community. The money goes towards communal activities, heating, and *Shabbat* and festival meals.

Visiting tourists to Kaifeng have probably been the single most important catalyst in the reawakening of the Kaifeng Jewish identity. Over generations there have been a constant string of visits. The Baghdadi Jews of the last century communicated with them, later some of the Jews of Russian origin made contact. But the most important are the hundreds, and by now thousands, of American Jews who have come on heritage tours to China and made their way to Kaifeng. Sometimes meeting and sharing an evening with them, sometimes spending a *Shabbat* dinner or other occasions, these experiences reinforced that it was a positive thing to be a Jew, it was associated with modernity, English-speaking ability, wealth, success, and so on. Of course, the financial support may have also been an important factor in the identity of many, but many Jewish communities have been assisted by Jews of better financial condition and it is natural to be encouraged by the material benefits offered.

In many ways the Jewish tourism to China served as a form of "shlihut," and served a remarkable historic service, which the tourists may or may not have understood at the time of their visit.

As the descendents talk about their future and speculate whether the authorities will allow them to freely express themselves and openly identify as Jewish descendents, the question of how far they wish to take their Jewish identity is inevitably raised and whether they wish to convert to Judaism or, for example, undergo circumcision.

The general interest in Judaism is high. Though strongly patriotic as Han Chinese, there is great interest in studying English and Hebrew and in modernizing. English is seen as a Jewish legacy, as most Jewish tourists have been English-speakers and association with Judaism is with the successful tourists. Many would take the opportunity to study in Israel and discover more about their identity.

Out of the seven original clans of Kaifeng Jews, the Zhang clan was said to have converted to Islam in the beginning of the twentieth century with the decline of the community and the problems in that period of China's history. The Gao clan migrated to other Chinese cities including Xian. The other five clans remain, including the Shi family, which numbers from 400 to 500 people, the Li, Jin, Ai, and Zhao clans, together numbering approximately 1,000 people including relatives and spouses. Of them about 200 are young members (up to age 30).

Modern Chinese Judaism has been a topic of interest for nearly half a century. In hindsight, it faced nothing but containment and restrictions from the government, despite great opportunities from other quarters. Struggling with pressure from the Chinese authorities not to be too public with their identity, and a lack of endorsement from Chabad in China, who fear that this would compromise their work, the Kaifeng Jewish descendents are not optimally placed to be helped. The Chabad movement is theologically opposed to the prospect that the descendents be recognized in any way as Jews until formal conversion. But they are also not prepared to accept them to learn or participate in gatherings due to government restrictions on missionary activity. The Israeli foreign diplomacy is also weary of becoming involved and risking its relations with the Chinese government and stirring Arab–Chinese–Israel instability for the sake of a few hundred Jewish descendents.

The ostensible reasons to restrain Chinese Judaism from any possible revival are government misgivings about state diplomatic policies, minority nationalities, and religion. Chinese officials make up a large bureaucratic pyramid. Local Kaifeng officials are often overcautious in their actions, fearful that inappropriate behavior will result in a demotion, throwing them to the bottom of the pyramid.

There is great caution regarding religion in China. Religious leaders have organized nearly every peasant rebellion that occurred in China over the past 3,000 years. This may explain why Chinese officials have been so conservative in their reaction to any efforts to revive the Jewish community of Kaifeng. Local rulers could not authorize religious autonomy without government control. While great hospitality was extended to Marc Polo and Mateeo Ricci, it seems this was nothing but curiosity from a central empire to an envoy of a foreign country. Eventually, both the Catholics and the local Chinese rebellion Boxers became the targets for elimination.

Another reservation is that the recognition of a small group of 300–1,000 Jewish descendents as an ethnic minority, could legitimize the claims and requests of many other small minorities, for formal recognition and rights.

These groups are also small, but number in their hundred of thousands and sometimes millions. The issue of formal recognition of the Jewish descendants may open a "Pandora's box" of other demands to receive formal recognition. There are various dimensions to this issue, which will be discussed further in an upcoming book entitled *Jews and Judaism in Modern China* (Routledge, 2008).

Although the revival of modern Judaism may fulfill some practical interests for the city of Kaifeng, such as tourism and foreign investment, officials have acted cautiously, fearful of losing positions that they worked hard to obtain. This lack of activity has prevented China from reaping any of the possible positive benefits. It is curious how so tiny a religion or ethnic minority group could be perceived to be so harmful to the unity and integrity of such a huge country and population. As things are, there are many challenges and obstacles in the way for Judaism in Kaifeng to be revived.

Most of the reasons for the limitations placed on Chinese Judaism are based in traditional Communist philosophy. Karl Marx, Vladimir Lenin, Josef Stalin, and Mao Zedong, the early patriarchs of communism, all strongly supported the abolition of both religious practice and social stratification. Through the implementation of this ideology, hundreds of Chinese nationalities have been deprived official recognition, making them legally part of a majority that has different customs, beliefs, and history. Moreover, according to this ideology, once an ethnic group has lost its independent identity, it is unacceptable for it to reappear from its historic remains. Today, the Chinese government recognizes 56 national minority groups. As seen with the Jews of Kaifeng, it is extremely difficult for a group to maintain individuality when they do not have freedom to exercise independence. Their support is coming from some secular or reform Jews in America, some human rights activists, Jewish tourists who had personal contact with the descendents, various historians, Jewish studies scholars, a number of pro-Jewish Christian groups, and a few Israeli groups interested in seeking out marginal Jewish communities to bring back to the homeland.

The constellation of support against those that are either indifferent or opposed to the developments amongst the Jewish descendants of Kaifeng is not always encouraging.

The question remains whether it is necessary or advantageous for the descendents of the Jews of Kaifeng to be officially recognized as Jews. While many argue for this right, were the ethnicity of an individual required to be written on an American or French passport, it would cause uproar and scandal. Jews have traditionally prided themselves on assimilation and only under oppressive regimes have been forced to be officially identified. However, various privileges are granted to registered ethnic minorities including the right to have more than one child under China's "one child" policy. The psychological pressure of perhaps doing something that could result in being arrested is too much for most average people, and this more than anything is the reason they would like to be recognized as a legitimate ethnic minority.

The future of the Jewish descendents of Kaifeng is probably one of steady growth. Short of disaster or a heavy government crackdown, enough of the descendants are aware and sufficiently interested in their identity to make it difficult to faze out. In the age of the internet, available information in the Chinese language on Jewish thought and culture, a strong interest and respect for Jews amongst the Chinese nation and the freedom of Jewish travelers to Kaifeng and of Kaifeng Jews abroad, make the re-emergence of a small but intact indigenous Chinese Jewry a very possible reality.

Notes

1 *Gazetteer of Xiangfu County*, the sixteenth year of Emperor Shunzhi, 1660.
2 "In Memory of Reconstruction of Kaifeng Synagogue," Monument, the second year of Emperor Hongzhi, 1489.
3 William C. White, *Chinese Jews: A Compilation of Matters Relating to the Jews of K'aifeng Fu*, Toronto: University of Toronto Press, 1966.
4 "A Memory of the Ancient Hall," Monument, the eighteenth year of Emperor, 1680.
5 "In Memory of Reconstruction of Kaifeng Synagogue," op. cit.
6 Instruction by the Committee of National Affairs of China to the Report "Present Situation of Kaifeng Jewish Descendants," 1956.
7 "Present Situation of Kaifeng Jewish Descendants," op. cit.
8 An Interview with Zhao Pingyu by Wang Yisha, 5 October 1980.
9 "Present Situation of Kaifeng Jewish Descendants," op. cit.

15

CHINESE GOVERNMENT POLICY TOWARDS THE DESCENDANTS OF THE JEWS OF KAIFENG

Xu Xin

China is the only country in the Far East where Jews have continually lived for over a 1,000 years. Their religious beliefs and practices developed under unique circumstances. Jews who came to China before 1840, that is to say Jewish Persian traders, from the tenth to the eighteenth centuries, who settled in Kaifeng or stations on the Silk Route, had been assimilated into Chinese society. In contrast, Jews who arrived after 1840, that is to say the Iraqi–Indian migration, did not assimilate into broader Chinese society. Chinese policy, especially since the 1950s, views these Jews as two separate groups. This chapter addresses the difference in treatment between the assimilated Jews of Kaifeng and the later immigrations from a historical perspective, granting special consideration to those who settled in Kaifeng, and how their conditions have changed over the last 50 years.

Historical Overview

Over the past 1,000 years, what, if any, has been China's official policy towards Jews and their religious practices? Documents related directly to this issue are rare;[1] however, historical documents indicate that the Chinese government carried out a liberal policy of "respecting their religion and changing not their customs and traditions." This policy was applied to all ethnic groups and their faiths, including Jews and Judaism. Accordingly, the dynasties and governments instituted lenient policies towards Jews, permitting them to live within the country, practice normal religious activities, and allowing them to erect synagogues.

Chinese acceptance of Jews is well reflected in the case of the Kaifeng Jews. Records from Jewish sources indicate that the Emperor gave permission for Jews to both live in the capital of China and follow their own Jewish traditions and customs.[2]

Respect for Jews is also illustrated through land grants, which indicate that officials from different dynasties allowed the building and rebuilding of the synagogue in Kaifeng, first constructed in 1163. Permission to renovate was requested and granted each time the synagogue was destroyed, by either fire or flood. The reconstruction of the synagogue in 1421 was sponsored by the Prince of Zhou, the younger brother of Ming Emperor Chen Zu. The Imperial Cash Office subsidized the project. Forty years later, a flood completely destroyed the synagogue, save its foundation. After the floodwaters subsided, the Jews of Kaifeng, headed by Ai Qin, petitioned the provincial commissioner, requesting the right of the community to rebuild the demolished synagogue on its original site. Permission was granted, and Kaifeng Jewry was able to reconstruct their house of worship.[3]

It is believed that the population of the Kaifeng Jewish community reached its height before the Yellow River flood in 1642. At that time, the community numbered approximately 5,000 individuals. The population dropped to 1,000 or less in the eighteenth century. The dedication of the repaired synagogue was celebrated throughout the Chinese community. This was clearly displayed through one plaque inscribed by a Qing Emperor, and several vertical plaques and scrolls donated by local officials.[4]

The Jews of Kaifeng had absolute freedom of religion, and their customs were respected. At one point in history the local government enacted a regulation that stated "strangers and carriers of pork cannot pass near the synagogue."[5] No equivalent period in the entire history of other historical Diasporas shows Jews enjoying this level of respect.

Kaifeng Jews Since 1950

As a community, the Kaifeng Jews always lived according to their own traditions, as both observant and assimilated Jews. Relations between the Kaifeng Jews and the Chinese government have always been good. Nobody interfered with their distinct lifestyle. Compared with China's enormous population, the Kaifeng Jews were so small in number that they went completely overlooked.[6] It was not until recent history that any policies were implemented to place restrictions on their way of life.

The Chinese government has never prevented foreigners from practicing Judaism within China. However, they handled Kaifeng Jews differently. Why was a different policy implemented for the Kaifeng Jews? Why did the government pay so much attention to them?

Over time, the Jewish community in Kaifeng deteriorated. However, the Jews of Kaifeng never lost their sense of identity. Today, their customs and traditions are not very different from other Chinese. They do not practice traditional Jewish rites; however, they remember their ancestry and insist on their Jewish roots when discussing their identity. In a 1952 government census, many of the Kaifeng Jews classified themselves as "Jew" when filling out the census forms. As a result, their residence registration booklet and ID card (issued in late 1980s) marked them as "Jew." The local government accepted their claim and never challenged their Jewish identity.

However, the local and central governments handled things differently. After defeating most of the Guomindang's forces and with the end of the Korean War in sight, the Chinese government started to look inward and paid more attention to the stability of its own country. Of specific importance was the unity of all ethnic groups within Chinese territory. In August 1952, the central government issued three decrees to strengthen unity. These decrees established autonomous regions and protected the equal rights of all ethnic groups. One decree was the "Resolution on Ensuring That All Minority Groups That Live in China Enjoy Equal National Rights."[7] The resolution was implemented to ensure that all minorities, regardless of the size of their populations, were permitted to establish their own autonomous region. The resolution also protected small nationalities, who either lacked the requisites for establishing autonomous areas, lived in mixed communities, or scattered across the country. These minorities were to enjoy national equality all the same. In addition, all small nationalities were given representation at the National People's Congress, at least one deputy each.

In order to fulfill this resolution the Chinese government ethnically identified the population. This was the first time individual minorities and their areas of habitation were ever recorded. Such facts needed clarification in order to ensure the rights and political representation of minorities promised under the new resolution. The government introduced a list of traits in order to define what constituted a separate ethnic group. The list included five criteria:[8]

1. a common language;
2. an area of habitation;
3. unique set of customs;
4. attitudes and beliefs; and
5. traditional means of livelihood.

Investigation groups comprised of ethnologists, linguists, historians, and other specialists who were organized by the central government to assist local governments in areas that housed ethnic groups under question. In order to gain official recognition as an ethnic group, the investigation groups had to declare that the community met with the five criteria listed above.[9] Obviously, the Kaifeng Jews did not qualify as an ethnic minority based on those five criteria, and were therefore not granted government recognition.

It is argued that the Chinese government was doing something impossible: to identify each and every ethnic group by one set of criteria, as there are always exceptions. It is, however, clear that the government was well intended.

National Day in 1952 was one of the biggest events in the history of Chinese politics. The theme of all festivities was the unity of individual minorities. Local governments across the country were asked to select representatives from every ethnic group living in their region. Those selected would be invited to go to Beijing to participate in the National Day celebrations. This demonstration showed the whole world that China was giving equal rights to all.

Although the Kaifeng Jews were not declared an individual ethnic group, the Bureau of Central South and the Kaifeng Municipal Government chose two Jewish descendants from Kaifeng to represent them in Beijing. Ai Fenming was a communist who worked in an air force unit in Kaifeng; Shi Fenying worked for Henan Province in the Foreign Affairs Office. The Jewish descendants were selected because the local governments were aware of their existence and wanted to ensure that they too be granted equal rights.

While in Beijing, Ai Fenming and Shi Fenying introduced themselves as Jews. They were well received at the National Day celebration. They participated in all activities including a state banquet hosted by Premier Zhou Enlai on 16 October. *The People's Daily*, a major newspaper run by the Central Committee of the Communist Party, cited the Jews as one of 46 ethnic groups[10] that participated in the banquet,[11] an indication that the Kaifeng Jews were considered one of the separate ethnic groups.

One may feel that Jews in Kaifeng were lucky in New China. They were honored simply because they were Jews. This was the first community recognition they received in the 1,000 years they had been in China. No Jews elsewhere had ever enjoyed the same honor. Seemingly, their identity was no problem at all.

In April 1953, a policy-seeking telegraph was sent from the United Front[12] of the Bureau of Central South to the Central United Front in Beijing to inquire if it was appropriate for them to recognize the Kaifeng Jews as an individual ethnic group.[13] Why the issue arose at this time is still not clear. Regardless, this telegraph questioned the political status of the Kaifeng Jews for the first time in history. It resulted in a far-reaching Chinese policy towards Kaifeng Jews. According to the policy, Kaifeng Jews would have had political representation automatically had they been recognized as a separate ethnic group. It is only because they did not receive initial recognition that their status was in question.

The Central Unity Front of the Community Party of China sent an official written reply to the United Front of the Bureau of Central South on 8 June 1953. They explained that the Jews who reside in Kaifeng

have no direct connections economic wise. They don't have a common language of their own and a common area of inhabitance. They have completely mixed and mingled with the majority Han population, in terms of their political, economical and cultural life, neither do they possess any distinctive traits in any other aspect ...

therefore, "it is not an issue to treat them as one distinctive ethnic group, as they are not a Jewish nation in themselves."

However, the document also explains that this was an intricate issue because there were Jews residing in other Chinese cities as well. The document refers specifically to the stateless Second World War refugees who were still living in Shanghai at that time.[14] It points out that recognition as a separate ethnic group "could cause other problems and put us in a passive position politically." We have no idea what they meant by "other problems" and no clear understanding of why the Chinese government believes they might have found themselves "put in a passive position politically." Nothing specific is mentioned in the document. However, the expression "in a passive position politically" is used here to warn that the local government should do everything possible to avoid political confrontation. The document's final conclusion read, "your request of acknowledging Kaifeng Jewry as a separate nationality is improper. Kaifeng Jewry should be treated as a part of the Han Nationality."

Nevertheless, the document stressed that:

> we should take the initiative to be more caring to them in various activities, and educate the local Han population not to discriminate against or insult them. This will help gradually ease away the differences they might psychologically or emotionally feel exists between them and the Han.

The document was hand written and reworked many times.[15] For instance, originally, the document stated that, "in order to avoid unnecessary misunderstanding and problems, it is better not to say anything if we recognize them or not, but to keep the above principle in the mind of leaders." However, those words were crossed out before the document was sent out. The document also showed that it was read and approved by top Chinese leaders such as Chairman Mao, Liu Shaoqi, Zhou Enlai, and Deng Xiaoping. It is highly possible that some of the corrections were made by one of these leaders. Regardless, their approval finalized the document permanently.

Although the document was initially written to deal with ethnic identification, it became the guideline for all future issues concerning the Kaifeng Jews.

Clearly, this document was written solely to clarify the ethnic identification of the Kaifeng Jews. It contains no discrimination against the Kaifeng Jews. Had the Kaifeng Jews maintained their traditional way of life, observed Jewish *kehillah*, maintained their own temple, followed the Jewish calendar, abided by the rules of *kashrut*, and taken part in Hebrew prayer, things would probably have turned out differently.

This policy did not affect everyday life for the Kaifeng Jews. However, any hopes that the Chinese government would acknowledge the Kaifeng Jews as a separate ethnic group were permanently ended. Although they lacked official political status, they still received outside attention. The Chinese government encouraged foreigners to visit Kaifeng and see the Jewish community. For instance, Timoteus Pokora, a Czech sinologist, and Rene Goldman, a Canadian, visited Kaifeng Jews in 1957.[16] This indicates that although the government did not qualify them as a separate ethnic group, they still recognized the Kaifeng Jews as a unique community. However, the issue dissolved as other political changes caused China to become increasingly isolated from the rest of the world.

China implemented the Open-Door Policy in the late 1970s, dramatically changing all policies relating to both domestic and international affairs. In January 1980, the Ministry of Foreign Affairs of China arranged for a small group of foreigners to visit Kaifeng. This group included four Canadians, and one American journalist named Aline Mosby; several Chinese reporters were also commissioned to make this special trip. Their goal was to meet with the Jews of Kaifeng and see how the Cultural Revolution affected them.

Why was this trip organized? Mosby requested that the trip be organized, and the Chinese government granted permission.[17] After their visit to Kaifeng, the Westerners wrote and published articles about the current situation of the Kaifeng Jews.[18] This newfound attention re-introduced the question: should the Chinese government formally recognize the Kaifeng Jews as a separate ethnic group? For the first time, the issue was given both national and international attention.

More and more foreigners were entering China, a direct result of the Open-Door Policy.[19] The local government of Kaifeng predicted that an increasing number of tourists would come to see Kaifeng's Jewish community. In preparation for this, the Unity Front of Henan Province re-opened the case of the Kaifeng Jews, challenging the central government's decision to deny them special status yet again. The Unity Front of Henan Provence sent a report to the office of the Central Unity Front in March 1980. In the report, the Unity Front of Henan Provence asked two fundamental questions:

1. Should the Kaifeng Jews be treated as a minority group?
2. How should the Kaifeng Jews be referred to and treated in foreign affairs?

Why did the Unity Front of Henan Province do this? Surely, they were aware of the previous policy sent from Beijing in 1953. It is highly possible that they were seeking a new policy altogether. In this period of Chinese history, the late 1970s to early 1980s, it was not uncommon for people to seek new policies in order to make changes. Still, the actual reason for their request remains unclear.

The Central Unity Front responded to the Unity Front of Henan Province's questions on May 8, 1980.[20] It was obvious that the Central office was not willing to make changes. First, the response quoted the policy stated in the document of 1953. It went on to explain that the Kaifeng Jews did not seek recognition as a minority people after 1953, and as far as they understood, the majority of Kaifeng Jews did not desire special classification. Most young and middle-aged people felt indifferent about the issue. In conclusion, the Central Unity Front declared:

> We believe, as it was not necessary in the past, it is not necessary now for us to recognize Kaifeng Jewry as an ethnic group. However, when we deal with them, we should give consideration to the customs they still keep, help them to solve possible problems they may have, and more important, do not discriminate against them.

The document suggests at the end that "some appropriate arrangements be made for representative figures among them," a common method of dealing with ethnic groups and political issues in China.

The reaction of the local government on this issue is still unknown; however, their prediction regarding tourism was correct. Every year more and more Westerners visit China. Many of them are Jewish and, in the hope of meeting some of the Kaifeng Jews, they include Kaifeng on their travel itineraries.[21]

Local authorities responsible for receiving these visitors needed a specific guideline to deal with the new situation. They wanted to ensure that they properly represented the Kaifeng Jewish community. On 2 July 1984, the Foreign Affairs Office of the Henan provincial government drafted another document, this time dealing directly with political policy towards the Kaifeng Jews. The document outlined three main points. After completion it was sent to Beijing for approval. The three points read:

1. Stick to the principle of denying Kaifeng Jewry as an ethnic group of its own. Various periodicals and newspapers should carry objective reports both domestically and internationally. Recognize the fact of historical migration, but put emphasis on the freedom and happiness that they have today. Use the terminology 'descendants of Kaifeng Jews' when we address them without implying any country or ethnic group in order to avoid any unnecessary controversy.

   Be lenient to foreign scholars and tourists with the request of visiting Kaifeng synagogue relics, stone tablets and meeting with Jewish descendants. The Kaifeng Foreign Affairs Office will be in charge of their visits politically.

2. From the standpoint of historical materialism, we may consider opening the original site of Kaifeng synagogue and stone tablets to the public. Kaifeng

Municipal Museum could keep historical files of Kaifeng Jewry in one of its exhibit rooms for viewing. Related introduction could also be made in books and paintings for publicity abroad and in tourist brochures.

3. Regarding donations made to Kaifeng by Jewish persons from other countries, acceptance could be considered if the donor has no political intentions, and is only doing it out of kindness for renovating historical sites, museums or other welfare purposes. If the donor's purpose is religiously oriented or implying 'a Jewish nation,' the donation should be turned down with grace.

As we can see here, the points emphasized the major concerns of Henan province's Foreign Affairs Office. Most issues deal with matters other than ethnic identification. In short, the points introduced a set of guidelines for tourist issues: what can and cannot be done when receiving foreign visitors.

The three points were highly politically oriented. They raised two fundamental issues related to the Kaifeng Jews:

1. They address the Kaifeng Jews as "descendants" in order to deny the Kaifeng Jews' connection with the Jewish people and Israel as a Jewish state. This was done to avoid controversy.
2. They made the Jewish religion taboo, and classified anything related to Judaism unacceptable, even donations.

Response to the three points from the authorities in Beijing remains unknown. However, this document provided a guideline for dealing with foreign visitors in Kaifeng. Those who are familiar with the situation concerning Kaifeng and those who have been to Kaifeng can confirm that the policy works even now.

For the past 1,000 years Jews have lived, worked, and thrived in China. However, big changes have occurred over the last 50 years. After the Second World War, many Jews left China. Today, Jewish presence is increasing steadily. Western Jews now reside in major cities throughout China, bringing customs and religious practices with them. The arrivals of coreligionists and tourists have caused the Jewish descendants of Kaifeng to show a renewed interest in their heritage. New links are being established between Kaifeng and Israel. On both fronts, all bodes well for a continued, mutually advantageous relationship between both Jewish communities.

The full text of the 1953 document reads as following:

> The United Front of the Bureau of Central South:
> The telegraph dated Apr 3rd regarding the Kaifeng Jewry is received.
> Judging from your telegraph, the Jews scattered in Kaifeng have no direct connections economic wise, they don't have a common

language of their own and a common area of inhabitance. They have completely mixed and mingled with the majority Han population, in terms of their political, economical and cultural life, neither do they possess any distinctive traits in any other aspect. All this indicates that it is not an issue to treat them as one distinctive ethnic group, as they are not a Jewish nation in themselves.

Secondly, aside from the Kaifeng Jewry, there is stateless Jewish population in Shanghai. Jewish presence in some other large and mid-sized cities are also possible, however scarce it might be. It is an intricate issue. It could cause other problems and put us in a passive position politically if we acknowledge the Jews of Kaifeng. Therefore, your request of acknowledging Kaifeng Jewry as a separate nationality is improper based solely on the historical archival evidence you found. You have only seen the minor inessential differences between the Kaifeng Jews and their Han counterpart, and fail to see their commonality and the fact that they're essentially the same. (The publication found in *People's Daily* during National Day celebration time last year regarding "a Jewish nationality" was provided by the Central Ethnic Affairs Committee.) Kaifeng Jewry should be treated as a part of the Han Nationality.

The major issue is that we should take the initiative to be more caring to them in various activities, and educate the local Han population not to discriminate against or insult them. This will help gradually ease away the differences they might psychologically or emotionally feel exists between them and the Han.

The United Front of the Central Committee
of the Communist Party of China
June 8, 1953

Notes

1 A few documents still exist from the Yuan Dynasty (1271–1368) that refer to the Mongol's policy concerning Jews. For details, please refer to Donald D. Leslie, *The Survival of the Chinese Jews*, E. J. Brill, 1972, pp. 11–16.
2 The 1489 stele records "the three-points covenants" made by Chinese Song emperor with the Kaifeng Jews: "Become part of Chinese, honor and preserve the customs of your ancestors, and remain and hand them down in Kaifeng." This could not be proved genuine by other reference.
3 Cf. the 1489 stele.
4 To read the full text see William C. White, *Chinese Jews*, pt. II.
5 White, *Chinese Jews,* pt. I, p. 80.
6 Traditionally speaking, Chinese use the word "minority" to refer to all non-Han ethnic groups, as they are all small in number compared with the majority — Han people. In fact, the word "Chinese" refers to "Han." As a result, Chinese people often use the word "nationality" when referring to their ethnic group. Another word which is very much used is "nationality" to refer to which ethnic group one belongs.

7 The other two are "Implementing Program for Regional National Autonomy" and "Resolution on Measures of Setting Up Local national Democratic United Government."

8 *Questions and Answers about China's National Minorities*, New World Press, 1985, p. 144.

9 A power mechanism in Central China set up by the Central Committee of the Communist Party. The whole country was then divided into several regions, each governed by a bureau that was higher in political structure in China than provincial government.

10 The number rose to 55 in 1960s. Today 56 national minorities are recognized by the central government.

11 "People's Daily," 17 October 1952, p. 1.

12 An office set up by the Chinese government in charge of affairs of multiparty and multiethnic groups in general.

13 That telegraph is not available to this author but we could figure out the main point from the reply document, which repeats the request. The date of the telegraph is 3 April 1953.

14 Obviously, this refers to Jewish refugees from Central Europe and still staying in Shanghai though the majority had left after the Second World War.

15 It should be pointed out that not every word, especially those corrections, is legible as far as the copy I have is concerned.

16 Michael Pollak, *Mandarins, Jews and Missionaries: The Jewish Experience in the Chinese Empire*, Philadelphia: Jewish Publication Society of America, 1980, pp. 248–49.

17 This document is not available to this author but its purpose was repeated in the reply.

18 Michael Pollak, op. cit., p. xiv.

19 Pollak lists a number of such visits: Pollak, op. cit., p. xix.

20 The document is titled "Reply for the Issue on the Kaifeng Jews" and is marked as No. 2, 401.

21 It is estimated a few hundred Jews visit Kaifeng annually.

16

THE JUDAISM OF THE KAIFENG JEWS AND LIBERAL JUDAISM IN AMERICA

Anson Laytner

Back in 1942, when he first shared the history and cultural materials of the Kaifeng Jewish community with the English-speaking world, Bishop William Charles White noted:

> No attempt has been made to interpret the religious or moral philosophical ideas of the Chinese Jews, or the permeation and influence of Chinese non-Jewish ideas upon their beliefs, as may be revealed in these inscriptions. Such a study would require considerable time, and would bring this monograph to undue dimensions. As a matter of fact, a Part IV, PHILOSOPHICAL, would be necessary to deal adequately with this subject.[1]

Indeed, since these words were penned, few have attempted to analyze or discuss the religious ideas of this isolated Jewish community. Michael Pollak devoted several chapters to a general review of the synagogue, the inscriptions, and the practices and customs of the community in his *Mandarins, Jews and Missionaries*.[2] In Jonathan Goldstein's volumes based on the historic 1992 Harvard conference on the Jewish Diasporas in China, essays by Nancy Shatzman Steinhardt, Irene Eber, and Andrew Plaks, in particular, have expanded on this subject.[3] And most recently, Tiberiu Weisz has devoted a slim volume to a re-translation and interpretation of the Kaifeng stele.[4] But, by and large, this field of study has remained relatively unexplored and the research on it meager.[5]

These notes, written by an amateur scholar with little knowledge of classical Chinese language and culture, hopefully will stimulate a more complete examination of the religious ideas of the Kaifeng Jews, treating them with the respect they inherently deserve. I say this because, when it comes to the so-called "exotic" Jewish communities, the cultural bias of the dominant Jewish communities shows through. We have no trouble with – and often no idea of – the extent to which our own varieties of Judaism have borrowed from other theologies and philosophies. However, when it comes to Chinese Jews, the influence of Confucian thought is seen somehow as a *lian*, or contaminating, or as evidence of the Kaifeng Jewish community's assimilation.

Consider though Biblical Judaism's foundations in ancient Egyptian, Mesopotamian, and Canaanite cultures; the influences of Zoroastrian, Hellenistic, Aristotelian thought (the latter via Islamic thinkers), and the borrowings from medieval Christianity and the European philosophers from the seventeenth to twentieth centuries, to mention but a few. Thus, while it may indeed be said that the Chinese Jews absorbed foreign ideas into their faith, the same may be said, and indeed ought to be said, for the Jewish communities of Europe and the Middle East as well. What is fit for the Beijing duck ought to be fit for the goose and gander as well!

The only difference between what happened in Europe and the Middle East on the one hand and China on the other is that, in no small part due to population size, the Chinese Jews ended up virtually assimilating, while further to the West foreign ideas were assimilated but the people flourished.

But what would happen if, instead of viewing the incorporation of Confucian ideas into the Jewish religious thought of the Kaifeng Jews as something regrettable and unfortunate, we chose to look at the phenomenon as a unique amalgam of two great schools of thought, as syncretism of the highest order? While admittedly this Confucianized Judaism has not had any influence in the history of Jewish thought as did, for example, the pre-rabbinic incorporation of Hellenistic thought into the Judaism of that era, which in turn became rabbinic Judaism, i.e. the Judaism that is practiced today, it is nonetheless significant in its own right.[6]

I have an ulterior motive for proposing a more intensive study of this Confucian–Judaic hybrid. As a rabbi/teacher, I have observed how many contemporary Jews struggle with the theological impact of the Holocaust on our concepts of God and our understanding of the divine–human relationship. What impact might the unique synthesis of Confucian/Taoist concepts and Judaism potentially hold for contemporary Jewish thought and life? Given the interest of many Western Jews in Eastern faiths (itself a parallel of the European and North American general society's interest in the same[7]), I thought it might be intellectually and spiritually worthwhile – and "fun" – to explore the Kaifeng Jewish materials for what they might offer to our own Western-style Judaism.

Primary Sources

The primary sources for constructing a Chinese Jewish theology are the texts of the stone stele and the *bian* and *lian*, the inscriptions that respectively adorned the beams and columns of the synagogue, some of which were transcribed by the Jesuits and later by the "Chinese delegates," and thereby were preserved for posterity once the synagogue was demolished.[8] One has to regret the loss over time of two books, which are mentioned in the 1663 stele. One of these, entitled *A Preface to the Illustrious Way*, apparently was an introduction by a Chinese Jewish scholar to the Jewish way of life as he knew it.[9]

In the following sections, I have grouped material from the steles, the *bian* and the *lian* thematically. One general preliminary comment: when one reads the texts of the steles, one notes that they say little about God, more about the Way (*Dao/Torah*), and the most about the practices, customs, and history of the Kaifeng community. This is both very Jewish and very Confucian.

God

Although the Chinese Jews used a number of common Chinese terms for God (including *Shang Di*, *Tian Zhu* and the most common appellation, *Tian*), what is interesting theologically speaking is that the most commonly used term "Heaven" has a parallel in a commonplace rabbinic Hebrew synonym for God, *Shamayim*.[10]

What do the Chinese Jewish sources say about "Heaven?" Very little, as it turns out. *Tian* is impersonal, creative, and mysterious.[11] The steles instead focus on "*Dao*," i.e. the Way of Heaven, which, as we will see, also referred to the Scriptures/*Torah*, whereas the *bian* and *lian*, perhaps because they were affixed to the synagogue columns, arches and gates, offer succinct and inspirational slogans, such as one still sees in China today albeit for a different faith. These phrases were either direct quotes from Chinese sources (the Book of Odes, for example) or innovative sayings.

The *bian*:

- "August Heaven the Supreme Ruler"
- "He Daily Regards This Place"
- "Lord of the Pure and True Religion"
- "The Religion Honors (that which/he who) Has No Form".

The *lian*:[12]

- "When looking up, in contemplating the creative works of Heaven, you dare not withhold your reverence and awe"
- "Its presence is not impeded by visible form, its absence does not imply an empty void; for the Way is outside the limits of existence or non-existence"
- "Before the Great Void, we burn fragrant incense, entirely forgetting its name or form"
- "The ever-living lord, who produces life without ceasing/The creating Heaven, whose transmutations never end"

209

- "(He is) intelligent, (He is) clear-seeing; let us with enlightenment worship his majesty".

Torah/Dao

As can be seen even in the *lian* quoted above, closely related to "Heaven" is their use of the word "Dao" or "Way," which apparently was their term of choice for "Torah" but which, obviously, also simultaneously connected their Chinese Jewish reader with the Confucian/Daoist concept. Their choice was a good one because the concepts of *Torah* and *Dao* can fit neatly together. For the rabbis, *Torah* – which literally means instruction, and in this case, divine instruction – existed in multiple forms. Most common is the written *Torah*, the actual text of the Five Books of Moses. Then there is the oral *Torah*, the gradually unfolding rabbinic interpretations of the written *Torah*, both of which traditionally are believed to have been given to Moses in their entirety on Sinai. Third, there is the mystical *Torah* of the *kabbalah* (of which the Chinese Jews may have been acquainted in its more ancient Biblical or classical rabbinic forms if at all); and fourth, there is the primordial *Torah*.

According to classical rabbinic *midrashim*, this primordial *Torah* existed before Creation and God used it, as an architect might use a plan, to effect Creation.[13] In this form, *Torah* suggests something greater than "Torah" as we generally understand the word but, at the same time, it is markedly similar to the concept of the *Dao*.

It is good to heed Donald Leslie's advice:

> It is best, I think, not to look for a Jewish interpretation of this word *Tao*. It is the Way of Heaven, *T'ien Tao*, of the religion, the Moral Order which should be followed. There are occasionally mystical aspects, and the Christian "Word" or Greek *Logos*, and Jewish *Shechina* or "Presence" of God, may spring to mind. But the Confucian and Taoist *Tao* covers all that is intended.[14]

The key point, however, is that both *Torah* and *Dao* are accessible to human beings. Through meditation, prayer, and study, a person can gain both an understanding of the mysteries of Creation and knowledge of how to live one's life in harmony with this heavenly order. The most glaring difference between the two, of course, has to do with the Chinese and Jewish perspectives on God/the Source of Creation, the former generally stressing an impersonal but immanent force, with the latter generally emphasizing a transcendent and anthropomorphic deity. Somehow, the Chinese Jews were able to reconcile the two concepts, although mostly at the expense of the anthropomorphic qualities rabbinic Judaism generally ascribed to God.

Torah/Dao of Heaven

The 1489 Stele:[15]

> Above, it is ethereal and pure; it is most honorable beyond com-
> pare. The Way of Heaven (*Tian Dao*) does not speak, yet 'the four
> seasons pursue their course, and all creatures are produced.' It is
> evident that things come to life in the springtime, grow during the
> summer, are harvested in the autumn, and stored up in the winter.
> Some fly, others swim, some walk, and other grow. Some are lux-
> uriant, others despoiled, some blooming, others falling. Living
> things are produced from the sequence of life; transformations are
> due to the process of change; shapes are the outcome of the parti-
> cular form, and colors are developed from their color source.[16]

The Ai Shi Archway:

- "Intelligence Penetrates the Profound Mysteries."

The *bian*:

- "The Invisible Source of the Law"
- "Religion Follows the Truth of Heaven"
- "Religion is Derived from Heaven."

The *lian*:

- "The Way has its source in Heaven, and the fifty-three sections record
  the facts concerning the creation of Heaven, Earth, and Man/The Religion is based on holiness, and the twenty-seven letters are used to
  transmit the mysteries of the Mind, the Way, and Learning"
- "The Scriptures were written to co-ordinate Heaven, Earth, Man, and
  Things. Bonds and Virtues, Relationships and Arrangements, have been
  orderly maintained for all time; and Moral Principles existed before
  Names and Forms."

Torah/*Dao: The Transmission of Revelation/Enlightenment*

The texts make a point of stressing the continuity of the chain of transmission,
much like the classic rabbinic text *Pirkei Avot* does. It does so to highlight
the antiquity of their faith in a culture that put the highest premium on the
most ancient of things. This principle, when linked with Chinese characters
from antiquity like PanGu and NuWa,[17] referenced to Chinese dynastic
history, and playing into the syncretistic Chinese approach to religion,
served to firmly root the Kaifeng Jews in the soil of Chinese society.

The 1489 Stele:

Abraham, the patriarch who founded the religion of Israel, was of the nineteenth generation from PanGu Adam. From the creation of heaven and earth the patriarchs handed down successively the traditions which they had received ... So (Abraham) meditated upon Heaven ... The patriarch suddenly awakening as out of sleep then understood these profound mysteries.[18] He began truly to seek the Correct Religion, with a view to assisting the true Heaven ... Through transmission (the Religion) reached Moses, who was also a patriarch of the Correct Religion ... Again (the Religion) was transmitted to Ezra ... His way of honoring Heaven and performing worship fully revealed the mysteries of the Way of the ancestors ... Truly, the Way of the Religion has been handed down, but the transmission and reception have been in sequence. It came out from TianZhu (usually identified as India); in obedience to the divine command it came.

The 1512 Stele:[19]

As for the Religion of Israel, the first ancestor Adam originally came out from India of the West country ... The founder of this religion is Abraham who is thus the ancestor of the religion. After him Moses, who transmitted the Scriptures, is thus the master of the religion. Then this same religion, from the time of the Han Dynasty, entered and established itself in the Middle Kingdom ... The Scriptures of the Way, in their transmission, had a beginning. From creation down, the Patriarch Adam handed them on to Noah; Noah handed them on to Abraham; Abram ... to Isaac ... to Jacob ... to the Twelve Tribes ... to Moses ... to Aaron ... to Joshua ... to Ezra.

The 1663 Stele:[20]

It began with Adam ... and it was continued, at first by Noah, and then by Abraham. Abram comprehended the purpose of the union of Heaven and man, as well as the principles of moral cultivation and of human destiny. He knew also, that the Way of Heaven "has neither sound nor smell", and is very mysterious and profound, and that from it creatures are endowed with movement and with life, and are transformed and nourished in orderly manner. That is why he modeled no images, nor did he allow himself to be deluded by ghosts and spirits. He made the honoring of Heaven as the only principle, leading men to 'develop completely their minds,' and to

212

conform to Heaven, so that they could follow their minds and see the Way.

After it had been handed down through several lines, the holy Patriarch Moses was born. Endowed wit spiritual intelligence and heavenly sincerity, his extraordinary penetration excelled that of other men. Seeking the Way with a sincere heart, he repressed sensual appetites, forgetting both sleep and meals, and finally he received the Scriptures on Mount Sinai.

The holy Patriarch (Moses) ... penetrated in quietness to the very heart of God (Di), away from the midst of forms and sounds and all confusion. He alone comprehended the abstruse principles, and thus composed the fifty-three sections of the Sacred Literature (the *Torah*). They are most easy and most simple, they may be known and may be practiced, and they teach men to do good, and forbid men to do evil.

The Scriptures contain the true doctrine, and the interpreter dares not blend with them anything evasive. The Scriptures in themselves are easy and simple, and the interpreter dares not mix with them anything complex or difficult. From them men learn [the Five Cardinal Relationships] have their foundation in the good faculty of knowing and doing. All men may manifest goodness and return to their original condition, which is in accordance with the principle which underlay the compiling of the Scriptures by the holy Patriarch (Moses), and the reason why the ancestors venerated the Scriptures.

The *bian*:

• "The Superior Doctrine Comes from the West."

The *lian*:

• "Through Abram the Religion was established, and the Laws had no visible image/ From Moses the Scriptures were handed down, and their Doctrines were grounded on the one center"
• "The Heavenly Writings are fifty-three in number; with our mouth we recite them, and in our heart we hold them fast; praying that the Imperial Domain may be firmly established/ The Sacred Script has twenty-seven letters; these we teach in our families; and display on our doors; desiring that the land and grain[21] may continually prosper."

Torah/Dao on Earth

The stele and the inscriptions devote the bulk of their texts to descriptions of how the *Torah/Dao* is practiced and how it was transmitted through time.

How the community preserved its scriptures and its temple is a major topic that is beyond the scope of this paper. Of great importance to the Kaifeng community was its need to show how closely aligned the *mitzvot* were with Confucian observance, both in theory and practice.

The 1489 stele:

> ... the Way must be based on Purity (*Ching*), Truth (*Zhen*), Ritual (*Li*), and Worship (*Bai*). *Ching* means pure unity without duplicity, *Zhen* signifies genuineness without depravity, *Li* denotes simply reverence, and *Bai* is an act of obeisance. In the midst of daily occupations men must not forget Heaven even for a single moment, but morning, noon, and night, three times a day should pay due reverence (*li*) and offer worship (*bai*). This is the basic principle (*li*) of the true Way of Heaven (*T'ian Tao*) ... The Way has no form or figure, but is just like the Way of Heaven which is above. [The text goes on to describe the traditional Jewish prayer postures with a "Chinese" interpretation, "ancestor worship"[22] and holy days.[23]]

The 1512 stele:

> It is commonly said that the Scriptures were for the purpose of communicating the Way. What is the Way? It is a principle (*li*) of daily usage and common practice, which has been followed by all men from antiquity to the present.
>
> Therefore, in great things like the Three Cardinal Virtues of duty and the Five Constant Virtues, and in small matters like the fine details of events and objects, there is nothing in which the Way is not, and no moment when it is not functioning; in short it is concerned with everything.
>
> Without the Scriptures the Way cannot be conserved, but without the Way the Scriptures cannot be put into practice. Suppose the Scriptures did not exist, then the Way would not be supported, and men would wander blindly, not knowing where to go, and would finally put credence in absurd gossip and walk in gloomy darkness. Therefore, the Way of the saints and sages has been transmitted through the Six Scriptures,[24] for the instruction of after generations up to the present, and will reach finally to myriads of succeeding generations.
>
> Although the written characters of the Scriptures of this religion are different from the script of Confucian books, yet on examining their principles (*li*) it is found that their ways (*tao*) of common practice are similar. That is why when the Way reigns between father and son, the father extends loving-kindness and the son

responds with filial love ... the prince is benevolent and the minister reverential ... the elder (brother) is friendly and the younger respectful ... the husband conciliatory and the wife complaisant. When the way reigns between friends, they will be mutually helpful and faithful.

In the Way there is nothing greater than Love (*Ren*) and Righteousness (*Yi*), and when these are put into practice, the 'feeling of commiseration' and the 'feeling of shame and dislike' will be the natural results. In the Way there is nothing greater than Propriety (*Li*) and Wisdom (*Zhi*),[25] and when they are put into practice, the 'feeling of modesty and complaisance,' and the 'feeling of approving and disapproving' will be the natural results.

The 1663 Stele:

Filial piety and brotherliness, loyalty and faithfulness, have their foundation in the heart; benevolence and righteousness, propriety and wisdom derive their origin from nature. Heaven and earth, and all things, and the moral obligations and laws controlling human relationships, are the great themes of the Scriptures. The greatest of the items are the ritual ceremonies and the sacrifices.

He who performs the ceremonies of worship, puts away from him that which is evil, and models himself on that which is true; he overcomes in himself the things which do not conform to the rites, and renders himself conformable to them.[26]

The 1679 Stele:[27]

The Scriptures have been propagated in accordance with the principles of both Heaven and Humanity (*T'ian Ren*), and in harmony with the teachings of Confucius and Mencius ... The religion (taught them) to venerate August Heaven, to reverence the Scriptures, and to exercise frugality in the use of things.

The Zhao Shi Archway:

- "Honor Heaven and Pray for Country"
- "Reverence the Scriptures and Cultivate the Social Duties."

The Ai Shi Archway:

- "Reverently Accord with August Heaven"
- "Honor and Fear August Heaven"
- "Happiness."

The *bian*:

- "Honor and Fear August Heaven"
- "Honor Heaven and Pray for Country"
- "In Obedience to Heaven Proclaim Transforming Law"
- "With Enlightenment Serve the Supreme Ruler"
- "Render Pure Service to Majestic Heaven"
- "Reverence Heaven and Respect Men."

The *lian*:

- "Acknowledging Heaven, Earth, Prince, Parent and Teacher, you are not far from the correct road of Reason and Virtue/ Cultivating the virtues of Benevolence, Righteousness, Propriety, Wisdom and faith, you reach the first principle of Sages and Philosophers"
- "Worship consists in honoring Heaven, and righteousness in imitating Ancestors; but the human mind has always existed before worship or righteousness"
- "Before the Great Void, we burn the fragrant incense, entirely forgetting its name or form/ Tracing back to the Western World, we resist our evil desires and solely attend to purity and truth."

The *Mitzvot*

However much the Kaifeng community presented a synthesis of Jewish and Confucian theology, when it came to practice, the Jews of Kaifeng observed a traditional Jewish lifestyle. In this they were most pragmatic, because how one lives life is far more important than what one thinks or believes. It is also the key to transmitting one's culture/faith. The texts speak for themselves in terms of delineating how closely Chinese Jewish custom paralleled that of Jews elsewhere. For those who need details, both White and Weisz, the former from afar and the latter from within the fold, document the connections between the Chinese practice and mainstream Jewish observance.

The 1512 stele:

> When men follow the Way in their fastings or purifications, they necessarily show themselves dignified and respectful. When men follow the Way in the sacrifices to the ancestors, they necessarily show themselves filial and sincere.
>
> When men follow the Way in their acts of worship in blessing and praising Heaven above, the Author and Preserver of all things, they make sincerity and reverence, in all their motions and attitude, the sole foundation of their conduct.

216

Concerning widows and widowers, and orphans and childless old men, and the lame and infirm of every sort, there is not that is not succored and relieved by compassion, so that no one becomes shelterless.

If anyone through poverty is unable to arrange a marriage, or to carry out a necessary funeral ceremony, there is not but will hasten to bring him help, so that he may have the funds for a wedding, or the needed equipment for a funeral.

If anyone is in mourning, meat and wine are for bidden to him, and at funerals he does not make ostentatious display, but follows the ritual regulations, for he does not believe at all in superstitious practices.

Coming down to the accuracy of scales and the dimensions of measures, they do not, in the slightest degree, dare to cheat other men ... [28]

However, their fear of the decrees of Heaven, their observance of the imperial laws, their high esteem for the Five Social Relations, their veneration for the Five Constant Virtues, their respect for the customs received from their ancestors, their filial piety towards their parents, their respect for their superiors, their harmony with their neighbors, their attachment for their masters and their friends, the teaching they give to their sons and grandsons, their diligence in their vocations, their accumulation of secret merit, their patience when confronted with small resentments, and their ideas of carefulness, attentiveness, exhortations, and encouragements — all these belong to this.

Truly, such are the Scriptures, in their applications of the Way in regard to daily usages and common practices.

Therefore it is, that from what 'Heaven has conferred, and nature has obeyed,' there is perfection; that from 'instruction through keeping the Way,' there is progress; and that from the virtues of love and righteousness, propriety and wisdom, there comes preservation.

As to the modeling of statues and figures, and the painting of forms and colors, they are vain matters and empty practices, meant to startle and dazzle the ears and eyes, which is a depraved theory ...

Therefore all who practice this religion think only of imitating that which is good, and forbidding themselves that which is evil.

Morning and evening they are careful and watchful, and give themselves sincerely to improving their moral nature. They practice fasting, and keep the festival days, and in their meat and drink they are careful to observe the distinction between what is permitted and what is not. In all of these things they strive to take the Scriptures as their rule of conduct, and they hold them in veneration and believe in them with reverence.

Thus they hope that the favors of Heaven will come upon them in abundance, and that the benefits of Providence will not be lacking. Men will be praised for their virtues and goodness, and families rejoice in the rearing of their young. In this way the intention of the Patriarchs of the Religion will not be frustrated, and the ceremonies of the cult will be performed unchanged.[29]

The 1663 stele:

Because there is not a day when Heaven is not among men, therefore each day, morning, noon, and night, three times there are the acts of worship — and these are just the times when men see Heaven.

In rendering a rational awe, men honor the Way and honor virtue; exerting to the utmost their reverence and sincerity, day by day they are constantly renewed. The Book of Odes says, 'Heaven ascends and descends about our doings; it daily watches us wherever we are' (Ode 288); does this not express the very same meaning?

During the acts of worship the Sacred Literature which is recited and sometimes chanted along, and in this the honoring of the Way is manifested. Sometimes there is silent prayer, and thus the Way is honored in secret. Advancing to the front (the worshipper) sees It in front of him; receding backwards suddenly It is behind him. Turning to the left, It seems to be at the left; turning toward the right It seems to be at the right.

[The text goes on to describe worship, offerings, holy days, and fasting, drawing out the similarities between the Jewish and Confucian practice.]

It is difficult completely to describe the broad lines and the detailed items of the Scriptures ... In them this Way is set forth in a manner shining with clarity and perfections, like the brilliant sun suspended in the empty void. There is no man who is incapable of perceiving the Way, and so there is no man who does not know how to honor the Scriptures.

The composition of the Scriptures, although written in an ancient script and of a different pronunciation, is in harmony with the principles of the Six Classics, and in no case is there anything not in harmony with them.

Analysis and Application of Kaifeng Judaism for Liberal Jews Today

The Kaifeng Jews wanted very much to have their faith and practices be understood in light of the dominant culture, much as Jews everywhere always have. It is not only a matter of community relations, but also a matter of spiritual survival because, by comparing and contrasting one faith with the other, what it means to be a Jew is more clearly delineated. In the Chinese situation, they were fortunate to live in a society that fostered syncretism and was indifferent to doctrinal differences in a way unimaginable in the Middle East or Europe. Consequently, the Kaifeng community was able to embrace basic Confucian and Daoist concepts, and blend them relatively easily with their own Jewish ones. The focus of both faiths on human relationships rather than theology made this syncretism particularly rich and it was able to sustain the community for many centuries.[30] That the Kaifeng community went into decline is due to its isolation, to the integration of its members into the larger society and literati class, and to China's own long eclipse during the late Qing dynasty and the subsequent turmoil of the early Republic.

Perhaps what is most striking about the Kaifeng Jewish materials is their humanistic focus. While neither atheist nor agnostic, the texts do not present a theistic perspective either. The standard term for God, *Tian*, is neither a proper name, like YHVH, nor even a word meaning "God," like *Elohim*; it is impersonal, even abstract. At best, like its Hebrew counterpart *Shamayim*, *Tian* is a word with a dual meaning, referring both to the actual sky and to a figurative or symbolic "Heaven." Absent from both terms are the anthropomorphic god-concepts of the *Torah* and *Talmud* and the *siddur* (prayerbook). Instead, in what is almost standard for mystical traditions, the texts assert that the divine, i.e. Heaven, is a mystery and ultimately unknowable.

Nonetheless, as in traditional Jewish thought, God – or *Tian* – can be known both through the creative power of nature and through the *Torah/Dao*. In the texts, *Tian Dao* provides a singular ordering of the natural world and the human world. By following the *Dao* of Scriptures, a person puts himself in harmony with the *Dao* of the natural world and, simultaneously, with the *Dao* of Heaven. The *mitzvot* are intended to help the practitioner put himself in harmony with the *Dao* so that all is one. For the Chinese Jews as for other Jews, the *mitzvot* are also what provide for Jewish continuity.

But the biggest difference between the Chinese Jewish "theology" and mainstream Jewish theology has to do with the concept of revelation and God's intervention in history. In Western religious traditions, God intervenes in history both to execute justice and effect mercy — the Jewish paradigm is Exodus from Egypt and the Revelation at Sinai. In the Chinese Jewish texts, Heaven's only intervention – if it is that at all – is the giving of Scriptures. Here revelation is only the attunement of the human being to something that is omnipresent and immanent. In the traditional Jewish perspective, revelation is something God gives to Moses and, through him, to Israel and the World. However, in the Chinese Jewish view, it is through human endeavor and self-improvement – not unlike Maimonides' views on the levels of the intellect and of the prophetic mind – that an outstanding person like Abraham or Moses can gain enlightenment and perceive the *Dao* of Heaven. In Abraham's case, his enlightened state made him the first to "know" Heaven and, therefore, he is honored as the founder of the faith. In Moses' case, his highly developed personal character led to his perceiving the mystery of Heaven and, thereafter, to his composing the Scriptures. But the revelation is theirs to achieve, not God's to bestow.

Absent from the texts is any real reference to Israel's miraculous exodus from Egypt or its Biblical years. Were these ignored because slavery was ignominious, the idea of an intervening God inconceivable, or because the Chinese Jews did not believe it or were ignorant of it? The latter seems unlikely, as the earlier generations knew Hebrew and had teachers. In traditional Judaism, God uses both history and nature as either reward or punishment. None of this is apparent from the Chinese texts. It seems that the only ways by which *Tian* manifested It/Himself were by being receptive to the perceptive human being and by ordering all life according to *Dao*.

And what of prayer? The texts amply attest to the fact that the Chinese Jews worshipped in traditional Jewish ways and observed most of the same holy days. But what happened when they read the *Torah* or uttered the traditional prayers? Probably in the beginning they understood and accepted what they recited. But as they absorbed more Chinese ideas into their faith, how did they process the radically different god-concepts? Was there a profound disassociation? Or did they recite *Torah* and the prayers out of respect for their antiquity, in other words, as a rite? This we do not know.

To summarize: *Tian* exists, without description. *Dao/Torah* is *Tian's* ordering of both the natural world and the human world. It too exists in some abstract but also immanent way. It is the role of the exceptional human being to perceive it, experience it, understand it, and try to communicate it to other people. Accepting this, the ordinary person has only to practice the *Dao* as expressed in the Scriptures – honoring Heaven with appropriate rituals, respecting one's ancestors, and living ethically – and thereby live his/her life in harmony with the *Dao* of Heaven. It is a faith that is firmly planted on earth and rooted in the proper doing of daily deeds, yet its practice allows one to feel a sense of unity with the totality of existence and to aspire to a perception of the Whole. This emphasis on human behavior and on the potential awareness of an immanent Presence/Being, rather than a system based on a transcendent and intervening God's giving of *Torah* and on our obligation to observe God's commandments (whether out of fear or love, or both), is also possibly more in keeping with the humanistic tenor of our age.

First, for many people today, the sciences have wreaked havoc on our ancient traditional god-concepts, and yet the experience of the divine in some form remains vital. Second, as modern communication methods have resulted in a smaller world in which we know more about other human beings, their perceptions of the divine are increasingly seen as being legitimate. Third, the Holocaust and other modern genocides significantly challenge the optimistic traditional perception that whatever happens is part of God's good plan. Skepticism about God's job description and/or God's job performance are the order of the day for many Jews and questions about whether or not God has ever intervened in history are increasingly common.

What better way to express our changing perception of the physical universe, of humanity's multiple perceptions of the divine, and of our despair at the enormity of human suffering than to embrace the concept that God/ Heaven is something beyond our comprehension? And, of course, this is precisely what Jewish tradition teaches by having God self-described as "I am who/what I am" or "I will be who/what I will be," and by having at its core the unpronounceable name of YHVH, which combines the present and future tenses of the verb "to be."

What Vera Schwarcz wrote about the Kaifeng Memorial Book applies equally to the Kaifeng community in general, and to us as well:

> That the flame of historic memory was not totally extinguished among the Jews of Kaifeng testifies to the perdurance of both Chinese and Jewish tradition ... Chinese and Jewish customs of memory transmission ... show us a two-way road: they offer a pathway back to the ancients as well as a trail ahead into the unforeseen.[31]

The Kaifeng Jewish community blazed a trail that was unique both for its history and for its cultural adaptation. For too long, we Jews in other parts of the world have seen only what they borrowed from Chinese civilization and not what they created; we presumed to judge their assimilation rather than admire their synthesis of Chinese and Jewish thought. Today, when so many Western Jews are falling away from traditional Jewish practice and their identity as Jews, whether because of scientific progress or the failure of Jewish theology to adequately explain God's apparent absence during the Holocaust, perhaps we can turn to the novel interpretation of Judaism by the Kaifeng Jews for a reinvigorated form of faith.

Notes

1 William Charles White, *Chinese Jews*, Toronto: University of Toronto Press, 1942. Preface to Part II.
2 Michael Pollak, *Mandarins, Jews and Missionaries: The Jewish Experience in the Chinese Empire*, Philadelphia: Jewish Publication Society of America, 1980, pp. 274–316.
3 Nancy Shatzman Steinhardt, "The Synagogue at Kaifeng: Sino–Judaic Architecture of the Diaspora;" Irene Eber, "Kaifeng Jews: The Sinification of Identity;" and Andrew H. Plaks, "The Confucianization of the Kaifeng Jews: Interpretations of the

Kaifeng Stele Inscriptions," in Jonathan Goldstein, (ed.) *The Jews of China, Volume I, Historical and Comparative Perspectives*. Armonk, NY: M.E. Sharpe, 1999, Chapters 1–3, pp. 3–21, 22–35, 36–49, respectively. In the same book, Nathan Katz studies the Judaisms of Kaifeng and Cochin, pp. 120–138. In an email to the author, dated 25 July 2005, Andrew Plaks noted that his Hebrew translations of the first two stele inscriptions appeared in *Pe'amim*, (the monthly periodical of Machon Ben-Zvi) in 1989 and that a student of his at Hebrew University, Noam Urbach, recently did a fine Hebrew translation of the 1663 stele for an M.A. project. Urbach now teaches at Shandong University under Avrum Ehrlich.

4 Tiberiu Weisz, *The Kaifeng Stone Inscriptions: The Legacy of the Jewish Community in Ancient China*, New York: iUniverse, Inc., 2006.

5 One other study, from the Chinese side, is Chen Yuan's "A Study of the Israelite Religion in Kaifeng, 1920, revised 1980," in S. Shapiro (ed.) *Jews in Old China: Studies by Chinese Scholars*, New York: Hippocrene Books, 1984, pp. 15–45.

6 Kudos to Andrew Plaks for arguing for the same culturally-neutral, but appreciative, perspective in his essay in Goldstein, *The Jews of China*, pp. 38–39.

7 This interest is hardly new. It goes back well into the nineteenth century. Irene Eber, for one, has studied the subject from the perspective of a European Jewish theologian's exploration and adaptation of Daoist ideas in what is probably the most in-depth study of the two "theological" streams. See her article "Martin Buber and Taoism" in *Points East*, vols 20:2 and 3, July and November 2005, an excerpted version of her article of the same name which appeared in *Monumenta Serica, Journal of Oriental Studies*, Vol. 42, 1994. In a different vein, Vera Schwarcz has compared crosscultural perspectives on historical memory in her book *Bridge Across Broken Time: Chinese and Jewish Cultural Memory*, New Haven: Yale University Press, 1998.

8 See Pollak, op. cit., pp. 287–289, for a brief description of the *bian* and *lian*, and White, *Chinese Jews*, II, p. 121–153 for a complete listing.

9 See White, *Chinese Jews*, II, p. 66. For more on this, and other, lost works, see Wang Yisha, "New Trends and Achievements in Chinese Research on Ancient Chinese Jews," in J. Goldstein, (ed.) *The Jews of China*, vol. II, A Sourcebook and Research Guide. Armonk, NY: M.E. Sharpe, 2000, pp.26–2, and Donald Daniel Leslie, *The Survival of the Chinese Jews: The Jewish Community of Kaifeng*. Leiden: E.J. Brill, 1972, pp. 129-130.

10 See Leslie, op. cit., p. 97.

11 The translations are from White's book and, I think, reflect an understandable religious desire on his part to personalize Heaven. I know enough Chinese to know that many of the personal pronouns are added into the text. White occasionally is honest enough to admit this – see II: 132 – "The words 'He Whom' must be supplied, for the object of reverence of the Jewish religion was God." As mentioned in note 4, Tiberiu Weisz has recently completed a new translation of the stele, the accuracy of which I cannot measure but the language of which is sometimes incomprehensible (as is White too for that matter).

12 The *lian* are couplets. For the purpose of this paper, I have sometimes separated the paired verses in order to better present ideas thematically.

13 See Genesis Rabbah 1:1. Sometimes the opening sentence of Genesis was translated/interpreted as "With Wisdom (i.e. Torah), God created heaven and earth."

14 Leslie, op. cit., p. 98.

15 White, op. cit, II, pp. 8–16. I generally have omitted words in parentheses from the quotation because they are additions by the translator, perhaps meant to clarify, but they also obscure the original meaning. Weisz, op. cit., pp. 3–19.

16 Plaks, "The Confucianization of the Chinese Jews," in Goldstein, *The Jews of China*, vol. I, pp. 40-42, discusses the apparent conflict between the Confucian and the Jewish views of Creation and basically he is correct in asserting the dominance of the creation *ex nihilo* school of thought among rabbinic thinkers. However, *midrash* allowed for multiple rabbinic perspectives and, besides, the Kaifeng community may not have been aware of these philosophical controversies as they developed in the Western realms. Plaks mentions the term *tiandi kaipi*, the opening up of the cosmos, and I would only point out that in Torah, the way God creates is by splitting and separating, opening up a space and place for life to begin and, furthermore, it is by no means self-evident from Scriptures that God created *ex nihilo*—it just depends on how one translates the Hebrew and what one wants to read into the story. See also his article "Creation and Non-Creation in Early Chinese Texts," in *Genesis and Regeneration*, Shaul Shaked (ed.), published by the Israel Academy of Sciences in 2005.

17 See Plaks, op. cit., pp. 39–40, for a discussion of Pan Gu and other names.

18 Of particular interest is the transliteration of Abraham's name to include the Buddhist term "luohan," one who has attained enlightenment — which is consistent with what the stele says Abraham achieved.

19 White, op. cit., II: 58–68, 88–90; Weisz, op. cit., pp 20–30.

20 White, *Chinese Jews*, II: 42–46; Weisz, op. cit., pp. 31–49.

21 White's translation says "Commonwealth."

22 Plaks is right in his take on the congruence of so-called "ancestor worship" among the Kaifeng Jews and its counterpart in rabbinic Judaism [see Plaks, in Goldstein (ed.), pp. 43–44]. In addition to the *avot* prayer in the "eighteen benedictions," classical rabbinic Judaism embraced the concept of *zechut avot*, the merit of the fathers/ancestors, according to which the Patriarchs and Matriarchs in Heaven continue to intercede with God on the Jewish people's behalf. Given this belief, which was reflected in prayer, and the *mitzvot* related to honoring and fearing one's parents, the corresponding Chinese concept is not so much of a stretch.

23 Plaks' analysis (ibid., pp. 44–45) of the Sabbath and the "Sabbath of Sabbaths," a.k.a. *Yom Kippur*, is brilliant.

24 White identifies these as six classics of Confucian thought and this is the generally accepted view. I suggest that in the context of this document it might instead refer to the six books that comprise the *Mishnah*, the premier classical text of Rabbinic Judaism that may have been familiar to the Kaifeng Jews because of its early date of origin.

25 The corresponding Jewish terms for these values may be *hesed* and *tsedek, derekh eretz* and *hochmah*, respectively.

26 It is interesting to see the more "humanistic" way Weisz deals with this text (p.33): "Filial piety, brotherhood, loyalty and faithfulness/were sources of the heart./ Benevolence, righteousness, ritual and wisdom/were sources of (human) nature, and/ (that) of heaven, earth and all creatures./Laws, customs, and relationships and regulations/ were the rules of the Scriptures./Activity, passivity, work, rest,/ daily drinks and foods/were the topics of the Scriptures./But its greatest (topic)/were prayers and sacrifice./Those who prayed/discarded the extravagant and modeled the truth./They were able to cause those who did not pray/ to return to praying."

27 White, op. cit., II, pp. 97–101. Weisz does not translate this stele.

28 This section reads like a summary of the basic social *mitzvot* as laid down, for example, in Leviticus 19.

29 Weisz translates the last lines as "Then many (will accord) with/the meaning of the patriarchs of the religion./Nothing will be discarded/And in honor of the rituals/Nothing will be made in excess" (pp. 29–30).

30 Xu Xin, in his article "Some Thoughts on our Policy toward the Jewish Religion – Including a Discussion of our Policy toward the Kaifeng Jews," in *Points East*, vol. 15:1, March 2000, notes the basic similarity between the two cultures: "So the Jewish religion does not just mean the religious beliefs of Jews but also the visible shape of the culture of the Jewish people, and so it is frequently used to indicate generally Jewish culture or the kernel of Jewish culture. This is similar to the term 'Confucianism' which in reality points to the heart of Chinese culture."

31 Schwarcz, op. cit., p. 108.

Part VI

PHENOMENA OF THE JEWISH–CHINESE NEXUS

17

THE ADOPTION OF CHINESE CHILDREN BY JEWISH FAMILIES AND THE EFFECT ON NORTH AMERICAN JEWISH IDENTITY

David Straub

The Jewish community in North America is as diverse as the Diaspora itself. While there has been extensive research into the various ethnic groups that make up the continent's Jewry, one subgroup of this community that has historically lacked recognition is Jews of East Asian descent. This changed in the 1990s when demographic circumstances in China and North America combined to create an entirely new Jewish subgroup: children from China adopted by Jewish families in the US and Canada. As hundreds, if not thousands, of Chinese children have been adopted by North American Jewish families, news media and Jewish social circles have debated what effect Chinese adoptees are having on the North American Jewish identity. What has also made this group notable is that it is one of first Jewish–Chinese groups in North America that has consciously formed social groups in large urban areas, such as New York City and Toronto, and social networks that have spanned the distance of the US and Canada. As the number of Chinese adopted by Jewish families continues to grow rapidly, the impact that these children have on the identity of the North American Jewish community will only increase.

Until recently, there has been very little research into the history of Chinese Jews in North America. One problem has been that, unlike other Jewish subgroups that immigrated to North America and settled together in communities, Chinese Jews are scattered across the continent individually; this has made it difficult even to provide an estimate of the group's total size, which includes not only Chinese adoptees but also the offspring of mixed Jewish–Chinese marriages and Chinese who converted to Judaism. Two studies, the National Jewish Population Survey of 2002 and the Institute for Jewish and Community Research survey in 2002, found that just over 7 per cent of America's 6 million Jews identify themselves as African

American, Asian, Latino/Hispanic, or Native American or mixed-race, for a total of about 435,000 individuals.[1] One of the few experts on the subject of Asian Jews is Patricia Y.C.E. Lin, a Taiwanese–American who converted to Judaism in the 1990s, and currently is a staff member at the Center for Educational Partnerships at the University of California, Berkeley. In a survey beginning in 2004, Lin interviewed individual Asian Jews from across the US and she estimated that the total number of American Jews of East Asian descent is between 32,000 and 60,000.[2] Jews of Chinese descent must be a sizable portion of this group, perhaps numbering in the tens of thousands, and Chinese adoptees raised in Jewish families are one of the fastest growing subgroups of Chinese Jews.

The Adoption of Asian Children by North American Families and China's One Child Policy

The adoption of Asian children by non-Asian parents in North America is not a new phenomenon. In the decade and a half after the end of the Second World War, several thousand Japanese and Chinese orphans were adopted by American parents, a trend that continued until the early 1960s when the availability of needy children ceased as a result of economic prosperity in Japan and political isolation in China. Orphaned children first began to arrive from the war-torn Korean peninsula in the 1950s, where a large number of biracial children fathered by American soldiers were abandoned.[3] By 1981, some 38,000 Korean children had been adopted by American families and Korea has continued to be a source of adoptions, though the rate of adoptions has slowed as a result of efforts by the government to decrease the number of international adoptions. In the 1960s and 1970s, Indochina experienced a refugee crisis as the American-led war in Vietnam displaced millions of civilians, and the unification of Vietnam by the North Vietnamese in 1975 unleashed a wave of millions of "boat people;" among these refugees were thousands of orphaned children who found homes with families in the US.[4] Most of the families that adopted Asian children were ethnically "white," and, while it is unknown how many children have been adopted by Jewish families since the 1940s, the number of Asian adoptees that have grown up in Jewish households is likely large.

By the 1980s, the number of East Asian countries that parents in North America could turn to for adoptions had dwindled. The communist government in Vietnam had closed its doors to adoptions and Korea, while still a destination for prospective parents, did not have enough children available for adoption to satisfy the international demand. At the same time, China was opening up economically and socially after decades of internal turmoil and isolation from the outside world. One aspect of the post-Cultural Revolution reforms that the new Deng Xiaoping government instituted in China had an unintended consequence that created a large number of orphaned baby girls who were in need of international adoptions: the "one child family" policy. In the late 1970s and early 1980s, the Chinese government instituted a strict set of rules for the number of children a family could have in order to limit the growth of China's population, which more than doubled in size under the rule of Mao Zedong and numbered more than one billion. New government regulations limited parents to one child per family in urban areas, and two to three children per family in rural areas and for ethnic minorities.

The effect the one child policy had on Chinese demographics was profound, as the rules on family size were strictly obeyed by both government officials and married couples, who faced severe fines and punishment for giving birth to more than their quota of children. The social ramifications of this policy were great, especially for mothers who gave birth to daughters. In traditional Chinese society, family lineage is passed on by the son, who receives his father's surname. For millions of fathers of female infants in China the one child policy meant that their family line would die with them; thousands of fathers could not bear this ignominious outcome and their newborn daughters were abandoned. Traditionally in China, adoptions were arranged by biological and adoptive parents through informal arrangements and, each year, thousands of infant boys and girls were adopted by Chinese parents, but by the 1990s hundreds of thousands of children were living in orphanages, far outpacing the demand of domestic adoptive families.

The 1990s and the Growth of Chinese Adoptions in North America

In 1989, the first batch of Chinese orphans, totaling thirty-three children, found new families in the US. That spring, mass student demonstrations in Tiananmen Square in Beijing were followed by a bloody massacre of thousands of protestors and bystanders, an event that left China isolated and abruptly, but temporarily, halted the foreign adoption program. The number of adoptions by American families rebounded to about 1,300 children from 1991 to 1994, and leaped to 2,049 in 1995 and 4,491 in 1998.[5] By the end of the decade, China had become the largest source of foreign adoptions in the US and more than 18,000 Chinese children, 90 per cent of them girls, had been adopted by American families. Across the border in Canada, a similar pattern occurred and, in 1995, there was an estimated 800-1,000 annual adoptions of Chinese children by Canadian families.[6]

To extract from these numbers how many Chinese children lived with Jewish families is not possible, as no statistics were kept for Chinese adoptions by Jewish families on a national level in either the US or Canada. One of the few pieces of empirical evidence for Chinese adoptees in Jewish families was a 1997 survey conducted by Stars of David, a Boston-based nationwide Jewish adoptive parents group. The survey found that, out of a set of 204 parents and 302 adoptees from across the US, 13 children, or 4.3 per cent, were from China; of the non-white children in the survey this number ranked fifth behind adoptees from Latin America, Korea, Eastern Europe/Russia and African Americans.[7] It also must be noted that at the time of the survey China had only been open for adoptions for less than a decade, and, thus, the percentage of Chinese children would certainly rise in later surveys. A second survey, The United Jewish Communities' National Jewish Population Survey of 2000–01, measured the total number of adopted children in Jewish families. This study found that more than 5 per cent of American Jewish families had adopted children, accounting for about 35,000 children, though it did not take into account the race of adoptees.[8] If the percentage of Chinese children in 1997 was the same as the 2000–01 survey, then it could be extrapolated that approximately 1,500 adopted Chinese children lived with Jewish families at the turn of the century. Though this number is unscientific and could be considered little more than an educated guess, it is certain that by turn of the century the total number of Chinese children in American Jewish adoptive families numbered in the high hundreds, if not thousands. The adoption of Chinese orphans by Jewish families in Canada most likely saw similar percentages, and the trend of adoptions from China was not limited to North America, as the 1990s saw a growing number of Israelis travel to China to adopt.

The appeal of China for families seeking to adopt was enhanced by a number of economic and social factors. Perhaps most important was the relative efficiency of China's adoption regulations; families reported the entire time to complete an adoption, once the paperwork was approved, at 3–10 months, and the average cost at around US$15,000, along with a US $3,000 "donation" to the Chinese orphanage.[9] Chinese children were also much less likely to suffer severe health problems or disabilities, which were common in children adopted from Eastern Europe.[10] Another sensitive issue that drove many North American families to seek Chinese orphans was the increased number of instances of birthmothers in the US seeking to regain custody of their children. In the 1990s, there were numerous well-publicized incidents of birthmothers reneging on promises to give up their child for adoption, contacting the adoptive families after legally signing over the rights to their child, or even going to court to regain custody of the adopted child. Many prospective parents choose overseas adoptions because they wanted to avoid the problem of dealing with the birthmothers, which is typically not even a question in China, considering that most children available for adoption have been abandoned.[11]

The greatest number of adoptive Jewish families with Chinese children was in New York, a region that has the largest concentration of Jews in North America. But the phenomena of Chinese adoptees living in Jewish families was not limited to one region or state; a search of the Lexis-Nexis news database by the present author revealed articles about Jewish adoptions of Chinese children published in newspapers in California, Connecticut, Florida, Indiana, Kentucky, Massachusetts, New York, Ontario, Oregon, South Carolina, Virginia, and West Virginia, and it is safe to assume that many more states and provinces are home to Jewish families with Chinese adoptees. The origin of Chinese adoptees was equally widespread across China; the most common areas mentioned in articles about Jewish adoptions were located in the south of China, namely the provinces of Anhui, Guangdong, Hunnan, Jiangxi, and the city of Shanghai, though adoptions took place all across the country.

The Cultural and Religious Aspects of Jewish–Chinese Adoptions

Unlike the generation of parents who adopted Asian children in the first few decades after the Second World War, the families that adopted Chinese children in the 1990s were keenly aware of the "cross-cultural" issue of bringing a Chinese child into North American culture. Today, it is widely recognized that the advice given to adoptive parents from the 1950s to the 1970s to allow their children to fully assimilate and become "Americans" had been nearsighted and damaging.[12] Many adopted Asians children grew up with little knowledge of their biological homelands and were raised in predominantly white neighborhoods and suburbs, where they may have been one of only a small number of Asian students in their schools and neighborhoods. In late adolescence or early adulthood, these children all too frequently experienced an identity crisis between their "white" families and the fact that society categorized them as "Asian Americans." Compounding this problem for Jewish parents of Chinese adoptees, was the fact that while Jews are considered to be "white," they are also recognized as a unique minority with distinct religious and cultural traditions. The question then facing these families was to what degree a child could be Jewish and Chinese. By the 1990s, numerous resources were available for these families, from seminars to books to online email groups, many of which were tailored specifically for Jewish families. While each family made decisions according to their personal desires, general trends emerged in the blending of Chinese and Judaic culture and traditions.

In North America, there are hundreds of support groups and online forums for families with adopted Chinese children. While many of these groups cater exclusively to Jewish families, the group most often cited in articles and books about Jewish–Chinese adoptees is Families With Children From China (FCC), a non-denominational organization that has thousands of members and dozens of chapters in the US, Canada, Europe, and Australia. FCC provides information for prospective adoptive parents and organizes events for families with Chinese adoptees. Jewish families frequently participate in FCC events and activities, and a number of profiles of Jewish–Chinese children have been posted on FCC websites.[13] Jewish families have also come to depend on resources created exclusively for the Jewish community; an online group that is exclusive to Jewish families with Chinese adoptees is Jewish Families with Children from China. This online support community, created in 2000 on the free yahoogroups.com website (yahoo id: jfwcc; url:http://groups.yahoo.com/group/jfwcc/), has nearly 350 members and more than 1,000 posted messages. Topics discussed range from options for conversion to enrolling children in Mandarin or Hebrew school and family trips back to China.[14] An example of a more traditional support group for Jewish families is the Canadian Jewish–Asian Association (CJAA) in Toronto, where there are at least 40 Jewish families with adopted Chinese daughters. The family of Jeffrey and Linda Cutler founded the support group, and has organized events for Jewish and Asian families to come together for major Asian and Jewish holidays in the hope of instilling an understanding and appreciation for both cultures.[15]

Chinese adoptions by Jews have frequently been covered in the media, most commonly in regional newspapers. Hundreds of stories have appeared across North American in local papers, including the touching story of Barbara Fields Karlin. In 1938, Karlin's father fled Berlin in the aftermath of Kristallnacht for sanctuary in Shanghai, a war-time refuge for thousands of European Jews, and eventually settled in Rhode Island in the US. Sixty-five years later, Karlin and her husband traveled to China, a "magical, mysterious land" that her father often spoke of, to adopt a baby girl.[16] There has also been news coverage of the adoption of Chinese children by notable Jews including novelist Tama Janowitz of the US, novelist Lillian Nattel from Canada, American musician Merryl R. Goldberg, and American talk-show host Maury Povich, who is married to Chinese–American journalist Connie Chung. Povich and Chung's adoption of their son Mathew, in 1998, became a news sensation and a prominent subject in their television interviews with Larry King and Barbara Walters. Memoirs and guide books were also written by Jewish individuals that had adopted Chinese children, including the illustrated children's book *I Love You Like Crazy Cakes* (2000) by Rose Lewis; the adoption guidebook *Dim Sum, Bagels and Grits* (2001) by Myra Alperson; and *The Bamboo Cradle: A Jewish Father's Story* (1988), the memoir of a visiting American–Israeli professor in Taiwan who found an abandoned newborn at a railway station that he and his wife adopted; this is one of the few examples of literature about adoptions from Taiwan, where in 2001 there were only thirty-two adoptions by Americans.[17] The theme of Chinese adoptions has even made its way into fiction; Talia Carner's 2006 novel *China Doll* told the story of a Jewish rock star who has a Chinese infant thrust on her during a tour in China and fights for the right to keep her; and Daniel Goldfarb's play *Sarah, Sarah*, performed in 2004 at the Manhattan Theater Club in New York, is about a Jewish family from Toronto that adopts a baby girl from China.[18]

For adoptive families across North America, the question of the degree to which their children should be exposed to Chinese culture is a subject of great debate. Many families enroll their children in Chinese language classes, participate in cultural events, and celebrate traditional Chinese holidays such as the Lunar New Year and the Moon and Mid-Autumn Festivals. In New York City, which has a sizable Chinese immigrant population, parents have unique opportunities that are unavailable in much of the rest of the US and Canada, including a number of Chinese language schools where students are immersed in Chinese and their primary courses are taught in Chinese. While the large majority of students attending Chinese-language schools come from Chinese families, many white families, including Jewish parents, have enrolled their Chinese adopted children in these schools. In 2002, *The New York Times* ran a story covering one of these schools, the Shuang Wen Academy, and exposed a wide degree of opinions from parents looking to enroll their children in these schools. One Jewish family was eager for their child to "look Chinese and feel Chinese" and readily enrolled their children at Shuang Wen Academy, while another family chose to have their daughter attend the Ramaz School in Manhattan, where she studied Hebrew and Judaism.[19]

The issue of race is another sensitive topic for Jewish families with Chinese adoptees, especially for those that live in areas with few or no other Asian families. Adam Pertman, Executive Director of the Evan B. Donaldson Adoption Institute in New York, states that Chinese adoptees are changing the definition of what it means to be a Jew. He points out that Chinese adoptees are likely to face both anti-Semitism and racism from outsiders, as well as prejudice from within the Jewish community itself. "We should expect it," Pertman said, "It would be foolish for us not to acknowledge that race is an issue in our culture."[20] The issue of sexual orientation has also entered the public discussion of adoptions, as a growing number of single gay and lesbian individuals or same-sex couples have decided to adopt children. As states across America passed laws limiting the rights of gays and lesbians to adopt children in the state's custody, an increased number of prospective gay and lesbian parents looked towards China, which has allowed single individuals to adopt; although China bans adoptions by homosexuals, many adoption agencies have advised clients to hide their sexual orientation.[21] This trend may be coming to an end, as in 2007 the Chinese government banned adoptions by single parents, a restriction meant in part to end adoptions by gays and lesbians.

The Jewish faith has also been influence by the arrival of Chinese adoptees. Adoption is ingrained in Jewish religion, as is evinced in Sanhedrin 19b from the *Talmud*, "whoever brings up an orphan in his home is regarded, according to Scripture, as though the child had been born to him." Among adoptive Jewish parents, there is a consensus that their Chinese children are Jewish. Some parents freely mix their Jewish faith with traditional Buddhist practices, and may include statues of Buddha and Buddhist prayers in religious ceremonies. All families, whether liberal or conservative in their beliefs, face religion-based questions, most notably surrounding the issue of conversion. Most literature surrounding Chinese adoptees in Jewish families does not even mention the religious implications of adoption, while race and culture appear as more prominent topics. One member of the clergy to address the issue of religion is Reform Rabbi Yoel Kahn, executive director of the Stanford University Hillel Foundation, and the father of an adopted child. Rabbi Khan believes that it is not necessary for Reform Jewish families to get an Orthodox conversion for their child, which for boys entails both circumcision and *mikvah* immersion and for girls immersion. Khan recommends that during the conversion ceremony families include some elements of the child's Chinese background, e.g. their Chinese name or a Chinese story. Khan also points out that a conversion ceremony is "the binding of family," which may provide a way for extended family members to deal with hesitations of adopting non-Jewish children.[22]

In recent years, as the original adoptees from the early 1990s have come of age, more and more Chinese children have had *bar* and *bat mitzvahs*. While *bar* and *bat mitzvahs* for Chinese adoptees include the same religious rituals as for any other Jewish children, the ceremonies commonly include Chinese stories and customs. As the large majority of adoptees are girls, *bat mitzvahs* for Chinese girls have become commonplace in New York, including that of Cecelia Nealon-Shapiro. In March 2007, Nealon-Shapiro's *bat mitzvah* was the centerpiece of a cover story for *The New York Times*, which commented extensively on her mixed racial family and gave no hint that the ceremony was different than for other Jewish girls.[23] One recent example of how a Chinese adoptee's biological heritage has affected their *bat mitzvah* is that of Lily Jacobs, who was adopted by an American Jewish family when she was four months old and returned to China at the age of two because her mother had the opportunity to work in Beijing. In 2007, Jacobs' had a solicitation posted on the front page of the FCC website calling for other adopted Jewish–Chinese girls to send her their personal stories and photos for a special project for her *bat mitzvah*. On her webpage, Jacobs displayed the flags of the US, Israel, and China, and wrote extensively of her pride of being Jewish, American, and Chinese.[24] Perhaps the most important aspect of *bar* and *bat mitzvahs* for Chinese adoptees, is that the ceremony represents an acceptance of their adopted religion, as was aptly stated by an 11-year-old New Yorker preparing for her *bat mitzvah*, "When you're adopted, you get to choose whether you're Jewish or not. At my bat-mitzvah, I'm going to say I'm choosing to be Jewish."[25]

The total number of Chinese children adopted by American families alone has reached more than 60,000 and continues to grow by thousands each year, ensuring that the phenomena of Chinese children growing up in North American Jewish families will continue well into the future. While there is no consensus in the Jewish community as to what is the best method to confront the cultural, religious, and racial questions surrounding Jewish–Chinese adoptions, it is likely that as time passes Chinese Jews will be increasingly accepted as "normal" by those within and outside of the Jewish community. Use of the labels "Asian," "Jewish," "Chinese," "American," and "Canadian" will likely still be controversial and confound those who want to categorize Jewish–Chinese adoptees, but what is most important for the individual adoptees is that Jewish families across North America have found their own personal comfort in calling their children both "Jewish" and "Chinese."

Notes

1 "The Growth and Vitality of Jewish People," *Institute for Jewish & Community Research*, < www.jewishresearch.org/projects_growth.htm > (accessed 30 September 2007).

2 "Patricia Lin's 2004 Abstract," *PANA Institute*, < www.psr.edu/pana.cfm?m=210 > (accessed 30 September 2007).

3 Adam Pertman, *Adoption Nation: How the Adoption Revolution Is Transforming America*, New York: Basic Books, 2000, pp. 72–3; Arnold R. Silverman, "Outcomes of Transracial Adoption," *The Future of Children ADOPTION*, Vol. 3, No. 1, Spring 1993.

4 Silverman, op. cit.

5 Pertman, op. cit., p. 88.

6 "Foreign adoptions: issues and answers," *Canadian Jewish News*, Vol. 36, No. 49, 12 April 1996. *Lexis-Nexis Universe:General News Topic*, op. cit.

7 Rita James Simon and Howard Alstein, *Adoption Across Borders: Serving the Children in Transracial and Intercountry Adoptions*, Lanham: Rowman & Littlefield, 2000, pp. 127–129.

8 Leslie A. Pappas, "Chinese adoptions accelerating trend toward more diversity," *Philadelphia Inquirer*, 13 April 2005, *Lexis-Nexis Universe:General News Topic*, op. cit.

9 Elaine Louie, "Now Chosen, Chinese Girls Take to U.S.," *The New York Times*, 27 April 1995, *Lexis-Nexis Universe:General News Topic*, op. cit.

10 Pertman, op. cit., p. 201.

11 Pertman, op. cit., p. 72.

12 Myra Alperson, *Dim Sum, Bagels, and Grits: A Sourcebook for Multicultural Families*, New York: Farrar, Straus and Giroux, 2001, pp. 4–7.

13 "FCC Chapters and Local Contacts," 25 September 2007, *Families with Children from China*, < catalog.com/fwcfc/contacts.html > (accessed 29 September 2007).

14 Membership in the jfwcc group must be approved by its administrator and this author was not granted access to the group, though information concerning membership and the number of messages sent were available without membership. Daniela Gerson, "So, How Do You Say 'Happy Chanukah' In Mandarin?" 23 December 2003, *The New York Sun, Lexis-Nexis Universe:General News Topic*, op. cit.

15 "Discover the world in Toronto," *The Toronto Star*, p. A20, 16 May 2006, *Lexis-Nexis Universe:General News Topic*, op. cit.

16 Barbara Fields Karlin, "Viewpoint – Journey to adopt spans generations," *Providence Journal-Bulletin*, p. C-03, 18 February 2003, *Lexis-Nexis Universe:General News Topic*, op. cit.

17 "Taiwan Adoption," *Adoption.com*, < taiwan.adoption.com/ > (accessed 30 September 2007).
18 Donald Lyons, "Engaging 'Sarah' Breaks Up," *The New York Post*, p. 42, 2 April 2004, *Lexis-Nexis Universe:General News Topic*, op. cit.
19 Yilu Zhao, "Living in 2 Worlds, Old and New; Foreign-Born Adoptees Explore Their Cultural Roots," *The New York Times*, 9 April 2002.
20 Pappas, op. cit.
21 Pertman, op. cit., pp. 86, 216–18.
22 Karen Koenig, "Rabbi probes issues around non-Jewish adoption," 11 December 1998, *The Jewish News Weekly of Northern California*, < www.jewishsf.com/content/2-0-/module/displaystory/story_id/10144/edition_id/194/format/html/displaystory.html > (accessed 1 October 2007).
23 Andy Newman, "Journey From a Chinese Orphanage to a Jewish Rite of Passage," 8 March 2007, *New York Times*, < www.nytimes.com/2007/03/08/nyregion/08batmitzvah.html > (accessed 9 October 2007).
24 Lily Jacobs, "Be a part of my Bat Mitzvah," 2007, *Families with Children in China*, < www.fwcc.org/LilyJacobsBatMitzvah.pdf > (accessed 29 September 2007).
25 Merri Rosenberg, "Jewish Moms, Chinese Daughters," *LILITH*, spring 2006, < www.lilith.org/pdfs/asiangirls.pdf?PHPSESSID=70b66fc0ce38c68f9f81852d2ab08315 >.

Part VII

CHINA–ISRAEL RELATIONS

18

SINO–ISRAEL RELATIONS AT THE START OF THE SECOND DECADE

A view from Shanghai and Jerusalem

Ilan Maor

It is 15 years since Israel and China established formal diplomatic relations. A short period of time in the history of two nations, but a rich one in terms of events and developments.

If to borrow a concrete metaphor from life, in many ways, the relationship between Israel and China resembles the relationship between a couple: dynamic, interesting, and most of the time fruitful, but also sensitive and evolving, demanding commitment, investment, and perseverance.

Just like in a marriage, in which each person brings his or her own unique character, background, and personal history, so too in the case of the bilateral relations, national character and heritage (Jewish and Chinese), and the political and economic developments of each country are all expressed.

Unless the couple opts to live on a desert island, their marriage will be influenced by surrounding events and by their neighbors and allies. There is no doubt that similar factors on the political level very strongly influence the bilateral relationship, and we see the effect that Israel's relations with her neighbors in the Middle East and that Israel–US as well as China–US relations have on Israel's relations with China.

In the past decade, I have been fortunate to observe different aspects of this special relationship from several different angles: first in the capacity of my work in Israel's Economic and Cultural Office in Taipei (1994–96), then in my posting to the North East Asia Department at the Foreign Ministry in Jerusalem (1996–2001), in my term as Israel's Consul General in Shanghai (2001–04), and now, through my position as the director of the Economic Department responsible for Asian affairs in the Foreign Ministry, during the past two years.

This chapter will try to offer a broad outline of developments in the relationship, mainly viewing its future from the vantage of my former seat in Shanghai, the economic capital of rejuvenated China, and my current posting in Jerusalem. As my work has mainly been concentrated on the economic sphere for the past six years, I will put the emphasis on the economic component of the relationship, which has been an important factor in the development of relations so far, and I believe it will continue to play a pivotal role in future.

To present the analysis in a structured and methodical way, I have reviewed four features of the relationship: starting with a historical overview, followed by a look at the first decade of relations from honeymoon to obstacles, followed by a discussion of the foreign and domestic issues affecting the bilateral relations. To conclude, I will present several aspects of the development of the second decade, while looking ahead to maintaining progress in future.

Historical Background

It is difficult to analyze the relationship between the two countries without discussing the historical background and friendship that has formed over the past several hundred years between the Jewish and Chinese people. As so much has been written about the Jewish presence in China, I will only touch on this briefly.

Throughout history, there was Jewish settlement by communities and individuals in different areas throughout China, the foremost of these being Kaifeng, Harbin, Dalian, and Shanghai. The Jewish settlement in China was highly diversified – with Jews from a variety of ethnic backgrounds, from White Russians to Iraqis – settling at different periods in different locales. There was, however, one thing they all shared, namely that, in China, Jews were never confronted with the black cloud that has dogged the Jewish people for generations — the cloud of anti-Semitism. Outside cultures have influenced Chinese life in many ways from dress and music, to food and science. But they did not whip up prejudices against Jews. Thus, rather than hostility and suspicion, the Chinese developed an esteem for the Jewish nation, and its rich culture and history, from which its strength and resilience were drawn.

Chinese academics and the public in general found areas of similarity between the two ancient cultures, which had both struggled against threats and influences throughout history but preserved their uniqueness and values. In the past, like today, common values, stress on education, the importance of family ties, and even the qualities of Jewish and Chinese mothers, are often raised in discussions between Israelis, Jews, and Chinese.

The friendship between the peoples became etched onto the history of the two nations, when China, and in particular, the people of Shanghai, opened its doors and hearts to thousands of Jewish refugees who were fleeing the menace of the Holocaust in Europe. The refugees found haven with the population, who, despite the misery of war and the hardships of the time, never lost sight of their compassion and value of helping others.

In time, the relationship between the two peoples served as a strong and deep foundation for the development of relations between two young countries: the State of Israel (established May 1948) and the People's Republic of China (established a year later, in October 1949).

The unofficial relationship between Israel and the Chinese People's Republic began in the early years after the establishment of each country. Israel was among the first nations (and the first in the Middle East) to recognize China, as early as January 1950.

Initial contact between the two countries failed to develop into an official relationship. Different factors, including Israel siding with the US in the Korean War, China's rapprochement with the Arab world, and the emergence of the bipolar international order – with China and Israel at opposing poles – prevented the development of relations, which were limited to informal and spasmodic contact.

Nonetheless, it should be noted that the lack of diplomatic relations did not deter the continuity and development of mutual respect and admiration within both public and other circles: officialdom, academia, and the scientific establishment. This basis of mutual appreciation and friendship played an important role in the speedy development of relations after obstacles were removed and doors opened.

Changes in the international arena and the development in Chinese foreign policy, along with China's interest in Israel–US relations and the influence of the Jewish communities in the United States, and, of course, progress in the Middle East peace process, in the early 1990s, led to a significant change in relations between the two countries. Discussions between the two countries began in the mid-1980s, and included the first clandestine meeting between the two foreign ministers at the 1987 UN Assembly, followed by a negotiation process that prepared the ground for establishing informal representation: an office of China International Travel opened in Tel Aviv in 1989 and the office of the Israeli Academy of Science opened in Beijing in 1990.

The period of "courtship" was relatively short, and on 24 January 1992 the Israeli and Chinese foreign ministers signed an agreement establishing diplomatic relations between Israel and China, which heralded a new era in relations between the peoples and countries.

Sino–Israel Relations: The First Decade – Honeymoon and Hurdles

It took more than four decades from the time the State of Israel and the People's Republic of China were founded, until full diplomatic relations were established and the gates opened to leaders and civilians from both countries to see, learn, understand, and grow closer.

The long waiting period before formalizing relations, the mixture of curiosity and reciprocal esteem, and the desire to "make up" for the delay in relations led to warm, friendly bilateral relations and, above all, to a rapid rate of development — call it a successful, extended honeymoon.

Four clear indicators of the speed in development of bilateral relations are the exchanges of official visits, the establishment of bilateral agreements, the development of reciprocal economic relations, and, finally, the cooperation in the areas of training (MASHAV).

Visits by Senior Officials

Establishing official relations gave the green light for a long succession of bilateral exchange visits by senior officials. In the first year of relations, Chinese Foreign Minister Qian, visited Israel, and Israeli president, Haim Herzog, paid a state visit to China.

Intensive official visits continued in the following years, peaking in 1998–2000. Prominent Israeli visitors to China in this period were Prime Minister Netanyahu (1998), President Weizman (1999), Defense Minister Mordechai (1998), and Supreme Court President Barak (1998). The Chinese visits were by People's Congress Chairman, Li Peng (1999); Chinese Minister of Defense, General Chi Haotian (1999); and the jewel in the crown, an official visit by Chinese President Jiang Zemin who stayed in Israel for about a week (April 2000) — this visit was much longer than usual for a Chinese president.

Bilateral Agreements

The signing of the agreement establishing diplomatic relations between Israel and China removed the obstacle to developing ties between the two countries both formally and publicly, and was the first step in a complex and important process of forming bilateral agreements between the two countries. The bilateral agreements were essential both for establishing a clear, legal basis and for encouraging ties in different spheres.

Negotiations towards bilateral agreements usually last a long time. With Sino–Israeli relations, however, goodwill and efforts on both sides led to impressive achievements: in the first two years alone (1992{-{93), seven agreements were signed, including the agreement to open a consulate general in Shanghai (opened summer 1994); an aviation agreement (enabling Israel's national airline, El Al, to fly commercial flights to Beijing and cargo to Shanghai); a trade, taxation, and investment protection agreement; an agricultural cooperation agreement; and others.

In the first decade of Sino–Israel relations, 15 bilateral agreements were signed between the countries — with more to come.

Size of Bilateral Trading

In the first year of Sino–Israeli relations, bilateral trade between Israel and China was a modest $49 million. The magnitude of bilateral trade rapidly increased in the first decade of relations, reaching $1.2 billion in 2002.

Israeli economic activities in China, which were initially focused on agriculture and water, expanded during this decade to include a wide range of commercial areas, including a strong hi-tech component. The rapid increase in bilateral trade and the economic development on both sides were solid grounds for assuming continued growth in the future.

MASHAV (Israel Center for International Cooperation)
Cooperation

An important role in establishing and expanding the basis for bilateral relations is played by the Foreign Ministry's Center for International Cooperation. As relations were established between the two countries, thousands of Chinese trainees have attended courses in Israel and China in various fields, ranging from education, health, and social services to agriculture, and regional and technological development. Three model farms were also built in China, and visits were made by specialists in different fields to advise and promote cooperation.

The MASHAV cooperation has helped to enhance mutual understanding and respect and to promote academic, scientific, and trade cooperation. Chinese course graduates and their Israeli instructors play an important role in extending the bilateral relations from the government level, to the public and business spheres, and to the wider public.

Optimism and Hopes

Flourishing relations and rapid growth in different spheres gave rise to a feeling that "the sky's the limit," with both sides looking forward to ongoing rapid development.

The first half of 2000 is an excellent example of the honeymoon, peaking with President Jiang's visit to Israel, which reflected the amicability of the relations and the importance attached by countries to fostering them. This visit also boosted the feeling that President Jiang was personally interested in fostering the relationship, and that he had not hid his admiration for Israel and its achievements.

Influences and Developments on the Domestic and
International Scenes

Early in this article, I mentioned events on the bilateral level that preceded the establishment of relations and characterized the first decade of relations.

In order to better understand the background to how relations developed in that the first decade, we need to examine, at least briefly, three factors, which influenced the relations: the Middle East situation and the peace process, the two economies, and the triangular relationship between America, China, and Israel.

Middle East Events and the Peace Process

Relations between Israel and China were established against a background of wide-reaching changes in the Middle East and Israeli arenas. The Madrid Conference heralded a new era in discussions between Israel and her neighbors through various channels, and was followed by important gains including the Israel–Palestinian Declaration of Principles (1993), the Peace Agreement between Israel and Jordan (1994), and the Interim Agreement (1995), signifying the achievements of the process.

The positive developments in the peace process produced a significant change in Israel's relations with the international community. Israel–Asia relations are a good example of this: in one month, January 1992, Israel established diplomatic relations with the two largest countries in the world, China and India. The Foreign Ministry's network of representation quickly grew: on the Asian continent alone, the early 1990s saw the inauguration of four new embassies, in Beijing, Delhi, Seoul, and Hanoi.

The peace process between Israel and her neighbors, developments in Chinese foreign policy, and greater international involvement by China, produced increasingly warm bilateral relations in all spheres. Furthermore, China's Middle East policy became more moderate and generally more balanced. China also developed an interest in becoming involved in the peace process and even appointed an ambassador-at-large to this end.

The continuing wave of terrorism kept clouding these developments, and seriously damaged efforts towards trust building and promoting the peace process. An almost complete breakdown in positive momentum occurred following the failure of the Camp David negotiations (July 2000) and the resumption of intensive rioting and violence by Palestinians in September 2000.

Difficulties regarding the peace process carried direct and indirect implications for the bilateral relations. Growing tension in the Middle East (as well as the developments on the Iranian nuclear issue) threatened to affect China's interest in a steady oil supply, Chinese trade with the Middle East, its interest in ensuring the Arab vote in the United Nations, etc., affecting the balance in its Middle East policy.

Economic Development

In the 1990s, Israel enjoyed rapid economically growth, supported by a long-term investment in research and development (R&D), innovation spirit, and government investment in infrastructure and growth incentives, as well as the optimism brought by the peace process.

Israel's economic growth, which relied largely on achievements in initiatives and R&D, earned Israeli industry a respected place as a global technological center. It also sparked considerable potential in China for the Israeli model of initiative and development and for Israeli technology, first in the field of agriculture and then in other areas, chief of these being the information and communication industries (ICT).

China's economic development in this decade increased its relevance and importance as a potential partner for the Israeli economy, and steadily increased the interest shown by Israeli companies for working with the Chinese industry and penetrating the Chinese market.

The crisis in the global hi-tech sector and a slowdown in the US and European economies, combined with setbacks in the peace process and an escalation in Palestinian violence, caused a significant slowdown in growth of the Israeli economy at the end of the last decade of the twentieth century and beginning of this one.

The US–China–Israel Triangle

At one of the staff meetings we held at the Consulate, I updated my colleagues about the chapter I was writing on Sino–Israel relations, and the metaphor I had used comparing the bilateral relationship with marriage between a couple. One colleague, Jackie Huang, immediately asked: "But what about the third party in the relationship — the United States?"

"The American connection" has accompanied Sino–Israel relations for the last 50 years. America's stance was an important factor in the deliberations leading up to Israel's decision to recognize the People's Republic of China (in contrast with America's recognition of the Republic of China – Taiwan – under General Chiang in Taipei), and, as noted before, Israel's siding with the US in the Korean War, and subsequently, presented an obstacle to relations at the time.

The close strategic partnership between Israel and the US has strengthened in recent decades. The American administration (both the present and its predecessor) is a dependable and continuous source of support for Israel: in voting at the Security Council of the UN Assembly, in the international sphere in general, and in reinforcing Israel's defense, etc. Relations between countries are obviously a two-way affair, and Israel also gives great credence to America's position and interests on a variety of issues. A good illustration of the influence of Israel–US relations, with far-reaching consequences was the cancellation of the Phalcon deal in 2000.

Navigating the middle path between a strong desire to continue developing warm, high impetus relations with China, on the one hand, and a desire and interest in a strategic and close alliance with the US, is the complex challenge that Israel faces in the second decade of relations.

End of Honeymoon and Obstacles to Relations

The optimism and high hopes attached to the relations, which reached a high in the first half of 2000, were overshadowed in a few months. As with most married couples, the honeymoon faded.

The Phalcon affair, about which much has been spoken and written, was a clear signal that Israel's honeymoon with China was fading. The cancellation of the deal affected various aspects of the bilateral relations: from undermining Chinese defense apparatus hopes of Israel being a major source of advanced technology; to reservations within the Chinese leadership concerning the balance of Israel–China–US ties and China's place in this triangle; and ending with a grave sense of unease, which rankled with the Chinese leadership, chiefly President Jiang due to the cancellation of the project and the surrounding chain of events.

The eruption of events in the territories, and the slowdown of the peace process also contributed to a slowdown in ties between the countries. Chinese criticism of Israeli policy and disagreement regarding the stance on Arafat and other subjects widened the gulf in this sphere.

One of the clearest and most immediate symptoms of the honeymoon ending was a downturn in the flow of visits by senior Chinese officials to Israel. Only a few visits by high-ranking Chinese were made between the years 2001–03.

Sino–Israeli Relations: The Second Decade – Looking Ahead

The first decade ended "under a cloud," still I believe there is a solid base for optimism in regards to the future development of the bilateral relations.

The historical and cultural track record is an important basis for the future relations between the countries. Looking back, we see a positive historical background: in the distant past, it is a history of religious acceptance and tolerance by the Chinese, offering sanctuary to Jewish refugees, and the common qualities and similarities shared by these two ancient peoples with their rich cultures.

In the recent past, we see a decade of relations based on partnership and friendship, despite the "dark clouds" that overshadowed these relations at the decade's end. Moreover, the friendship and mutual regard between the leaders of the two countries represents a solid foundation for the development future ties.

The second factor is the international environment – both immediate and overall – in which the relations exist. In this regard, we can note a significant improvement.

Yasser Arafat's death and the ascent of a new Palestinian leadership within the Palestinian authorities, coupled with the Israeli government's efforts to break the deadlock in the peace process (as manifested in the disengagement from the Gaza strip), contribute to expectations of positive developments in the Middle East situation. Such developments would further additional positive developments in Sino–Israeli relations.

Hamas taking over the Gaza strip and its effort to continue terrorist activities against Israel, is a serious setback in this positive development, still, it is now confronted jointly (at least partially) by Israel and the Palestinian authorities — with the support of the international community.

Another factor relating to this area has been China's enlistment in the international struggle against terrorism. Dealing with the menace of global terror will naturally increase China's understanding of the constraints under which Israel operates in this regard, and will increase mutual understanding between the countries.

The third influential factor is economic interests and potential which, in the modern era, is a primary motivating factor in cultivating bilateral relations. The Israeli and Chinese economies are extremely different. First, there is fundamental difference in size and scale (land mass, population, natural resources), with consequences for the domestic market, the workforce, etc. The two countries' national industries are also very different: in China, one finds large-scale manufacturing industries, which are the mainstay of the economy, while the Israeli economy is largely technological and innovation-based. Still, there are various interfaces between the economies. China's lightening economic growth, its technological development and economic reforms create great potential for cooperation and the expansion of economic and commercial ties with Israel.

The interest in developing economic ties shown by both government and business sectors in the two countries has led to impressive growth in bilateral trade and contacts between industries. The target of Israeli industry was traditionally the US and Europe. However, China's rapid growth and speedy technological development have produced a significant increase in interest from Israeli industry, and, indeed, the recent years have shown a rapid rise in operations by Israeli companies in China.

The commercial work of the Israeli Consulate General in Shanghai accurately reflects the upsurge in Israel's economic and commercial activities in China in general, and particularly in the district surrounding the Yangtze River estuary. The number of Israeli firms seeking consulate assistance has risen from about 60 in my first year in Shanghai (2001) to 330 in 2004, and the activity of the consulate remains vital and productive.

Besides ongoing cooperation in agriculture and traditional industries, we have seen a considerable increase in the hi-tech sphere, focusing on telecommunications, semiconductors, life sciences, and venture capital. The number of Israeli projects in China is growing steadily and we now find

Israeli-established projects all over China, in Shanghai and in almost every sector, from a telecom venture in Hangzhou, to a group of chemical projects throughout Jiangsu province, to water and environmental projects in North and Central China, as well as an innovative joint venture capital project in the city of Suzhou.

Hi-tech trade delegations, mainly for telecommunications and semiconductors, regularly visit the region and organize seminars and business meetings. The Israel Business Conferences held in Shanghai and Beijing (June 2004) was definitely one of the high points in developing Sino–Israeli economic ties, and clearly symbolizes the momentum of those ties at the start of the second decade of relations. Some 200 business people, from over 100 Israeli companies, participated in the mission led by the Israeli Deputy Prime Minister and Minister of Trade and Industry, Mr Ehud Olmert (currently the Israeli Prime Minister). This was one of the largest, most impressive economic missions ever sent by Israel overseas and clearly demonstrates Israeli government and industry interest in developing ties with China.

The impressive reaction from the Chinese indicates that the desire to develop ties is not one-sided: some 500 Chinese participants attended the Conference, taking part in panels and business meetings. Over 300 prearranged business meetings were held during the Conference held in Shanghai, and also a large number of ad hoc meetings.

Ties between the economies have great potential: in terms of bilateral trade and also in other forms of cooperation with considerable potential to contribute to the prosperity of both economies. The next section describes some important areas of cooperation.

Bilateral Trade

Since establishing diplomatic relations, bilateral trade has developed at a remarkable rate. In the first half of the second decade of relations, bilateral trade has demonstrated an exciting pace of growth in both directions: exports to China and imports from China (though not equivalent in size).

During this period, Chinese exports to Israel have witnessed rapid growth. In 2006, Chinese exports to Israel came to $2.43 billion, a rise of 28 per cent compared with the year 2005. Strengthening ties and the constant development of Chinese technology has gradually increased the potential in this regard, so that now in Israeli shops we stock the finest products produced by Chinese hi-tech manufacturers, e.g. Shinco, Panda, and others.

Israeli exports to China have also shown impressive growth in recent years. In 2006, Israeli exports to China totaled more than $958.4 million, a 29 per cent increase compared with 2005. The rapid development of Chinese industry hand-in-hand with intensive investment in infrastructure (with emphasis on telecommunications) and impressive growth in the Chinese consumer market, means great potential for Israeli technology and goods.

Chinese State Counselor, Mr. Tang Jia Xuan, who visited Israel in December 2004, said he believed in the ability of Israel and China to achieve an ambitious goal, namely doubling bilateral trade to $5 billion by 2008. We can deduce from the rate of growth so far, and from the great potential for further trade development, that this goal is indeed achievable.

R&D and the Use of Technology in the Next Generation of Industry

Investment in R&D is a key factor in Israeli industrial growth ranging from hi-tech, to other sectors, such as chemicals, security, agriculture, etc. More-over, continuing investment in this area is a vital part of ensuring the future and prosperity of Israeli industry.

R&D cooperation can and should take place along several channels:

1. There is clearly great potential in combining Israeli and Chinese cap-abilities in the field of industry, and this applies to cooperation between Chinese and Israeli firms in developing new technologies and products.
   Recognizing the potential in R&D cooperation, the two governments signed a R&D Cooperation Agreement, which represents the confidence of the two governments in the potential of this avenue of cooperation. The next phase will hopefully involve signing more R&D agreements at the provincial level and establishing a joint R&D found, to help finance joint projects between Israeli and Chinese companies.
2. Dozens of international companies and corporations have chosen Israel as an important site for their R&D centers, as these enjoy the benefit of highly qualified personnel and a unique technological operating envir-onment, for technological and product development. The list of compa-nies includes major international companies (Intel, Motorola, HP, IBM, and others), as well as some Asian companies (e.g. Samsung). There is no doubt in my mind that leading Chinese companies such as HuaWei, ZTE, Haier, Panda, and others would benefit from joining this list and establishing centers in Israel.
3. Various international companies have found the Israeli hi-tech industry a reliable source of technologies that can help develop their capabilities and improve their range of products for their customers. Companies like Cisco, SAP, Lucent, Microsoft, and others repeatedly invest in Israeli technological companies, in many cases through mergers or acquisitions — an excellent proof of what Israeli technology can offer fast-growing Chinese companies.
4. Another avenue of technological cooperation is cooperation between Israeli manufacturers of technologies, parts, sub-systems, and mobile equipment, and leading Chinese manufacturers operating in China and

the international arena. Major international companies now offer Israeli equipment as part of their product packages or as complementary products for solutions that they supply, and we can reasonably assume that the future will reveal major Chinese companies doing the same thing in their China-based operations and elsewhere.

Venture Capital Cooperation

Israel's venture capital (VC) sector has undergone rapid growth and development in the past 12 years, and Israel now has dozens of Israeli and international funds, which contribute significantly to technological development and R&D. Israeli funds have outstanding experience in raising capital, identifying investment opportunities, and international operations.

The development of China's market economy alongside reforms in the area of finance, have led to the gradual development of a VC sector. This opens possibilities for cooperation between VC funds in both countries, for investment in Israeli venture funds, for forming joint funds, or for cooperation in identifying investment opportunities in Israel and China. Quite a few Israeli funds already operate in China, and it is reasonable to expect further expansion in this area in the future.

The first joint Sino–Israel venture capital project involves Israel Infinity VC and the management company of the Singapore hi-tech park in Suzhou. This joint venture, which is also the first of its kind in China, began operating about a year ago. It aims to promote capital investment in Israeli and Chinese business ventures, with emphasis on hi-tech.

Cooperation in Reform and Upgrade Process of Chinese Industry

Under the heading of China's industrial reform, many local companies and factories have felt the need to cooperate with foreign companies and thus enhance their capabilities on the domestic and international fronts. Thus, many state and non-state companies want to upgrade technological and management capabilities, improve performance in a competitive market, and enhance their handling of the international arena.

Cooperation between Israeli and Chinese companies can, in my view, help significantly in this, benefiting mainly from two unique characteristics of the Israeli business sector:

1. First, the constraints of the Israeli domestic market, which is limited in size (in terms of land size, population, natural resources), forces Israeli companies to mostly depend on overseas activities. Companies have thus gained experience and acquired contacts overseas in everything from sales and marketing, to imports, exports, production overseas, and strategic cooperation, to raising international capital and finance.

2. Second, decades of investment in advanced technological production and development have resulted in a diversified pool of advanced technologies and technical and management expertise, capable of enhancing the modernization and effectiveness of established companies wishing to develop and improve the effectiveness of their operations.

Israeli Manufacturing and Technology in China

For more than a decade, Israeli companies have set up manufacturing operations in China through wholly Israeli-owned or joint venture projects. These companies represent diverse sectors, such as telecommunications (e.g. ECI, Galtronics), agriculture and water (e.g. Bermad, Amiad, Netafim), chemicals (e.g. ICL, Gadiv), and others.

A good example of an Israeli company intensively active in this area is the leading Israeli chemical company ICL-IP, which operates a production network in several locations in China, making Jiangsu Province the center for its China operations, with a joint venture in the city of Lianyungang, five more ventures in the pipeline in Jiangyin, a logistics center shaping up in the city of Jiangjagang, and at least one more project planned.

It is important to bear in mind that in many cases, Israeli companies bring advanced technologies and a wealth of experience to production management, which involves integrating R&D, etc. In this way, they contribute to the expertise and technology of their local partners.

International Events – From the Olympics Games to Expo 2010

During the next four years, China is scheduled to host several large-scale international events; the two main ones are the Olympic Games in Beijing in 2008, and Expo 2010 in Shanghai. These events and many other smaller scale events, obviously provide a great opportunity for Sino–Israeli cooperation. Israeli technology can help ensure the quality of the events in many ways. The following are some opportunities for cooperation in this area:

- Monitoring and management technologies that greatly assist organizers to ensure smooth and systematic event management.
- Systems for ICT operations, water management and irrigation, smart construction, energy saving, and other areas can improve events infrastructure performance and ensure site compatibility with events.
- Israeli security solutions, which have proven themselves in numerous sites and events, among them the Athens Olympics, can certainly contribute considerably to securing the safety of participants and visitors to the events at a time of growing threat from international terrorism.

These are special opportunities for cooperation, as they fully exploit the relative advantages of each country. Thus, both partners enjoy added value, as "the whole is greater than the sum of its parts."

At a time when the economy has a primary function in the international arena, there is no doubt that economic ties which concentrate on the areas listed above could contribute significantly to cultivating Sino–Israel ties and for ensuring a happy (and prosperous) union between Israel and China.

Summary

A combination of a past – based on friendship and esteem, between China, the Jewish people, and the State of Israel – alongside a host of positive influences and joint interests substantiates the assessment that relations between the two countries will continue to develop, and that in future we will witness even more vigorous growth and cooperation.

If the freezing of Chinese visits in 2000 marked the end of the honeymoon of Sino–Israel relations, then it is reasonable to assume that the series of visits in the past few months, by senior Chinese and Israeli leaders, is clear proof of a renewal in the momentum of relations. In November 2004, Israeli Foreign Minister Shalom, visited China, and a month later, State Counselor Tang visited Israel. During the years 2005–07 we have witnessed an ongoing and intensive flow of visits from both side, topped by the recent visit of Prime Minister Olmert to Beijing in January 2007.

For most of the first decade, Sino–Israel relations were like a honeymoon fueled by the initial emotional enthusiasm of the partners. Now, in their second decade, the partners have entered an adult, mature, stable stage of their relationship, which is underpinned by structure and realistic expectations regarding the potential for both, and by a realistic understanding of the limitations and obstacles accompanying the package.

19

ECONOMIC AND CULTURAL RELATIONS BETWEEN CHINA AND ISRAEL SINCE THE ESTABLISHMENT OF DIPLOMATIC RELATIONS IN 1992

Jonathan Goldstein

Background: Sino–Israeli Relations and Non-Relations, 1948–92

When Israel was established on 15 May 1948, its founding fathers took the position that the nation's long-term international interests would be better served by relations with the newly formed People's Republic of China (PRC) and informally known as both "China" and "Communist China," than with that nation's offshore rival, the Republic of China on Taiwan, known informally as "Formosa," the "ROC," and "Nationalist China." On 9 January 1950, the State of Israel became the first Middle Eastern nation to recognize the People's Republic of China, long before any other Middle Eastern country, and at time when, outside of the Communist bloc, China only had relations with Denmark, India, and Sweden. Sporadic contacts continued between the two nations until December 1954, when China made a conscious effort to distance itself from Israel. The specific incident that marks the beginning of a "frozen" period between the two nations was the Bogor, Indonesia organizational meeting for the Afro Asian summit conference in Bandung, Indonesia. China was scheduled to participate in Bandung. The Bogor organizers resolved, despite stiff protests from Ceylon, to exclude Israel from the summit, establishing a precedent for Israeli exclusion from "Third World" and "Non-aligned" gatherings thereafter. Within a month, Israel began to feel the brunt of the Bogor decision and observed that China went along with it. On 28 January 1955, a delegation headed by Israeli Ambassador to Burma David Hacohen, arrived in Beijing for a long-scheduled, four-week visit. The commission was only met by a Chinese vice foreign minister and lesser officials. It was not received by Chinese Premier and Foreign Minister Zhou Enlai, who had met Hacohen previously in Burma and who had authorized the visit. The signals of diplomatic frigidity were unmistakable.[1]

The Bogor organizational conference also excluded the Republic of China on Taiwan. After the Bandung summit, which lasted from 18 to 24 April 1955, both Chinas strove to cultivate relations with different Arab states. In both cases, these efforts were at Israel's expense, as Arab states customarily used hostility toward the Jewish state as their litmus test, if not major criterion, for friendship. The ROC's greatest success was with Saudi Arabia, which supplied Taiwan with much of its oil and shared a visceral anti-communism with the ROC. The PRC, for its part, established full diplomatic relations with Egypt, Syria, and Yemen in 1956, Iraq in 1958, and Algeria, Morocco, and Sudan shortly thereafter.[2]

In spite of these setbacks, Israel continued to seek Chinese friendship in various ways. But it met with frustration and hardship at almost every turn. An issue that highlights Israel's dilemma in dealing with both Chinas in the 1950s through the 1970s was the question of China's admission to the United Nations (UN). Israel supported China's admission to the UN on the grounds that its inclusion would promote peace and stability in Asia. In choosing to vote in this way, Israel resisted pressures from the US, its major ally, to discontinue all friendly gestures toward China. By the mid-1960s, the PRC's virulent anti-Israeli rhetoric in international forums, plus the 1965 opening of a Palestine Liberation Organization office in Beijing, caused Israel to reverse its position and oppose the PRC's UN admission. By 1971, after the United States switched sides on the UN membership issue, Israel also reversed its position. According to Israeli diplomat and Sinologist E. Zev Sufott, "Israel (and the US, ed.) relented and cast her vote in favour of the proposal which removed Taiwan and seated China in its place at the United Nations."[3] Perhaps the fullest expression of Israel's frustration with respect to both Chinas in this period was the instruction from Jerusalem to Israel's Washington embassy in 1959 "to restrict contacts with Nationalist China to a minimum despite the bitter disappointments in our relations with People's China."[4]

Ending China's Repudiation of Israel: the Establishment of Full PRC–Israel Diplomatic Relations (24 January 1992) and of Regularized Israeli Commercial and Cultural Dealings with Taiwan

After bitter Sino–Vietnamese border hostilities in 1978–79, the PRC made concerted efforts to find overseas sources for advanced weapons that had been combat-tested against those of the Soviet Union. Such armament would also be useful on China's Laotian, Indian, Mongolian, and, of course,

Soviet frontiers. Israel was a skilled, state-of-the-art arms manufacturer and a logical supplier of such weaponry. From the Chinese point of view, a strictly clandestine arms trade with Israel would not hamper the PRC's overt support of Arab states and causes. The US, which had been in a reconciliation mode with the PRC for eight years, did not oppose weapons sales directed against America's arch-rival, the Soviet Union. Menachem Begin was Israel's Likud Party Prime Minister at that time and was at least as anti-Soviet as the US. Begin would have probably armed the devil if he pledged to make war against the Soviet Union. The Chinese were especially impressed with Israel's seaborne invasion of Egypt in 1970, in which Israel exclusively used upgraded weapons of Soviet origin that had been initially captured from Egypt and Syria.

In February 1979, with all of these factors working to his advantage, Israeli arms dealer Shoul Eisenberg won Israeli and Chinese approval to send a delegation of military experts to China. Their task was to show the Chinese the prowess of Israeli military industries in upgrading and counteracting Soviet weaponry, and to strike an arms export deal. The team arrived incognito aboard Eisenberg's private jet. The Chinese were eager to deal them after the beating they took from the Vietnamese and soon signed contracts with Eisenberg's Israel Corporation. Several factors favored Eisenberg over other contractors. First, his sales were never contingent on any human rights considerations. Second, instead of just selling new equipment to China, he promised to use existing material to upgrade some 30,000 antiquated Chinese T-34 tanks. To replace them at $1 million each would have amounted to $30 billion, which China did not have. But at the cost of $100,000 each, for a total of $3 billion, Israel could widen and strengthen existing tank treads and install 105-millimeter tank barrels, thereby producing functionally new tanks.

Under the terms of Eisenberg's contracts, technical teams began going back and forth on a regular basis beginning in 1980. Two events encapsulate the overt and covert nature of Sino–Israeli relations from the period of 1979–92. On the one hand, in 1982, in a widely publicized gesture, the PRC donated $1 million to the Palestine Liberation Organization. That was a miniscule fraction of the amount the PRC was already paying Israeli arms salesman and manufacturers. On the other hand, in October 1984, when China's newly-retrofitted T-34 tanks with their 105-millimeter cannons were paraded in Beijing on China's national day, there was no public mention whatsoever of the source of the new armament.[5]

Clandestine Sino–Israeli commerce also provided the openings for diplomatic contact. In 1984, Israeli Labor Party Prime Minister Shimon Peres affirmed that "we shall knock once again on China's door — (for) there is no need for the geographical distance between us to be translated into a pointless diplomatic distance."[6] On 30 September 1987, the then Foreign Minister Peres met Chinese Foreign Minister Wu Xueqian at the United

Nations, the first time that an Israeli foreign minister met his Chinese counterpart.[7]

On 22 December 1988, the Basic Policy Guidelines of the Israeli government re-emphasized "the establishment of diplomatic relations with China." The foreign ministers of the two countries again met at the United Nations in the fall of 1989 and agreed on the exchange of unofficial missions. In June 1990, the Basic Policy Guidelines of the Israeli government once more reiterated the importance of establishing diplomatic ties.[8] In the following month, Israel opened its mission in Beijing. It was technically a branch of the Israel Academy of Sciences and Humanities and was headed by Dr. Yosef Shalhevet, an agronomist from the Volcani Institute in Rehovot, with the assistance of Israeli Foreign Ministry technical expert (and later Ambassador) Yoel Guilatt. Guilatt was soon replaced by the aforementioned Zev Sufott, a veteran diplomat and professionally trained Sinologist who had most recently served as Israel's Ambassador to the Netherlands. A Chinese mission was set up in Tel Aviv under Luxingshe, the China National Travel Service. Israeli visas for China were processed by this office but were technically issued by the Chinese Embassy in Cairo. The liaison offices functioned smoothly. By September 1990, 15 PRC students were studying Hebrew in Jerusalem and five Israelis were studying Chinese in Chengdu, all under tacit host-government sponsorship. The first weekly El Al Israel Airlines flights between Tel Aviv and Beijing commenced in September 1991, technically under contract to an Australian firm. Sufott conducted a discrete, "officially unofficial" political dialogue with the Chinese Foreign Ministry.[9]

The fullest expression of Sufott's negotiations came on 24 January 1992, during Israeli Foreign Minister David Levy's visit to Beijing. Forty-two years after Israel's recognition of the PRC, Israel and China established full diplomatic relations. The particulars of this event are analyzed in detail in Sufott's 1997 book, *A China Diary: Towards The Establishment Of China-Israel Diplomatic Relation*, and 2002 article, as well as in my 1999 book *China and Israel, 1948-1998: A Fifty Year Retrospective*, to which Sufott contributed.[10] The immediate consequence of the establishment of full diplomatic relations was that the liaison offices in China and Israel were elevated to fully fledged embassies. As of August 2007, there is a modern Israeli Embassy in Beijing near the Great Wall Hotel, headed by veteran diplomat Ambassador Amos Nadai. The PRC has its embassy and residence on Ben Yehuda Street in downtown Tel Aviv, employing 28 Chinese and two Israelis.

The establishment of Sino–Israeli diplomatic relations put an end to long-term clandestine Israeli military ties with the ROC. Israeli political scientist and Sinologist Yitzhak Shichor writes that Eisenberg, also the major intermediary in Israeli–ROC arms deals between 1975 and 1985, withdrew from ROC sales in order to pursue far more lucrative contracts with the PRC.

His key role in Sino–Israeli military relations was aptly demonstrated in 1992 when Taipei was supposedly interested in buying Israeli Kfir (jet) fighters … Aware that such a deal would damage if not ruin his business in the PRC, Eisenberg had done his best to abort it well before the potential customer declined the offer.[11]

When Chinese Foreign Minister Qian Qichen visited Israel on September 17, 1992, Labor Party Prime Minister Yitzhak Rabin publicly announced that Israel had decided not to sell Kfir jet fighters to Taiwan.[12]

Post-1992 PRC–Israel Economic Ties

A host of commercial treaties followed the exequaturs, which established diplomatic relations in January 1992 and paved the way for Yitzhak Rabin's October 1993 visit to Beijing and Shanghai, the first by an Israeli Prime Minister. Treaties signed in 1993 governed technological and scientific partnership and cooperation in medicine and telecommunications. In 1994, the two nations signed specialized agreements on the standardization of products and shipping. A formal aviation agreement was also signed, superseding the informal arrangements for El Al and Air China flights, which began in 1991 and 1992, respectively. In 1995, both nations signed agreements to enhance financial cooperation, encourage investment in each other's countries, and, most importantly, prevent double taxation, an important commercial privilege that Israel does not have with the ROC. Following Likud Prime Minister Benjamin Netanyahu's August 1997 visit to Beijing, four Sino–Israeli working groups were set up to promote relations in agriculture, electronics, health, and communications. The first product of these bilateral committees was an agreement signed in 2000 governing collaboration and exchange of leading scientists. Since the signing of these agreements, approximately 250 PRC scientists and technicians have annually visited Israel and 130 Israeli biologists have traveled to China. Agreements and memoranda of understanding signed in 2002 governed hydrological and agricultural projects and the development of startup companies. Much of this activity has been initiated by MASHAV, the Israeli Foreign Ministry's Center for International Development. MASHAV established an agricultural research farm in China and conducts many agricultural training courses there.[13]

These treaties, arrangements, agreements, memoranda of understanding, and working groups have fueled an upsurge in PRC–Israeli trade. It has always been difficult to get precise figures on Israel's trade with both Chinas because of secret military deals and indirect trade through Hong Kong. Beginning in the 1990s, there has also been a massive upsurge in Taiwanese trade to the PRC. Indeed, Taiwan has now surpassed Japan as the single largest investor on the Chinese mainland. Israeli firms have and will continue to participate in that branch of indirect trade as well.

Bearing in mind these variables, we can still get some sense of the para-meters of Sino–Israeli trade. In 1992, official figures revealed that Israel imported $5 million worth of goods from China and exported $56 million. Within a decade, bilateral trade had expanded 40-fold to approximately $2.4 billion, with imports in 2003 amounting to $1.8 billion and exports to $613 million. Similar statistics exist for the year 2004. While these totals are less than Israel's trade with small EEC countries, and marginal even by Israeli standards, there is significant potential for Sino–Israeli trade. Israeli firms are engaged in negotiations with the PRC for two communications satellites to broadcast the August 2008 Beijing Olympic Games. If successfully con-cluded, that deal alone could amount to as much as $350 million. Addi-tionally, the Israeli diamond export industry, a major source of Israel's foreign currency earnings, has taken special note of the opportunities of the market in China. In 2003, its Diamond Exchange in Ramat Gan undertook a major initiative to develop exports to China, which it sees as surpassing the heretofore largest Asiatic market, Japan.[14]

Israel's Post-1992 Economic and Cultural Ties with Taiwan

As a byproduct of PRC–Israeli diplomatic recognition, there has been sig-nificant progress in ROC–Israeli economic and cultural ties. The establish-ment of full PRC–Israeli diplomatic relations gave the ROC and Israel the leeway to open liaison offices in Taipei and Tel Aviv, an arrangement similar to that which the ROC has with the US and many other countries. Until 1992, during Israel's negotiations for recognition by the PRC, most "offi-cially unofficial" contact between Taipei and Jerusalem was conducted via Tokyo and, on rare occasions, Hong Kong. As of 2007, a Taipei Economic and Cultural Office in Israel is located in the Azrieli Center 1, Round Building, Twenty-first Floor, 132 Petach Tikva Road, Tel Aviv 67021 (Tel.: 972-3-607-4791; Fax: 972-3-607-4787). Its long-term Chief of Mission, as of 2005, is Charles Teng, who previously served in the ROC's Washington, D. C., Embassy. Six Chinese and five Israelis work in the office. Israel has a corresponding Economic and Cultural Office in Taiwan in the International Trade Building, Suite 2408, 333 Keelung Road, Section 1, Taipei, Taiwan 110, Republic of China (Tel.: 886-2-27577221; Fax: 886-2-27577197; email: taipei@israel.org). As of 2005, it is headed by Ambassador Ruth Kahanoff, a professionally trained Sinologist who was Israel's first Deputy Chief of Mission in Beijing. Four Israelis and five Chinese work in that office.

These offices have promoted an upsurge in Israel–ROC economic activity. As in the case of the PRC, official figures on ROC–Israeli trade must be considered carefully, because of trade via Hong Kong and elsewhere. According to official figures, between 1991 and 1997, total Israeli exports to the ROC rose from $49 million to $202.8 million and imports from the ROC increased from $185.3 million to $362 million, creating an Israeli balance of payments deficit of $159.5 million. In 1997, Israeli exports to and imports from the ROC were nearly double those to and from the PRC, exclusive of arms. Between January and December 2002, Israel exported $331 million worth of goods to the ROC and the ROC exported $430 million worth of goods to Israel, once again resulting in an approximate $100 million balance of payments deficit in favor of the ROC. However, since 1998, Israel's trade with China's booming economy has far surpassed Israel's trade with the ROC.[15]

There has also been an upsurge in ROC–Israeli cultural interchange since 1992. In 1995, one of the ROC's premier musical conductors, Lu Shao-chia, led Israel's Haifa Symphony Orchestra in a series of concerts in Haifa Auditorium.[16] In 1997, Gad Modai, then Director-General of Israel's Taipei office, published the first Hebrew-language history of, and guidebook to, Taiwan. This 102-page volume included sections on trade associations, credit information services, law offices, translators, and interpreters. Modai won an official commendation from the ROC's Ministry of Economic Affairs. Other important cultural exchanges included a July 1999 visit by Taipei's mayor to Israel, a January 2000 performance of a kibbutz dance company in Taipei, and a 2002 exhibit of Taiwanese at Haifa's Tikonin Museum. In December 2003, Ambassador Jackson Lee and other prominent Taiwanese officials participated in Israel's annual non-governmental security conference at Herzliya's Interdisciplinary Center.[17]

Recent Difficulties in Sino–Israeli Relations: The "Patriot," "Lavi," "Phalcon," "Harpy," and "Einstein" Incidents

There have been some awkward bumps in the road as Sino–Israeli relations have evolved since 1992. In the 1970s, there were allegations that Israel transferred to the ROC elements of American technology for the "Lance" surface-to-surface missile.[18] Since January 1992, the US government has expressed similar concerns over actual and potential transfer of purely Israeli, plus derivative American military technology to China. Those concerns have resulted in four well-publicized controversies, over the American-made "Patriot" anti-missile missile, the Israeli-made "Lavi" jet fighter aircraft, the Russian-built "Illuyshin 76" jet transformed by Israel into an airborne reconnaissance platform known as the "Phalcon," and the Israeli-made "Harpy" drone, an unmanned reconnaissance and assault aircraft.[19] The "Phalcon" incident had further repercussions in the cultural realm, in that it sparked China's cancellation of a long-scheduled, pre-approved exhibit from the Hebrew University archives about the physicist Albert Einstein. P. R. Kumaraswamy, a Sino–Israeli relations expert at Jawaharlal Nehru University, sees Israel's dilemma in each of the technology transfer cases as having to choose between "relations with a strategic ally (the United States)" and "its newly found friendship with its strategic customer (China)."[20]

The "Patriot" Incident

The United States deployed "Patriot" anti-missile missiles, made by the Massachusetts-based Raytheon Corporation, in Israel during the 1990 Iraq War. In that war, Israel was hit by 39 Scud missiles launched from Saddam Hussein's Iraq. The "Patriot" sites were manned by both American and Israeli crews. Yitzhak Shichor writes that:

> allegations that Israel had transferred Patriot technology to China were particularly humiliating. Following its denials, Israel agreed that its Patriots would be examined by a joint US State-Defense Department team. The team found no evidence of unauthorized transfer and Israel was cleared by the State Department in early April 1992, yet not by the CIA and the Defense Department, which still believed that Israel had provided Beijing with technical documents that an on-site inspection could not reveal.[21]

There is no unclassified version of the team's report and the State Department did not even issue a press release on it because the issue was so sensitive. In a 2 April 1992 press conference, State Department spokeswoman Margaret Tutweiler stated publicly that "our team found no evidence that Israel had transferred a Patriot missile or Patriot missile technology. We plan no further action on this question with Israel and consider the matter closed."[22]

There has been one recent development with respect to the "Patriots." A Massachusetts Institute of Technology study indicated that the "Patriot" missile, at least in its early incarnations, was a failure. It was incapable of bringing down Iraqi Scud missiles. Israel Aircraft Industries has now had to develop its own anti-missile missile, the Hetz ("Arrow"). If Israel wanted to harm the Chinese it should have sent them "Patriots." Nevertheless, allegations of Israel transferring this technology to China continue to surface in the media, to the detriment of American–Israeli relations.[23]

The "Lavi" Incident

Close on the heels of the "Patriot" flap came the "Lavi" incident. There is a long Israeli defense forces tradition of trying to develop its own advanced weaponry whenever possible. The tradition dates back to Israel's harrowing experiences with erratic Czech arms deliveries during Israel's War of Independence and a total French arms embargo during and after the June 1967 Six Day War. By the mid 1980s, to offset dependence on foreign suppliers, the Israeli government authorized Israel Aircraft Industries (IAI) to design and produce the prototype of a multipurpose jet fighter called the "Lavi."

Problems plagued the "Lavi" from its inception. It was to have been manufactured in Israel but with some foreign-built components, notably its engine. The major proponents of the "Lavi" scheme were IAI and Likud's Moshe Arens, an aeronautical engineer who served variously as Foreign Minister, Defense Minister, and Chairman of the Knesset's (Parliament's) Defense and Security Committee. The Israeli Air Force opposed a "95 per cent" Israeli-built jet, fearing it too was vulnerable to the vacillations of foreign suppliers. Equally significant, the "Lavi" initiative depended on American financing at a moment of downturn in the Israeli and American economies. When American financing did not materialize, IAI scrapped the project, igniting a domestic public relations firestorm. IAI was accused of compromising Israel's security plus sacrificing important jobs. IAI then attempted to revive the project, and its tarnished image, by trying to export the "Lavi" to China, much as it tried to export the "Kfir" to Taiwan in 1991–92. Kumaraswamy writes that "Israel began to collaborate with the PRC for production of a new multipurpose fighter aircraft that incorporates 'Lavi' technology. The new jet, designated F-10, is to go into production at the Chengdu Aircraft Corporation of Sichuan in south China by 2000."[24] There is no hard evidence that Israel transferred to China either its own "Lavi" technology or technology imported from the United States for the "Lavi" project. Nevertheless, these allegations remain along with collateral damage to American–Israeli relations.[25]

The "Phalcon" Episode: When Israel's "Good Uncle" Became "Uncle Scrooge"

The "Phalcon" incident may well be the most serious rift in American–Israeli relations American since America's arrest and conviction of Israeli spy Jonathan Jay Pollard in 1985. It can also be considered the low point in Sino–Israeli ties since the establishment of full diplomatic relations in 1992.[26] The "Phalcon" is an airborne reconnaissance platform that enables its owner to "see" the territory beneath it in real time. It uses purely Israeli technology, which is functionally similar to that of American AWACs, whereby the Pentagon can eavesdrop on enemy communications and "observe" actual battles being fought thousands of miles away. Because of America's concern about China's use of such technology over Taiwan and the Taiwan Straits, it is extremely unlikely that the US would have ever sold it to China. That possibility became non-existent after China's June 1989 crackdown on students in Tiananmen Square and America's consequent embargo on all arms sales to China.

In 1989, with full diplomatic support, IAI signed a contract to produce a "Phalcon" for Chile. In 1994, IAI delivered its first fully outfitted plane, a Boeing 707, without as much as a peep of international protest. On the heels of that success, also in 1994, the Labor Party government of Prime Minister Yitzhak Rabin began negotiations with China on a deal estimated at over a billion dollars, whereby Israel would install reconnaissance platforms on at least four, and perhaps eight, large jet aircraft which were yet to be acquired. In July 1996, Prime Minister Benjamin Netanyahu finalized the avionics and electronics part of the deal in a formal agreement with China. However, both countries still lacked appropriate jet aircraft. During a March 1997 state visit to Moscow, Netanyahu convinced the Russians to provide Illuyshin 76 jets as the vehicles into which Israeli electronics would be installed. In 1998, Netanyahu worked out the final details of the package during a state visit to Beijing. China then gave Israel a $190 million down-payment for the entire project.[27]

On 25 October 1999, the first unmodified Russian aircraft arrived at Israeli's Ben Gurion International Airport. The giant "Phalcon" was there for all to see, on the tarmac alongside the road to Petach Tikva. It was visited by high level Chinese delegations in widely publicized events, including one led by Chinese President Jiang Zemin in April 2000.[28] IAI declined to build a hangar for the substantial aircraft, citing the 30,000 shekel cost factor. It may have also viewed the "Phalcon" project as a publicity asset after its earlier public relations debacle with the "Lavi."

Although the "Phalcon" did not involve American technology, its sale to China worried the Clinton administration, because of concerns about Taiwan and the Taiwan Straits. It is unclear at what level the "Phalcon" deal, personally struck by IAI Chairman Moshe Keret with the cooperation of several Israeli Prime Ministers, had been pre-approved with American officials in Washington. Nor is it clear whether the deal involved the cooperation of the Israeli embassy in Washington, which almost surely would have told Keret (and Jerusalem) that there was no support for such a proposition on either side of the aisle within the US Congress. Clinton himself was surely aware of so public a deal before 2000. His administration was, however, paralyzed by other concerns, notably the Monica Lewinsky affair and election scandals involving Vice President Albert Gore. In those dark days of the Clinton administration, the President's domestic base had eroded. Questions about the "Phalcon" and related security concerns about Taiwan were relegated to the backburner. In early 2000, with Clinton exonerated, allegations and finger-pointing over the "Phalcon" deal commenced. US Secretary of Defense William Cohen tried to pressure Israeli Prime Minister Ehud Barak to abort the deal completely. Clinton, however, also wished to retain whatever goodwill he still had with then Labor Party Prime Minister Ehud Barak, in order to gain flexibility in negotiations with the Palestinians. Matters came to a head during the tri-lateral Camp David negotiations of 12 July 2000. On that day, according to Kumaraswamy,

> Barak buckled ... Israel cancelled the deal, apologized to Beijing, and agreed to pay huge financial compensation for reneging on its commitment. In response, the US agreed to Israel's decision to sell

the Phalcon to India. For its part, Israel agreed to exercise caution and exhibit transparency in its military dealings with China.

The Director General of Israel's Defense Ministry thereupon flew to Beijing to cancel the "Phalcon" deal and on to New Delhi to attempt a sale to the Indian government. On 15 March 2002, the Likud government of Prime Minister Ariel Sharon announced a formal agreement under which Israel would return China's $190 million deposit plus an additional $160 million in compensation. In agreeing to pay China $350 million, Sharon became the fourth Israeli Prime Minister, from both major political parties, to be involved in the "Phalcon" affair.[29] As will be explained below, it took nearly five years of fence-mending after the collapse of the "Phalcon" deal for Sino–Israeli relations to be even partially restored to where they were in the heyday of 2000.[30]

The "Harpy" Incident

The most recent blip on the American–Israeli–Chinese technology transfer front involved Israel's "Harpy" drone, an unmanned reconnaissance aircraft. Like the "Phalcon," the "Harpy" is exclusively the product of Israeli technology. This gigantic model plane, with components from Tadiran, Elbit, and other Israeli firms, flies from fixed bases at Palmachim in the Northern Negev and elsewhere in Israel. Because of the risk of inclement weather, it has a mobile, trailer-based landing apparatus that enables it to alight on almost any tarmac surface. For years, it has hovered over Arab areas and conveyed real-time footage to operators within Israel. More recently, according to *The Washington Post*, the "Harpy" has been upgraded into a predator drone that can loiter over enemy territory for hours and then fire radar- and laser-guided munitions onto land-based targets, which could include enemy radar sites and missile systems.[31]

As with the "Phalcon" airborne reconnaissance platform, the "Harpy" would be invaluable to China over the Taiwan Straits and Taiwan. "Harpy" technology, like that of the "Phalcon," is unavailable to China from the US. Indeed, the US may well lag behind Israel in the development of this particular form of reconnaissance and weaponry.

It is unclear at what level Israel's sale of the "Harpy" to China was preapproved in Washington. In the mid-1990s, having received permission from the Clinton administration, Israel sold the espionage version of the drone to China. At some point thereafter, Israel saw its commitment to "repair" the drone as an opportunity to upgrade the drone's offensive capabilities, an arrangement which greatly pleased the Chinese. In December 2004, while at least one Chinese drone was in Israeli workshops, Chinese State Councilor Tang Jiaxuan visited Israel and invited Prime Minister Ariel Sharon to visit Beijing. The importance of both Tang's visit and the reciprocal invitation cannot be overemphasized. It was the highest level visit of a Chinese official to Israel, and invitation of an Israeli official to China, in the four-and-a-half years since the cancellation of the "Phalcon" sale. The visit effectively ended a four-and-a-half year freeze on higher level political visits and contacts and, at least temporarily, cemented the Sino–Israeli reconciliation process. However, simultaneous with Tang's visit, US Deputy Secretary of Defense Paul Wolfowitz and Undersecretary of Defense Douglas Feith vigorously protested the "Harpy's" upgrading. They asked Israel to confiscate the plane, even though it was Chinese property. To stress the seriousness with which America viewed the issue, US Air Force Chief of Staff General John P. Jumper cancelled a trip to Israel planned for that same month.[32]

Israel, according to Kumaraswamy, "eventually bowed to American dictates. After weeks of wrangling, pressure tactics, and behind the scene negotiations, the issue was resolved ... Israel settled for a compromise and, according to a senior Chinese official, returned the drone without upgrading." Kumaraswamy concludes:

> Israel's strategic decision to resume military deals with Beijing appears to have boomeranged ... US Undersecretary of Defense for Policy Douglas Feith, the third most senior official in the Pentagon, demanded the resignation of Amos Yaron, the top bureaucrat in Israel's Defense Ministry, over the 'Harpy' controversy. However, having learned from the 'Phalcon' controversy, all parties decided to quietly resolve the dilemma.[33]

As of September 2007, Amos Yaron has assumed other responsibilities and Israel and the US are in the process of negotiating a new and explicit set of rules for technological transfer to China. Those "rules of play" will, at some point, have to be communicated to the Chinese. It is anyone's guess at this point as to how the Chinese will respond. One indication of Chinese displeasure appeared in an article in spring 2005 by Jin Liangxiang, a research fellow at Shanghai's government-linked Institute for International Studies. Jin threatened in that month's issue of the *Middle East Quarterly* that "if Israel does not meet its commitments to upgrade the drones, contractual terms would lead Beijing to launch sanctions on Israeli enterprises not only on the Chinese mainland but also in Hong Kong."[34] Jin's article needs to be taken seriously. He could not have published it without approval of higher authority, at least the head of his institute. It was written in December 2004 at the height of the "Harpy" crisis and at a time when China may indeed have been debating retaliating against Israel, if not severing diplomatic relations. The debate was at least temporarily resolved in favor of improving relations with Israel.

The "Einstein" Incident

The "Phalcon" deal had repercussions in the cultural sphere, as well as in the areas of military, economic, and political relations. The cultural dimension evolved as follows. In the fall of 2002, at the height of public controversy over the "Phalcon" debacle, China cancelled a long-scheduled "Einstein and China" exhibition. The objects in this proposed display were drawn from the famous professor's own archives in the Hebrew University Library. The show featured photographs and other evidence documenting the world famous physicist's long-term sympathy for, and visit to, China. Just as the exhibit was about to open, PRC officials raised objections to previously approved panels. The panels that were now considered objectionable featured Einstein's support of Israel and the fact that Israeli Prime Minister Ben Gurion offered Israel's presidency to Einstein, a proposition that the ailing and elderly professor declined. Israel refused to re-edit the panels, seeing the Chinese request as diplomatic fallout after the cancellation of the "Phalcon" deal. The Einstein exhibit was then moved to Taiwan where, between October and December 2002, it showed to record crowds in three of the island's largest cities, Taipei, T'ai-chung, and Kao-hsiung. It then moved on to even larger audiences in Los Angeles and Boston. As the exhibit reflects so favorably on both Einstein and China, it may yet be shown in the People's Republic. Its abrupt cancellation can be seen as one more blip in a Sino–Israeli relationship which, even since 1992, has been fraught with ups and downs.[35]

Conclusion

Perhaps most significantly, 15 years earlier the Einstein exhibit almost surely would not have been permitted in Taiwan either. That the exhibit was shown in Taiwan at all, is testimony to how far ROC–Israeli relations have advanced since the 1980s. As of 2007, Israel and Taiwan have achieved a modus vivendi. Taiwan maintains its contacts with Israel, but also retains its long-term ties with nations of the Arab and Islamic world, most notably Saudi Arabia, which chose to recognize the PRC in July 1990 and is now one of China's major suppliers of oil. As of this writing in September 2007, relations between Israel and the PRC, and between Israel and Taiwan both remain strong, albeit on different levels of engagement. The regularization of Israel's non-governmental economic and cultural ties with Taiwan was made possible, in no small measure, by the establishment of full diplomatic relations between Beijing and Jerusalem.

Notes

Copyright Jonathan Goldstein, used here with permission. An earlier version of this chapter was presented on 24 October 2004 in a panel on "Mainland China,

Taiwan, and Smaller Countries" at the American Association for Chinese Studies annual conference in Williamsburg, Virginia. The author wishes to thank the following for their assistance with this research: Cai Weiming, Embassy of the People's Republic of China to the State of Israel; Teddy Kaufman, President, Israel–China Friendship Society, Pan Zhanlin, Ambassador (Ret.) of the People's Republic of China to the State of Israel; Dr. Joseph Shalhevet, Israel Academy of Sciences and Humanities, Beijing Office; Charles Teng, Representative, and Eugene Y. T. Chen and Terry G. C. Ting, Directors, Taipei Economic and Cultural Office, Tel Aviv; and Ambassador and Deputy Director (Ret.) Moshe Yegar, State of Israel Ministry of Foreign Affairs, Jerusalem.

1 *Asia Recorder*, New Delhi, April 23–29 1956, pp. 191–92; David Kimche, *The Afro-Asian Movement: Ideology And Foreign Policy Of The Third World*, Jerusalem: Israel Universities Press, 1973, pp. 52, 67, 73; E. Zev Sufott, "Israel's China Policy," *Israel Affairs*, London, 7, no. 1, Autumn 2000, pp. 94–118; David Hacohen, *Yoman Burma: Rishmei Shlichut 1953–55* (Burmese Diary 1953–55) (Tel Aviv: Am Oved, 1963).

2 Bau Tzung-ho, "The Policy of the Republic of China Toward the Middle East," in Yu San Wang (ed.), *Foreign Policy Of The Republic Of China On Taiwan*, New York: Praeger, 1990, pp. 116–17; *China Yearbook* 1958–1959, pp. 202–08.

3 Sufott, "Israel's," pp. 97, 106.

4 "Relations with People's China," Asian and African Division memorandum, 16 October 1959, Israel Ministry of Foreign Affairs, cited in Sufott, "Israel's," p. 106.

5 Hao Bocun, *Ba nian canmou zong zhang ri ji* (Chinese: Eight-year diary as Head of the General Staff) (Taibei Shi: Tian xia yuan jian wen hua chu ban gu fen you xian gong si, 2000), p. 799.

6 "Address in the Knesset" by Shimon Peres, 13 September 1984, in Meron Medzini (ed.) *Israel's Foreign Relations. Selected Documents* 1984–88, vol. 9, Jerusalem: Ministry of Foreign Affairs, 1992, p.10; "Airport Statement and Press Conference with President Herzog," 21 November 1986, in Medzini, *Israel's*, vol. 9, p. 531.

7 Medzini, *Israel's*, vol. 10, pp. 576, 707.

8 Medzini, *Israel's*, vol. 10, p. 985; vol. 11, p. 1; vol. 12, p. 346, 373.

9 Medzini, *Israel's*, vol. 18, p. 89; Interviews with Yossi Shalhevet and Yoel Guilatt, Beijing, 23–29 August 1990.

10 E. Zev Sufott, *A China Diary: Towards The Establishment of China–Israel Diplomatic Relations*, London: Frank Cass, 1997; Sufott, "The Crucial Year 1991," in Jonathan Goldstein, *China And Israel, 1948–1998: A Fifty Year Retrospective*, Westport, Conn., and London: Praeger, 1999, pp. 107–26; Sufott, "Israel's," pp. 94–118; Medzini, *Israel's*, vol. 12, pp. 720–21, 733; vol. 13, pp. 10–11.

11 Yitzhak Shichor, "Israel's Military Transfers to China and Taiwan," *Survival* (London) 40, no. 1, Spring 1998, p. 8; P.R. Kumaraswamy, "Israel–China Relations and the Phalcon Controversy," *Middle East Policy* 11, no. 2, Summer 2005, pp. 99–100; Hao Bocun, *Ba nian*, pp. 68–70, 254, 799, 893.

12 Summary of meeting between Yitzhak Rabin and Foreign Minister Qian Qichen, 17 September 1992, in Medzini, *Israel's*, vol. 13, pp. 52–53.

13 "Address by Yitzkak Rabin, 25 October 1993," in Medzini, *Israel's*, vol. 13, pp. 372, 375; "Summary of a meeting between Benjamin Netanyahu and Chinese Minister of Foreign Affairs Qian Qichen," in Medzini, *Israel's*, vol. 16, pp. 456–57; "Summary of a meeting between Alon Liel and China's Ambassador Pan Zhalin (SIC), 2 January 2001," in Medzini, *Israel's*, vol. 18, p. 439.

14 Interview with Simcha Lustig, Israel Diamond Exchange, Ramat Gat, 29 December 2003; "China Bound," a special issue of *Israel Diamonds* (Ramat Gan) no. 191, December 2003.

15 *Foreign Trade Statistics Quarterly,* Jerusalem: State of Israel Central Bureau of Statistics, 43, no. 2, April–June, 1992, p. 40; 49, no. 2, April–June, 1998, pp. 30–33, and "Trade Countries-Imports and Exports," *Foreign Trade Statistics Monthly,* Jerusalem: State of Israel Central Bureau of Statistics, February 2003; *Preliminary Statistics Of Export And Import, Taiwan Area, Republic Of China,* Taipei: Department of Statistics, Ministry of Finance, 7 January 1998, table 9. Shalom Salomon Wald, "China is the next great power," *Jerusalem Post Online Edition,* 9 July 9 2005.

16 "Taiwan Straits: The Best Musicians Go Abroad, " *Jerusalem Post,* February 13, 1995, p. 5.

17 Interviews: Charles Teng, Representative, and Eugene Y. T. Chen and Terry G. C. Ting, Directors, Taipei Economic and Cultural Office, Tel Aviv, June 2004; Gad Modai, Taivan (Hebrew: Taiwan) (Taipei: Israel Economic and Cultural Office, 1997).

18 Warren Strobel and Bill Genz, "U.S. Can't Pin Israel, Drops Probe," *Washington Times,* 2 April 1992, pp. 1, 4.

19 Jin Liangxiang, "Energy First," *Middle East Quarterly* (Spring 2005), pp. 9–10.

20 Kumaraswamy, "Israel–China," p. 93.

21 Shichor, "Israel's," pp. 82–83; Kumaraswamy, "Israel, China, and the United States: The Patriot Controversy," *Israel Affairs,* London: 3, no. 2, Winter 1996, pp. 12–33.

22 Shichor, "Israel's Military Transfers," pp. 72–73; Hao Bocun, *Ba nian,* p. 68.

23 *Aviation Week And Space Technology,* 18 January 1993, p. 20.

24 P. R. Kumaraswamy, "South Asia and PRC–Israeli Diplomatic Relations," in Goldstein, China, pp. 145–46.

25 25 May 1999 US House of Representatives *Report Of The Select Committee On US National Security And Military/Commercial Concerns With The People's Republic Of China.*

26 *Washington Post,* 13 July 2000, and the following articles by Jonathan Goldstein: "Phalcon Indemnification," *Jerusalem Post,* 18 January 2002, p. 4A; "The Phalcon phenomenon," *Jerusalem Post Internet Edition,* 22 January 2002; Shichor, "Mountains out of Molehills: Arms Transfers in Sino–Middle Eastern Relations," *Middle East Review Of International Affairs* (MERIA) 4, no. 3, Fall 2000, p. 73; Jin, "Energy," p. 9.

27 IAI's contract with Chile was signed in 1989. Chile was willing to pay only $180 million. See articles by Amnon Barzilai in *Ha-Aretz:* 22 April 2000, and especially "China to Get $350 M for Lost Phalcon Deal," 14 March 2002; Kumaraswamy, "Israeli," pp. 96, 100.

28 Jin, "Energy," p. 8; Shichor, "Mountains," passim.

29 "Joint press conference with Ehud Barak and US Defense Secretary Cohen, 3 April 2000," in Medzini, *Israel's,* vol. 18, pp. 216–17; "Summary of a meeting between David Levy and Chinese President Jiang Zemin, 13 April 2000," in Medzini, *Israel's,* vol. 18, p. 219; "Statement on the sale of Phalcon system to China, 12 July 2000," in Medzini, *Israel's,* vol. 18, p. 267; Kumaraswamy, "Israeli," pp. 96, 100.

30 *Jerusalem Post,* 16 August 2000; AFP Report, 26 March 2002, in *FBIS-CHI-2002-0326,* 26 March 2002; Goldstein, "Shimon Peres' Visit to Beijing in Historical Perspective," *Points East 17,* no. 2, July 2002, p. 4.

31 *Washington Post,* 13 November 2004.

32 *Ha-Aretz* (Tel Aviv), 22 December 2004.

33 Kumaraswamy, "Return," n.p.

34 Jin, "Energy," p. 10.

35 Jonathan Goldstein, "Einstein and Sino–Israeli Ups-and-Downs," *Points East 17,* no. 3, November 2002, p. 4; Interviews: Charles Teng, Representative, and Eugene Y. C. Chen and Terry G. C. Ting, Directors, Taipei Economic and Cultural Office, Tel Aviv, June 2004.

20

CHINA'S POTENTIAL CONTRIBUTION TO MIDDLE EAST COOPERATION

Liang Pingan

New China and the Middle East

Since the Han Dynasty, the Middle East has been an important neighbor of China. Economic and cultural ties were first established along the Silk Road and reached a high point during the seven ocean voyages headed by Zheng He, a Chinese Muslim eunuch during the Ming Dynasty. The modern era of China's relations with the Middle East began after the People's Republic of China was founded in October 1949. Even before this point, the Palestine–Israel conflict, the main root of conflict in the Middle East, had been ongoing for decades. China, with numerous domestic and external problems to face, was rarely free enough to concern itself with the Middle East, which is geographically and psychologically remote from the Chinese perspective. But soon, political hostility and economic embargo against China by major Western powers made the Chinese extend their international space into new realms. The Non-Alignment Movement of Bandung in 1955 offered a chance for Chinese leaders to shake hands with Gamar Abdul Nasser, and other Arab leaders from Iran, Iraq, Jordan, Lebanon, Saudi Arabia, and Syria. Except for Egypt, the other Arab countries showed little interest in China because of their special traditional ties with the Western countries.[1] But the similar colonized background, the self-identification as "Third World" countries, and the common antipathy against the Western "oppressors" produced a big enough stage for China and those radical Middle East countries to find close approaches and positions on many international affairs. China has expressed pro-Palestinian and pro-Arab positions, but that policy has been limited mainly to rhetoric during disputes, as Israel has maintained its hospitality to China after it first gained independence. This true intermediate position has produced both negative and positive results for China, which regained its permanent member seat in the Security

268

Council of UN after 1972. Based on the UN and its Security Council decisions or statements in recent decades, there has been a strong enough Chinese voice in approval or disapproval on the Palestine affairs, but China's statements were of little concern to the Israelis or the Arab states. That was why there was no presence of Chinese diplomats in the Camp of David Accords, the Middle East Peace Conference in Madrid, or the recent Road Map initiative. All these seem to indicate that China could not influence the Middle East countries before, now, and even in future. Nevertheless, this kind of non-behavior policy based on traditional Taoism and Confucianism has created for China an international reputation as a "fair judge" and built a solid path for its involvement in Middle Eastern affairs. In addition, a vast population of Muslims, scattered mostly in Northwestern China, has been another unavoidable consideration in expression of China's position concerning Middle Eastern events.[2]

In the twenty-first century, with its highly sustained economic growth, China can no longer estrange itself from the Middle East, even if it does not wish to be involved in it, because this area has become a target of China's necessary strategic extension.

Israel was the first country in the Middle East to recognize the People's Republic of China,[3] though the two countries did not establish formal diplomatic relations until as late as in January 1992. Frankly speaking, this separation was not caused by a mutual hostility but that of each nation's strategic interests. It is true that Chinese UN representatives have condemned Israel many times for its "aggression and occupation of Palestine territories" in different UN council resolutions and statements, but China only went along with the majority and never initiated resolutions.[4] Karl Marx's Theory of Materialism, accompanied by idealism, has been practiced as a major thought in China's strategy both in its domestic and international policies. The re-establishment of China as a UN and permanent Security Council member would have been harder without the strong appeal, favor, and support from the Arab world and other Muslim countries;[5] nobody would expect the Chinese government to favor Israel over the much larger Arab world. Thus, an overall and one-sided diplomatic policy towards Palestine Arabs was designed and carried out until the early 1990s.

The Middle East Peace Conference in Madrid in 1990, and the realization of China as a global power brought Beijing back to a realistic review of its diplomatic policies. Followed by a "fine-tuning" of its Middle Eastern policies, a reasonable and pragmatic transformation appeared gradually, but steadily, between China and Israel. In the first professional academic conference on Jewish Studies held in Shanghai in late 1991, which was approved by higher authorities from Beijing, a section chief of the Chinese Foreign Ministry described the development of Israel–China relations as "small steps, but running fast." On the other hand, China realized that Israel laid its foundation in world politics through its own initiative, especially through the five Middle Eastern wars. China could not, or would not, be an "onlooker" any more if it wished to join in the game as a world power. Consequently, "intermediate or transcendent," another major principal of Confucius philosophy, was applied in the revision of China's Middle Eastern programs.

Since January 1990, both China and Israel have appreciated their late-coming bilateral relations, and it seemed that both sides were trying to make up for those wasted years of past decades. In Israel, almost 400 local students have taken Chinese language courses at Tel Aviv University, Hebrew University, Ben-Gurion University, and other universities. Different Israeli institutions were keen on various Chinese studies, and some scientific institutes offered China advanced technology in agriculture and energy products. It was a public secret that Israel was favoring China to upgrade its arms technology. More Jews, both from America and Israel, wished to express their thanks to China for its acceptance of the Jewish Diasporas both in ancient and modern times. Correspondingly in China, Jewish Study centers were established in Shanghai, Kaifeng, Nanjing, Beijing, Harbin, and Jinan, approved by the government after being taboo for decades. More and more Chinese civilians were getting to know that the images of Shalok in the "Merchant of Venice" by William Shakespeare, and Judas in the New Testament of the Bible, are only exceptions to the long history of notable Jews such as Karl Marx, Albert Einstein, Pablo Picasso, Sigmund Freud, and Henry Kissinger. Many Chinese scholars and literati were beginning to take a reasonable and objective view on the Palestine conflicts, and official media reported daily non-interference on these disputes. It seemed that a Sino–Israel honeymoon finally had arrived after a long-term separation, without realizing that this kind of enthusiasm caused concern and worry from some US authorities.

The blockage of Israel's sale of the Phalcon Surveillance system to China by America was the first unpleasant event that occurred between China and Israel. No Chinese could blame Israel for its withdrawal, while the US and European Union were still practicing an embargo of weapon technology against China based on the Varssena Arrangement. From 12–28 April 2000, Chinese President Jiang Zemin started his six-states visit to Israel, Palestine (recognized at this time by Chinese official media as a normal state), Egypt, Turkey, Greece, and South Africa. The first leg of the tour was in Israel, which indicated nothing but to stress Jiang's concern for this country. Jiang stayed in Israel for almost six days, while he only shared two hours with Yasser Arafat. More meaningful is that the President was also chairing the seats of both the MCCPC (Military Committee of Communist Party of China) and MCPRC (Military Committee of the People's Republic of China). According to the *World Tribune* on 3 April 2000, Chinese President Jiang Zemin's visit to Israel aroused concern in the US, because Israeli officials said such issues as agriculture and military cooperation would be

270

on the agenda. Not long after that, in November of the same year, Li Peng, China's number two leader visited Israel, stressing the same project. Jiang visited Israel Aircraft Industries Ltd, which was manufacturing the Phalcon system that was to be sold to China. Jiang's visit came under the shadow of increased US criticism of Israel's military relations with China. The Clinton administration was trying to stop the sale of airborne early warning systems to the Chinese air force. Just on the eve of the Chinese President's visit to Israel, US Defense Secretary William Cohen arrived in Israel, where he discussed Israeli arms sales to China. The *Ha'aretz Daily* said Prime Minister Ehud Barak appeared ready to approve the early warning airborne deal with China. Israel's final withdrawal from the military deal caused Jiang's visit to end without success, which caused him to refuse to meet with Ehud Barak again in New York, following a UN Summit Conference in September that year. In addition, the US took the negative decision to take more serious military sanctions against Israel after it sold and prepared the Harpy drone for China; history again proving that a small country can become the victim in a dispute between powers. The Americans declared that this kind of deal runs against its will.[6]

According to *Ha'aretz* on 12 June 2005, the Americans were to quit a series of existing support programs for Israel, including financial aid, joint research plans on the JSF fighters, delayed transmission of military systems to Israel, and freezing the night-vision system. Meanwhile, the US Defense Department forced Israel to reveal the details of its arms sales list with China, which included more than 60 deals in recent years. Otherwise, the bilateral relations between the two countries could not be expected to be formalized. Pentagon officials even refused to accept any phone calls from their Israeli partners. The Israeli–American meeting for Strategic Discussion, which had been held regularly every six months, was cancelled. And some of the Pentagon officials even claimed that "it's not worthy to deal with the Israelis."[7] The sanctions mentioned above were approved by the US at the end of 2004. This was a rare crisis between the two traditional allied countries in the past half-century. And it seems that the US administration is determined to carry out what it previously declared. Is there a better choice for Israel in such a dilemma? Moshe Yaalong, the former Chief Staff and three other senior officials were fired to please the Americans. Hertz Bodinger, the former Israeli air force commander-in-chief, was appointed as the envoy to deal with Washington to improve the situation.

China is Invited to the Middle East Cooperation as One of the "Fair Judges"

The Arab states turned their sights to China after the terrorist attacks in the US on 11 September 2001. Actually, all the present files and surveys predict the possibility of cooperation development and enlargement between China and the Middle East. The Chinese leaders stressed on different occasions that if East Asia, where China is located as a power, is united and collaborated with those Arab countries in West Asia and North Africa, this would definitely influence international affairs and help to promote a multipolar international political mechanism, which would not be favored by the Americans. Thus, the US administration built up a huge agency attached to its embassy in Beijing to watch over and trace the bilateral development between China and the Arab countries, of which the bilateral relations between China and Iran, Syria, and Libya have been a major concern to the Americans.[8]

From the Arab side there is a practical need to strengthen bilateral relations in order to build up a stable, continuous, and balanced relationship with China, particularly in economic terms. Both China and the Arab countries are now in the process of establishing open economic freedom and privatization, of which China may offer more experience to its Arab partners.

There has been an understanding and cooperative base between China and the Arab world in the past half-century. It is clear to the latter that China has had neither historic hospitality and territory claims, nor expansion or intrusion against the Arab world, whereas permanent Chinese support for the Palestine Arabs has assured them of a safe and intimate relationship China, while the Americans are striving to promote their Greater Middle East Partnership (GME).

In the past decades, China has maintained its Middle Eastern positions quite differently from the US, other Western powers, and even from the Soviet Union. During the Cold War era, five Arab–Israeli wars involved the Western powers, headed by the US and the Soviet Union. Most Arab countries had upheld strong anti-West tendencies, except Iran and Iraq, before Ayatollah Khomeini's time. Anwar Sadat's decision to expel the Russians in July 1972 indicated a desperate disappointment and frustration of the Arabs toward the global powers. A fine-tuning of Egyptian diplomacies towards the US showed nothing but the Arabs' powerlessness to face their communal rivals. The Westerners' natural and instinctive inclination to the Israelis assured the Arab leaders of their inability to solve the Palestine–Israeli conflict, thus they showed little interest in suppressing the Islamic radicals, urged by the Westerners unless the radicals threatened their own powers. Based on the common colonized background and underdeveloped conditions, almost all of the Middle Eastern countries are keeping harmonious, if not so close, relations with China, whereas the September 11 attacks in 2001 drew a historic and psychological boundary or gap between the Arabs and the Western civilized countries. This, together with Samuel Hentington's Theory of Civilizations Conflict, caused cultivation of a new identity for the Arabs in the international world. The theory identified the Arabs as natural foes to the Westerners, and only China, a symbol of another civilization also repelled by Western civilizations, could have a successful relationship with them in this world.

Most Arab governments are worried about the Greater Middle East Partnership (GME) initiated by the Western world. Even Saudi Arabia, Egypt, and Kuwait, the traditional allies of the US in the Middle East, are cautious and sensitive to this initiative.

On 14 September 2001, just three days after the attack at the New York World Trade towers, Li Zhaoxing, the Chinese Foreign Minister, signed the Action Plan Bulletin on Arab–Sino Cooperation Forum in Cairo, with all Arab foreign ministers participating. As early as January 2004, President Hu Jintao met with Amor Musa, the General Secretary of the Arab Union in Beijing, expecting this forum to consolidate bilateral relations and cooperation in the twenty-first century. From 4–7 July 2004, six financial ministers of the Gulf States visited Beijing, which passion on developing relations with China surprised other world powers.

The Need for Middle Eastern Oil and High Technology from Israel Will Make China Maintain a Positive and Neutral Position in Middle Eastern Cooperation

Before 2001, China placed great importance on the supply of oil from Central Asia, most notably in bidding for oil fields in Kazakhstan, and building transmission pipes in the Caspian countries. But after 11 September 2001 and America's subsequent occupation of Afghanistan and Iraq, the Chinese realized the weakness of relying on too narrow an area for energy supplies, just as Western countries had realized in the 1970s.[9] Thus, the Middle East became a focus of New China's strategy based on the fact that, in 2001, China imported 53.7 million tons of crude oil (10.85 million tons from Iran, 8.78 million tons from Saudi Arabia), and 20.1 million tons of finished oil products. In 2002, China imported 69.41 million tons of crude oil from Saudi Arabia, Iran, and Oman, 43.3 per cent of its total imports. Iran (10 per cent), Saudi Arabia (8.2 per cent), Oman (22.3 per cent), Angola (12.3 per cent), and Sudan have been the five major oil suppliers to China, which exported 42.2 million tons of crude oil to China, with 60 per cent of its total import that year.[10] It was predicted that in 2005 China could only produce 170 million tons of crude, in 2010 175 million tons and in 2015 185 million tons. Without oil imports, there would have been an oil supply shortage of 95 million tons in 2005, and predicted shortages of 137 million tons in 2010 and 194 million tons in 2015. According to the IEA analysis in 2005, China will import 50 per cent of its oil in 2010 and 80 per cent in 2020. Thus, we may say China will definitely maintain its traditional ties with these Arab countries for its energy supply. But energy supply has never been China's sole need from the Middle East. The import of advanced technology is another vital element to make China a true global power; for this, Israel is the only partner available in this region.

On 24 June 2004, an Israeli delegation headed by Vice Prime Minister Ehud Olmert,[11] visited Shanghai for Hi-Tech & Venture Capital Conferences. Before that, the Israel–China Business Cooperation Conference was held in Beijing on 22 June. Mr. Ehud Olmert and Xu Guanhua, Chinese Minister of Science and Technology, gave presentations and delivered speeches. Mr. Olmert said China is the major target of Israeli business in next decades. Israel has wide variety of interests in the Chinese market. Its key interests are hi-tech, biotech, homeland security, telecommunications, information technology, environmental protection, agriculture, and infrastructure. He hoped to expand cooperation with China in these fields. Xu Guanhua said China has regarded Israel as an important economical and technological partner. The Chinese government appreciates Israeli cooperation with China. He hoped the conference would be able to push forward long-term cooperation between the Chinese and Israeli governments and enterprises, and stated that China welcomes investment from Israeli enterprises.[12]

Since China and Israel established diplomatic ties in 1992, the two countries have enjoyed a steady development of diplomatic ties. The total trade volume between the two countries reached US$1.23 billion in the first 11 months of 2001, a 28 per cent increase over the same period of 2000. In just the first three months of 2005, the trade volume between the two countries was US$654.37 million, another 28.6 per cent increase over the same period of 2004.[13]

One of the centerpieces in Sino–Israeli relations has been China's need for advanced technology from Israel. As early as May 1998, Benjamin Netanyahu, the former Israeli Prime Minister, made an official visit to China, trying to boost his country's agricultural and hi-tech exports to the booming Chinese market. He said a special relationship was developing between China and Israel, since the two countries established diplomatic relations in 1992. Ties had blossomed as China sought investment and technology to spur its development efforts. He held out bright hopes for future cooperation between the two nations. He said Israel's hi-tech base was sufficiently flexible to design products according to China's needs. One Israeli hi-tech export that the Chinese have developed a taste for is military equipment. According to Western experts in Beijing, China is the largest customer in Asia for Israeli military-related exports, and Israel is second only to Russia in the volume of its military sales to China. Western military attaches in Beijing have presumed that the defense ties of the two countries run quite deep; they believed Israel's military industries were providing cruise missile-related technology to China, except the Phalcon early warning system. They said RAFAEL – the Israeli Defense Ministry's Research and Development Agency for Air-Launched Weapons – had sold Python-3 air-to-air missiles to the Chinese and was seeking to sell them the more advanced Python-4. US navy intelligence has long maintained it believes Israel has passed American-provided technology to the Chinese for China's F-10 fighter program. Israel refused to discuss American suspicions over the F-10 and other programs. But Mr. Netanyahu and other Israeli officials categorically denied US technology had been made available to China. Netanyahu declared that there were two conditions and two rules for Israel's military sales engagements around the world: one is to honor contracts avoiding certain technology transfers; the other is to consider any implications for Israel's own security. Some Western politicians suspected that China provided Iran and Saudi Arabia with sophisticated weaponry, and neither of those states is friendly to Israel. They believe Israel's military relationship with China involves a calculated risk, and that as these ties progress they might influence China's policy toward the Middle East.[14]

The Israel–China–US arms triangle is complex and has placed restrictions on Sino–Israel relations. As long as Israel depends on Washington for political support, economic largesse, and strategic backing, Israel's ability to pursue an independent arms export policy with China will continue to be limited and circumspect.[15] After a brief hiatus, US–Israel tensions over China returned. This time the dispute was over Israel's desire to upgrade the Harpy drone that it had sold to China in the mid-1990s. The US feared that the drones could upset the delicate strategic balance between mainland China and Taiwan, as well as upset its interests in the Asia–Pacific region. What was initially described as "repairing" later turned out to be "upgrading," thereby igniting a new controversy in bilateral relations between Israel and the US. As the controversy continued, Chinese State Councilor Tang Jiaxuan visited Israel in December 2004 and invited Prime Minister Ariel Sharon to visit Beijing; this was the highest visit from China in nearly five years. There were even suggestions that, contrary to American fears and misgivings, the deal would not only consolidate Sino–Israeli ties but also further American intelligence capabilities vis-à-vis China.

Israel, however, eventually bowed to US dictates and after weeks of wrangling, pressure tactics, and behind the scene negotiations, the issue was resolved. While China was keen to upgrade the Harpy drone, the US demanded Israel "confiscate" it. Israel settled for a compromise and, according to a senior Chinese official, returned the drone without upgrading. Since the end of the Cold War and the disappearance of the Soviet Union, bilateral relations between the US and Israel have been marked and marred by periodic controversies over Israel's military relations with China. Long before formal diplomatic relations were established in January 1992, both countries forged close military ties. Despite public acrimony and criticism over Israel's policy vis-à-vis the Palestinians, China found Israel to be an important player in its drive for military modernization. The US-led sanctions following the Tiananmen controversy in 1989 merely enhanced Israel's role as the proverbial "backdoor" to Western technology.

Likewise, Israel found China to be a prime customer, especially in the 1980s, when its lucrative arms markets in Latin America and South Africa were either drying up or becoming politically untenable. Strategically, the military sales to China smoothed the political differences between the two countries and eventually paved the way for Sino–Israeli normalization in January 1992. Thus, both Israel and China benefited from increased military relations. While demanding its European allies continue military sanctions against China, the US remained indifferent towards the Sino–Israeli arms trade. Seeing the military route as a means of promoting the interests of the Jewish state, Washington was not concerned about Israel upgrading Chinese military equipment and technology.

The end of the Cold War, however, altered erstwhile US indifference towards Sino–Israeli ties. A reasonable explanation to this could be that it no longer needed Beijing as a counterweight to Moscow, and Washington began to perceive Sino–Israeli relations, especially the military deals, as a threat to its interests both in the Pacific region and the Middle East. The looming prospect of China emerging as a global player that could one day threaten US influence in Asia resulted in the US becoming concerned over the entire development. It is, however, undeniable that Beijing occupies a prime position in US global interests, especially its policy towards the Middle East.

As a result, since the end of the Cold War, both the Republican and Democratic parties in the US began viewing Sino–Israeli military ties with suspicion and periodically sought to slow down, contain and, if possible, scuttle any military deals between Israel and China. Unlike in the past, mainstream US leadership, including those committed to strong US–Israel relations, began to disapprove of Sino–Israeli military ties. In early 1992, Israel was accused of the unauthorized transfer of US technology to China; the *Washington Times* argued that Israel had given China technological details on the Patriot anti-missile system that was deployed in Israel during the Gulf War. Despite it being a strong ally, an official team was sent to Israel to verify the allegations. While the team was unable to confirm the allegations, the political damage was significant. This was followed by charges that Israel had re-transferred US technology from the Lavi fighter program to China. The Lavi fighter plane that was to have been developed by Israel depended heavily upon US funding and technology. Having eventually canceled the project under intense US pressure, Israel was later accused of seeking to export Lavi technology to China.

Yet, Israel could not avoid using the time-tested military means to regain the trust and confidence of China. Its ability to restore Sino–Israeli relations, especially against the background of growing international criticism and isolation due to the al-Aqsa Intifada, entirely depended upon the military route. Over the years, the military dimension has become the indicator to measure Israel's relations with the outside world. For example, military sales play a pivotal role in the close ties that Israel maintains with Turkey and India. Hence, the Harpy upgrading, to avoid US suspicion, was initially described as a "repair" rather than an "upgrade." Israel's strategic decision to resume military deals with Beijing appears to have boomeranged. Israeli media admits that US Undersecretary of Defense for Policy Douglas Feith, the third-most senior official in the Pentagon, demanded the resignation of Amos Yaron, the top bureaucrat in Israel's Defense Ministry, over the Harpy controversy. However, having learned from the Phalcon controversy, all parties decided to resolve the dilemma quietly.

The continuing nature of the Sino–Israeli–US controversy underscores a number of important but often forgotten lessons. Astonishingly, Israel has yet to recognize and reconcile with the negative consequences of the end of the Cold War. It continues to dwell on the benefits of the new world order, whereby countries such as Syria were forced to seek a negotiated political settlement with the Jewish state. It is rarely recognized in Israel that the disappearance of the "evil empire" also meant Israel losing some of its relative importance to the US. This has resulted in Israel not appreciating the new US concerns vis-à-vis China and its potential threats to US interests in the Pacific and elsewhere. Moreover, by focusing on the non-US nature of its military exports to China, Israel is unable to comprehend the real issues involved. The problem is not whether they contain technology supported or funded by the US; indeed, both the Phalcon and Harpy programs do not appear to contain any US component or technology. Nevertheless, Israel's dependence upon the US has limited its foreign policy leverage when dealing with countries about which Washington has strategic concerns. The controversies surrounding Sino–Israeli military ties and Israel eventually yielding to American demands also undermines Israel's ability as a reliable arms supplier. At one level, Israel's ability to promote its foreign policy vis-à-vis the rest of the world largely depends upon it being a reliable arms supplier. At the same time, arms supplies to China bring Israel into a conflict situation vis-à-vis the US. It is said that the new Israeli Defense Minister has decided "to take lessons in the historical experiences and manage its own ways in the arms deal with China."[16] On the other hand, China has to, and is fine-tuning its policies toward the Middle East, getting rid of those traditional inclining approaches in the different Palestine–Israel conflicts. China will be a good player in the game to keep everything in balance.

Notes

1 China only built up formal diplomatic relations, respectively, with Egypt and Syria in 1956, Iraq in 1958, Iran in 1971, Lebanon in 1971, Jordan in 1977, and Saudi Arabia as late as in 1990 — from Chronology of Chinese Foreign Ministry.
2 According to the 1990 census, the Muslim population in China was 8,602,978, only after Han, Zhuang, and Manchu nationalities.
3 *People's Daily*, 17 January 1950.
4 UN resolutions and statements on Palestine affairs after 1973.

5 *People's Daily*, 28 October 1971.
6 *Ha'arez*, 12 June 2005.
7 *Global Times*, 15 June 2005.
8 "Cooperation between the Arabic World and China in the 21st Century," by Mohammed Abdul Wahab Sagit, *Journal of Arab World Studies*, the 3rd Edition, 2005, Shanghai, p. 31.
9 "China's Choice for Its Oil Supply," *CNN*, 8 October 2002.
10 *New Wealth*, May 2003.
11 He is one of the Ashkenazi scions in China, with his grandfather still buried in the Jewish cemetery of Harbin, Northeast China.
12 *People's Daily*, 22 June 2004.
13 Census of State Customs of PR China, April 2005.
14 *Voice of America*, 28 May 1998.
15 See Dr. P.R. Kumaraswamy for PINR, 27 May 2005.
16 A talk with an anonymous official of the Israeli diplomat vacationing in Shanghai, China, 6 July 2005.

SELECTED BIBLIOGRAPHY

Books

Adler, Solomon, *The Chinese Economy*, London: Routledge & Kegan Paul Ltd, 1957.

Alperson, Myra, *Dim Sum, Bagels, and Grits: A Sourcebook For Multicultural Families*, New York: Farrar, Straus and Giroux, 2001.

Berthrong, John, *All Under Heaven — Transforming Paradigms In Confucian Christian Dialogue*, New York: SUNY Press, 1994.

Betta, Chiara, 'Silas Aaron Hardoon (1849–1931), Marginality and Adaptation In Shanghai,' Ph.D. Dissertation, School Of Oriental and African Studies, 1997.

Cohen, Israel, *The Journal Of A Jewish Traveller*, Plymouth: Mayflower Press: 1925.

Crook, David, Crook Isabel, *Revolution In A Chinese Village: The Mile Inn*, London: Routledge & Kegan Paul Ltd., 1959.

Crook, David, Crook Isabel, 'An Anglo-Canadian Couple's 30 Years In New China,' In *Living In China By Twenty Authors From Abroad*, Beijing: New World Press 1979.

De Bary, William Theodore, *The Trouble With Confucianism*, Cambridge: Harvard University Press, 1991.

Dicker, Herman, *Wanderers and Settlers In The Far East*, New York: Twayne Publishers, 1962.

Ehrlich, M. Avrum (ed.), *Encyclopaedia of the Jewish Diaspora*, Santa Barbara: ABC-CLIO, 2008, Macmillan, 1971–72.

Epstein, Israel, *The People's War*, London: Victor Gollancz, 1939.

Epstein, Israel, *The Unfinished Revolution*, Boston: Little Brown and Company, 1947.

Epstein, Israel, 'Vignettes Of Past and Present,' in *Living In China By Twenty Authors From Abroad*, Beijing: New World Press, 1979.

Epstein, Israel, *My China Eye. Memoirs Of A Jew and A Journalist*, San Francisco: Long River Press, 2005.

Fu Xiaowei, *What Is God: Isaac Bashevis Singer's Creation and His Reception and Influence In China*, Beijing: People's Literature Publishing House, 2006. (In Chinese)

Ginsbourg, Sam, *My First Sixty Years In China*, Beijing: New World Press, 1982.

Goldstein, Jonathan, *Philadelphia and The China Trade, 1682-1846: Commercial, Cultural and Attitudinal Effects*, University Park: Penn State University Press, 1978.

Goldstein, Jonathan (ed.), *China and Israel, 1948–1998, A Fifty Year Retrospective*, London: Praeger Publishers, 1999.

279

Goldstein, Jonathan, (ed.), *The Jews Of China, Volume I: Historical and Comparative Perspectives*, Armonk: M.E. Sharpe, 1999.

Goldstein, Jonathan (ed.), *The Jews Of China, Volume II: A Sourcebook and Research Guide*, Armonk: M.E. Sharpe, 2000.

Heppner, Ernest G., *Shanghai Refuge: A Memoir Of The World War II Jewish Ghetto*, Lincoln: University Of Nebraska Press, 1993.

Jackson, Stanley, *The Sassoons*, New York: E. P. Dutton & Co. Inc., 1968.

Kranzler, David, *Japanese, Nazis and Jews: The Jewish Refugee Community Of Shanghai, 1938–1945*, New York: KTAV Publishing House, 1988.

Kublin, Hyman (ed.), *Jews In Old China: Some Western Views*, New York: Paragon Book Reprint Corp, 1971.

Kublin, Hyman (ed.), *Studies Of The Chinese Jews: Selections From Journals East and West*, New York: Paragon Books, 1971.

Lange, Thomas, 'Exotische Wahlverwandtschaften – Dshu Bailans JÜDisches China,' In W. Kubin (ed.) *Mein Bild In Deinem Auge*, 1995, pp. 187–218.

Leslie, Donald Daniel, *The Survival Of The Chinese Jews: The Jewish Community Of Kaifeng*, Leiden: E. J. Brill, 1972.

Leslie, Donald Daniel, *The Chinese–Hebrew Memorial Book Of The Jewish Community Of K'aifeng*, Belconnen: Canberra College Of Advance Education, 1984.

Leslie, Donald Daniel, *Jews and Judaism In Traditional China: A Comprehensive Bibliography*, Sankt Augustin: Monumenta Serica Institute, 1998.

Leventhal, Donald, Leventhal, Mary W. (eds.), *Faces Of The Jewish Experience In China*, Hong Kong: Hong Kong Jewish Chronicle, 1990.

Liberman, Yaacov, *My China: Jewish Life In The Orient: 1900–1950*, Jerusalem: Geffen Publishing House, 1998.

Lin, Jianfa, Qiao, Yang, *A General Survey Of Contemporary Chinese Writers: Chinese Writing and World Literature*, Shenyang: Chunfeng Literature Publishing House, 2006. (In Chinese)

Liu, Hongyi, *Toward Cultural Poetics: Studies In American Jewish Fiction*, Beijing: Beijing University Press, 2002. (In Chinese)

Malek, Roman (ed.), *From Kaifeng … To Shanghai: Jews In China*, Sankt Augustin: Monumenta Serica Institute, 2000.

Medzini, Meron (ed.), *Israel's Foreign Relations: Selected Documents*, Jerusalem: Ministry For Foreign Affairs, Vol. 1–18, 1976–2002.

Michael, Nylan, *The Five Confucian Classics*, New Haven: Yale University Press, 2001.

Milton, David, Milton, Nancy Dall, *The Wind Will Not Subside: Years In Revolutionary China 1964–1969*, New York: Pantheon, 1976.

Needle, M. Patricia (ed.), *East Gate Of Kaifeng: A Jewish World Inside China*, Minneapolis: China Centre: The University Of Minnesota, 1992.

Pan, Guang, *The Jews In Shanghai*, Shanghai: Shanghai Pictorial Publishing House, 1996.

Pan, Guang, Wang, Jian, Yi, Ge, *Jews In Shanghai Since One-and-A-Half Century (Ban Shiji Yilai De Shanghai Youtairen)*, Shanghai: Shehui Kexue Wenxian Chubanshe, 2002. (In Chinese)

Pertman, Adam, *Adoption Nation: How The Adoption Revolution Is Transforming America*, New York: Basic Books, 2000.

Pollak, Michael, *Mandarins, Jews and Missionaries: The Jewish Experience In The Chinese Empire*, Philadelphia: The Jewish Publication Society Of America, 1980.

Rickett, Allyn, Rickett, Adele, *Prisoners Of Liberation: Four Years In A Chinese Communist Prison*, New York: Cameron Associates, 1957.

Rittenberg, Sidney, Bennett, Amanda, *The Man Who Stayed Behind*, New York: Simon & Schuster, 1993.

Roland, Joan G., *Jews In British India: Identity In A Colonial Era*, Hanover: University Press Of New England For Brandeis University Press, 1989.

Roth, Cecil, *The Sassoon Dynasty*, New York: Robert Hale, 1941.

Rudavsky, David, *Modern Jewish Religious Movements: A History Of Emancipation and Adjustment*, New York: Behrman House, Inc., 1967.

Rutland, S.D., 'Waiting Room Shanghai: Australian reactions to the Plight of the Jews in Shanghai After World War II', *Leo Baeck Year Book* London 1987, pp. 407–433.

Sacks, Jonathan, *Crisis and Covenant — Jewish Thought After The Holocaust*, New York: Manchester University Press, 1992, p. 268.

Schwarcz, Vera, *Bridge Across Broken Time: Chinese and Jewish Cultural Memory*, New Haven: Yale University Press, 1998.

Shapiro, Michael, *Changing China*, London: Lawrence & Wishart, 1958

Shapiro, Sidney, *Experiment In Sichuan: A Report On Economic Reform*, Beijing: New World Press, 1981.

Shapiro, Sidney, *Jews In Old China: Studies By Chinese Scholars*, New York: Hippocrene Books, 1984.

Shapiro, Sidney, *I Chose China: The Metamorphosis Of A Country and A Man*, New York: Hippocrene Books, Inc., 2000.

Siao, Eva, *Peking. Eindrücke Und Begegnungen. Eingeleitet Von Bodo Uhse*, Dresden: Sachsenverlag, 1956.

Siao, Eva, Hauser, Harald, *Tibet*, Leipzig: F.A. Brockhaus, 1957.

Siao, Eva, *China. Photographien 1949–1967. Herausgegeben Von Reinhold Misselbeck*, Köln:Museum Ludwig, 1996.

Siao, Eva, *China – Mein Traum, Mein Leben*, Berlin: Econ-Taschenbuch-Verlag, 1997.

Sufott, E. Zev, *A China Diary: Towards The Establishment Of China-Israel Diplomatic Relations*, London: Frank Cass, 1997.

Tobias, Sigmund, *Strange Haven: A Jewish Childhood In Wartime Shanghai*, Urbana: University Of Illinois, 1999.

Valler, Shulamit, *Women and Womenhood In The Stories Of Babylonian Talmud*, Tel-Aviv: *Hakibbutz Hameuchad*, 1993. (In Hebrew)

Weber, Max, *The Religion Of China: Confucianism and Taoism*, trans. Hans H. Gerth, Glencoe: The Free Press, 1951.

Weisz, Tiberiu, *The Kaifeng Stone Inscriptions: The Legacy Of The Jewish Community In Ancient China*, New York: Iuniverse, Inc., 2006.

White, William Charles, *Chinese Jews: A Compilation Of Matters Related To The Jews Of Kai-Feng Fu*, second edn, New-York: Paragon Book Reprint Corporation, 1966.

Xu, Xin, *The Jews Of Kaifeng, China: History, Culture, and Religion*, Jersey City: KTAV Publishing House, 2003.

Yang, Zhidong, *Klara Blum – Zhu Bailan (1904–1971). Leben Und Werk Einer Österreichisch-Chinesischen Schriftstellerin*, Frankfurt: Peter-Lang-Verlag, 1995.

Zeng, Yanbing, *Kafka and Chinese Culture (Kafu Ka Yu Zhongguo Wenhua)*, Beijing: Shoudu Shifan Daxue Chubanshe, 2006. (In Chinese)

Zhang, Ping, *Avoth: The Wisdom Of Our Fathers*, Beijing: CASS Press, 1996.

Zhang, Ping, *Bridging Between The Actual and The Ideal In Early Rabbinical and Confucian Literature*, Ph.D Dissertation, Tel-Aviv University, 1999.

Zhang, Zhong, She, Shusen, Hong, Zhicheng, Wang, Jingtao, *An Introduction Of Contemporary Chinese Literature*, Beijing: Beijing Daxue Chubanshe, 2002. (In Chinese)

Zhou, Xun, *Chinese Perceptions Of The Jews and Judaism: A History Of The Youtai*, Richmond: Curzon Press, 2001.

Articles and Academic Papers

Abraham, Wendy, 'Conversations with Kaifeng's Jewish Descendants, August, 1985,' *Points East,* August 1993, pp. 1–11.

Allinson, Robert Elliot, 'Hillel and Confucius: The Proscriptive Formulation Of The Golden Rule In The Jewish and Chinese Confucian Ethical Traditions,' *Dao: A Journal Of Comparative Philosophy*, December 2003, Vol. 3, No. 1, pp. 29–41.

Brady, Anne-Marie, 'Red and Expert: China's "Foreign Friends" In The Great Proletarian Cultural Revolution 1966–1969,' *China Information*, Autumn/Winter 1996, Vol. XI, Nos. 2–3, pp. 110–137.

Brady, Anne-Marie, 'Who Friend, Who Enemy? Rewy Alley and The Friends Of China,' *The China Quarterly*, September 1997, No. 151, pp. 614–632.

Buber, Martin, 'The Spirit Of The Orient and Judaism,' in Nahum N. Glatzer (ed.) *On Judaism*, New York: Schocken Books, 1967.

Chen, Yiyi 'A Brief Survey Of The History Of Chinese Translations Of The Hebrew Bible,' *SBL Forum*, November 2005.

Chen, Yiyi, 'Understanding Israelite Religion: New Challenges For Chinese Bible Translations,' *Religion Compass,* Vol. 1, 2006.

Clarke, Duncan, Johnston Robert, 'U.S. Dual-Use Export To China, Chinese Behaviour, and The Israel Factor,' *Asian Survey*, March–April 1999, Vol. 39, No. 2.

Eber, Irene, 'Social Harmony, Family, and Women In Chinese Novels, 1948–1958,' *China Quarterly*, 1989, No. 117.

Eber, Irene, 'The Jews Of Kaifeng - Sinification and The Persistence Of Identity,' *PE'AMIM*, 1989, Vol. 41.

Eber, Irene, 'China and The Jews,' *China and The Jews, A Sampling Of Harvard Library Resources*, 1992.

Eber, Irene, 'Translating The Ancestors: S. J. Schereschewsky's 1875 Chinese Version Of Genesis,' *Bulletin Of The School Of Oriental and African Studies*, October, 1993, Vol. LVI, No. 2.

Eber, Irene, 'Kaifeng Jews Revisited: Sinification As Affirmation Of Identity,' *Monumenta Serica* 41. 1993, pp. 231–47.

Eber, Irene 'Martin Buber and Taoism' *Points East*, July–November 2005, Vol. 20. Nos. 2–3.

Eckstein, Mathew A., 'Identity Discourse and The Chinese Jewish Descendants,' *Sino–Judaica: Occasional Papers Of The Sino–Judaic Institute*, 2000, Volume 3. pp. 23–38.

Elazar, Daniel J., 'Are There Really Jews In China?' *Jerusalem Letter*, Vol. 82, No. 1–4, September 1985.

Goldman, Rene, 'Moral Leadership In Society: Some Parallels Between The Confucian "Nobleman" and The Jewish Zaddik,' *Philosophy East and West*, 1995, Vol. 45. No. 3.

Hacohen, David, 'Behind the Scenes Of Negotiations Between Israel and China,' *New Outlook* 6, November–December 1963, No. 9, pp. 29–44.

Knowles, Christopher, 'The Sephards Of Shanghai,' *China Review*, 1992.

Kumaraswamy, P. R., 'Israel, China, and The United States: The Patriot Controversy,' *Israel Affairs*, Winter 1996, Vol. 3, No. 2, pp. 12–33.

Kumaraswamy, P. R., 'Israel and China Collaborate On Military Aviation,' *Middle East International*, 1995, No. 510, 6 October, pp. 18–19.

Li, Yang, 'Dr. Hans Müller – Ein Aussergewöhnlicher Kämpfer Im Weissen Kittel,' *Beijing Rundschau*, 1992, No. 28, pp. 29–32.

Meng, Zhenhua, Yiyi, Chen, 'The Hebrew Studies Program At Peking University, Beijing, China,' *Point East*, 2007, Vol. 22, No. 1, pp. 1–6.

Messmer, Matthias 'Chinas andere Wirklichkeiten. Das Reich Der Mitte In Den Augen Der Ehemaligen "Foreign Experts,"' *China-Report*, January 2002, No. 36, pp. 21–24.

Patt-Shamir, Galia, 'Way As Dao; Way As Halakha: Confucianism, Judaism and Way Metaphors,' *Dao,* Summer 2006, Vol. 5, No. 2, pp. 137–158.

Qiu, Chengzhong, '"Mi-Daifu" – Ein Leben FÜR China. Der Deutsche Arzt Prof. Dr. Hans Müller: "Ich Bin Ein Chinese,"' *China Heute,* March 1990, pp. 42–45.

Rhee, Song Nai, 'Jewish Assimilation: The Case Of Chinese Jews,' *Comparative Studies In Society and History*, January 1973, Vol. 15, No. 1, pp. 115–126.

Shichor, Yitzhak, 'Hide and Seek: Sino–Israeli Relations In Perspective,' *Israel Affairs*, Winter 1994, Vol. 1, No. 2, pp.188–208.

Shichor, Yitzhak, 'Israel's Military Transfers to China and Taiwan,' *Survival: The IISS Quarterly*, Spring 1998, pp. 68–91.

Sufott, E. Zev, 'Israel's China Policy,' *Israel Affairs* (London), Autumn 2000, Vol. 7, No. 1, pp. 94–118.

Tu, Weiming, 'The Creative Tension Between *Jen* and *Li*,' *Philosophy East and West,* 1968, Vol. 18, Nos. 1–2, pp. 29–39.

Yutkowitz, E., 'Shanghai Fortunes' *Jewish Monthly,* March 1987, No. 7.

Zhang, Ping, 'Israel In Chinese Cyber Space,' *Zmanim*, No. 85, 2004, pp. 15–23. (In Hebrew).

INDEX

Abish, Walter 128
Abraham 63, 99, 212, 220
Abraham, Wendy 180, 186
Adam 212
Adelson, Sheldon 12
Adler, Pat 23
Adler, Solomon 22–24
adoption of Chinese children 227–35
Agnon, S.Y. 119, 165–70
Ai Dianyuan 176
Ai Fenming 200
Ai Qin 198
Akivah, Rabbi 52, 58
Aleichem, Sholem 118, 127, 164
Alley, Rewy 34
Almog, Ruth 168
Alperson, Myra 232
Amichai, Yehuda 165–70
Analects 63–65
Andi Wu 159
anti-Semitism 12, 49, 99, 107, 233, 240
Appelfeld, Aharon 165, 167, 170
Approaching Israel website 104–5, 110
Arafat, Yasser 146, 246–47, 270
Arens, Moshe 147, 261
Aryeh, Sivan 168
Asch, Sholem 118–19
Auster, Paul 128
Australia 135–49
avant-garde culture 121
Avins, Carol 130
Avtzon, Mordechiai 43
Azerbaijan 9–10

Babel, Isaak 31, 119, 129–30
Baidu's Israeli Bar website 105
bar and *bat mitzvahs* 234
Barak, Ehud 262, 271
Bar Gal, Dvir 10
Bar-On, Hanan 143
Bartov, Hanoch 170
Bauer, Yehuda 84–85
Beckett, Samuel 118
Begin, Menachem 255
Bei Cun 122, 125–26
Bellow, Saul 118–23, 127, 131
Ben Gurion, David 138, 265
Ben Shay, Simicha 43
Berenbaum, Michael 92
Berg, Irvin 187
Bergson, Henri 101, 118
Berstein, David 147
Berthrong, John 68–69
Bible, the 89, 152–62, 270; read as literature 164
bilateral relations between China and Israel 242–43, 247–49, 270–71
biological parents 230
Birnbaum, Eliyahu 189
Birstein, Yossel 168
blogs 113–15, 128–29, 159–60
Blum, Klara 35–38
Bodinger, Hertz 271
Bowen, John 144
Brender, Gerda 139
Brender, Joseph 139
Brenner, Yosef Haim 168
Brod, Max 123

Brodsky, Joseph 118, 128
Buber, Martin 66–67, 70, 101
Buddhism 49, 79–80, 87, 156, 170, 234
Buxbaum, Elisheva 43

Calwell, Arthur 136–37
Can Xue 122
Canaan Forum website 104–10
Canadian Jewish-Asian Association
    232
Caplan, Leslie 143
Carmel School, Hong Kong 14
Carner, Talia 232
Center for Jewish Studies, Shanghai
    105
Center for Judaic and Inter-Religious
    Studies, Shandong University 105,
    186, 188
Central Conference of American
    Rabbis 75–76
Central Database of the Shoah Victims'
    Names 90
Chabad 5–12, 43–45, 186, 194
Chang, Iris 85, 93
Chantepie de la Sausaye, P.D. 68
Chen Boda 21
Chen Cun 120
Chen Duxiu 77
Chen Yiyi 167
Chen Zhongyi 171
Cheng Chung-ying 68
Cheng Siyuen 147
Chi Haotian 242
Chi Li 168
Chiang Kai-shek 18, 26, 245
China National Knowledge
    Infrastructure 119
Christianity 49, 76, 78, 87
Chung, Connie 232
Clinton, Bill 262, 271
Cohen, Michael 140, 148
Cohen, Nilli 171
Cohen, Pinchas 13
Cohen, William 262, 271
Confucianism 49–58, 61–70, 78–81, 87,
    158, 175, 208–10, 214, 216, 219, 269
Conservative Judaism 73–74, 79, 101
Corrie, Rachel 106
Cowen, Sir Zelman 142
Crook, David 23
Crook, Isabel 23
Crystal, Jack 43

Cultural Revolution 21–24, 28–32, 37,
    42, 145, 178–79, 202
Cutler, Jeffrey and Linda 232

Dai Huikun 168
Daizong 130
Daoism 49, 67, 156, 210, 219
Darfur 94
David, King of Israel 89
de Bary, William Theodore 68
Deng Xiaoping 22, 30, 143, 147, 177,
    179, 201, 228
Diaso Haifeng 168
Ding Fan 168
Dinstein, Yoram 142, 148
diplomatic relations 111, 135, 138, 143,
    147, 149, 165, 183, 239–45, 253–57,
    264–65, 269, 274
Dongxi 126
Du Yuesheng 34
Dweck, Zakki 43

Eber, I. 160–61, 207
Ehrenburg, Ilja 32
Ehrlich, Avrum 50, 149, 158, 189
Eichmann, Adolf 84, 90, 170
Eijlenberg, Mark 43
Einhorn, Ephraim F. 15
Einstein, Albert 152, 259, 265, 270
Eisenberg, Shoul 179, 255–56
El Al 5, 14
Elkin, Stanley 128
embassy staff in China 8
Epstein, Israel 18, 23, 25, 28
ethnic minorities in China 194–95, 199–
    200
European Union 270
Exploring Jewish World website 104–5
Expo 2010 251

Fairbank, John K. 23
Families with Children from China
    (FCC) organization 231–32
family relationships 55–57
Fan Hongsheng 167–68
Fan Yuchen 114
Feith, Douglas 264, 277
Fraser, Malcolm 142–45
Frazer, J.G. 68
freedom of speech 110
Freud, Sigmund 101, 152, 270
Freudlich, Shimon 44

Freund, Michael 187–89
Freundlich, Dini 9
Frey, Richard 29–30, 35
Fu Hao 165–71
Fu Youde 13, 158
Fuhrman, Osmond Carl William 137

Gao Qiufu 168–70
Gao Sui 168
Garden of Eden 62–63
Ge Fei 122
Geiger, Abraham 73
Ginsbourg, Sam 13, 27–28
Glassgold, Adolph C. 137
god, different concepts of 219–21
Goldberg, Merryl R. 232
Goldfarb, Daniel 232–33
Goldman, René 58, 64, 69, 202
Goldmann, Nahum 140
Goldstein, Jonathan 135, 207
Gordimer, Nadine 118, 128
Gore, Al 262
Gotel, Jerry 189, 192
Gould, Randall 16
Granich, Max 23
Great Leap Forward 18, 21, 28, 33
Greenberg, Shalom 11, 44
Greenspan, Alan 152
Grossman, David 167–70
Guillat, Yoel 146, 256
Guo Hongtao 167
Guori, Haim 170

Hacohen, David 253–54
Hammer, Hedda 33
Han Xu 146
Harlev, Raphael 147
Harpy reconaissance drone 263–64,
    271, 275–77
Hawke, Bob 144
Haylen, Leslie 137
Hazaz, Haim 167
He Xiaozhu 120–21, 124–26
Heard, John 12
Hegel, G.W.F. von 73
Heiler, Friedrich 68, 70
Heller, Joseph 118
Herzog, Haim 242
Hinduism 50
Hirschberg, David 43
Hitler, Adolf 82, 87
Holdheim, Sammuel 73

Holocaust, the 11, 82–85, 89–90, 93–94,
    140, 147, 170, 208, 221, 240–41
homosexuality 233
Hong Kong 13–14, 107, 143–44
Hong Man 114
Horn, Joshua S. 30–31
Hu Jintao 273
Hu Yuzhi 164
human rights 191
humanism 219
Huntington, Samuel 272
Hussein, Saddam 260
Husserl, Edmund 101

ICL-IP (company) 251
identity: cultural 72, 80; ethnic 191;
    Jewish 8, 11, 193, 198–200, 227
image of Israel and the Jewish people
    110–15
India 244, 262–63
Institute for Jewish and Community
    Research 227
internet resources 103–15
Islam 68, 176, 194
Israel, Shavei 188–89
Israel, State of 89–90, 103, 106, 111,
    191, 241, 253; Consulate General,
    Shanghai 247; Embassy, Beijing 105,
    110
Israel China Chamber of Commerce 5

Jacobs, Lily 234
Jakubowicz, Andrew 148–49
Janowitz, Tama 232
Japan 82–93, 228
Jewish Net website 104
Jewish Soul website 104
Ji Chaoding 22–23
Ji Chen 126
Jiang Qing 22
Jiang Zemin 29, 242–43, 246, 262, 270–
    71
Jin Guangyuan 184–85
Jin Liangxiang 264
Jin Wenjing 184
Jinan 6–7, 12–13
John of Montecorvino 153
John Paul II, Pope 98
Jordan, Charles 136
Josephine, Maven 181–82
Joshua, Rabbi 52
Jumper, John P. 264

Kafka, Franz 118–25, 129, 167
Kahana-Carmon, Amalia 170
Kahanoff, Ruth 144, 146, 258
Kahn, Yoel 234
Kaifeng 6, 175–221
Kanaz, Yehoshua 168
Kanee, Sol 147
Kaniuk, Yoram 168
Kant, Immanuel 156
Kaplan, Mordechai 74
Karlin, Barbara Fields 232
Ka-Tzetnik 170
Ke Ju system 80
Ke Yanbin 167
Kenaz, Yehsoshua 170
Keret, Moshe 262
Kimche, David 143
King, Larry 232
Kinsman, Nathan 12
Kissinger, Henry 270
Klausner, Joseph 165–66
Kniuk, Yoram 170
Kolet, Ezra 142
Kong, H.P. 144–45
Kong Xianyi 179
Kotlarsky, Moshe 43
Kumaraswamy, P.R. 259–64
Kundera, Milan 118
Kung, H.H. 22

Lang, Olga 34
Lavi jet fighter 260–62, 276
Lee, Archie 159
Lee, Jackson 259
Lee Kuan Yew 41
Leibler, Isi 135, 140–49
Leibniz, Gottfried 102
Lenin, Vladimir 195
lesbianism 233
Lesley, Daniel D. 50
Leslie, Donald 210
Lestz, Michael 91
Levenson, Joseph R. 80
Levin, Aura 142
Levy, David 147, 256
Lewis, Rose 232
Lexis-Nexis database 230–31
Li Chuwen 144
Li Geng 120–21
Li Keran 32
Li Peng 29, 242, 271
Li Shenzhi 145

Li Wenjun 168
Li Xiannian 20
Li Zehou 77–78
Li Zhaoxing 273
Liang Gong 158
Liang Pingan 189
Liao Huixang 168
Liberman, Yaacov 15
Liebrecht, Savyon 170
Lilley, James 181–82
Lin, Patricia Y.C.E. 228
Lin Xianghua 169
Link, Perry 88–89
Lippmann, Walter 26
Lipski, Sam 144–45
Lipson, Roberta 6, 9
literature, Hebrew 164–71
Liu Hongyi 167
Liu Shaoqi 20, 177, 201
Liu Shipei 77
Liu Shu-hsien 68
Lu Fan 119
Lu Fenyan 147
Lu Han 115
Lu Jiande 124, 171
Lu Peiyong 165
Lu Shao-chia 259
Lu Xun 34, 118, 127
Lu Yang 125–26
Lü Zhenzhong 153
Luo Han 168
Lv Wenling 165

Ma Xiaolin 114
Ma Xulun 77
Ma Yueran 130
Macao 12
McCarthy, Joseph 25
Magid, Isador 135–38
Mai Lijuan 167
Mailer, Norman 118
Maimonides 219–20
Malamud, Bernard 118–19, 123, 127, 131
Mann, Thomas 32, 118
Mao Dun 118, 127, 164
Mao Zedong 20–28, 31–35, 138, 176–81, 195, 201, 229
Marshall, David 41
Marshall, George C. 20
Marx, Karl 101, 152, 195, 269–70
Masel, Alec 136

MASHAV Center 243
Maugham, W. Somerset 30
May 4th Movement 77–80, 164
Mei Lanfang 32
Mei Shaowu 124
Mencius 69
Mendelssohn, Moses 74
Meng Jian 168
Merhav, Reuven 143–46
Messmer, Matthias 3
Meyer, Nachum 136
Middle East peace process 244–46, 269
Mo Yan 122, 171
Modai, Gad 259
modernity and modernization 72–73, 76, 121
Moruo, Guo 32
Mosby, Aline 202
Moses 212–13, 219–20
Moshinsky, Sam 138
Mou Tsung-san 68
Moustafine, Mara 149
Müller, Hans 28–29, 139
Muller, Max 68
Musa, Amor 273

Nadai, Amos 256
Nanjing Massacre 82–93
Nanjing Massacre Memorial Hall 90
Nasser, Gamal Abdul 268
National Jewish Population Survey (2002) 227, 230
National Library of China 118
Nattel, Lillian 232
Nazism 86–87
Nealon-Shapiro, Cecelia 234
Neruda, Pablo 32
Netanyahu, Benjamin 242, 257, 262, 274–75
Neville, Robert Cumming 68
New York Times 234
Nie Rongzhen 20
Nimoy, Leonard 185
Noah 212

oil supplies 273
Olmert, Ehud 248, 252, 274
Olympic Games 251, 258
One Child policy 195, 229
Open Door policy 143, 191, 202
Opium Wars 102, 107
Orlev, Uri 168, 170

Oz, Amos 167–71
Ozick, Cynthia 119, 128

Palestine 108, 111–14, 244–45
Paley, Grace 128
Pan Guang 11
parental responsibilities 56
Patriot missile system 259–60, 276
Peng Dehuai 29
Peres, Shimon 147, 255–56
Peretz, Isaac Leib 118
Pertman, Adam 233
Phalcon reconnaissance platform 261–65,270–71, 274, 277
Picasso, Pablo 270
Pinski, David 118
Pinter, Harold 128
Plaks, Andrew 50, 170, 207
poetry 169
Pollak, Michael 207
Pollard, Jonathan Jay 261
Polo, Marco 194
population, Jewish: in China 4, 75; of Chinese descent 227–28, 234–35
Povich, Maura 232
Powell, John W. 25
Proust, Marcel 118

Qian Hongjia 165
Qian Mansu 121
Qian Qichen 147, 257
Qingdao 6, 13
Qiu Huadong 171

Rabin, Yitzhak 257, 261
Rabinovitch, Abraham 136
racism 233
Rathner, Kurt 140
Ravikovitch, Dalia 169
Rebbe, Lubavitcher 43
Reform Judaism 73–76, 101, 234; relevance for Chinese culture 76–81
religious freedom 5, 9, 191, 194–98
research and development (R&D) 249–50
Ricci, Matteo 153, 194
Riegner, Gerhard 140
Riskin, Shlomo 189
Rittenberg, Sidney 19–24
Rocha, Bachman 73
Rong Yi-ren 182
Rosenfeld, Jacob 12–13

Roth, Henry 139
Roth, Philip 118, 128
Rousseau, Jean-Jacques 156
Sachs, Nelly 118
Sacks, Jonathan 51
Sadat, Anwar 272
Salinger, J.D. 118
Sartor, Frank 139
Sassoon, David 107
Schereschewsky, S.I.J. 156, 160–61
Schulz, Bruno 130
Schuman, Julian 25–27
Schwarcz, Vera 221
Schwartz, Yigal 170
Seiroko, Kajiyama 92
Semel, Nava 170
September 18th 1931 incident 82, 87, 91
September 11th 2001 incidents 271–73
Shabtai, Yaakov 167, 170
Shaked, Gershon 166–67
Shakespeare, William 270
Shalev, Meir 168, 170
Shalev, Zeruya 169
Shalhevet, Yosef 146, 256
Shamir, Moshe 167, 170
Shand, Adam 138–39
Shandong 12–13
Shapiro, Michael 23–24, 35
Shapiro, Sidney 17–19, 24–25, 145–46
Sharon, Ariel 263, 275
Sharpre, Eric 68
Shen Zhihong 168
Shi Fenying 200
Shi Lei 186–89, 192
Shi Xin Guang 186, 193
Shichor, Yitzhak 256–57, 260
Shigeru, Yamaoka 87–88
Shintaro, Ishihara 92
Shippe, Hans 34
Shuang Wen Academy 233
Shultz, Shlomo 180–81
Siao, Emi 31–32
Siao, Eva 31–35
Sicher, Efraim 130
Sights of True Israel website 106
Silverstein, Alisa 9
Simon Wiesenthal Center 182
Singer, Isaac Bashevis 118–20, 123–31
Singer, Israel 143–44
Smedley, Agnes 34
Snow, Edgar 30

Solarz, Stephen 146
Solomon, King 89
Song, T.V. 22
Song Jian 183
Song Lihong 158
Spinoza, Baruch 101, 156
Stalin, Josef 93, 177, 195
Stars of David group 229–30
Stein, Richard see Frey, Richard
Steinhardt, Nancy Shatzman 207
Strong, Anna Louise 20
Su Tong 124, 126, 130–31
Sufott, E. Zev 146, 254–56
Sui Lijun 168
Sun, Madame 23–25, 34
Sun Ganlu 120
Sun Yatsen 111–12
synagogues 9–10, 43–45, 135, 177–83, 187–88, 193, 197–98, 202, 207

Taiwan 14–15, 112–13, 232, 253, 257, 259, 262, 265
Talmud, the 51, 54, 56
Tammuz, Benjamin 167–70
Tan Wen Zui 143
Tandler, Julius 34
Tang Danhong 114
Tang Jiaxuan 263–64, 275
Tang Xuzhi 164
Tannebaum, Gerald 24–25
Taoism 79–80, 176, 269
Taylor, L.A. 136–37
Teng, Charles 258
Tiananmen Square incident (1989) 146, 181, 229, 261, 275
Tibet 18
Tiele, C.P. 68
Timoteus, Pokora 202
Tokayer, Marvin 187
Tong Jian Hua 42
Torah, the 52, 73, 99, 210
tourism 4, 7, 10–11, 179–81, 187, 193–95, 202–4
Tower of Babel 62–63
trade relations between China and Israel 242–43, 274
traditional values: Chinese 76–81; Jewish 75, 89
translation process 165–66
Triguboff, Harry 138–39, 148
Trusch, Matt 186–87
Tshuva, Elad 13

Tshuva, Yitzhak 13
Tu Weiming 57, 61, 68
Tutweiler, Margaret 260

United Nations 147, 241, 245, 254–56, 268–69
universities 7–8
Urbach, Noam 187–88

Valler, Shulamit 57
Veliz, Claudio 145
venture capital 250–52
Vico, Giovanni Battista 73
Vietnam 228
Vogel, David 168

Wallah, Yona 169
Walters, Barbara 232
Wan Li 147
Wang Bingman 23
Wang er Kong 144
Wang Guangmei 20
Wang Meng 130
Wang Mingqian 168
Wang Runhua 165
Wang Tianbing 130–31
Wang Yang-ming 70
Wang Yisha 179–80, 185, 189–92
Washington Times 276
Weber, Max 68
websites: academic 105, 110; official and semi-official 105–6; personal 104–5, 110
Wei Jinsheng 22
Wei Yuan 78
Weis, Isaac Mayer 73
Weiseltier, Meir 169
Weiss, Karel 43
Weiss, Ruth 33–35
Weisz, Tiberiu 207, 216
Weizman, Ezer 242
Werblowsky, Zwi 148
White, Theodore 16
White, William 178, 207, 216
Williams, Dick 42
Wisse, Ruth 128
Wittgenstein, Ludwig 101
Wolfowitz, Paul 264
World Jewish Congress 140–44, 147–48
World Literature magazine 167, 169
Wu Xueqian 148, 255–56

Xiao Lin 113
Xiao Yaozhen 168
Xie Yong 167
Xiun Xin 169
Xu Chongliang 168
Xu Guanhua 274
Xu Kun 168, 171
Xu Xiangqun 185
Xu Xin 131, 158, 165, 167, 170, 185–86

Yaalong, Moshe 271
Yaffe, Rafi 109
Yan Hui 58
Yan Lianke 171
Yang Dongxia 168
Yang Fan 168
Yang Fuchang 182
Yang Haihong 168
Yang Hengda 168
Yang Rong 168
Yang Yugong 168
Yao Renku 145
Yao Yi'en 127
Yao Yongcai 167
Yao Yongqiang 167
Yaron, Amos 264, 277
Yehoshua, Abraham B. 167, 170
YeTingfang 129
Yin Gang 114–15
Yizhar, Smilansky 167, 170
Young, Katherine K. 50
Yu Haijiang 168
Yu Hua 120–26, 130
Yuval, Moshe 137–38

Zhang, Moshe 189–92
Zhang Chong 168
Zhang Jingxiang 183
Zhang Ping 158
Zhang Qiong 168
Zhang Taiyan 77
Zhang Yueran 171
Zhang Zhidong 77–78
Zhao Xiang-ru 183–84
Zhao Ziyang 18
Zheng He 268
Zheng Yalan 168
Zhidong Yang 38
Zhong Zhiqing 114, 167–71
Zhou, Prince of 198
Zhou Enlai 19, 200–201, 254
Zhou Xiaoping 169

Zhu Bailan 37; *see also* Blum, Klara
Zhu Biyun 165
Zhu Meihui 168
Zhu Rongji 29
Zhu Weizhi 158
Zhu Xi 65
Zhu Xiangcheng 35

Zhu Zhencheng 180–81
Zim (company) 14
Zion, Yakov 43
Zionism 76, 103, 111, 147
Zong Pu 122
Zweig, Arnold 32
Zweig, Stefan 118

Lightning Source UK Ltd.
Milton Keynes UK
UKOW06f1155031116
286785UK00005B/57/P

9 780415 593410